GUIDE TO USING
LOTUS™ 1-2-3™

THE OSBORNE **McGRAW-HILL**

GUIDE TO USING LOTUS™ 1-2-3™

SECOND EDITION

COVERS VERSION 2

Edward M. Baras

Osborne **McGraw-Hill**
Berkeley, California

Published by
Osborne **McGraw-Hill**
2600 Tenth Street
Berkeley, California 94710
U.S.A.

For information on translations and book
distributors outside of the U.S.A., please write to
Osborne **McGraw-Hill** at the above address.

1-2-3 is a trademark of Lotus Development Corporation.
The Osborne/McGraw-Hill Guide to Using Lotus™ 1-2-3™ is not sponsored
or approved by or connected with the Lotus Development Corporation.
All references to 1-2-3 in the text of this book are
to the trademark of Lotus Development Corporation.

Hyperion is a registered trademark of Bytec-Comterm, Inc.; Rainbow is a trademark
of Digital Equipment Corporation; GRiD is a trademark of GRiD Systems Corporation;
HP is a trademark of Hewlett-Packard Co.; IBM is a registered trademark of International
Business Machines Corporation; TI is a registered trademark of Texas Instruments, Inc.;
Victor is a registered trademark of Victor Technologies, Inc.; Wang is a registered
trademark of Wang Laboratories, Inc.; Zenith is a trademark of Zenith Data Systems.

The Osborne/McGraw-Hill
Guide to Using Lotus™ 1-2-3,™ Second Edition

Copyright ©1984, 1986 by Edward M. Baras. All rights reserved. Published 1984.
Second Edition 1986. Printed in the United States of America. Except as permitted under the
Copyright Act of 1976, no part of this publication may be reproduced or distributed in any form or
by any means, or stored in a data base or retrieval system, without the prior written permission of
the publisher, with the exception that the program listings may be entered, stored, and executed
in a computer system, but they may not be reproduced for publication.

1234567890 DODO 89876

ISBN 0-07-881230-5

Cindy Hudson, Acquisitions Editor

Judy Ziajka, Developmental Editor

Jean Stein, Senior Editor

Rick Finocchi of Applied Computer Consultants(Oakland, Calif.) and
Mary Campbell of Campbell & Associates (Grand Rapids, Mich.) Technical Reviewers
Elizabeth Fisher, Editorial Assistant

Donna Behrens, Composition

Yashi Okita, Cover Design

This book and its author are dedicated
to Sondra
wife, pal, mother, attorney —
the sum is greater than the parts

Contents

Acknowledgments

I'd like to acknowledge the following individuals for their advice and assistance:

Rick Finocchi and Mary Campbell, who reviewed the manuscript, giving generously of their time and expertise.

Judy Ziajka, whose daily editorial assistance contributed immeasurably to the quality of this book.

Most of all, Kevin Quinn, Director of Financial Analysis and Profit Planning at Standard & Poor's Corporation. His unqualified support and insightful advice helped transform this project from a lark of an idea to a finished product.

EMB

Preface

In less than a year, Lotus 1-2-3 became one of the most important and popular programs in the world of 16-bit microcomputers. By integrating spreadsheet analysis, information management, and graphics into a single program, 1-2-3 allows its users to develop applications more comprehensively and easily than ever before.

It is not a complicated program to use, once you have learned it. However, with over 110 commands and over 80 functions—not to mention the concepts and techniques involved in using them—you will need to invest time learning to use 1-2-3 efficiently and effectively.

The Osborne/McGraw-Hill Guide to Using Lotus 1-2-3, Second Edition, teaches 1-2-3 commands, concepts, and techniques through applications. It is a tutorial that elevates the reader from a beginning to an advanced level. Not only will you learn what the commands are, you will see how to put them together into comprehensive, integrated applications.

This book is wholly dedicated to the "learn by example" approach. Each chapter guides you, step-by-step, through the development of an application. Commands and concepts are fully explained. While the primary focus is on learning by doing, you will derive an additional bonus by developing and implementing functional, practical models.

Applications include income forecasting, portfolio management, billing, simulation, acquisition analysis, consolidations, and market surveying. The techniques involved in developing these applications apply to almost anything you would do with 1-2-3.

How This Book Is Organized

This book has been updated to include 1-2-3 Version 2. Version 2 adds a number of important enhancements to 1-2-3, including character string manipulation, increased macro programming capability, and temporary suspension of the worksheet session. The first twelve chapters of the book cover both versions 1A and 2, and owners of either version may rely on this text as a thorough guide. The last chapter deals exclusively with Version 2.

. The book consists of three major parts. Part 1 deals with spreadsheet analysis and graphics. Chapter 1 introduces 1-2-3, its uses, and its capabilities. Chapters 2 and 3 comprise a spreadsheet application, a forecast of the revenues and expenses of a corporation. These chapters cover the basics of the spreadsheet, such as entering and editing data and formulas, copying cells, formatting, saving and retrieving disk files, and printing a worksheet. Chapter 4 features 1-2-3's ability to consolidate worksheets. It also introduces graphics and macros (user-defined procedures that can be executed automatically with the stroke of two keys).

Part 1 concludes with Chapter 5, a production simulation model based on two functions: @RAND, which generates a random number, and @VLOOKUP, which performs table lookups. Having read Part 1, the reader will be well equipped to tackle spreadsheet applications like job costing, tax and depreciation schedules, sales forecasting, real estate analyses, and price estimation.

Part 2 explores database management. Chapter 6, an application to track invoices, centers on the Data Sort command, which sorts a data file in alphabetical or numerical order. Chapter 7, a continuation of the invoice tracking system, covers the Data Query commands, which locate, copy, and delete records from a database.

Chapter 8 applies macros to database management in a sales ranking task. A series of macros is developed, then combined into a user-defined command menu that allows non-technical users to run a tailor-made application with a minimum of training. Chapter 9, covering 1-2-3 database-specific functions and the data table capability, rounds off Part 2.

The techniques covered in Part 2 apply to many other database management projects, such as payroll, purchase order and inventory tracking, accounts payable and receivable, baseball statistics tracking, time sheet tracking, and cataloging.

While the first two parts of the book focus on the most used aspects of 1-2-3, Part 3 concentrates on more advanced techniques. You should be thoroughly familiar with the commands and techniques introduced in Parts 1 and 2 before you begin Part 3. Chapter 10 builds on the invoice tracking system developed in Chapters 6 and 7. This chapter introduces forms-oriented input and output, which allows users to simulate a paper form on the screen and to use this form to store and retrieve data. The chapter also shows how 1-2-3's advanced printing options give you a great measure of control over the appearance of your reports.

Chapter 11 uses forms-oriented data management to develop a stock portfolio tracking system. Macros are used to create an interactive environment.

Chapter 12 presents a spreadsheet model for valuing acquisitions. This model uses some of 1-2-3's advanced financial functions and shows how powerful a tool the data table can be when used to answer what-if questions.

The last chapter, Chapter 13, deals exclusively with Version 2 of 1-2-3. This chapter uses a purchase-order tracking system to illustrate such important Version 2 enhancements as text manipulaton functions and the ability to suspend a 1-2-3 session temporarily to perform DOS functions.

Who Should Read This Book

This book is for both beginners and experienced users of 1-2-3. Beginners should proceed sequentially through the chapters. Chapters 2 and 3 are especially important. Experienced users will benefit most from Part 2 on database management, and from the advanced techniques covered in Part 3. Class instructors will also find this book especially appropriate as a classroom workbook.

To get the most out of the book, you should implement its examples on your microcomputer as you read each chapter. The text provides all the guidance you need, but if you should require additional explanation, the Lotus User's Manual is an excellent source of reference. In addition, while you are in the Lotus system, you may press the F1 (Help) key to get on-screen assistance.

By the time you finish this book, you should be an accomplished 1-2-3 user, applying the concepts and techniques you've learned here to your own computer projects. 1-2-3 can do much more for you, however. An advanced book by the same author (Osborne/McGraw-Hill, 1986), will begin where this book ends, giving special attention to macro programming and many advanced techniques.

A Word From the Author

The author has striven to make this book as valuable and helpful to you as possible. You could restrict your entire experience of 1-2-3 to the spreadsheet capabilities alone, and probably be content. But 1-2-3 does so much more than spreadsheets. To get the most out of your software and this text, don't be satisfied with Part 1 alone. Please make sure you've covered at least Part 2, if not Part 3. Learning the many facets of 1-2-3 requires an investment of time and effort, but the rewards far exceed the price.

PART 1
Introduction to The Worksheet And Graphics

Although 1-2-3 integrates several functions, the worksheet is basic to all aspects of the software, including information management and graphics. Part 1 introduces the capabilities of 1-2-3's worksheet.

Chapter 1 opens with a description of 1-2-3's capabilities and uses. After you learn how to start the program, you will be introduced to the 1-2-3 worksheet, the blank grid of columns and rows that houses your data. You will also learn how to issue commands to 1-2-3.

Chapters 2 and 3 develop the first worksheet application of the book, a model for forecasting business revenues and expenses. In these chapters you will learn how to enter data, develop formulas, correct mistakes, change the appearance of the worksheet, use the special formula functions, and print the worksheet. You will use the Copy command to copy entries from one part of the worksheet to another.

Chapter 4 uses the same forecasting model to demonstrate how to combine files and graph data. In Chapter 5 a simulation model uses the worksheet to emulate business operations. This chapter focuses on 1-2-3's functions, including the @RAND function and its extensive calculation features.

Chapter 1
Introducing
Lotus 1-2-3

The Three Capabilities
Of 1-2-3

Memory, Amnesia,
And 1-2-3

The Keyboard

Loading 1-2-3

The 1-2-3 Worksheet

Commands and Menus

Exiting 1-2-3

Within a year of its release, Lotus 1-2-3 topped the microcomputer software market in both sales and popularity. It has been called the most powerful spreadsheet on the market. However, it is far more than a spreadsheet.

This chapter describes what 1-2-3 is and what it can do for you. You will learn about memory and disk storage. Then you will learn how to enter the

1-2-3 environment, move around the *worksheet* (the electronic grid that appears on your computer's display), issue 1-2-3 commands, enter data, and correct mistakes. Reading this chapter will provide you with the background you will need to implement the models of this book.

The Three Capabilities of 1-2-3

Until recently, the decision-making uses of desktop computers—spreadsheet analysis, information management, and graphics—were segregated into discrete, incompatible software packages. The evolution of 16-bit microcomputers, coupled with innovations in software design, has given rise to a new generation of spreadsheet software that integrates the three decision-making functions of the microcomputer into a single program.

The first decision-making function of 1-2-3, *spreadsheet analysis*, applies the memory and speed of the computer to problems that would be solved manually with paper, pencil, calculator, and a host of formulas. The worksheet provides 8192 rows (2048 in Version 1A) and 256 columns, far larger than worksheets provided by most of its predecessors. The size of 1-2-3 does not detract from its speed, however. Change some numbers, and the worksheet recalculates formulas instantly, so that you can test alternatives without waiting for an answer.

The 1-2-3 worksheet contains data in the form of words, numbers, and formulas. It includes a large number of functions that perform a variety of special calculations—financial, statistical, calendar, logical, and mathematical. Furthermore, 1-2-3 has extensive formatting capability to control the appearance of the worksheet, and its printing options provide complete control over reports.

The 1-2-3 worksheet alone is impressive, but that is only one of its three major capabilities. Its designers realized that the spreadsheet framework lends itself to a second decision-making function, *information management*. People want to organize the information contained in the worksheet. To this end, 1-2-3 can sort a worksheet alphabetically or numerically in ascending or descending order. You can instruct 1-2-3 to locate or extract data on the worksheet, using up to 32 selection criteria. No longer is there a clear delineation between spreadsheet and database functions.

The third major capability of 1-2-3 is *graphics*. A graph may be worth a thousand words, but not if it takes a thousand keystrokes to generate it. With just a few keystrokes, you can cause 1-2-3 to graph information contained in the worksheet. And if you change the data that underlie the graph, you need only press a single key to view the revised graph on the screen. When the graph is to your liking, you may produce a hard copy on any of a variety of plotters and printers supported by the software.

How does 1-2-3 do it all? You need not understand computer programming in order to derive full benefits from the program's many talents. It is important, however, to have an understanding of computer memory and of the hardware environment in which 1-2-3 operates. Your microcomputer's configuration affects the way you use 1-2-3. Therefore, if you are new to computers, you should read the next section carefully before going on.

Memory, Amnesia, and 1-2-3

In some respects, a computer "thinks" very much as you do. Suppose you are asked to write down all of the telephone numbers listed in Elyria, Ohio. You probably don't have any of the numbers in your head, but there is an Elyria telephone book in your bookshelf. With pen and paper in hand, you open to the first page and read the first phone number. It jumps from the page into your memory. Once it is in your memory, your main processing unit (sometimes known as your brain) can instruct the output device (your hand) to copy the contents of your memory onto a piece of a paper. Next you look at another number, load it into memory, and output it onto the list. When you get to the fifth number, you will probably have forgotten the first one. This is because your memory is limited and transitory; it has been erased in order to make room for the next piece of information.

Before you switch on your computer, its memory is blank. You wish to use the 1-2-3 program, but the microcomputer has no knowledge of 1-2-3. However, a computer absorbs information quickly. If you take the 1-2-3 System Disk from its envelope, place it in the disk drive, and turn the machine on, your computer reads the 1-2-3 program and loads it into *random access memory* (RAM). Once the program is in RAM, your computer understands the 1-2-3 language.

Random access memory is temporary, however. Turning off your computer gives it a severe case of amnesia—anything that was in RAM is erased. To bring back the 1-2-3 program, you must reload it into the computer's memory.

Memory is also finite. The amount of memory available for 1-2-3 use depends on how much memory has been installed in your computer. To function at all, 1-2-3 requires a minimum of 256K* of RAM (1K equals 1024

---

*For Version 1.A, the minimum is 192K.

characters). The 1-2-3 program itself takes up a large portion of this 256K. The remaining free memory is used to store the data and formulas of your own worksheet. If your worksheet is going to be large, it may not fit into 256K of RAM. This is why many owners of 1-2-3 install more than 256K in their computers. The standard memory limit of an IBM PC is 640K, but special memory expansion boards that conform to the Lotus/Intel/Microsoft Expanded Memory Specification can extend memory up to 4 million bytes beyond the 640K limit for 1-2-3 Version 2.0.

Because of this memory constraint, you won't be able to realize the full potential of the 8192-row by 256-column worksheet. You might be able to use all of the rows but only some of the columns, or all of the columns but only some of the rows. The important point is that memory limits the size of the worksheet you can actually use.

Disk Storage

If memory is temporary, how do you store information permanently? By saving the worksheet onto a diskette. Turning the machine off erases memory, but it does not erase the diskette. By way of a radical analogy, if you were struck by lightning, your memory might be destroyed, but the list of telephone numbers you wrote on paper would remain intact.

Even if memory is erased, you can retrieve your worksheet from diskette by loading it back into memory. If memory is temporary storage, a diskette is permanent storage. However, it is possible to erase information from a diskette, either deliberately or accidentally. A diskette is also subject to damage.

Formatting Data Diskettes

If you intend to store anything on a diskette, the diskette must first be *formatted*. Blank diskettes cannot be used for data storage straight out of the box. First they must be formatted so that the computer can find its way around the diskette.

You can format a diskette using the Format command of the Disk Operating System (see your DOS User's Manual for details). You can use the Format command only within the DOS environment. With Version 2.0, you can format diskettes either before or after the 1-2-3 session or during the 1-2-3 session by selecting the System command to temporarily leave 1-2-3 and enter the DOS environment. The System command is covered in Chapter 13.

With Version 1A, you cannot format data diskettes while you are within the worksheet.

The Keyboard

As you use 1-2-3 both with this book and on your own, you will need to use many keys that you may not be familiar with. To reduce the time you might later spend searching the keyboard for an F6 or a PG DN, we will take a moment here to introduce the keyboard.

Figure 1-1 shows the IBM standard keyboard. It is labeled to show several special keys that appear in the text as key names, printed in small capital letters. For example, the carriage return key (the key marked ↵ on the right side of the IBM PC keyboard) is represented in this book as the ENTER key. The four directional arrow keys (←, →, ↑, and ↓ on the far right of the keyboard) are described as the left, right, up, and down arrow keys. The key marked ↹ on the keyboard is the tab key, represented as the TAB key in this book. The key marked ⇧ is the SHIFT key, and ← is the BACKSPACE key. Other special key names will also be printed in small capital letters. For example, F5 is function key 5, HOME is the Home key, and PG UP is the Pg Up (page up) key.

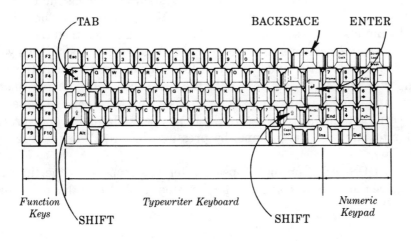

Figure 1-1. The IBM keyboard

A Note to Users of Non-IBM Versions of 1-2-3

The models in this book are described for use with an IBM PC or PC XT or with a completely compatible machine. Versions of 1-2-3 for other microcomputers are essentially the same as that for the IBM microcomputer, except for certain differences in the keyboard and operating system.

For your convenience, Appendix A at the back of this book details the differences between the IBM and other keyboards. If you are using a non-IBM version of 1-2-3, be sure to consult this appendix and also your 1-2-3 User's Manual, particularly with regard to preparing diskettes and loading the 1-2-3 program.

Loading 1-2-3

When you use the 1-2-3 program diskettes for the first time, you must prepare the program diskettes that come with the package, following the instructions in the 1-2-3 User's Manual. This process serves to install "drivers," programs that tell 1-2-3 how to interact with your particular set of hardware. Once the program disks have been prepared, you may load the 1-2-3 system. See the 1-2-3 documentation for instructions on installing the program for your particular system.

To load 1-2-3, you first load the DOS system by placing the DOS diskette into drive A (the left-hand disk on the IBM PC) and turning on the computer.* Prompts on the screen request the current date and then the time of day. The operating system uses the date and time to keep track of when you saved files onto a diskette, and 1-2-3 uses these for calendar calculations. If it is important to you to date your data files, or if you will be using the current date and time in 1-2-3 calculations, then be sure to respond to these prompts (according to the instructions in the DOS User's Manual). However, it is possible to skip over the prompts by pressing the ENTER key as each prompt appears.

The DOS "A:>" prompt appears after you respond to the time prompt. Replace the DOS disk with the 1-2-3 System Disk. From this point, there are

---

*Hard disk users have a different procedure for loading 1-2-3, described in the Lotus documentation.

two ways to enter the 1-2-3 worksheet. The most direct method is to type **123** and press the ENTER key. Another method is to type **LOTUS** and press ENTER. The LOTUS command invokes the *Lotus Access System*, which permits you to enter the worksheet, print a graph, or translate files to and from other program formats. In addition, the Access System of Version 2.0 allows you to begin the Install program or the disk-based tutorial, whereas in Version 1A the Access System allows you to perform diskette and file maintenance.

For now, you will simply enter the worksheet. You may either type **123** and press ENTER, or type **LOTUS** and press ENTER. If you choose the LOTUS command, the Access System menu appears at the top of the screen, and "1-2-3" appears in reverse video. Press the ENTER key to select the 1-2-3 worksheet.

The 1-2-3 logo appears on the screen. With Version 2.0, the worksheet appears automatically after a few moments, while with Version 1A, you must press a key to invoke the worksheet.

The 1-2-3 Worksheet

Figure 1-2 displays the 1-2-3 worksheet. A worksheet is a table of rows and columns that intersect to form many cells. Each cell has an address composed of the cell's coordinates (its column and row). Columns of the worksheet are designated by letters and rows by numbers. The highlighted border areas on top and to the left of the worksheet identify the columns and rows. For example, the address of the top-left cell of the worksheet is A1 (columns come before rows in cell addresses).

Cell Pointer, Control Panel, And Mode Indicator

Notice that cell A1 is highlighted in the worksheet. A movable highlight, called a *cell pointer*, currently rests on A1. If you press the right arrow key, the pointer moves one cell to the right, to B1.

The three lines above the worksheet border area are called the *control panel*. The control panel is used to display the current pointer position, command menus, information about the current cell location of the pointer, prompts, and the keystrokes that you have typed already to enter or edit data. At present the control panel displays the address of the cell pointer.

A *mode indicator* resides at the top right of the worksheet. It currently displays the word READY in inverse video, indicating that 1-2-3 is in Ready

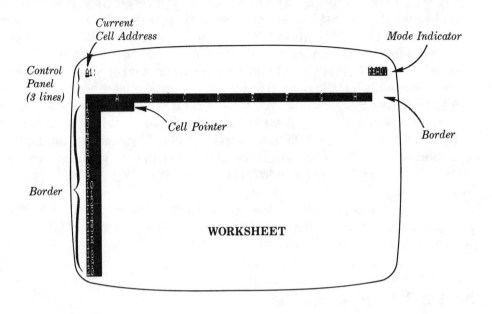

Figure 1-2. The 1-2-3 worksheet

Mode. *Ready Mode* means that 1-2-3 is ready to accept a command or a data entry. Before taking either step, we will become more familiar with the worksheet display.

Exploring the Worksheet

If you view a football game through binoculars, you can focus on a particular part of the playing field. To see another part of the field, you must focus the binoculars elsewhere—the field is too big for you to see its entirety through the lenses. Similarly, the screen is a window through which you can view a section of the worksheet. But the screen is too small for you to view the entire worksheet at once. What you are seeing now is a corner of a much larger area. To see a different part of the worksheet, you must shift the position of the window.

Press the right arrow key several times, until the pointer is in cell H1. If you press the right arrow key once more, column I appears in the window;

the pointer is in I1. However, because there is no room on the display for an extra column, column A *scrolls* off the screen at the left. Press the right arrow key again, and you will gain column J but lose column B. The right arrow key is moving the window to the right.

Holding down an arrow key causes the keystroke to repeat. (This is the case with almost any key on the keyboard.) Hold down the left arrow key. The pointer moves to the left, eventually causing the window to shift to the left. The pointer cannot go beyond column A, though. If you try to move the pointer beyond any of the worksheet limits, 1-2-3 will sound a "beep."

The up and down arrow keys move the pointer vertically. Whereas the arrow keys move the pointer one cell at a time, other pointer movement keys cause the pointer to skip. For example, pressing the HOME key transfers the pointer directly to cell A1, at the top left of the worksheet. The PG UP and PG DN keys move the pointer vertically by an entire screen. The TAB key moves the pointer horizontally by an entire screen. (Pressing the TAB key alone causes the pointer to move to the right; pressing SHIFT and TAB simultaneously moves it back to the left.)

You can also go directly to a specific cell using F5, the GoTo key. When you press the F5 (GoTo) key, 1-2-3 asks for the address to go to. If you type IV2048 and press the ENTER key, the pointer skips to column IV, row 2048. Using the arrow keys to get back home (cell A1) would be quite slow. But if you press the HOME key, you will see how fast the pointer movement can be.

Commands and Menus

Now that you know your way around the worksheet, you are ready to learn how to invoke a command menu, select a command, and "undo" a command selection.

Issuing commands to 1-2-3 is similar to ordering a meal in a restaurant in at least one sense: you select a command from a command *menu*.

The first step is to invoke the main menu by pressing the / (slash) key, located near the bottom right of the IBM PC keyboard.

1. Press the / key.

Throughout this book, all instructions that require you to type or enter commands are presented as numbered steps. Keys that you must press to enter commands or data are printed in boldface, as is the / in step 1.

Pressing the / key causes the main menu to appear in the control panel, as shown in Figure 1-3.

The top line of the control panel still shows the pointer address and the

Main
Menu
Line

Description
of Current
Selection

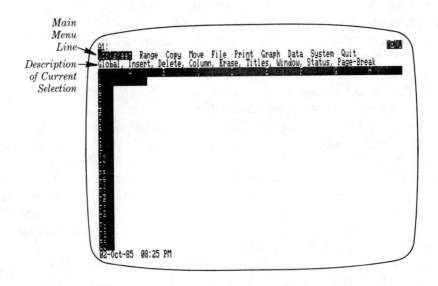

Figure 1-3. The main menu

contents of that address. (In this case, cell A1 is empty, so no characters appear beside it.) The second line displays the menu, a list of command names. The first command of the menu is highlighted by a *menu pointer*, which may be moved to other menu options by using the pointer movement keys, as we shall soon see.

Beneath the menu is a short description of the command that is highlighted by the menu pointer. This description consists of either a list of options (a submenu) pertaining to the command or a sentence about what the command does. The description for the Worksheet command, for example, is a list of options available with the Worksheet command:

Global, Insert, Delete, Column, Erase, Titles, Window, Status, Page-Break

(Version 1A substitutes "Column-Width" for "Column" and does not include the "Page-Break" command.)

Pressing the right arrow key moves the menu pointer to the next command of the main menu, the Range command.

2. Press the right arrow key.

Notice that the description on the third line of the control panel has changed; it now displays the submenu of the Range command.

3. Press the right arrow key once more.

The menu pointer now rests on the Copy command, whose description is

Copy a cell or range of cells

Because the Copy command does not involve a submenu, 1-2-3 can use the third line of the control panel to display a phrase describing what the command does.

You can use other keys to move from one menu selection to another. The left arrow key moves the pointer leftward in the menu. You can "jump" in a menu by pressing the END key to transfer the pointer to the last menu command or the HOME key to skip back to the first command. Once the pointer is on the command that you want, pressing the ENTER key selects that command. We will be exploring the capabilities of each of the main-menu commands as we proceed through the book. For now, though, we will issue one exemplary command, the Worksheet command.

4. Press the HOME key to move the menu pointer to the Worksheet command.

5. Press the ENTER key to choose the command.

Selecting the Worksheet command brings the Worksheet submenu to the control panel. This menu contains the same options as the Worksheet command description of the main menu. Now that we are in the submenu, however, the third line of the control panel displays a descriptive phrase about the option being pointed to.

You can see that several layers of menus can pertain to a single 1-2-3 command. Selecting a command from a menu brings you to the next layer. But what if you made the wrong menu selection by accident?

Correcting Menu Selections
With Escapes and Breaks

Fortunately, 1-2-3 is a very forgiving program. If you get into trouble with a menu, you can always leave the menu by pressing the ESC (escape) key at the upper-left corner of the IBM PC keyboard. The ESC key brings you one step backward. If you are in a submenu, ESC returns you to the previous menu, as if you had never made a mistake. If you press ESC while in the main menu, you are returned to Ready Mode—where you were before you typed the / key to get into the main menu.

To escape from the submenu of the Worksheet command to the main menu,

1. Press the ESC key.

Escaping is the gradual way of getting out of trouble. The more abrupt way is to issue a *break* by holding down the CTRL key (on the left side of the IBM PC keyboard) and pressing the SCROLL LOCK/BREAK key. No matter how deeply into the layers of menus you are, a break whisks you directly into Ready Mode.

To get back into the Worksheet menu, you would select the Worksheet option. Actually, 1-2-3 offers two ways to select a menu option. The first is to use the pointer, as we have done. The other way is to press the first letter of the option you want to select. Thus, to select the Worksheet option, you would

2. Type the **W** key.

Using this method, there is no need to press the ENTER key. The second method is faster because you do not move the pointer and then press the ENTER key. Instead you press only one key. The pointing method may be more intuitive, but as you become familiar with the menus, you will find the typing method both comfortable and quick. You may choose the method that suits you best.

Checking Memory: The Worksheet Status Command

Recall from the previous discussion of memory that there is a limit to the amount of worksheet that you can actually use. As you store data on the worksheet, you use up memory. It is important to keep track of how much memory is available to you.

The Worksheet Status command reports how much free memory is available at the moment that you issue the command. It also gives other information about the worksheet, but for now we restrict our attention to the status of memory. Currently, we are in the Worksheet submenu.

1. Select the Status option either by pointing to Status and then pressing ENTER or by typing **S**.

The screen displays the amount of memory in bytes (characters) along with other information. Remember that 1K of RAM equals 1024 bytes. If you know how much RAM is installed in your machine, multiply that number by 1024 to derive the number of bytes. Compare this number to the amount of memory available, and you will see how much RAM is taken up by the 1-2-3 program and the operating system. Your worksheet is now empty, so the number you see as available memory is the most you can have with the amount of RAM installed. After you use up a section of the worksheet, you should issue the Worksheet Status command periodically to check the available memory. You will be able to tell when you get close to running out, and you can then decide whether you want to install more memory in your computer.

To return to the blank worksheet display,

2. Press any key.

You are now back in Ready Mode, ready to invoke another command, enter data, take a coffee break, or begin the next chapter.

Exiting 1-2-3

You will conclude this chapter by learning how to exit from the program. Simply

1. Type /, press END to move the pointer to the Quit command, and press ENTER.

A prompt will ask whether you are sure you want to leave the current work session.

2. Select the Yes option.

If you used the 123 command to enter 1-2-3 from DOS, you will be returned to DOS (provided that the disk in the main drive is a system disk, such as the DOS system disk containing the COMMAND.COM file). If you entered 1-2-3 through the Access program using the LOTUS command, you will be returned to the Access System menu.

Note that you don't have to select the Quit command to leave 1-2-3. If you are finished with a 1-2-3 session and you have no need to exit into either Access or DOS, simply remove your diskettes and turn off your machine. The purpose of the Quit option really is to enable you to continue doing something else with your computer. If you have nothing else to do, there's no need to stand on formality.

Now that you are familiar with the worksheet, you can proceed directly to the first application. But make sure you have a formatted data diskette or two handy. Roll up your sleeves, rev up your mind, and turn the page.

Chapter 2
Using
The 1-2-3
Worksheet

———————————————————————————

———————————————————————————

———————————————————————————

Most spreadsheet applications are financial in nature. This chapter, together with Chapter 3, develops a financial tool for forecasting the revenues, expenses, and profits of a business or service enterprise. In the process, these chapters also serve as an introduction to basic spreadsheet concepts. You will learn how to enter and edit data, develop formulas, save and retrieve worksheets, copy cells from one part of the worksheet to another, format cells, and insert columns.

Completing these two chapters will give you a working knowledge of the spreadsheet facility, as well as a working model to use in forecasting the income statement of an organization. More importantly, you will have the necessary tools to develop your own worksheets for such applications as personal financial planning, budgets, cost projections, and checkbook registry.

Financial forecasting has many different definitions, but essentially it is a method for predicting financial performance. One barometer of financial performance is the income statement, which is an enumeration of the revenues and expenses associated with an organization's operation in one or more periods of time. Our model will be based on assumptions relating to the change in each line item of the income statement over time. We will build a model adaptable to many situations, though we will focus on a particular firm.

Rags to Riches' Income Statement: First Steps

Two years ago, Lesley and Sandy Rich began the lucrative business of manufacturing designer dishtowels. The dishtowels were produced by sewing the *L&S Rich* label onto secondhand rags. The designer dishtowels were quite successful—so much so that the innovators named their corporation Rags to Riches and grossed $10 million in revenues during their first year of operation.

The Riches believe that demand for the dishtowels will continue to be strong for years to come. They would like to have a forecast (or *pro forma*) income statement to predict the levels of sales, expenses, and profits over the next five years. The pro forma model should be able to reflect changes in assumptions about sales and expenses, because the financial future of a business rarely can be known with absolute certainty.

Figure 2-1 gives us a preview of the type of pro forma income statement we will be developing in this chapter and in Chapter 3. Step by step, we will make assumptions pertaining to the financial performance of Rags to Riches. We will use these assumptions to create the formulas that underlie the pro forma income statement.

	A	B	C	D	E	F	G	H	I
1									
2			INCOME STATEMENT						
3			RAGS-TO-RICHES CORPORATION						
4					($ IN THOUSANDS)				
5			0	1	2	3	4	5	NOTES
6	REVENUE		10000	12000	15600	18720	20592	22651	
7	% GROWTH OVER PREVIOUS YEAR			20.00%	30.00%	20.00%	10.00%	10.00%	
8									
9	COST OF GOODS SOLD								
10	MATERIALS			2040	2652	3182	3501	3851	% OF SALES
11	WAGES			1680	2184	2621	2883	3171	% OF SALES
12	FRINGE BENEFITS			252	328	393	432	476	% OF WAGES
13	OTHER			100	108	117	126	136	% GROWTH RATE
14									
15	GENERAL & ADMINISTRATIVE EXPENSE								
16	COMPENSATION: OFFICE			1200	1320	1452	1597	1757	% GROWTH RATE
17	COMPENSATION: SALES			960	1248	1498	1647	1812	% OF SALES
18	FRINGE BENEFITS			367	437	501	552	607	% OF COMP.
19	ADVERTISING & PROMOTION			300	390	468	515	566	% OF SALES
20	DEPRECIATION			20	20	20	20	20	DIRECT INPUT
21	MISCELLANEOUS			10	20	30	40	50	CONSTANT GROWTH
22									
23	TOTAL OPERATING EXPENSES		6400	6929	8706	10282	11313	12446	
24									
25	INTEREST EXPENSE		10	10	10	10	10	10	DIRECT INPUT
26									
27	PRE-TAX INCOME		3590	5061	6884	8428	9269	10196	
28									
29	TAX		1867	2632	3580	4383	4820	5302	% OF PRE-TAX INC.
30									
31	NET INCOME		1723	2429	3304	4045	4449	4894	

Figure 2-1. A pro forma income statement

Entering Worksheet Titles

Load 1-2-3, as described in Chapter 1. Your first step in building the Riches' pro forma income statement is to enter worksheet titles.

1. Use the arrow keys to move the cell pointer to cell C1.

Here we will enter the worksheet title, INCOME STATEMENT. The words INCOME STATEMENT constitute a *label*, which is defined as a string of characters that form the contents of a cell. Before entering the label into cell C1, notice that the mode indicator on the top right of the control panel says READY. 1-2-3 is prepared to accept data or to receive a command.

2. Press the CAPS LOCK key near the bottom right of the keyboard.

The word CAPS appears in inverse video on the bottom of the screen. Every letter you type while the CAPS indicator is on will appear in uppercase. If you press the CAPS LOCK key again, the CAPS indicator will vanish from the screen, and typing will revert to lowercase except when the SHIFT key is used.

When entering this label, we will find it convenient to remain in uppercase mode so that we need not bother with the SHIFT key to capitalize each letter. Note that CAPS LOCK affects only letters, not numbers or other keys.

3. Type the letter **I**. (If you make a mistake when typing, you can erase it by pressing the BACKSPACE key.)

Observe the mode indicator: it has switched from READY to LABEL because 1-2-3 has guessed that you have begun to enter a label into a cell. The letter I is on the second line of the control panel, followed by a blinking cursor which indicates where the next character typed will be placed.

4. Finish typing the title **INCOME STATEMENT** and press the ENTER key.

Pressing ENTER stores the label in cell C1 and returns 1-2-3 to Ready Mode. If you discover a typing error before pressing ENTER, you can correct it by using the BACKSPACE key, located above the ENTER key. The BACKSPACE key works just like the backspace key on a typewriter, except that it erases the characters over which you backspace.

If there are too many errors to bother correcting and if you have not yet pressed ENTER, you may escape from the situation by pressing the ESC key at the top left corner of the keyboard. The ESC key totally negates the entry and returns you to Ready Mode, as if you had never begun this data entry in the first place. We will see that ESC provides an escape route in many other situations as well.

Once you press ENTER, the entry is stored in the cell. If you find an error in the entry, simply leave the pointer on the cell and type the entry over again. Whatever you type will overwrite the previous contents of the cell when you press ENTER again. Later, we will see another means of editing an entry that has already been stored in a cell.

Initially, each cell in the worksheet has a width of nine characters. The INCOME STATEMENT title, however, is 16 characters wide, and so it does not fit entirely into cell C1. The last seven characters spill over into the next cell, D1. (Some less lenient spreadsheet packages would have truncated the label to nine characters.)

Notice the first line of the control panel. It displays the location of the pointer, cell C1, as well as the contents of this address. An apostrophe precedes the label. The apostrophe is called a *label-prefix*, and it serves as proof that the cell contains a label. Moreover, the apostrophe means that the label will be left-justified in the cell. The label-prefix appears only in the control panel, not in the cell itself. Actually, 1-2-3 has internally stored the prefix with the label in order to classify the display format of the entry and to distinguish the entry as a label rather than a *value*, which is interpreted arithmetically. There are other label-prefixes, and we will encounter them later in this book.

To further identify the worksheet, we will add a second title line, giving the name of the company to which this income statement pertains.

5. Go to cell B2 by pressing the F5 (GoTo) key and typing **B2** ENTER.

6. Type **RAGS TO RICHES CORPORATION**, and then press ENTER to store the label in the cell.

Using Edit Mode

Because the second title line is longer than the first, we began it one column to the left (in Column B) with the hope that it would end up centered beneath the first title line. Unfortunately, the company name is not quite long enough to be centered below the INCOME STATEMENT title. The label INCOME STATEMENT is 16 characters long, while RAGS TO RICHES CORPORATION is 26. The difference of 10 characters would dictate that the second title line must begin five spaces to the left of the top line in order to be centered. Because each column of the worksheet has a default width of nine characters, the second title actually begins nine characters to the left of the title above it. We need to insert four spaces in front of RAGS TO RICHES CORPORATION. This is accomplished by using Edit Mode.

1. With the pointer remaining on cell B2, press the F2 (Edit) key to enter Edit Mode.

Observe that the mode indicator now reads EDIT. *Edit Mode* permits you to add to, delete from, or otherwise alter the contents of the cell currently indicated by the position of the pointer.

Pressing the F2 (Edit) key causes the cell contents to appear on the second line of the control panel, along with the blinking *edit cursor.* The edit cursor indicates the point at which the next editing action will take effect.

Initially, the edit cursor appears at the end of the cell contents. To change the contents of a cell, you need to position the edit cursor beneath the portion you want to edit and then type the characters to be added to the cell contents. With the edit cursor at the end of the cell contents, the effect of typing additional characters would be to append these characters to the end of the current contents. We want to insert spaces at the beginning of a label, so we must move the cursor to the far left of the cell contents.

There are several ways to move the cursor in Edit Mode. The left arrow and right arrow keys move the underscore left or right one space each time one of them is depressed. The TAB key moves the edit cursor five characters to the right. To tab left, hold down the SHIFT key while pressing the TAB key. The END key makes the cursor skip to the last character of the cell, whereas the HOME key skips to the first character.

2. Press the HOME key.

The edit cursor is now situated at the beginning of the cell contents, the label-prefix. Any entry you make at this point will be inserted before the apostrophe, causing the apostrophe and all characters to the right of the apostrophe to shift to the right. However, it is not our intention to insert spaces *before* the apostrophe. Because the label actually begins *after* the apostrophe, we must position the edit cursor after the apostrophe, beneath the letter R of RAGS.

3. Press the right arrow key once to move the edit cursor one space to the right of the label-prefix.

4. Press the space bar four times to insert four spaces.

The revised contents, on line 2 of the control panel, now appear as

'   RAGS TO RICHES CORPORATION

Until the ENTER key is pressed, the old label will still be stored and displayed in cell B2, but do not press ENTER yet—there is still more editing to be done.

Perhaps you made a typing error somewhere in the second title. Even if you did not, the company chairpersons have just decided to hyphenate the firm's name: instead of RAGS TO RICHES, the second title should be written as RAGS-TO-RICHES.

5. Press the right arrow key four times to position the edit cursor beneath the space directly to the right of RAGS.

6. Press the - key once. (The character - is used both as a hyphen and as a minus sign. You may use either the - key near the upper right of the keyboard or the - key on the numeric keypad.)

The hyphen has been inserted above the cursor, but the space that has now been shifted to the right of the hyphen should be deleted. You can extract characters with the aid of the DEL (delete) key. First

7. Press the DEL key once.

The DEL key deletes the character above the cursor. Next, insert the second hyphen after the word TO. This time, delete the space before you insert the hyphen, as follows:

8. Use the right arrow key to position the edit cursor beneath the space to the right of TO.

9. Press the DEL key to delete the space.

10. Press the - key to insert the hyphen.

If you made any other mistakes, correct them, and then

11. Press ENTER.

Pressing ENTER while in Edit Mode stores the edited line of the control panel into the current location of the cell pointer (replacing any former contents), clears the second line of the control panel, and returns you to Ready Mode.

Entering Column Headings

The pro forma income statement will include six years of information. The first column of data contains actual profit-and-loss figures for the previous year of operations. We refer to this period as Year 0. The next five columns of the spreadsheet will contain the forecasted results for the next five years of operations. Column A of the spreadsheet will be used for row headings of the statement, such as REVENUE and NET INCOME. Therefore, Year 0 figures will be stored in column B, Year 1 in column C, and so forth. Let us enter the headings for these columns in row 4 of the worksheet. Each heading will consist of the number corresponding to the year: 0, 1, 2, 3, 4, or 5.

1. Use the F5 (GoTo) key to move to cell B4.

Here we will enter the heading for Year 0.

2. Press the **0** (zero) key on the top row of the keyboard.

The numeric keypad on the far right of the standard IBM keyboard serves two functions. It can be used to move the pointer or it can be used as a standard keyboard. However, the keyboard can perform only one of these two functions at a time. As a rule, it is best to use the keyboard for pointer movement only, using the keys on the top row of the keyboard to enter numbers. When you first start up 1-2-3, the numeric keyboard has the pointer-movement function. If you wish to use the keyboard to enter numbers, press the NUM LOCK key. This disables the pointer-movement function, activates the numeric keyboard, and causes the NUM indicator to appear on the bottom right of the screen. Pressing NUM LOCK a second time switches the keyboard back to its pointer-movement function.

The character 0 is numeric, and 1-2-3 considers it a value rather than a label. Notice the mode indicator. 1-2-3 enters Value Mode because it knows that you pressed the number 0, not a character. The distinction is very important because 1-2-3 is able to do certain things (such as arithmetic) with values that it cannot do with labels.

3. Press ENTER to complete the data entry.

Look at the control panel. Its first line reads

B4: 0

Observe that there are no prefixes for values as there are for labels.

A Formula for Numeric Column Headings

The heading for Year 1 could similarly be entered by pressing **1** and ENTER, but we will use a different method to illustrate how 1-2-3 uses formulas.

There are two types of values. One is a number, such as the 0 we entered in cell B4. The other type of value is a formula. A *formula* is a set of instructions that tell 1-2-3 to make calculations. When a formula is placed in a cell, 1-2-3 stores the instructions, carries out the calculation according to the formula, and displays the results of the calculation in the cell.

1. Move to cell C4.

Because the income-statement years are sequential, the formula for each year after Year 0 can be expressed as 1 plus the previous year. Thus, the heading for Year 1 is derived from the formula $1+0=1$. In terms of cell coordinates, the formula for the Year 1 heading can be entered as 1+B4. Upon receiving this formula, 1-2-3 examines the value of cell B4 (which is 0), adds 1 to it, and stores the result (1) at the current position of the pointer, C4.

2. Press the **1** key on the top row of the keyboard.

Notice that the mode indicator shows that 1-2-3 has entered Value Mode, because the first key pressed for the entry was a number. Now continue entry of the 1+B4 formula:

3. Type **+B4** and press ENTER.

Pressing ENTER stores the formula, displays the result in cell C4, and resumes Ready Mode. The control panel indicates that the formula 1+B4 has been assigned to the cell.

If we were to use formulas to enter the headings for Years 2 through 5, we would find that the formulas are nearly identical. In each cell, the formula is 1 plus the value of the previous cell. The formulas are not *exactly* the same; the formula 1+B4 for Year 1 differs slightly from 1+C4, the formula for Year 2. However, because the formulas are similar, the Copy command can be used to copy the formula in C4 to another cell or to several other cells.

Introducing the Copy Command

The Copy command replicates a range of cells from one location of the worksheet (the *source*) to another (the *target*). Ranges of cells are used frequently in 1-2-3 commands and functions, so before we go on to experiment with copying, we will take a moment to discuss ranges.

Cell Ranges

A *range* is a rectangle of cells. This rectangle can be a row of two or more adjacent cells, a column of adjacent cells, or a block containing two or more rows and columns. A single cell also qualifies as a range; it is a block made up of a single row and a single column.

Lotus 1-2-3 identifies a range by its first and last coordinates. As we will see later, there are several ways to specify a range. The one we will use here is to enter the addresses of the two ends of the range, separated by a period.*

---

*Actually, 1-2-3 allows you to type one, two, or three periods between the two addresses of the range. Thus A1.J1, A1..J1, and A1...J1 all have the same meaning.

The row of cells from A1 through J1 is entered as A1.J1. The column A1 to A15 is entered as A1.A15.

A rectangular block of cells is fully described by specifying any two of its diagonally opposite corners. For example, the rectangle whose corners are A1, J1, J15, and A15 could be entered as A1.J15 or J1.A15. When 1-2-3 sees either of these sets of coordinates, it realizes that the range's width spans columns A through J and that its length spans rows 1 through 15.

There is little choice in how to designate a single-cell range. The cell's address is both the beginning and the end of the range. For example, the range consisting only of cell A1 would be entered as A1.A1. Now that we know the rules of range notation, let us proceed to the Copy command.

How the Copy Command Works

The Copy command copies a source range to a target range. The following table summarizes the various types of replications you can do with the Copy command:

SOURCE	TARGET
One cell	One cell
	A horizontal range (row)
	A vertical range (column)
	A rectangular block
A column	A column
	A rectangular block (several columns)
A row	A row
	A rectangular block (several rows)
A rectangular block	A rectangular block

The Copy command generally involves four steps.

First, move the pointer to the source to be copied. If the source is a single cell, position the pointer at that cell. If the source is a range of cells, position the pointer at the top-left cell of the range.

Next, initiate the Copy command by typing the / and C keys.

Third, identify both the source and target in response to 1-2-3 prompts.

Finally, press the ENTER key to activate the copy procedure.

The simplest type of copy is from one cell to another cell. This is the type of procedure that we will use to copy the formula stored in cell C4 (1+B4) into cell D4.

Copying to a Single Cell

To implement the four steps just described,

1. Position the pointer at cell C4, the source.

2. Type /Copy to invoke the Copy command.

Now 1-2-3 gives the response, "Enter range to copy from: C4..C4". (When 1-2-3 displays a range, it always uses two dots between the two addresses, even though it allows you to use one, two, or three dots.) Automatically, 1-2-3 assumes that the beginning of the source range is the cell where the pointer is located. It also recommends the same cell as the end of the source range. In other words, 1-2-3 recommends a source range of a single cell, C4. This is precisely the desired source, so

3. Press ENTER to lock in the source range.

Now that 1-2-3 knows the source cell, it awaits the designation of the target cell or range by prompting "Enter range to copy to: C4". By default,* 1-2-3 recommends the current pointer position (C4), but this is unacceptable. The cell we would like to copy to is D4. One way of overriding 1-2-3's recommendation is to

4. Type **D4**.

This tells 1-2-3 where you want the target cell to be. To signal to 1-2-3 that you have finished entering the target,

5. Press the ENTER key.

Instantly, the sum of 1+C4, which is 2, appears in D4. The pointer is returned to C4, its position prior to the Copy procedure. Move the pointer to cell D4, and then inspect the control panel. The first line, indicating the contents of the cell, shows its value to be a formula, 1+C4.

---

*A default value is something the worksheet automatically assumes or uses unless you tell it otherwise.

Relative Copying

When someone stops you on the street to ask directions to a road in your neighborhood, you would be more apt to say "three blocks up, then two blocks to the right" than to give the precise latitude and longitude of the destination. Your instructions would be *relative* to your location.

Unless you tell it otherwise, 1-2-3 also thinks in relative terms. As you see, Copy does not necessarily copy exactly. Although the source cell contained 1+B4, the target cell contains 1+C4 after the copy. This is because 1-2-3 performed a *relative copy* by replicating the relative positions of cells referenced in the source's formula. In other words, 1-2-3 interpreted the contents of the source cell as *1 + the contents of the cell to the left of the source*, not as *1 + cell B4*. The cell referenced in the source formula (B4) is interpreted in terms of its position relative to the source cell (C4). Therefore, when the formula is copied to the target cell D4, it is copied as *1 + the contents of the cell to the left of D4*, so the target contents become 1+C4.

To obtain the headings for Years 3, 4, and 5, simply use the Copy command to replicate cell D4's formula to cells E4 through G4. This constitutes copying from a single-cell source to a target range. The first step is to move the pointer to the source of the copy, cell D4.

1. Move the pointer to cell D4.

Next, begin the command.

2. Type /Copy.

1-2-3 recommends D4..D4 as the source, which is correct, so

3. Press the ENTER key.

The desired target is the range E4.G4, but 1-2-3 is suggesting D4. Override the recommendation by entering the correct range.

4. Type **E4.G4**.

5. Press the ENTER key.

The column headings for the forecasted years are now complete.

Using formulas and the Copy command to produce column headings may seem unduly complicated as a substitute for entering numbers. However, the Copy command is the cornerstone of electronic spreadsheets. Once mastered, it acts as a significant time-saver in applications development, as we will demonstrate shortly.

Repeating Labels and Underscores

To set off the column headings from the rest of the spreadsheet, we should put underscores beneath the headings. We cannot put a series of underscore characters within the heading cells themselves because these characters would replace the heading characters. However, it is possible to put a row of underscores in the cells beneath the headings.

1. Press the F5 (GoTo) key, and then type **B5** and press ENTER. This will place the pointer at cell B5, the cell beneath the heading for Year 0.

To fill the cell with hyphens, you would expect to press the - key several times.

2. Press the - key once.

Examine the mode indicator. Note that 1-2-3 is in Value Mode, even though you think you are entering a label. Remember that 1-2-3 classifies a data entry by examining the first key typed—in this case, the - key. When 1-2-3 sees a - as the first character of an entry, it assumes that you are about to enter a negative value (for example, -5). Here is an instance where we do not intend to enter a numeric character, but 1-2-3 assumes a value. Therefore, we must explicitly override the default assumption.

First, exit Value Mode. To do this,

3. Press the ESC key.

To override the program's default assumption that our - entry is a value, we must begin the entry by typing a label-prefix character.

Which label-prefix character? The apostrophe has already been introduced. When you entered titles earlier in this chapter, 1-2-3 assumed they were labels and automatically inserted the apostrophe label-prefix.

It is permissible, though, to type the label-prefix yourself. Thus, one way to enter a string of hyphens would be to explicitly type '-----. 1-2-3 would recognize the initial apostrophe as a label-prefix, would enter Label Mode, and would display only the hyphens in the cell entry. To use this method, however, you would have to count exactly how many hyphens to enter in order to fill up the entire cell.

1-2-3 provides an easier way, using a different label-prefix. The \ (backward slash) label-prefix is used to enter a repeating label into a cell from Ready Mode. With the pointer still on B5,

4. Type the \ key.

1-2-3 enters Label Mode (check the mode indicator) and awaits a repeating label. Any character(s) you type before pressing ENTER will be repeated until the cell is full. Thus \- will fill the cell with dashes.

5. Type the - key and press ENTER.

The \- could be used in each of cells C5 through G5 to underscore the rest of the headings. Here is where the Copy command can be used to save some keystrokes. (Copy can be used for labels as well as values.) The pointer is already on the source, so proceed with the command:

6. Type /Copy.

7. Press ENTER to accept B5 as the source.

The target is the range of C5 through G5, so

8. Type **C5.G5** to enter the target range.

9. Press ENTER to conclude the copy.

Imagine how useful the Copy command would be if the forecast covered 20 years instead of only five.

Saving and Retrieving Files: How to Avoid Zapping

Have you ever been "zapped?" "Zapping" occurs when you lose something valuable for no good reason. A police zap occurs when you get ticketed for $30 because you forgot to renew your automobile registration. Similarly, a worksheet zap occurs if you neglect to save your file onto disk periodically as you develop a worksheet. A worksheet zap can happen because your colleague turned off the computer before you saved the file, or because of a power failure or perhaps a disk-drive failure. Like all zaps, the worksheet variety can be prevented with a little due care. Simply issue the File Save command to store the worksheet onto disk.

1. Type /**F**ile Save.

In response to the program's request for a save-file name,

2. Type **IS** and press the ENTER key.

We chose IS as an abbreviation for income statement. We could have picked any name.* Generally, however, it is better to choose a name that will jog your memory about the contents of the file. It takes only a few moments to copy the worksheet from memory onto diskette.

To retrieve the file from diskette, issue the File Retrieve command. Then 1-2-3 will request the name of the file to be retrieved. On the third line of the control panel, it lists the names of worksheet files currently residing on the data disk. You may either point to the desired file and press the ENTER key or explicitly type the file name yourself.

Note that retrieving a file causes the worksheet that is currently on the screen to be erased. If you do not save the current worksheet before you retrieve a new file, you are exposing yourself to worksheet zap. Save your files, and save yourself a lot of headaches.

Building Rags-to-Riches' Revenue Forecast

The stream of revenues that a company receives for its product depends on various factors. Demand, of course, is a primary factor; the state of the economy is another. Price increases must also be taken into account in predicting sales, and returns of merchandise must be deducted from sales to arrive at a net figure. If historical figures were available, historical trends would be an integral part of the forecast. Inasmuch as Rags-to-Riches has no history to speak of, a trend analysis will not be feasible.

For the purposes of this model, we will assume high growth in the first two years, lesser growth in the third year, and stabilized growth in the fourth and fifth years.

Management predicts that year-to-year revenue growth will be as follows:

YEAR	% GROWTH OVER PREVIOUS YEAR
1	25%
2	30%
3	20%
4	10%
5	10%

---

*File names may be up to eight characters long, and they may include letters (A through Z), digits (0 through 9), or underscores (_). Spaces are not allowed.

This scenario may be an optimistic one—particularly considering the high growth rates in the first three years. Later we may choose to change these growth rates. Therefore, it is important to build the spreadsheet with a liberal amount of flexibility so that changing assumptions won't necessitate building another model.

1. Move to cell A6, and then enter the row label **REVENUE**.

2. Move the pointer to Year 0 REVENUE (cell B6).

3. Enter **10000** (no commas), which represents $10 million of sales last year.

The figures used in this statement are expressed in thousands of dollars, so that 10000 actually means $10 million. To make this clear on the worksheet,

4. Move to cell F1.

We will enter the label ($ IN THOUSANDS) here. However, 1-2-3 interprets a left parenthesis (like the - character) as the beginning of a value entry; parentheses are commonly used in formulas such as (5+4)+3. Accordingly, we must enter an apostrophe label-prefix before this label entry:

5. Type **'($ IN THOUSANDS)** and then press ENTER.

As soon as you enter the apostrophe, 1-2-3 enters Label Mode. Any further alphabetic or numeric entries are treated as part of a label.

In Year 1, the growth is 25% of the previous year's net sales of $10,000. Year 1 sales are therefore 1.25*$10,000, or $12,500 (1-2-3 uses a * to indicate multiplication). In fact, each year's sales can be expressed by the formula (1 + *percentage rate*) * *previous year's revenues*.

Parentheses enclose the first term of this formula to avoid ambiguity. If there were no parentheses, it would not be clear whether the rate is first added to 1 and the result multiplied by the previous year's revenue (correct), or whether the rate should first be multiplied by the previous year's revenue and the result added to 1 (incorrect).

The similarity in the way each period's revenue is derived implies that the Copy command can be used. If we were not worried about later changes in the annual growth rates, we would input equations into each year, such as 1.25*B6 for Year 1, 1.30*C6 for Year 2, 1.20*D6 for Year 3, and so forth.

The percentage growth rates should be variable, however, because we may want to adjust them later. Therefore, it would be more convenient to store the annual rates separately somewhere in the worksheet and to reference these rate cells in the formulas for revenue. If a rate must be changed, the rate cell will be altered, but none of the formulas referring to that cell will need revision.

For example, let us place the rate for Year 1 just below the cell containing Year 1 revenue.

6. Move the pointer to cell C7, the cell beneath Year 1 REVENUE.

7. Type **.25** and press ENTER to store a 25% growth rate.

The revenue formula, stored in the Year 1 REVENUE cell, should be (1 + *cell below revenue amount*) * *previous year's revenue*. With 1-2-3, it is easy to enter such a formula.

Entering Formulas by Pointing

When you are dealing with a small worksheet, it is no effort to specify cell coordinates in formulas or commands. Larger worksheets present a problem, though. Unless your mind is equipped with 5 megabytes of RAM, you may have trouble remembering the exact address of a particular cell when you need it.

Suppose you were developing this income statement with pen and paper and someone came over and asked you to show them where Year 0 REVENUE is. You would not say "second column, sixth row," even though this is a valid way of describing the location. Instead, you would point to Year 0 REVENUE and say, "Here."

Electronic spreadsheets are supposed to be at least as easy to use as manual ones, and cell referencing should be no exception. 1-2-3 does provide a way of *pointing* to cells rather than specifying their addresses. When you need to refer to a cell, use the arrow keys to place the pointer on that cell. 1-2-3 knows where the pointer is and figures out its address. Once you know how to use the pointer to refer to cells, you rarely have to think in terms of column letters and row numbers. We will use pointing to enter the formula for Year 1 REVENUE.

1. Move to the Year 1 REVENUE cell (C6).

The formula is (1 + *cell below*) * *cell to left*, so

2. Type **(1+**.

Now instead of typing the address of the cell below, use the arrow keys to move the pointer to the cell below:

3. Press the down arrow key once to move the pointer to the annual growth rate cell (C7).

Do not type anything else yet. First examine the mode indicator. The word POINT means that 1-2-3 understands that it is in Point Mode; this permits you to use the arrow keys to position the pointer to the cell whose address you would otherwise have had to type. Now look at the second line of the control panel. So far it contains

(1+C7

Note that 1-2-3 itself supplied the address C7; there was no need for you to know the cell address specifically. Pointing is a very natural way of using the spreadsheet. With pointing, you think in terms of "Year 1 REVENUE" rather than "C6."

The formula $(1 + rate) * Year \ 0$ REVENUE has not been completed.

4. Type) to complete the first expression of the formula.

The pointer returns to its initial position at the Year 1 REVENUE cell.

5. Type * to indicate multiplication.

Once more we must refer to a cell, and again we utilize the pointing capability.

6. Press the left arrow key once to point to the Year 0 REVENUE cell (B6).

The control panel now shows (1+C7)*B6. This is what we want, so

7. Press ENTER to conclude the formula entry.

The result displayed on the worksheet is 12500, or $12.5 million revenue in Year 1.

Copying to a Range by Pointing

To complete the revenue forecast, we must enter the other annual rates in the cells below the annual revenues, and then copy the Year 1 REVENUE formula to Years 2 through 5.

1. Enter the annual growth rates **.30, .20, .10,** and **.10** into the annual growth rate cells (D7, E7, F7, and G7, respectively). Instead of pressing ENTER after each entry, you may press the right arrow key, which has the dual function of storing the value and moving the pointer to the right.

Notice that 1-2-3 displays .3 rather than .30. Unless we tell it otherwise, 1-2-3 displays only enough information to accurately show the number. We will tell it otherwise later on.

2. Move the pointer to the Year 1 REVENUE cell (C6), the source of the copy.

3. Type /Copy to initiate the Copy command.

4. Press ENTER to designate the Year 1 REVENUE cell as the source.

1-2-3 is now awaiting the target, which is the range of revenue cells for Years 2 through 5. Instead of trying to determine the beginning and ending coordinates of the range, we can simply point to them. We do this by pointing to the beginning of the target range, typing a period to "anchor" the beginning of that range, and then pointing to the end of the range.

5. Move the pointer to the Year 2 REVENUE cell (D6), the first cell in the row of target cells.

6. Type the . key to anchor the range.

7. Move the pointer to the Year 5 REVENUE cell (G6), the last cell in the range.

8. Press ENTER to activate the copy.

Figure 2-2 shows the forecasted revenue stream along with the underlying formulas.

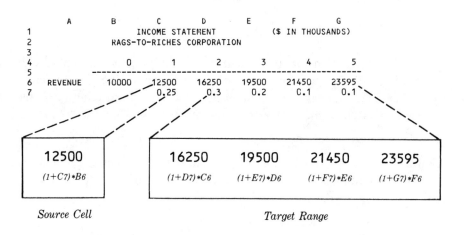

Figure 2-2. Revenue forecast showing source and target formulas

Improving the Worksheet's Appearance

Although the growth rates should be in decimal form for purposes of the revenue formulas, we would prefer to show them in percentage format (for example, 25% instead of .25). This may seem to be a matter of aesthetics, but it is also important for clarity. With 1-2-3, it is easy to make this change.

Using the Range Format Percent Command

The *Range Format command* assigns display characteristics to one or more cells.

1. Move to the first cell to be formatted, the Year 1 growth rate (C7).

2. Type /Range.

The Range menu will appear in the control panel. It consists of commands that operate on ranges of cells:

Format Label Erase Name Justify Protect Unprotect Input
Value Transpose*

The menu pointer highlights the Format option. You may choose the option either by pressing ENTER or by pressing the first letter of the option, F:

3. Press **F** to choose Format.

The Format command invokes a menu of its own:

Fixed Scientific Currency , General +/− Percent Date
Text Hidden Reset*

The Percent option formats a cell by multiplying its contents by 100 and appending a % sign to it. For example, a cell containing .250333 can be displayed as 25%. You can even control how many decimal places are displayed in the formatted number (for instance, 25.0%, 25.03%, or 25.0333%).

4. Type **P** to select the Percent option of the Format menu.

Now 1-2-3 requests the number of decimal places to display *after* multiplying the cell contents by 100. The default recommendation of two decimal places will serve our needs, so

5. Press the ENTER key.

---

*This menu differs slightly in Version 1A.

Now you must designate the range of cells you want to format as percentages. The control panel displays "Enter range of format: C7..C7". Notice that 1-2-3 assumes that the beginning of the range is the cell where the pointer was located prior to the Range Format command.

All 1-2-3 needs is the end of the range. If the end were the same as the beginning—that is, if you wanted to format only one cell—you would press the ENTER key at this point to complete the command. Otherwise, you can point to the end of the range.

Pressing the END key causes the END indicator to appear in inverse video on the bottom right of the screen. When this indicator appears, the arrow keys take on a different function. If the pointer is on a blank cell, then pressing the END key followed by an arrow key transfers the pointer to the next nonblank cell in the direction of the arrow. If the pointer is on a nonblank cell, then pressing the END key followed by an arrow key moves the pointer to the nonblank cell before the next blank cell. Once the END-arrow key sequence has been entered, the END indicator vanishes, and the arrow keys resume their normal function.

6. Press the END key.

7. Press the right arrow key.

The pointer expands to the end of the row of consecutive nonblank cells; in this instance, the pointer shifts to the annual growth rate for Year 5.

8. Press ENTER to activate the Range Format Percent command.

Figure 2-3 shows the result of the new format. Do not be deceived by looks, however. The actual contents of the cells are decimal numbers that have not been multiplied by 100. The Format command affects only the display of the cell, not its actual contents. Thus, Year 1 REVENUE is still computed as (1+0.25)*10000 rather than (1+25.00)*10000.

Using the Worksheet
Column Command

As a final measure of clarity, we will assign a row label to identify the row of growth rates. The label will be % GROWTH OVER PREVIOUS YEAR, and it should be indented three spaces.

1. Move the pointer to the cell beneath the REVENUE label (A7).

2. Press the space bar three times.

3. Type **% GROWTH OVER PREVIOUS YEAR.**

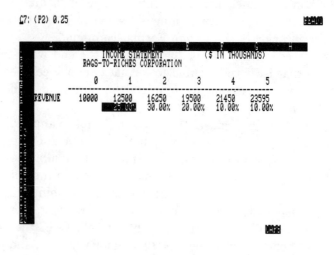

Figure 2-3. Revenue forecast formatted to show percentages

4. Press the ENTER key.

Some of the label is truncated on the worksheet, even though the control panel shows that the entire label was accepted into cell A7. Why was the label shortened here, whereas nothing like this occurred when we entered the income-statement titles?

Recall that each column of the worksheet is nine characters wide. If a label is longer than nine characters, the remaining part of the label spills over into the cells to the right—if the cells to the right are blank. Cell C7 is not blank, so some of the label is truncated in the worksheet display.

We will need to enter other long labels into this column later on, so it would be best to expand column A. The *Worksheet Column command** is used to expand or contract the width of any column of the worksheet.

With the pointer in the column whose width is to be changed (column A),

5. Type /Worksheet Column.

The *Set* and *Reset* options permit setting the width to a new value or resetting the width to the default value. Currently, the *global*, or general, column width defaults to nine characters (although even this default can be changed, using the Worksheet Global command).

---

*This command is called *Worksheet Column-Width* in Version 1A.

6. Choose the Set-Width option by pressing either **S** or ENTER.

Now 1-2-3 requests the new width and displays the current setting of 9. To maintain the current setting, you would press ENTER. There are two ways to revise the current width. One is to explicitly enter the new width (for instance, type 30 and press ENTER). The other is to use the pointing method. Pressing the right arrow key expands the pointer to a new width. As you continue to press the right arrow key, the control panel displays the new width of the pointer (and of the column). When the width is suitable, press ENTER to assign the new width to the column.

7. Press the right arrow key repeatedly until the control panel indicates a width of 30; then press the ENTER key.

Column A now differs from the default of nine, and the entire label is visible in cell A7 (see Figure 2-4).

Recalculating Projections Automatically

One of the principal features of an electronic spreadsheet is *automatic recalculation*. When the contents of a cell are altered, other cells that depend on the altered cell automatically reflect the change. Suppose you decide that 25% growth in Year 1 is too optimistic a projection. Changing the revenue growth rate in Year 1 necessitates changing the rest of the forecasted revenues, because each year's revenue depends on the previous year. The growth rate can be changed simply by placing the pointer at the appropriate

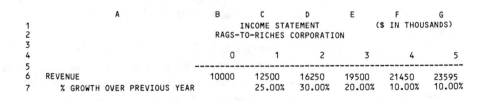

	A	B	C	D	E	F	G
1			INCOME STATEMENT			($ IN THOUSANDS)	
2			RAGS-TO-RICHES CORPORATION				
3							
4			0	1	2	3	4	5
5			---
6	REVENUE		10000	12500	16250	19500	21450	23595
7	% GROWTH OVER PREVIOUS YEAR			25.00%	30.00%	20.00%	10.00%	10.00%

Figure 2-4. Revenue forecast with column A expanded

% GROWTH OVER PREVIOUS YEAR cell and entering the revised growth assumption. For example:

1. Move the pointer to Year 1's % GROWTH OVER PREVIOUS YEAR cell (C7).

2. Type .2 and press the ENTER key. This will change the growth rate of Year 1 to 20%.

As a result of the Range Format Percent command issued earlier, the .2 that you entered is displayed as 20.00%. Look at the new revenue numbers on your screen. As soon as you pressed the ENTER key, the numbers changed. Year 1 REVENUE became 12000, a 20% increase. Without any further instructions, 1-2-3 automatically recalculated the revenue growth projections for Years 2 through 5.

So far we've been happily projecting revenues, but now it's time to come down to earth. Rags-to-Riches' pro forma income statement also must take into account all the expenses that will be incurred over the next five years.

These expenses fall into a few broad categories, including cost of goods sold, general and administrative expenses, and taxes. In the remainder of this chapter and in Chapter 3, we will be figuring these expenses into our projections.

Calculating the Cost Of Goods Sold

Expenses that are clearly associated with the goods produced are classified under *cost of goods sold*, which is defined as the sum of costs that directly enter into the production of the items sold. *Production materials*, such as rags, are a significant cost of manufacturing for Rags-to-Riches Corporation. The *wages* and *fringe benefits* paid to factory workers are the second and third ingredients in the cost of goods sold. In our model, we will include the three major expenses, and we will add an "other" category to include the remaining cost of sales.

Materials used in production are generally a function of sales. If sales are high, more goods are sold, and more material is used to produce the goods. Low sales would dictate less use of materials. It is reasonable, therefore, to forecast material expense as a percentage of sales. For example, based on the opinions of market analysts, the past performance of Rags-to-Riches, and the history of similar manufacturing firms, the Riches expect materials costs to amount to 16% of sales in each of the five forecast years.

Cost of Goods Sold
As a Fixed Percent

One way of setting material expenses at 16% of revenue is to enter the appropriate formula into the Year 1 material expense and then to copy this formula to the material expense cells of Years 2 through 5. Because materials represent a cost of goods sold, we will first enter the COST OF GOODS SOLD heading. Then we will enter the label MATERIALS, indented three spaces.

1. Move to cell A9 and enter the label **COST OF GOODS SOLD**.

2. Move to cell A10.

3. Press the space bar three times, type **MATERIALS**, and press the ENTER key.

The formula for Year 1 MATERIALS is .16 * *Year 1* REVENUE. Use the pointing facility to enter the formula, as follows:

4. Move to the Year 1 MATERIALS cell (C10).

5. Type **.16*** to begin the formula.

6. Move the pointer to the Year 1 REVENUE cell (C6).

7. Press the ENTER key.

We will replicate this formula into the forecast years in the same way that we copied the revenue formula. With the pointer already positioned on the source cell (C10),

8. Type /Copy to initiate the Copy command.

9. Press the ENTER key to accept the present pointer position (C10) as the source formula.

10. Move the pointer to the beginning of the target range (Year 2 MATERIALS at cell D10).

11. Type the . key to anchor the range.

12. Move the pointer to the end of the target range (Year 5 MATERIALS at cell G10).

13. Press the ENTER key.

The results are displayed in Figure 2-5, along with the underlying formulas for both the source cell and the target range.

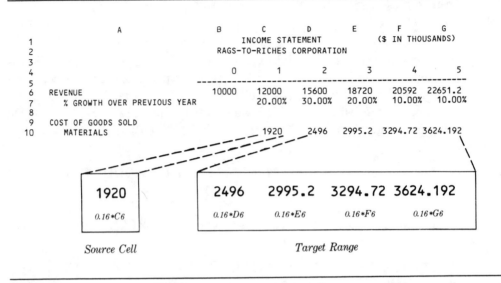

Figure 2-5. Cost of materials showing source and target formulas

A Variable-Rate Formula
For Cost Of Goods Sold

The method we just used is one way of calculating material expenses. It is not very flexible, however. What will happen if the Riches later find that their 16% estimate is unrealistic? We will have to reenter the entire Year 1 MATERIALS formula and then recopy it to the remaining years. There is a more efficient way to design the model.

When we developed the forecasting method for revenue, we used two rows—one for the revenue itself and the other for entering growth rates. This strategy permits us to change any year's growth without having to change other revenue formulas. The revenue formula itself refers to a rate cell whose contents can be varied without affecting the formula.

We can apply a similar concept to the material expense formula. Instead of entering a fixed-rate formula such as .16 * *revenue*, we will enter a variable-rate formula: a rate cell times the revenue cell.

Storing the percent of revenue in a cell and referring to that rate cell in the material expense formula allows us to alter the rate without altering the formulas. However, because the percent of revenues is going to be the same for all years (for example, 16% for Years 1 through 5), it is not necessary to create an entire row of rate cells as we did for revenue. Instead, we can designate a single cell to contain the percent of revenues that determines material expense for all five years.

Material expense is not the only expense that we will treat this way. It is common in financial forecasting to make one line item a percent of another. As a matter of foresight, let us create a column of cells to the left of the income statement that will serve as a variable-rate column, such as the one shown in Figure 2-6. When any given row of the income statement utilizes a rate, we can store that rate in the corresponding cell of the variable-rate column.

However, there is no room on the left side of the income statement. The income statement already occupies column A. If this model were being designed with pencil and paper instead of an electronic spreadsheet, it would be a thankless job to shift all columns to the right in order to make room for the rate column. One advantage of using 1-2-3 is that revisions to the model's format are easy, even after the model has been stored in the worksheet. In this instance, we can use the Worksheet Insert command.

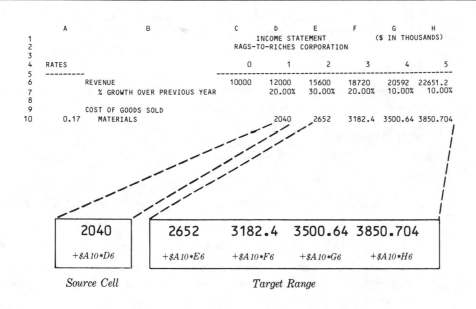

Figure 2-6. An absolute copy from one cell to a range

Using Worksheet Insert
To Create Extra Workspace

The *Worksheet Insert command* is used to insert columns or rows in the worksheet. Before using the command, you must position the pointer at the place where the rows or columns are to be inserted. If you wish to insert a column, then you must place the pointer in any cell of the column *to the left of which* the blank column will be inserted. For example, to insert a blank column before column D, you position the pointer anywhere in column D (cell D2, for example) and issue the Worksheet Insert Column command. Data stored in column D and in columns to the right of D will be shifted over to make room for the new blank column.

A row insertion operates in the same way as a column insertion. It involves placing the pointer in any cell of the row *above which* the blank rows are to be inserted. To insert a blank row at row 6, you would move the pointer to a cell in row 6 and invoke the Worksheet Insert Row command. The current contents of row 6 and any rows below it are shifted downward, leaving a blank row at row 6. The good news is that any formulas that referred to cells in the shifted rows or columns are automatically adjusted to address the new cell coordinates.

It may take some practice to remember where the new row or column goes relative to where the pointer is. Rows and columns are always added above and to the left of the pointer. Otherwise, with the pointer at A1, how could you add rows or columns at the top or left of the worksheet?

Back to the task at hand: inserting a blank column in which variable rates can be stored.

1. Move the pointer to a cell in column A (this can be done in a single keystroke by pressing the HOME key).

2. Type /Worksheet.

In response to the Worksheet menu,

3. Select the Insert option by typing **I**.

Now 1-2-3 responds with the Insert menu, prompting you to select Column or Row.

4. Select the Column option of the menu by typing C.

Now you have the option of inserting one or several columns. You communicate your intentions to 1-2-3 by indicating a column insert range. Following its prompt of "Enter column insert range:", 1-2-3 suggests a range of a single cell A1..A1 (the location of the pointer prior to entering the Worksheet command).

A blinking dash appears inside the pointer, indicating that you may use the pointing facility to expand the pointer over more than one column. To see how this works, press the right arrow key once; the pointer expands to span columns A and B, and the insert range automatically changes to A1..B1. By expanding the pointer over more than one column, you can insert multiple blank columns, beginning at column A. Naturally, the current spreadsheet will shift right as many columns as it takes to make room for the insertions. Press the left arrow key to shrink the pointer so that it includes only column A. The insert range also reverts to one cell, A1..A1.

5. Press the ENTER key to execute the insertion.

What used to be in column A now resides in column B, and all other columns have been shifted to the right. Formula references have also been adjusted. If you move the pointer to Year 1 MATERIALS at D10, you will find that the formula has changed to .16*D6 from the previous .16*C6.

6. Move to cell A4, and then enter the label **RATES**.

7. At A5, use \- ENTER to underscore the label.

Using Range Erase to Revise The Expense Formula

With the variable-rate column in place, we can now revise the formula for materials expense.

1. Move to the RATE coordinate corresponding to MATERIALS (cell A10).

2. Enter the rate of **.16**.

3. Place the pointer at the Year 1 MATERIALS cell (D10).

Before we enter the new formulas, let's get rid of the old ones. We can do this with the *Range Erase command.*

4. Type /**R**ange Erase.

1-2-3 prompts for a range to erase, suggesting the single-cell range of D10..D10. However, we want to erase the entire row of formulas. To indicate this to 1-2-3,

5. Press the END key, and then press the right arrow key to expand the pointer to the end of the range.

6. Press ENTER to complete the command.

Recall that the new formula for materials is the rate cell times the revenue cell for the appropriate year. To allow us to point to the rate cell as the first step in the formula entry, 1-2-3 must comprehend that we are entering a formula. The arrow keys affect formula entry only in Point Mode. Somehow we must force 1-2-3 into Value Mode so that it expects a formula.

Recall that 1-2-3 enters either Value Mode or Label Mode, depending on the first character typed in an entry. For example, typing a letter or a label-prefix invokes Label Mode. Typing a number, such as 5, throws 1-2-3 into Value Mode. Other symbols that have a mathematical connotation, such as +, -, ., and (, also invoke Value Mode when typed as the first character of an entry. For purposes of pointing, typing + is a good way to begin the entry.

Even if you choose to type coordinates directly instead of pointing to them, you may still need to start the formula with a special arithmetic character to force 1-2-3 into Value Mode. Consider the formula A10*D6. If you begin entering the formula by typing A, then 1-2-3 defaults to Label Mode because A is a character. Instead, enter + to activate Value Mode, and then enter the formula.

7. Type + to begin the formula.

The mode indicator shows VALUE, and you may now point to a cell.

8. Move the pointer to the RATE cell (A10).

9. Type * to continue the formula.

10. Move the pointer up to the Year 1 REVENUE cell (D6).

11. Press the ENTER key.

The new formula, +A10*D6, gives us the same result (1920) as that obtained with the old formula in Figure 2-5. The next step is to copy the Year 1 formula to the other years.

Absolute Versus Relative Copying

When we used the Copy command to replicate the revenue formula, we copied formulas in a relative manner. If the revenue for Year 1 equaled the previous year's revenue times Year 1's growth rate, then the revenue for Year 2 was copied as the previous year's (Year 1) revenue times Year 2's growth rate.

Actually, 1-2-3 does not understand the terms "Year 1" or "growth rate." To 1-2-3, the formula for Year 1 revenue was *one cell to the left * one cell below,* so that when the formula was copied, it was copied in terms of relative positions. Most uses of the Copy command are for relative replications like the one used for revenue (and the one used to create the column headings 1 through 5).

However, there are instances when relative copying is not desired, and the materials formula is one such case. The materials formula is a mixed breed with regard to copying. On the one hand, the reference to REVENUE should be relative. As the formula is copied from one cell to another, the target of the copy should always search four rows above itself to find the correct REVENUE amount. For example, the Year 3 materials formula should multiply the rate cell by the Year 3 REVENUE cell four cells above Year 3 materials; Year 4 should multiply the rate by Year 4 REVENUE four cells above, and so forth. The problem is the RATE cell. If the materials formula were copied relatively, 1-2-3 would interpret the source formula for Year 1 as "the cell three positions to the left" times "the cell four positions above." This formula works for Year 1, but if we apply it to the other years, something will be lost in the translation.

Our intention is not to copy the entire formula relatively, but rather to make the copied reference to the rate cell nonrelative, or *absolute*. Instead of "the cell three positions to the left," we want "the cell in column A, row 10." Returning to the analogy of someone asking you for directions to a street in your neighborhood, an absolute address would be equivalent to giving the geographical latitude and longitude of the street. No matter where in the world you are, you can identify the precise coordinates of the street. A relative address of "three blocks up, two blocks to the right" does not lead a person in Bangkok to the same street as it does a person in New York. An absolute address works for both people. To specify an absolute address in 1-2-3, we must alter the Year 1 source formula and designate A10, the rate, as an *absolute reference* to be copied in nonrelative terms.

The special character $ is used by 1-2-3 to make a column or row reference absolute. The $ must appear before the column letter or before the row number of the coordinate or in both positions. For the cell A10, $A$10 will always be copied without changing the A or the 10 in the target cell(s). However, $A10 (with no $ preceding the row number) will always retain A as the column letter in target formulas, but the row number will be changed relatively if the formula is copied to a different row. Similarly, A$10 (with no $ preceding the column letter) retains the row number 10 in the target, but the column letter changes if the formula is copied to a different column.

As far as Year 1 is concerned, it makes no difference whether the formula A10*D6 contains any $ signs or not. The difference comes into play only with regard to copying, when the appearance of a $ sign in one or more references of the source cell affects the formula copied to the target.

In the materials expense formula, the column of the address of the RATE cell must be copied absolutely, not relatively. Therefore, the formula should be either $A$10*D10 or $A10*D6. In the first form, no matter where the cell is copied to, the first term of the formula is copied absolutely as A10, not as a relative reference.

In the second form, the first term will always be copied referring to column A. However, if the cell is copied to another row, then the row reference of the rate coordinate will change. Thus, if the materials formula is copied from D10 to D12, the formula will assume the form $A12*D8, "the cell whose position is in the same row as the target, but in column A" times "the cell four rows above the target." We will choose $A10.

One way of inserting a $ sign into the formula is to enter Edit Mode:

1. Press the F2 (Edit) key.

The blinking edit cursor appears immediately to the right of the formula.

2. Press the HOME key to position the edit cursor at the left side of the formula.

3. Press the right arrow key once to place the edit cursor below the A of the A10 reference.

4. Type the $ key to insert the absolute symbol before the A.

5. Press the ENTER key.

The formula in the control panel should be +$A10*D6. Now copy this formula from Year 1 to the rest of the row.

6. Type /Copy, and then press the ENTER key.

7. Move right once to Year 2 MATERIALS (cell E10) to designate the first cell of the target range.

8. Type the . key to anchor the range.

9. Use the right arrow key to move to Year 5 MATERIALS (cell H10), the end of the target range.

10. Press ENTER.

Compare the results to those derived originally in Figure 2-5, and examine the formulas underlying the cells.

Now we can take full advantage of our new flexibility. For instance, when the Riches find that the cost of rags has increased, forcing them to raise materials expenses to 17% of sales, all we have to do is

11. Move to the MATERIALS RATE cell (A10), type .17, and press the ENTER key.

The model immediately recalculates the materials expense line, yielding the results shown in Figure 2-6. The underlying formulas are also displayed in the figure.

Saving the Worksheet

We now have the beginnings of the pro forma income statement for Rags-To-Riches Corporation. In the next chapter, we will complete the model and explore the Copy command even further. Before you leave this exercise, though, remember to save the current version of your model.

1. Type /File Save.

1-2-3 will recommend the last filename that was used to save the worksheet, IS.

2. Press the ENTER key to accept IS as the filename.

Before it begins overwriting the file, 1-2-3 ascertains whether you truly intend to erase the old one. If you save the worksheet under the old name, the previous version will be discarded, and the new version will take its place (another potential source of worksheet zap to be wary of). Because the old file is incomplete, go ahead and

3. Select Replace to replace the original version.

Your worksheet is now saved on diskette, ready for you to retrieve it when you begin work in Chapter 3.

Chapter 3
Using Copy, @SUM, and the Print Command

This chapter continues the income-statement forecast of Chapter 2. To complete the model, we will explore additional applications of the Copy command, use the @SUM function to total a group of cells, and format an entire worksheet with a few keystrokes. After completing the worksheet, we will use the Print command to obtain a hard copy of the model.

In order to follow the instructions, you must have the model developed in the last chapter, shown in Figure 2-6. If you already have the model on the screen, then skip to the next paragraph. If you saved the model, retrieve it again by typing the / key, then selecting **File** and **Retrieve**. Now 1-2-3 will prompt you for the name of the file to be retrieved, displaying the names of worksheets currently stored on the data diskette. Move the pointer to IS, and press ENTER.

Calculating the Remaining Costs Of Goods Sold

In Chapter 2, we began the income statement with revenues and then proceeded to the first cost of goods sold, materials expense. We will now move on to the next cost of goods sold, factory wages.

Using the F4 (Abs) Key For Wage Formulas

1. Move to cell B11, beneath the MATERIALS label, and enter the indented label WAGES by pressing the space bar three times and typing **WAGES**.

Like materials, the wages of factory workers can be assumed to depend on sales. As more units are sold, more workers are employed and more wages paid. Assume that Rags-to-Riches spends 14 cents of every sales dollar on wages. The formula for wages is essentially the same as that for materials: the rate cell at the left of the wages line multiplied by the revenue cell. Now that we are aware of the implications of absolute versus relative copying, we will not make the same mistake twice. When we enter the wages formula, we will make an absolute reference to the rate cell.

2. Move left once to the RATE cell (A11), and enter **.14** as the rate.

3. Move right to the Year 1 WAGES cell (D11).

The formula to be input here is *rate * revenue*.

4. Type + to begin the formula.

5. Move the pointer to the RATE cell (A11).

The control panel shows +A11 thus far. We could complete the formula and then backtrack by editing the formula, changing +A11 to +$A11. However, 1-2-3 provides a means for evading this roundabout method by allowing you to transform the cell reference to absolute form while remaining in Point Mode, *before* the formula has been completed. The function key F4, the Abs (absolute) key, is used for this purpose.

6. Press the F4 (Abs) key once.

The formula in the control panel has now been changed from +A11 to +$A$11. This is not what we want, so

7. Press the F4 (Abs) key again.

Now +$A$11 has become +A$11, which is unsuitable because the column reference A is what must be absolute.

8. Press the F4 (Abs) key once more.

Now the formula is +$A11, which is suitable. At this point we can proceed normally with the formula as if the absolute address had been entered originally. Incidentally, pressing F4 one more time would have produced +A11, devoid of any $ signs.

9. Type * to continue the multiplication formula.

10. Move the pointer to the Year 1 REVENUE cell (D6).

Before pressing the ENTER key, consider the fact that other income-statement items will have a similar relationship to revenue, so it may be advantageous to copy this formula to another row later on. If the formula were copied down to another row, the 6 in D6 would be altered. There is no harm in making the row reference absolute at this point, so

11. Press F4 as many times as it takes to arrive at D$6 (this requires two presses).

12. Press the ENTER key.

The formula for wages is now +$A11*D$6, which evaluates to 1680. The formula may now be copied to the rest of the row.

13. Type /Copy ENTER to invoke the Copy command and designate the current position of the pointer as the source.

14. Move right once to point to the Year 2 WAGES cell (E11) as the beginning of the target range.

15. Type the . key to anchor the beginning of the range.

16. Move the pointer to the Year 5 WAGES cell (H11), the end of the target range.

17. Press the ENTER key.

Calculating Fringe Benefits

Fringe benefits for factory workers can be approximated as a percent of wages because the more people are employed, the greater the fringe benefits expense will be. Again, we use the RATE cell to make the percent variable. Fringe benefits are 15% of wages at Rags-to-Riches.

1. Enter the indented label **FRINGE BENEFITS** beneath the WAGES label. (Move to cell B12, press the space bar three times, and type **FRINGE BENEFITS**.)

2. Move to the left, and enter **.15** in the RATE cell (A12).

3. Move to the Year 1 FRINGE BENEFITS cell (D12).

4. Type the + key to begin formula entry.

5. Move the pointer to the RATE cell (A12).

6. Press the F4 (Abs) key to make the cell reference absolute (either $A$12 or $A12 will do).

7. Type the * key to continue the multiplication formula.

8. Point to the Year 1 WAGES cell (D11) by moving the pointer up one space.

9. Press the ENTER key.

Now copy the formula to the other years:

10. Type /Copy, and press the ENTER key.

11. Move the pointer to the Year 2 FRINGE BENEFITS cell (E12).

12. Type the . key to anchor the beginning of the target range.

13. Move the pointer to the Year 5 FRINGE BENEFITS cell (H12).

14. Press the ENTER key.

Because FRINGE BENEFITS is a function of WAGES, which in turn is a function of REVENUE, the fringe-benefits expense (shown in Figure 3-1) grows at the same annual rate as REVENUE. Thus, the Year 2 FRINGE BENEFITS of 327.6 exceed the Year 1 expense of 252 by 30%, which equals the revenue growth from Year 1 to Year 2.

	A	B		C	D	E	F	G	H
1					INCOME STATEMENT			($ IN THOUSANDS)	
2					RAGS-TO-RICHES CORPORATION				
3									
4	RATES			0	1	2	3	4	5
5	---------								
6		REVENUE		10000	12000	15600	18720	20592	22651.2
7		% GROWTH OVER PREVIOUS YEAR			20.00%	30.00%	20.00%	10.00%	10.00%
8									
9		COST OF GOODS SOLD							
10	0.17	MATERIALS			2040	2652	3182.4	3500.64	3850.704
11	0.14	WAGES			1680	2184	2620.8	2882.88	3171.168
12	0.15	FRINGE BENEFITS			252	327.6	393.12	432.432	475.6752

Figure 3-1. Worksheet showing costs of wages and fringe benefits

Calculating Other Expenses

We will label the remaining cost of goods sold OTHER. The OTHER category incorporates production-related expenses (such as supplies, factory,
heating, lighting, and power) and miscellaneous expenses. Because this category of cost of goods sold is primarily associated with the factory as a whole,
it does not change as a function of sales. No matter what quantity of dish
towels are produced, factory expenses remain unaffected except by factors
such as inflation or plant expansion. Therefore, we assign an annual growth
rate to this category, assuming that it increases X% each year. The RATE cell
can be used to store the growth rate, but the formula for OTHER expense
differs from those for the costs of sales considered thus far. The formula is
(1 + *growth rate*) * *previous year's expense.* We will assume that OTHER
expense starts at 100 and grows by 8% per year. A start-up value must be
input for the first year:

1. Move to the cell below the FRINGE BENEFITS label (B13), press the
   space bar three times, and type **OTHER.**

2. Move to the RATE cell (A13), and enter **.08** as the growth factor.

3. Move the pointer to the Year 1 OTHER cell (D13).

4. Enter **100** as the start-up value.

5. Move the pointer to the Year 2 OTHER cell (E13).

6. Type **(1+** to begin the formula.

7. Move the pointer to the RATE cell (A13).

Additional items will be forecast using a growth rate, so it is important at this point to consider future potential for copying this formula. The rate cell's column reference, A, must be absolute because no matter where we copy the formula to, the rate cell will remain in column A. However, the row reference must be relative because if we copy the formula to another row, the target's rate will be contained in the target's row. Therefore,

8. Press the F4 (Abs) key three times, so that the formula appearing in the control panel is (1+$A13.

9. Type)∗ to continue the formula.

10. Move the pointer to the previous year's OTHER expense cell (D13).

This cell reference should be left relative; as you copy the formula to other columns, the column reference should change, and as you copy the formula to other rows, the row reference should change.

11. Press the ENTER key.

The Year 2 value of 108 is 8% higher than that for Year 1. Copy the Year 2 formula to the rest of the row:

12. With the pointer at E13, type /Copy and press the ENTER key.

13. Press the right arrow key once.

14. Type the . key to indicate a range.

15. Move the pointer to the Year 5 OTHER cell (H13).

16. Press the ENTER key.

Figure 3-2 shows what we have accomplished thus far in the model. Let's pause for a moment and review what it shows.

We have created a revenue forecast growing at an annual rate that we can specify for any year of the forecast. Cost of sales has been dissected into four parts: materials, wages, fringe benefits, and other. Materials and wages change as a percent of sales. Fringe benefits are a function of wages, while "other" grows at a constant rate. For each of these expenses, the associated rate can be changed simply by reentering the rate cell.

Within the general assumptions that we have imposed, it is quite easy to generate alternate scenarios with the model. If one of the general assumptions changes, however, the underlying formulas may have to be altered. Still, with the aid of the powerful Copy command, we can usually make changes to the model without expending much energy or time. In fact, now that the percent of sales and the constant growth rate assumptions have been incorporated into the wages and other expense items, respectively, it is a

	A	B	C	D	E	F	G	H
1				INCOME STATEMENT			($ IN THOUSANDS)	
2				RAGS-TO-RICHES CORPORATION				
3								
4	RATES		0	1	2	3	4	5
5	---------		---					
6		REVENUE	10000	12000	15600	18720	20592	22651.2
7		% GROWTH OVER PREVIOUS YEAR		20.00%	30.00%	20.00%	10.00%	10.00%
8								
9		COST OF GOODS SOLD						
10	0.17	MATERIALS		2040	2652	3182.4	3500.64	3850.704
11	0.14	WAGES		1680	2184	2620.8	2882.88	3171.168
12	0.15	FRINGE BENEFITS		252	327.6	393.12	432.432	475.6752
13	0.08	OTHER		100	108	116.64	125.9712	136.0488

Figure 3-2. Worksheet showing completed costs of goods sold

simple matter to use the Copy command to incorporate these assumptions into line items that follow.

Annotating the Worksheet

Looking at Figure 3-2, it is impossible to tell what assumptions were made to arrive at the forecast. If someone else is going to use this worksheet, it will be difficult for them to determine what formulas were used. Even if you are the only one using the worksheet, you may not remember how you derived the numbers. For this reason, it is a good practice to set aside an area of the worksheet where you can annotate what you have done.

To make our model clearer, we will add one more column to the right of the income statement for annotation. The column should be wide enough to contain the notes, so we will begin by using the Worksheet Column Set-Width command to override the default width of 9.

1. Move the pointer to cell J4.

2. Type /Worksheet Column Set-Width **17**.

3. Press the ENTER key.

The heading for this column is NOTES. If you entered the heading as is, 1-2-3 would insert an apostrophe label-prefix before the heading, causing the label to be left-justified within the 17-character cell. As mentioned earlier, there are other label-prefixes that format a label differently. The ^ (caret) label-prefix centers the label within the cell, and the " (double quotes) label-prefix justifies the label on the right.

4. Type "NOTES and press the ENTER key.

The label is right-justified. On second thought, though, the heading would look better centered.

5. Type ^NOTES and press the ENTER key.

Next use the repeating label-prefix to underscore the heading:

6. Move down one cell to cell J5, and type \- ENTER.

Now we can document the assumptions for the four cost-of-goods-sold expenses in the NOTES column.

7. Move to cell J10, and enter the label % OF SALES; then enter the same label in J11.

8. Move down the NOTES column to the FRINGE BENEFITS cell (J12), and enter the label % OF WAGES.

9. Move down the NOTES column to the OTHER cell (J13), and enter % GROWTH RATE.

Now the forecast is almost self-explanatory.

In order to set the NOTES column off from the model, we left column I blank. But we don't need column I to be nine characters wide. Let us shrink it down to two characters.

10. Go to cell I1, and type /Worksheet Column Set-Width 2 and press the ENTER key.

Using Copy for General And Administrative Expenses

Unlike the cost of goods sold, certain company expenses do not relate directly to production (at least in the short term). For example, Lesley and Sandy Rich are going to receive their $500 thousand salaries next year whether the company sells five rags or 5 trillion rags. Compensation for managerial staff and sales staff, as well as advertising and depreciation, come under the heading of GENERAL & ADMINISTRATIVE EXPENSES, the next set of deductions from revenue in our income statement.

Calculating Managerial Compensation

We begin by calculating the costs of compensating the managerial staff over the next five years. The first step is to enter labels.

1. Move to cell B15, and enter the label **GENERAL & ADMINISTRA-TIVE EXPENSE** (not indented).

2. Move down once to cell B16, press the space bar three times to indent the label, and type **COMPENSATION: OFFICE.**

The compensation of company management is not primarily a function of sales. Office compensation is more a function of inflation and the state of the job market. Therefore, office compensation is assumed to grow at some rate that reflects increases in the same factors that affect salaries. This assumption is the same as the one we used to forecast the OTHER cost-of-sales line. Therefore, that intuitive urge to use the Copy command should be welling up in you.

Copying From a Range to a Range

Until now, we have used the Copy command to replicate one cell to another cell and to replicate one cell to several other cells. We already have the tools to derive office compensation in three steps: first, enter a startup value in Year 1 COMPENSATION: OFFICE (cell D16); second, copy the Year 2 OTHER formula to Year 2 COMPENSATION: OFFICE (cell E16); and third, copy the Year 2 COMPENSATION: OFFICE formula to Years 3 through 5. It is possible to combine steps two and three into a single step. We can copy the row of OTHER formulas to the COMPENSATION: OFFICE row.

Copying from one row of cells to another row involves the same steps as the previous copies did. First, position the pointer at the beginning of the source from which formulas will be copied; then invoke the Copy command; identify the source range; identify the target range; and execute the copy. The source is the range of consecutive cells to be copied.

In specifying the target, however, you need not always identify an entire target range. In this case, 1-2-3 requires only the address of the first cell of the target. Why?

Put yourself in 1-2-3's shoes. The program knows what the source range is, and it knows the exact dimensions of the source. With only the beginning address of the target, 1-2-3 has sufficient information to copy the source, in its exact dimensions, to the target. There is no need to specify the end of the target range in this instance, because the dimensions of the source determine the dimensions of the target.

We will assume that office compensation in Year 1 amounts to $1200 thousand.

1. Move to the Year 1 COMPENSATION: OFFICE cell (D16), and enter the value **1200**.

Next set the annual growth rate to 10%:

2. Move to the RATE cell (A16), and enter **.1**.

Now for the copy.

3. Move to the beginning of the source range, the Year 2 OTHER cell (E13).

4. Type **/Copy** to invoke the Copy command.

Now 1-2-3 suggests a one-cell source range of E13..E13, and it highlights this range on the worksheet. Moving the pointer will expand the range. To expand the range to the end of the OTHER row,

5. Press the END key, followed by the right arrow key, to transfer the pointer to the Year 5 OTHER cell (H13).

6. Press the ENTER key to set the source range.

You must respond to 1-2-3's prompt, "Enter range to copy TO:", by specifying the beginning of the target:

7. Move the pointer to the Year 2 COMPENSATION: OFFICE cell (E16).

8. Press the ENTER key to activate the copy.

And finally, don't forget to document the assumption:

9. Move to the NOTE cell (J16), and enter **% GROWTH RATE**.

Figure 3-3 identifies the source and target ranges of the Copy procedure, and it also shows the underlying formulas.

Calculating Sales Compensation

Unlike office compensation, sales compensation is closely linked to revenues. As sales increase, so does the need to expand the marketing staff. The forecast assumption for sales compensation is the same as that for wages (calculated earlier under the COST OF GOODS SOLD heading), so we can use the Copy command to set sales compensation at 8% of sales.

1. Move to cell B17, and enter the indented label **COMPENSATION: SALES**.

2. Store **.08** in the RATE cell (A17).

3. Move to Year 1 WAGES, the beginning of the source range (cell D11).

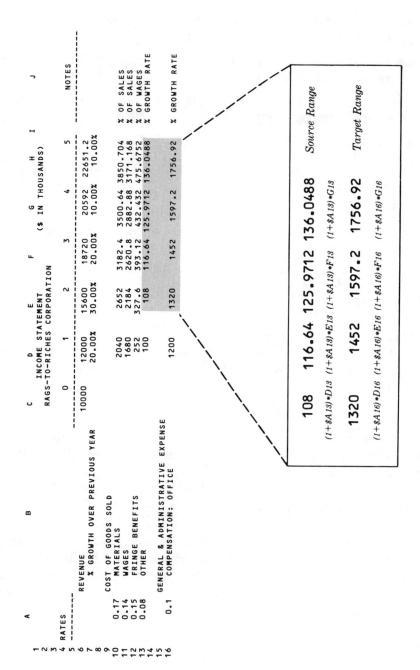

Figure 3-3. Source and target of copy, showing underlying formulas

4. Type **/Copy**.

1-2-3 prompts you for the end of the source range.

5. Press the END key, followed by the right arrow key, to transfer the pointer to the Year 5 WAGES cell (H11).

Since the assumption for sales compensation is the same as wages, we can copy the NOTE for WAGES too:

6. Press the right arrow key twice to expand the source range to encompass the NOTE cell (J11).

7. Press the ENTER key to set the source range.

8. Move down to the Year 1 COMPENSATION: SALES cell (D17), the beginning of the target range.

9. Press the ENTER key.

Your results, with the underlying formulas, should coincide with Figure 3-4.

Using Copy to Enter Remaining Expenses

Copying from row to row is a great time-saver once you get accustomed to it. But the Copy command has even greater potential. You can also copy from one column to another. Better yet, you can copy from one row to many rows or from one column to many columns.

There are four additional line items pertaining to general and administrative expense: fringe benefits for office and sales staff, advertising and promotion, depreciation, and miscellaneous. We will develop the formulas for these items for Year 1 only. Then, in one command, we will copy the Year 1 formulas to Years 2 through 5.

Fringe Benefits, Year 1

We can assume that fringe benefits of administrative and marketing employees will be a percent of office and sales compensation. Because these employees receive additional "perks" above and beyond those of the factory wage earners, we will apply a higher fringe rate than the 15% allotted to that group. A rate of 17% should be about right.

1. At cell B18, enter the indented label **FRINGE BENEFITS**.

2. Move to the RATE column (cell A18), and enter **.17**.

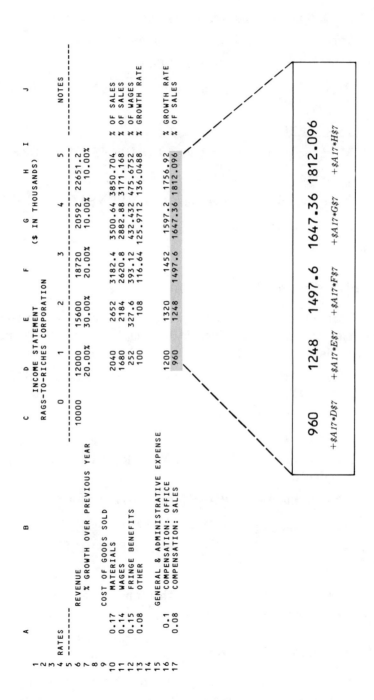

Figure 3-4. Worksheet showing sales compensation and underlying formulas

3. Move to the Year 1 FRINGE BENEFITS cell (D18).

The formula is *rate * (office compensation + sales compensation)*:

4. Type the + key to begin formula entry.

5. Move left to the RATE cell (A18).

6. Press the F4 (Abs) key three times to form $A18, a reference suitable for copying.

7. Type the *(keys.

8. Move the pointer to the Year 1 COMPENSATION: OFFICE cell (D16).

9. Type the + key to continue the formula.

10. Move the pointer to the Year 1 COMPENSATION: SALES cell (D17).

11. Type) and press the ENTER key.

The result is $367.2 thousand.

Advertising and Promotion, Year 1

Advertising and promotion expense is directly related to sales. The higher the sales, the greater the justification for increasing this expense. Rags-to-Riches plans to spend 2.5% of sales on advertising and promotion.

1. Move to cell B19, and then enter the indented label **ADVERTISING & PROMOTION**.

2. Store **.025** in the rate cell (A19).

Instead of entering the Year 1 formula from scratch, we can use the Copy command to duplicate the Year 1 WAGES formula we entered earlier, for this also depends on revenue:

3. Move to the Year 1 WAGES cell (D11), the source cell.

4. Type /Copy, and then press the ENTER key.

5. Move down to the Year 1 ADVERTISING & PROMOTION cell (D19).

6. Press the ENTER key to start the copy.

Your results should show $300 thousand in advertising and promotion expenses in the first year.

Depreciation, Year 1

Depreciation is a different type of expense from those we have encountered so far. Equipment is depreciated in order to reflect its decreasing value over time. No cash actually leaves the corporate till because of depreciation. Moreover, depreciation depends on several other factors: the value of the depreciable assets, the useful life of these assets, and the accounting method that the company uses to apportion the depreciation over the life of those assets.

If information were available about currently depreciable assets and future purchases of depreciable assets, we could develop a subsidiary worksheet to derive the forecast of depreciation expense (or we could input the line directly into this model). For Rags, no such details are provided, although company management assures us that depreciation will amount to a constant $20 thousand per year. Therefore,

1. Move to cell B20, and enter the indented label **DEPRECIATION**.

2. Store the value **20** in the Year 1 DEPRECIATION cell (D20).

Miscellaneous Expenses, Year 1

The miscellaneous classification of general and administrative expenses is independent of revenue. It is assumed to grow, but not at a percentage rate. Rather, we will assume that miscellaneous expenses increase at a constant rate, such as $10 thousand per year. In each year, miscellaneous expenses are $10 thousand greater than the year before.

The percentage growth was a multiplicative rate, but the constant increase is an additive rate. That is, each year's increase in miscellaneous expenses is simply added to the previous year's total. We can store the value 10 in the RATE cell and refer to it in the miscellaneous expense formula. In this way, it will be possible to change the additive rate at a later time.

1. Move to cell B21, and enter the indented label **MISCELLANEOUS**.

2. Move to the RATE cell (A21), and type **10**.

3. Move to the Year 1 MISCELLANEOUS cell (D21).

The formula for each year's miscellaneous expense is *rate + previous year's miscellaneous expense.*

4. Type the **+** key to begin the formula.

5. Move the pointer to the RATE cell (A21).

6. Press the F4 (Abs) key three times to make the column reference absolute.

7. Type the **+** key to continue formula entry.

8. Move the pointer to the Year 0 MISCELLANEOUS cell (C21).

9. Press the ENTER key.

Even though the Year 0 MISCELLANEOUS cell is blank, 1-2-3 considers it a numeric zero for purposes of calculation. Thus, the Year 1 result is $10+0 = 10$.

Copying From a Column to a Row

Now that we have entered the basic formulas for the last four general and administrative expense categories, all it takes to forecast Years 2 through 5 is a single Copy command.

The source range of the copy will be the Year 1 cells for fringe benefits, advertising and promotion, depreciation, and miscellaneous (cells D18 through D21).

For the target range, we need only specify E18..H18 (Year 2 FRINGE BENEFITS through Year 5 FRINGE BENEFITS). This target range refers only to the first row of the columns to which the Year 1 formulas will be copied, but it gives 1-2-3 enough information to do the entire job. Why? Because 1-2-3 knows that the source range is a column of four cells. It sees that E18 is the beginning of the target range, so it copies the D18..D21 range to column E, beginning in row 18. The dimension of the source range (four vertical cells) determines that the formulas will be copied from E18 to E21. Similarly, 1-2-3 sees F18, G18, and H18 in the target range, so it copies the source range to F18..F21, G18..G21, and H18..H21.

1. Move the pointer to D18, the beginning of the source range.

2. Type /Copy.

3. Move the pointer down to the Year 2 MISCELLANEOUS cell (D21) to designate the end of the source range.

4. Press the ENTER key.

5. Move the pointer to the Year 2 FRINGE BENEFITS cell (E18), the beginning of the target range.

6. Type the . key to indicate a range.

7. Move the pointer to the Year 5 FRINGE BENEFITS cell (H18).

8. Press the ENTER key.

With a single Copy command, we have just developed 16 forecast formulas and completed the operating expense section of the income statement. Figure 3-5 shows the results, highlighting both the source and the target ranges. For good measure, we should document the assumptions for the last four line items in the NOTES column.

	A	B	C	D	E	F	G	H	I	J
1					INCOME STATEMENT		($ IN THOUSANDS)			
2					RAGS-TO-RICHES CORPORATION					
3										
4	RATES									NOTES
5	-------		0	1	2	3	4	5		-------
6		REVENUE	10000	12000	15600	18720	20592	22651.2		
7		% GROWTH OVER PREVIOUS YEAR		20.00%	30.00%	20.00%	10.00%	10.00%		
8										
9		COST OF GOODS SOLD								
10	0.17	MATERIALS		2040	2652	3182.4	3500.64	3850.704		% OF SALES
11	0.14	WAGES		1680	2184	2620.8	2882.88	3171.168		% OF SALES
12	0.15	FRINGE BENEFITS		252	327.6	393.12	432.432	475.6752		% OF WAGES
13	0.08	OTHER		100	108	116.64	125.9712	136.0488		% GROWTH RATE
14										
15		GENERAL & ADMINISTRATIVE EXPENSE								
16	0.1	COMPENSATION: OFFICE		1200	1320	1452	1597.2	1756.92		% GROWTH RATE
17	0.08	COMPENSATION: SALES		960	1248	1497.6	1647.36	1812.096		% OF SALES
18	0.17	FRINGE BENEFITS		367.2	436.56	501.432	551.5752	606.7327		% OF COMP.
19	0.025	ADVERTISING & PROMOTION		300	390	468	514.8	566.28		% OF SALES
20		DEPRECIATION		20	20	20	20	20		DIRECT INPUT
21	10	MISCELLANEOUS		10	20	30	40	50		CONSTANT GROWTH

Source Range

Target Range

Figure 3-5. Source and target ranges for a column-to-row copy

9. In cells J18, J19, J20, and J21, enter the following labels consecutively: **% OF COMP; % OF SALES; DIRECT INPUT;** and **CONSTANT GROWTH.**

Calculating Total Operating Expenses: @SUM and Copy

The next step is to total the operating expenses by combining the cost of goods sold and general and administrative expenses. Begin by putting an underscore in the row below MISCELLANEOUS:

1. Enter an underscore in the Year 0 column (cell C22) by typing \ - and pressing the ENTER key.

2. At B23, enter the label **TOTAL OPERATING EXPENSES** indented three spaces.

We did not need Year 0 expenses in order to derive the Year 1 predictions. For informational purposes, however, we will include the total Year 0 expenses in the model. According to Lesley and Sandy Rich, there were $6.4 million of expenses in Year 0, most of which was office compensation (one way the Riches got rich) and materials expense.

3. Move to cell C23, the Year 0 TOTAL OPERATING EXPENSES cell, and type **6400.**

4. Move to the Year 1 TOTAL OPERATING EXPENSES cell (D23).

Using @SUM for Year 1 Expenses

Total operating expense in each of Years 1 through 5 is the sum of the MATERIALS through MISCELLANEOUS expenses of each year. Is it necessary to reference each and every expense cell in the formula? Fortunately, the answer is no.

Lotus 1-2-3 provides a function called @SUM that totals the contents of a range of cells. The format of the function is @SUM(*list*), where *list* is a cell, a range, or a list of cells and ranges separated by commas. For example, @SUM(D1..D100) totals the column of cells from D1 to D100. @SUM(A1..Z1) adds the row of cells from A1 to Z1. As usual, the range for the @SUM function can be specified by pointing to the beginning and ending coordinates.

1. With the pointer in cell D23, type **@SUM(.**

2. Point to the beginning of the range to be summed, the Year 1 MATE-RIALS cell (D10).

3. Type the . key to anchor the range.

4. Move the pointer to the Year 1 MISCELLANEOUS cell (D21).

Notice that 1-2-3 highlights the range, as it does whenever ranges are specified in Point Mode.

5. Type the) key to close the parenthesized range of the @SUM function.

6. Press the ENTER key.

Using Copy for Remaining Expenses

Year 1 operating expenses amount to $6929.2 thousand. Let us copy both an underscore and the Year 1 formula to the other years.

1. Move the pointer to cell D22, and enter an underscore by typing \-.

2. Type /Copy.

3. Expand the pointer to the Year 1 TOTAL OPERATING EXPENSES cell (D23), the end of the source range.

4. Press the ENTER key to complete the source-range entry.

5. Point to the beginning of the target range in the Year 2 column, cell E22.

6. Type the . key to anchor the range.

7. Expand the pointer to the Year 5 column (cell H22).

8. Press the ENTER key to activate the command.

Calculating Interest Expense

We will be developing lines for pre-tax income, tax expense, and net income, but first there is one more pre-tax expense to deal with: interest expense. Interest expense represents the amount of interest that the firm is required to pay in the current period. It includes interest payments due for notes, bonds, and both short-term and long-term loans. Like depreciation, interest expense is difficult to predict—it depends on the interest rate of each type of debt that the company owes. In our model, we will not attach an assumption to interest expense. Rather, we will provide a simple estimate, leaving you to adapt more complicated formulas and input them directly, if you wish.

Happily, Rags-to-Riches obtains most of its funding from only two types of riches: the Riches (Lesley and Sandy) who founded the company with their own capital, and the riches (company profits) which sustain both the company *and* Lesley and Sandy. There is a $100 thousand long-term loan, however, on which the firm pays 10% interest throughout the forecast period. No additional borrowing is anticipated, so interest expense will be a constant $10 thousand for all years of the forecast.

Interest expense, and the line items that follow it, is available for Year 0. Therefore, we will enter only Year 0 figures for the next few items. Later, we will copy the Year 0 formulas to the forecast years with a single Copy command.

1. Move to cell B25, and enter the indented label **INTEREST EXPENSE**.

2. Move to cell C25, and enter the value **10**.

3. Now use the TAB key and the right arrow key to move to the NOTE cell for INTEREST EXPENSE (J25), and type **DIRECT INPUT**.

Calculating Pre-Tax and Net Income

Pre-tax income can be calculated by subtracting operating expenses and interest expense from revenue.

1. Move to cell B27, and type the label **PRE-TAX INCOME**.

2. Move to Year 0 (cell C27).

3. Type the **+** key to begin the formula entry.

4. Move the pointer to the Year 0 REVENUE cell (C6).

5. Type the **−** key to continue with the subtraction of operating expenses from revenue.

6. Move the pointer to the Year 0 TOTAL OPERATING EXPENSES cell (C23).

7. Type the **−** key, and move the pointer to the Year 0 INTEREST EXPENSE cell (C25).

8. Press the ENTER key.

Year 0 pre-tax income was $3590 thousand.

Calculating Net Income

Net income is, of course, the pre-tax income minus tax expense. This is probably the most important line item of the income statement for owners, creditors, and investors. We will first calculate tax expense, then use these figures to calculate net income.

In Year 0, the company's tax expense came to 52% of pre-tax income. This percentage includes federal, state, and local taxes. Taxes are often forecast as a percent of income, and for Rags-to-Riches, we assume that this rate will remain constant throughout the forecast horizon. As you probably guessed, the RATE cell can store the effective tax rate, so that the rate can be altered if the assumption changes.

1. Move to cell B29, and enter the indented label **TAX**.

2. Move to the TAX line of the RATE column (cell A29), and store **.52**.

3. Move to the Year 0 TAX cell (C29).

4. Type the **+** key to begin the value entry.

5. Point to the RATE cell (A29).

6. Press the F4 (Abs) key to make the RATE reference absolute for future copying.

7. Type the ***** key to multiply this rate by pre-tax income.

8. Move the pointer to the Year 0 PRE-TAX INCOME cell (C27).

9. Press the ENTER key.

Taxes were $1866.8 thousand in Year 0.

10. In the NOTES cell (J29), type **% OF PRE-TAX INC**.

Now we are ready to calculate net income.

11. Move to cell B31, and type **NET INCOME**.

12. Move to the Year 0 NET INCOME cell (C31), and type the **+** key to begin the formula.

13. Point to the Year 0 PRE-TAX INCOME cell (C27).

14. Type the **−** key to continue.

15. Point to the Year 0 TAX cell (C29).

16. Press the ENTER key.

Of the $10 million of revenue in Year 0, $1723.2 thousand was net income, making for a profit of over 17 cents on every dollar of sales—a good performance. What about the other years?

Calculating Profits For Remaining Years

We can derive five years of data for the last four income statement items (20 formulas) with just one Copy command by copying the Year 0 formulas to Years 1 through 5. This is a replication of a column of cells to multiple columns. The source range consists of the five Year 0 formulas; the target range is the row of pre-tax income, Years 1 through 5.

1. Move the pointer to the first cell of the source range, the Year 0 INTEREST EXPENSE cell (C25).

2. Type /Copy to initiate the Copy command.

As always, 1-2-3 assumes that the beginning of the source range is the current position of the pointer. Move the pointer to the end of the source range:

3. Move to the Year 0 NET INCOME cell (C31).

4. Press the ENTER key to set the source range.

5. Move the pointer to the Year 1 INTEREST EXPENSE cell (D25), the first cell of the target range.

6. Type the . key to anchor the beginning of the target range.

7. Move the pointer to the Year 5 INTEREST EXPENSE cell (H25).

8. Press the ENTER key to activate the Copy command.

The cumulative number of keystrokes you would need without the Copy command is quite impressive. Imagine the work involved if this forecast were a monthly statement. You can see why the Copy command is perhaps the most important command of the worksheet. Figure 3-6 shows the significant growth expected by the company. Rags-to-Riches grows from $1.7 million in Year 0 to nearly $5 million in Year 5.

Finishing Touches: Formatting Numeric Displays

Before we save or print this model, there is a matter of neatness that we must attend to. The use of growth rates has led to a mixture of numeric displays. Some numbers have no decimals, while some have one, two, three,

	A	B	C	D	E	F	G	H	I	J
1										
2										
3			INCOME STATEMENT							
4			RAGS-TO-RICHES CORPORATION				($ IN THOUSANDS)			
5	RATES			0	1	2	3	4	5	NOTES
6		REVENUE		10000	12000	15600	18720	20592	22651.2	
7		% GROWTH OVER PREVIOUS YEAR			20.00%	30.00%	20.00%	10.00%	10.00%	
8										
9		COST OF GOODS SOLD								
10	0.17	MATERIALS			2040	2652	3182.4	3500.64	3850.704	% OF SALES
11	0.14	WAGES			1680	2184	2620.8	2882.88	3171.168	% OF SALES
12	0.15	FRINGE BENEFITS			252	327.6	393.12	432.432	475.6752	% OF WAGES
13	0.08	OTHER			100	108	116.64	125.9712	136.0488	GROWTH RATE
14										
15		GENERAL & ADMINISTRATIVE EXPENSE								
16	0.1	COMPENSATION: OFFICE			1200	1320	1452	1597.2	1756.92	GROWTH RATE
17	0.08	COMPENSATION: SALES			960	1248	1497.6	1647.36	1812.096	% OF SALES
18	0.17	FRINGE BENEFITS			367.2	436.56	501.432	551.5752	606.7327	% OF COMP.
19	0.025	ADVERTISING & PROMOTION			300	390	468	514.8	566.28	% OF SALES
20		DEPRECIATION			20	20	20	20	20	DIRECT INPUT
21	10	MISCELLANEOUS			10	20	30	40	50	CONSTANT GROWTH
22										
23		TOTAL OPERATING EXPENSES		6400	6929.2	8706.16	10281.99	11312.85	12445.62	
24										
25		INTEREST EXPENSE		10	10	10	10	10	10	DIRECT INPUT
26										
27		PRE-TAX INCOME		3590	5060.8	6883.84	8428.008	9269.141	10195.57	
28										
29	0.52	TAX		1866.8	2631.616	3579.596	4382.564	4819.953	5301.699	% OF PRE-TAX INC.
30										
31		NET INCOME		1723.2	2429.184	3304.243	4045.443	4449.187	4893.876	

Figure 3-6. Worksheet showing net income forecasts

or even four decimal places. Unless the numbers can be formatted differently, the output will look as sloppy as the display.

Back in Chapter 2, we used the Range Format Percent command to affect the display of the revenue in the % GROWTH OVER PREVIOUS YEAR row. It would be best to show the other income-statement line items rounded to the nearest integer or to some fixed number of decimal places. This can be accomplished with the Range Format command, but it would take several command sequences to format various ranges of the report. We will take an easier route here and set up a default format that will apply to all numeric cells *except* those that have been specially formatted with the Range Format command.

We use the Worksheet Global Format command to assign this global setting.

1. Type /Worksheet Global Format.

Notice that the resulting menu is the same one that appears for Range Format.

2. Select the Fixed option of the Format menu.

In response to the prompt for number of decimal places,

3. Type 0 (zero), and press the ENTER key.

Instantly, all values except the revenue growth rates appear as integers. They are not internally converted to integers; they are merely displayed as such. Internally, 1-2-3 stores the values with as much decimal accuracy as it can. Arithmetic calculations use the internally stored values, not the externally rounded integers.

But what has happened to the RATES column? Most of the rates have changed to 0—or at least they appear to have changed. The decimal rates were not specifically formatted with the Range Format command, and so they are subject to the new default integer format. To remedy this error, apply the Range Format Percent command to the RATE column.

4. Move the pointer to the first cell of the RATE column (cell A6).

5. Type /Range Format Percent.

To display two decimal places,

6. Press the ENTER key.

To indicate the end of the range to be formatted,

7. Press the PG DN key, followed by the down arrow key, thus skipping down the column past the last entry, NET INCOME, to cell A31.

INCOME STATEMENT
RAGS-TO-RICHES CORPORATION
($ IN THOUSANDS)

RATES		0	1	2	3	4	5	NOTES
	REVENUE	10000	12000	15600	18720	20592	22651	
	% GROWTH OVER PREVIOUS YEAR		20.00%	30.00%	20.00%	10.00%	10.00%	
	COST OF GOODS SOLD							
17.00%	MATERIALS		2040	2652	3182	3501	3851	% OF SALES
14.00%	WAGES		1680	2184	2621	2883	3171	% OF SALES
15.00%	FRINGE BENEFITS		252	328	393	432	476	% OF WAGES
8.00%	OTHER		100	108	117	126	136	% GROWTH RATE
	GENERAL & ADMINISTRATIVE EXPENSE							
10.00%	COMPENSATION: OFFICE		1200	1320	1452	1597	1757	% GROWTH RATE
8.00%	COMPENSATION: SALES		960	1248	1498	1647	1812	% OF SALES
17.00%	FRINGE BENEFITS		367	437	501	552	607	% OF COMP
2.50%	ADVERTISING & PROMOTION		300	390	468	515	566	% OF SALES
	DEPRECIATION		20	20	20	20	20	DIRECT INPUT
10	MISCELLANEOUS		10	20	30	40	50	CONSTANT GROWTH
	TOTAL OPERATING EXPENSES	6400	6929	8706	10282	11313	12446	
10	INTEREST EXPENSE	10	10	10	10	10	10	DIRECT INPUT
	PRE-TAX INCOME	3590	5061	6884	8428	9269	10196	
52.00%	TAX	1867	2632	3580	4383	4820	5302	% OF PRE-TAX INC
	NET INCOME	1723	2429	3304	4045	4449	4894	

Figure 3-7. Pro forma income statement reformatted

8. Press the ENTER key.

Your display is much more handsome now. If you want to change the default format, simply reissue the Worksheet Global Format command.

One more slight change. The RATE of MISCELLANEOUS was supposed to represent a constant increase of $10 thousand. The Range Format converted the 10 to 1000.00%. To change it back to the original value,

9. Move to the MISCELLANEOUS RATE cell (A21).

10. Type /Range Format General, and press the ENTER key.

General Format is in force when 1-2-3 is first loaded. It displays as many significant decimal digits as it can, if there are any. Your model should now resemble Figure 3-7.

Save the file as you did in Chapter 2.

11. Type /File Save ENTER Replace to replace the IS file with the current worksheet.

Printing the Worksheet

The Print command has a surprising amount of power and versatility. Still, it is an easy matter just to print the file exactly as it is. Prior to issuing the command, move to the first (top-left) cell of the section to be printed:

1. Align the printer paper at the top of the page; turn the printer on.

2. Press the HOME key to transfer the pointer to the top-left corner of the screen.

3. Type /Print to issue the Print command.

First 1-2-3 gives you the opportunity to send the printout either to the printer for hard-copy output or to a file on the disk. In general, as in this instance, you will respond to the File Print menu by choosing the Printer option:

4. Select Printer to send the output to the printer.

The Print Printer menu appears in the control panel:

Range Line Page Options Clear Align Go Quit

Unless told otherwise, 1-2-3 assigns a top margin of two blank lines, a bottom margin of two blank lines, a left margin of three spaces, and a right margin at position 76. Also, the printer is assumed to print 6 lines per inch,

66 lines per page. You should be familiar with these defaults because you will occasionally (perhaps frequently) want to change at least one of them. For example, the 73-space width is too narrow to contain our income statement.

Now 1-2-3 needs to know what section of the worksheet should be printed. This is the function of the Range option of the Print menu. Choose this option to designate a print range composed of a rectangular block of cells, which may contain one or more rows and one or more columns. As usual, specifying the range involves designating the top-left and bottom-right addresses of the rectangle. The range may be a single cell, a row, several rows, a column, several columns, a block of cells, or the entire worksheet. To print the entire worksheet,

5. Type **R** to select the Range option.

In response, 1-2-3 displays "Enter print range: A1". Typing a period to indicate a range and moving the pointer expands the range beyond A1..A1. The desired bottom-right corner of the print range is the bottom-right corner of the entire utilized position of the worksheet. You can jump to this position quite handily with a special use of the END key. By pressing the END key, then releasing it, and then pressing the HOME key, you can easily move the pointer to the bottom-right cell of the model.

6. Type the . key, then the END key, and then the HOME key.

The control panel informs you that the print range extends from A1 to J31 (the NOTE cell for the NET INCOME row).

7. Press the ENTER key to accept this range.

The Print menu reappears. As mentioned earlier, the right margin must be moved right to accommodate this print range. Overriding the right margin is a Print Option.

8. Type the letter **O** to choose Options.

The Options submenu offers the following options:

Header Footer Margins Borders Setup Pg-Length Other Quit

9. Select the margins option by typing **M**.

Now 1-2-3 asks which margin will be reset:

Left Right Top Bottom

10. Type **R** to reset the right margin.

Now 1-2-3 responds by displaying the current setting and asking for a new one. A right margin at position 132 will allow 129 characters to be typed because the left margin is at position 4. This is adequate for our needs since the width of the income statement is 125 characters.

11. Type **132** and press the ENTER key.

The Options menu returns. If you have a printer with a wide carriage, then you are ready to print, and you may skip to the next section. Otherwise, you may have to set up your printer so that it prints in condensed characters. Some printers can be put in condensed mode by setting the printer's switches. Others can be reset by sending special commands to the printer from the computer. These commands are called *setup strings*, and they may be sent to the printer using the Setup option of the Printer Options menu. See the 1-2-3 User's Manual and your printer manual for details.

12. Choose the **Q**uit option to exit the Options menu and enter the Print menu.

When you first turn your printer on, 1-2-3 does not know whether or not the paper has been aligned at the top of the page. It assumes that it has been, and therefore it begins counting its 66 lines per page wherever the page is actually positioned. This may cause spacing problems if there is a discrepancy between where 1-2-3 *thinks* the top of the page is and where the top actually is. The Align option of the Print menu makes 1-2-3 reset its internal line counter to 1. Wherever the paper is when Align is executed will be considered by 1-2-3 as the first of 66 lines of a new page. If you think that 1-2-3 may be "confused" about the location of the top of the page, choose the Align option of the menu. Then print out the report.

13. Choose the **G**o option.

Your report should now be printed, and it should look like Figure 3-7.

14. Choose the **Q**uit option to exit the Print menu and resume Ready Mode.

You must choose Quit in order to exit Print mode.

Resaving the model at this point also stores the current Print command options, including the print range. To do this,

15. Type **/**File **S**ave, and press the ENTER key; then type **R** to replace the earlier version of the IS file that contained no print settings.

Through extensive use of the Copy command, we have developed a general model to forecast the income statement of an organization. It may take a while before you can use the Copy command fluently, but its use does become quite easy and natural with a little practice. It is well worth the effort required to master this command.

Chapter 4
Using File Combine, Macros, and Graphics

Creating Divisional Income
Statements

Using File Combine to
Consolidate Worksheets

Macros: The Typing
Alternative

Using Graphics to Show
The Revenue Forecast

Suppose you have been using two worksheet files to hold your company's records. One file contains a detailed analysis of your company's sales, and the other contains an analysis of the company's expenses. You would like to have a single worksheet that shows both sales and expenses and also shows profit (based on the sales and expenses listed in the two files). How could you combine the two worksheets so that all of the information you need will appear in a single worksheet?

Here is another hypothetical problem. Suppose you are in charge of a chain of stores. Each of the branches uses a worksheet to keep track of its weekly sales and expenses, and each week they send you diskettes containing their worksheets. You need to consolidate the revenues and expenses of the branches into a total company worksheet. This problem differs from the first because you are not interested in showing the details of each branch on the screen. Rather, you want to add the numbers of the branchs' worksheets to obtain numbers for a consolidated worksheet.

As these two examples illustrate, there are times when it is necessary to combine worksheet files. Lotus 1-2-3's *File Combine* command allows you to do this. In this chapter, we will use the File Combine command to consolidate the income statement forecasts of the regional divisions of Rags-to-Riches, that hugely successful rag manufacturer introduced in Chapter 2. You will need the income-statement model that we completed in Chapter 3 and stored on diskette as IS. If you do not have the pro forma income-statement model saved on your diskette, you may create it by following the numbered steps in Chapters 2 and 3.

We also introduce *macros* (the "typing alternative") in this chapter as a means of automating the consolidation process. In addition, we introduce graphics, demonstrating how easily 1-2-3 can transform a table into a picture. The combination of spreadsheet and graphics in this application begins to scratch the surface of the integrated capabilities that have made this program so popular.

Whereas the previous chapters covered features of 1-2-3 that duplicate those of other spreadsheet programs, this chapter begins to deal with some of the innovative aspects of the package. As you proceed, bear in mind that the Rags-to-Riches worksheet is only a vehicle for illustrating the features of 1-2-3. The File Combine command, macros, and graphics can apply to your own particular projects in many ways.

Creating Divisional Income Statements

Consolidation presupposes the existence of component worksheets, but we have only one worksheet so far, IS. Rather than create separate income statements for the four divisions of Rags-to-Riches — a procedure that would involve more work than is necessary for our purposes—we will simply use the Rags-to-Riches model as a typical division, copying this model several times to "create" other divisions. The commands to combine worksheets will be easy to apply to other situations once you see how they are used here. With the data diskette containing the Rags-to-Riches model (file IS) in the disk drive, use the File Retrieve command to load the file into memory:

1. If the CAPS indicator does not appear in the lower-right corner of your screen, press the CAPS LOCK key.

2. Type /File Retrieve IS, and press the ENTER key.

The File Retrieve command erases whatever might previously have been stored in the worksheet on your screen (that is, in RAM), and it loads the file you designate. The fact that the worksheet is cleared before the file is loaded is significant, especially in contrast to other file-loading commands that do not clear the worksheet. (We will use these commands later.)

Our strategy is to save this worksheet four times, under different names, in order to simulate four divisional income statements. The consolidated statement will be the sum of the four divisions. We will begin the process by creating the individual worksheets for the divisions' income statements. Once these have been saved, we can proceed to the task of combining the worksheets to create the income statement for the total company.

When we consolidate the divisions, we will not want to combine all of the items of the income statement. Rags-to-Riches' revenue and operating expenses are likely to be recorded on a divisional basis, but interest expense and taxes are computed on a total corporate basis. Interest expense depends on the company's borrowings, and Rags-to-Riches' headquarters does not allow the divisions to borrow money independently. Headquarters decides when and what to borrow. Also, the divisions are not taxed individually; the company is taxed as a whole.

Therefore, the financial forecasts of the divisions should extend only to the TOTAL OPERATING EXPENSES line of the income statement, while a separate worksheet should store total-company items such as TAX and INTEREST EXPENSE. The IS worksheet that serves as our blueprint thus comprises two conceptual sections, as shown in Figure 4-1: the *divisional* section and the *total-company* section.

We will need to create two worksheets out of IS: a divisional worksheet, containing the divisional section of IS, and a total-company worksheet, containing the total-company section. In a moment we will split the IS income

INCOME STATEMENT
RAGS-TO-RICHES CORPORATION
($ IN THOUSANDS)

RATES		C 0	D 1	E 2	F 3	G 4	H 5	NOTES
	REVENUE	10000	12000	15600	18720	20592	22651	
	% GROWTH OVER PREVIOUS YEAR		20.00%	30.00%	20.00%	10.00%	10.00%	
	COST OF GOODS SOLD							
17.00%	MATERIALS		2040	2652	3182	3501	3851	% OF SALES
14.00%	WAGES		1680	2184	2621	2883	3171	% OF SALES
15.00%	FRINGE BENEFITS		252	328	393	432	476	% OF WAGES
8.00%	OTHER		100	108	117	126	136	% GROWTH RATE
	GENERAL & ADMINISTRATIVE EXPENSE							
10.00%	COMPENSATION: OFFICE		1200	1320	1452	1597	1757	% GROWTH RATE
8.00%	COMPENSATION: SALES		960	1248	1498	1647	1812	% OF SALES
17.00%	FRINGE BENEFITS		367	437	501	552	607	% OF COMP.
2.50%	ADVERTISING & PROMOTION		300	390	468	515	566	% OF SALES
20	DEPRECIATION		20	20	20	20	20	DIRECT INPUT
10	MISCELLANEOUS		10	20	30	40	50	CONSTANT GROWTH
	TOTAL OPERATING EXPENSES	6400	6929	8706	10282	11313	12446	
	INTEREST EXPENSE	10	10	10	10	10	10	DIRECT INPUT
	PRE-TAX INCOME	3590	5061	6884	8428	9269	10196	
52.00%	TAX	1867	2632	3580	4383	4820	5302	% OF PRE-TAX INC.
	NET INCOME	1723	2429	3304	4045	4449	4894	

Divisional Section

Total-Company Section

Figure 4-1. Income statement showing divisional and total-company sections

statement into two parts, but first we need to introduce a new concept: assigning names to ranges.

Assigning Names to Ranges

For reasons that will soon become apparent, it would be convenient to assign *names* to the two ranges of cells that make up the IS worksheet. When it becomes necessary to refer to a range in a command such as Copy or Range Erase, the range's name can be substituted for the range's beginning and ending coordinates. A name is assigned to a range of cells with the Range Name Create command.

The first step in assigning a range is to move the cursor to the first cell of the range you are about to name. Then issue the Range Name command. The divisional section begins in cell A1.

1. Press the HOME key to move the pointer to cell A1.

2. Type /Range Name Create.

Now 1-2-3 requests the name you would like to assign to the range. The name you select may contain from 1 to 15 characters or numbers. Avoid names that may be confused with cell references, such as A15 or IC256. Also refrain from using spaces or arithmetic operator symbols such as the hyphen (or minus sign). The underscore character ___ is a useful substitute for a space. Names serve as cues, so choose a name that will help you remember what range it describes. For example, the divisional section of the IS worksheet might aptly be named DIVISION.

3. Type **DIVISION**, and press the ENTER key.

Note that 1-2-3 assumes the current position of the pointer (A1) to be the beginning of the range (that is why we moved to A1 *before* selecting the Range command), and it now awaits the address of the end of the range. If you pressed the ENTER key again at this point, 1-2-3 would assign the name DIVISION to the single cell A1. Moving the pointer communicates your intention to name an entire range. The bottom-right cell of the desired range is in the NOTES column of TOTAL OPERATING EXPENSES, at cell J23.

4. Point to the NOTE cell in the TOTAL OPERATING EXPENSES row (cell J23).

As usual, 1-2-3 highlights the range to show you exactly what you are referring to.

5. Press the ENTER key to end the command.

Cells A1..J23 now have the range name DIVISION.

Using File Xtract to Save
A Partial Worksheet

Now we are ready to save the first divisional worksheet. Remember that the new divisional file should contain only the divisional section of this worksheet. When you issue the File Save command, 1-2-3 does not ask you whether you want to save all or part of the worksheet. The Save option assumes that you intend to store the entire worksheet. To save only a segment, you must use a different option of the File command, the Xtract option.

File Xtract permits you to save a range of the worksheet. Additionally, it allows you to specify whether you want to store the range with any formulas that may be contained in it, or whether you prefer the extracted file to contain only labels and values. In this case, "values" means numbers. Cells containing formulas are converted to the values resulting from the formulas. Later, when we use the File Combine command to add the divisions together, we will see that the values we want to combine must be stored as numbers, not formulas. Therefore, we will select the Values option of the File Xtract command.

1. Type **/File**.

2. Select the Xtract option of the File menu.

In response to the "Formulas Values" prompt,

3. Select the Values option.

We will call this file DIV1. Answer the prompt for the file name just as in a File Save procedure:

4. Type **DIV1**, and press the ENTER key.

Because you have distinguished the extract section with a name, you may specify this name in response to the prompt for the extract range:

5. Type **DIVISION**, and press the ENTER key.

At this point, it may be tempting to invoke the File Retrieve command to see whether the extraction worked. Recall, however, that the Retrieve command wipes out the current worksheet. Clearing the worksheet now would cause 1-2-3 to forget the range name DIVISION that we assigned earlier. We assigned the name to the current worksheet in memory, but until we save the worksheet onto diskette, the name is only temporary. Resaving the current worksheet as IS stores the range name onto diskette with the worksheet.

6. Type **/File Save IS**, and press the ENTER key.

7. Select **R** to replace the old version of IS.

Now we can fetch the DIV1 worksheet without being zapped. Retrieving an extracted file is no different from retrieving an ordinary worksheet.

8. Type **/File Retrieve**.

The files of the current diskette appear in the control panel.

9. Move the menu pointer to DIV1, and press the ENTER key.

Figure 4-2 shows the DIV1 worksheet. If you move the pointer to a cell that was originally created with a formula (such as Year 1 REVENUE, cell D6), you will find that the formula has been replaced by a number. By pressing the END and HOME keys and then scrolling toward the left, you can see that the bottom of the worksheet is the TOTAL OPERATING EXPENSES row. The total-company section is excluded from the DIV1 file.

Saving the Separate Worksheet Components

To "create" the other regional divisions of Rags-to-Riches, we need to save the DIV1 file with different file names. We should also replace the RAGS-TO-RICHES CORPORATION label in cell C2 with the name of the division (we will do this for Division 1 as well).

1. Move to cell C2, and type **DIVISION 1**.

2. Type **/File Save**, and press the ENTER key; then select **R** to replace the earlier DIV1 file.

3. With the pointer still at cell C2, either type the label **DIVISION 2** or use the F2 (Edit) key to replace the 1 with a 2.

4. Type **/File Save DIV2**, and press the ENTER key.

5. Next enter **DIVISION 3** in cell C2 either by typing or by using the F2 (Edit) key.

A	B	C	D	E	F	G	H	I	J
			INCOME STATEMENT			($ IN THOUSANDS)			
			RAGS-TO-RICHES CORPORATION						
1									
2									
3									
4 RATES									NOTES
5		0	1	2	3	4	5		
6	REVENUE	10000	12000	15600	18720	20592	22651		
7	% GROWTH OVER PREVIOUS YEAR		20.00%	30.00%	20.00%	10.00%	10.00%		
8									
9	COST OF GOODS SOLD								
10 17.00%	MATERIALS		2040	2652	3182	3501	3851		% OF SALES
11 14.00%	WAGES		1680	2184	2621	2883	3171		% OF SALES
12 15.00%	FRINGE BENEFITS		252	328	393	432	476		% OF WAGES
13 8.00%	OTHER		100	108	117	126	136		% GROWTH RATE
14									
15	GENERAL & ADMINISTRATIVE EXPENSE								
16 10.00%	COMPENSATION: OFFICE		1200	1320	1452	1597	1757		% GROWTH RATE
17 8.00%	COMPENSATION: SALES		960	1248	1498	1647	1812		% OF SALES
18 17.00%	FRINGE BENEFITS		367	437	501	552	607		% OF COMP.
19 2.50%	ADVERTISING & PROMOTION		300	390	468	515	566		% OF SALES
20	DEPRECIATION		20	20	20	20	20		DIRECT INPUT
21 10	MISCELLANEOUS		10	20	30	40	50		CONSTANT GROWTH
22									
23	TOTAL OPERATING EXPENSES	6400	6929	8706	10282	11313	12446		

Figure 4-2. The DIV1 worksheet

6. Type /File Save **DIV3**, and press the ENTER key.

7. And again, enter **DIVISION 4** in cell C2.

8. Type /File Save **DIV4**, and press the ENTER key.

That takes care of the divisional worksheets. As for the total-company section, let us save it in a file called TOT_COMP. To do this, we will need to retrieve the IS worksheet from diskette:

9. Type /File Retrieve **IS**, and press the ENTER key.

The total-company worksheet should contain only total-company items. Thus, we should erase the divisional section before we save the worksheet. Here is a good opportunity to illustrate another use of range names. You can use a range name whenever 1-2-3 expects a range—as it does in the Range Erase command.

10. Type /Range Erase.

Now 1-2-3 tries to help us out by suggesting a range, beginning with the current address of the pointer. But we know exactly what range we want:

11. Type **DIVISION**, and press the ENTER key.

As soon as you typed the D of DIVISION, 1-2-3 removed its suggestion and understood that it was about to receive a range name.

The resulting worksheet has formulas, beginning in row 25, that depend on the area we just erased. For example, PRE-TAX INCOME equals REVENUE (blank) minus TOTAL OPERATING EXPENSES (blank) minus INTEREST EXPENSE (10). Therefore, PRE-TAX INCOME is −10 for all years. The total-company section of the statement works, but right now there is no divisional data for it to work with. When we fill in the blank section with the divisions' revenues and expenses, the model will recalculate the bottom section and derive the correct figures.

Now we can save the total-company worksheet.

12. Type /File Save **TOT_COMP**, and press the ENTER key.

Using Worksheet Erase to Clear
The Screen

Now the stage is set to aggregate the worksheets into a single, consolidated financial forecast. To start the process with a clean slate, let us clear the screen with the Worksheet Erase command. Worksheet Erase erases the current worksheet from memory. It can be a dangerous command if you did not save the worksheet before erasing it because, once a worksheet has been erased, there is no way to retrieve it except from diskette.

1. Type / and select the **Worksheet** command.

2. Select the **Erase** option.

Because 1-2-3 is mindful of the common types of errors that people make, it prompts you with "No Yes" to make sure that you want to erase the worksheet.

3. Select **Yes**.

Now the worksheet is blank, and we can get on with the consolidation.

Using File Combine to Consolidate Worksheets

Imagine that you have a copy of the TOT—COMP worksheet on a sheet of clear plastic film (a transparency). You also have transparencies of each of the divisional worksheets. You take the TOT—COMP transparency and lay it on your desk top. Then you overlay the DIV1 transparency directly on top of the TOT—COMP sheet. You then see that, by some miracle, the PRE-TAX INCOME, TAX, and NET INCOME lines of the TOT—COMP sheet have changed; they now reflect the income statement of Division 1. By overlaying and combining the two plastic sheets, you have recalculated the formulas of TOT—COMP using the data of DIV1, as if this were a single worksheet.

This is similar to the effect of the *File Combine* command. This command overlays a worksheet from diskette onto the current worksheet (the worksheet on the screen) at any location you choose. There are three ways to use File Combine. *File Combine Copy* replaces entries of the current worksheet with entries of the incoming file. *File Combine Add* adds the value cells of the incoming file to corresponding cells of the current worksheet, and *File Combine Subtract* subtracts the value cells of the incoming file from corresponding cells of the current worksheet.

The File Combine command may seem similar to the File Retrieve command. After all, both load worksheet files from a diskette. There are important differences between the two commands, however. For one, the File Retrieve command clears the worksheet before the diskette file is loaded, whereas the File Combine command leaves the current worksheet on the screen. For another, the File Retrieve command loads the diskette file beginning at the top-left corner of the worksheet (cell A1), whereas the File Combine command loads the diskette file wherever you want it. The Copy option of the File Combine command replaces the section of the original worksheet upon which the incoming file is overlaid. With the File Combine Add or File Combine Subtract command, only the blank and numeric cells of the original worksheet are changed—labels and formulas of the original worksheet are unaffected.

Overlaying Two Files With File Combine Copy

The ability to add entire worksheets together in a single command fits perfectly with our purposes in this application. As in our description of the imaginary plastic transparencies, we will begin by laying the TOT—COMP worksheet on an empty "desktop"—or screen, in our case. We will do this by retrieving the TOT—COMP file. Then we will use File Combine Copy to overlay the DIV1 file onto the blank upper portion of TOT—COMP. We will use the File Combine Add command to add the other divisional income statements to the worksheet, one after the other. The final result will be a consolidated income statement for Rags-to-Riches.

1. To start, type /File Retrieve **TOT—COMP**, and press the ENTER key.

Because the total-company section begins in row 25, it does not appear in the window on your screen. If you like, you can scroll downward to verify that the total-company items are there.

The next step is to use the File Combine Copy command to overlay the DIVISION 1 revenue and expenses onto the divisional section of the worksheet. Before using a File Combine command, you must put the pointer on the cell at which you want the top-left corner of the incoming file to be placed. You must always be careful to pick the right spot because you don't want to replace the wrong cells. In this instance, the pointer should be at cell A1, the point at which the divisional section begins.

2. Go to cell A1.

3. Type /File, and select the Combine option.

In response to 1-2-3's "Copy Add Subtract" prompt,

4. Select the Copy option.

When you use the Combine command, you have the luxury of retrieving either an entire worksheet or a section of a worksheet from diskette. To retrieve a section, you must previously have assigned a range name to the section of the incoming file that you want to retrieve (the name must also have been saved previously as part of the incoming file), and then you must refer to that name in the Combine command. This is why 1-2-3 prompts you to select between two options, Entire File and Named Range.

5. Select Entire File.

Naturally, 1-2-3 needs to know the name of the file to retrieve from disk. The third line of the control panel displays the names of all files on the current disk.

6. Move the menu pointer to DIV1, and press the ENTER key.

Now 1-2-3 loads the file. For all intents and purposes, it is equivalent to the IS file shown in Figure 4-1, except that the division section is made up of values, not formulas. Change the title of the worksheet to reflect the fact that this is going to be a consolidation of income statements:

7. Go to cell C2, and then type the label **CONSOLIDATED INCOME STATEMENT**.

Before we go on, it would be a good idea to protect the work we have done so far. That way, if we make a mistake later on, we can always go back to this point. Let us save the worksheet, using a new file name.

8. Type /File Save **CON_DIV1**, and press the ENTER key.

Splitting the Screen
With Worksheet Window

As we retrieve the other divisional files, we will want to observe the effects on several line items. For one thing, we will want to know how the top portion of the statement is changing as we add the divisional files. At the same time, we will want to keep an eye on the bottom portion of the statement to see how it changes. There are not enough lines on the screen to display both items at once, and we certainly do not want to have to scroll up and down repeatedly. At times like this, it would be helpful to have two independent screens so that we could point at will to any section of the worksheet.

But you do have two screens; 1-2-3 gives you a second one for free with the *Worksheet Window* command. With the Window command, you can split the worksheet display into two vertical or horizontal portions. It is as if you were a TV director using two monitors to view the same object from different angles, or to view two different objects at once. You can scroll each window, just as you scroll the standard screen, to focus on a particular section of the worksheet. Using windows, you can also make a change to a cell in one section of the worksheet and see the effect immediately in another section of the worksheet.

To split the screen horizontally, you begin by moving the pointer to any cell in the row at which you want to divide the screen. For a vertical split, move the pointer to any cell in the column at which you want to divide the screen. Then invoke the Window command. We are going to use a horizontal window so that we can see both the REVENUE line in the top (divisional) portion of the statement and the NET INCOME line in the bottom portion. These two lines will reflect the changes that take place as we add the separate divisional worksheets to the combined file on the screen.

1. Press the HOME key to move the pointer to the home position (cell A1).

2. Use the down arrow key to move the pointer down to row 11.

3. Type **/Worksheet**.

4. Select the **Window** option of the Worksheet menu.

The Window menu lists the following options:

Horizontal   Vertical   Sync   Unsync   Clear

5. Select the **Horizontal** option.

The screen splits *above* the pointer location (in a vertical window, the screen splits *to the left of* the pointer's position). By placing the pointer in row 11, we divided the screen into halves. If we had placed the pointer in another row before issuing the Worksheet Window command, we could have made one window larger than the other. Notice that the pointer is stationed in the upper window. The pointer may be moved in the normal way, except that it will remain in this window until you press the *Window key*, key F6. The Window key transfers the pointer from one window to the other.

Use the F6 (Window) key to put the pointer in the lower window, and press the TAB key several times. Notice how scrolling the bottom window causes the top window to scroll as well. This is called *synchronized* scrolling. By default, scrolling is synchronized when the Window command is first invoked.

Now press the F6 (Window) key to transfer the pointer to the top window, and press the HOME key to display the top-left portion of the spreadsheet. This forces the bottom window to scroll back to the column on the far left. It is possible to disable the synchronization default by issuing the Worksheet Window Unsync command. This command causes the windows to scroll independently. Once you have issued the Worksheet Window Unsync command, windowing will remain unsynchronized until you invoke the Worksheet Window Sync command. We do not need unsynchronized windows, so we will focus our two "monitors" so that they show the parts of the worksheet we want to see.

6. Make sure that the upper window's top-left corner is in the home position.

7. Use the F6 (Window) key to transfer the pointer to the bottom window.

8. Using the down arrow key or PG DN key, scroll the bottom window so that it displays the NET INCOME label at row 31.

Your screen should now look like Figure 4-3.

9. Use the F6 (Window) key to transfer the pointer to the top window. Make sure that the pointer is in the home position.

The File Combine Add Command

Now we are ready to bring Division 2 into the picture. We want to add Division 2's revenue and expenses to the current worksheet, so we use the File Combine Add command. (If we used the File Combine Copy command, we would merely replace the Division 1 numbers without adding.) Watch the top section change as you combine the two worksheets.

1. With the pointer at A1, type /File Combine.

2. Choose the Add option of the Combine menu.

3. Type **E** to load the entire file.

4. Type **DIV2**, and press the ENTER key (or choose DIV2 with the menu pointer) to retrieve the DIV2 file.

Compare the results, shown as an entire worksheet in Figure 4-4, with those

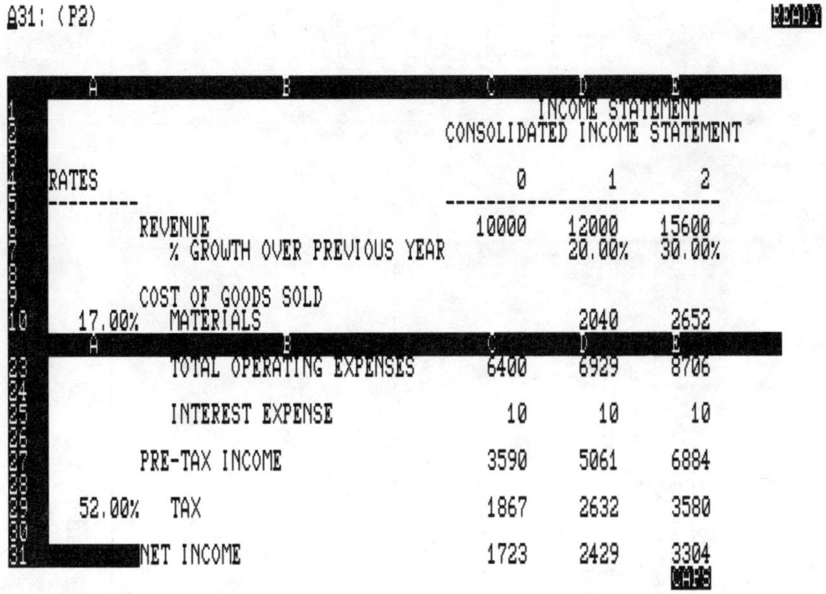

A31: (P2)

```
                                     INCOME STATEMENT
                          CONSOLIDATED INCOME STATEMENT
RATES                                 0       1       2
---------                     ---------------------------
            REVENUE                 10000   12000   15600
            % GROWTH OVER PREVIOUS YEAR     20.00%  30.00%

            COST OF GOODS SOLD
   17.00%   MATERIALS                        2040    2652
            TOTAL OPERATING EXPENSES  6400    6929    8706

            INTEREST EXPENSE           10      10      10

         PRE-TAX INCOME             3590    5061    6884

   52.00%   TAX                     1867    2632    3580

         NET INCOME                1723    2429    3304
```

Figure 4-3. Worksheet showing horizontal windows

of the previous display in Figure 4-3. The Year 1 REVENUE line has doubled with the addition of Division 2. In fact, all revenue and operating expense figures have doubled, which is to be expected because Division 1 and Division 2 contain precisely the same numbers.

What about the total-company section? The INTEREST EXPENSE row remains the same—it was set to a constant 10, independent of revenue and expenses. However, the PRE-TAX INCOME, TAX, and NET INCOME lines all depend on revenue and expenses. They are not affected directly by the Combine Add operation; they are affected only to the extent that they depend on the divisional portion of the worksheet.

Now that we know how to use the File Combine Add command, completing the consolidation is easy.

	A	B	C	D	E	F	G	H	I	J
			CONSOLIDATED INCOME STATEMENT	INCOME STATEMENT		($ IN THOUSANDS)				NOTES
5	RATES		0	2	4	6	8	10		
6		REVENUE	20000	24000	31200	37440	41184	45302		
7		% GROWTH OVER PREVIOUS YEAR		20.00%	30.00%	20.00%	10.00%	10.00%		GROWTH RATE
9		COST OF GOODS SOLD								
10	34.00%	MATERIALS	3400	4080	5304	6365	7001	7701		% OF SALES
11	28.00%	WAGES	2800	3360	4368	5242	5766	6342		% OF SALES
12	30.00%	FRINGE BENEFITS	420	504	655	786	865	951		% OF WAGES
13	16.00%	OTHER	185	200	216	233	252	272		% GROWTH RATE
15		GENERAL & ADMINISTRATIVE EXPENSE								
16	20.00%	COMPENSATION: OFFICE	2182	2400	2640	2904	3194	3514		% GROWTH RATE
17	15.0%	COMPENSATION: SALES	1600	1920	2496	2995	3295	3624		% OF SALES
18	34.00%	FRINGE BENEFITS	643	734	873	1003	1103	1213		% OF COMP.
19	5.00%	ADVERTISING & PROMOTION	500	600	780	936	1030	1133		% OF SALES
20		DEPRECIATION	40	40	40	40	40	40		DIRECT INPUT
21	20	MISCELLANEOUS	0	20	40	60	80	100		CONSTANT GROWTH
23		TOTAL OPERATING EXPENSES	12800	13858	17412	20564	22626	24891		
25		INTEREST EXPENSE	10	10	10	10	10	10		DIRECT INPUT
27		PRE-TAX INCOME	7190	10132	13778	16866	18548	20401		
29	52.00%	TAX	3739	5268	7164	8770	9645	10609		% OF PRE-TAX INC.
31		NET INCOME	3451	4863	6613	8096	8903	9793		

Figure 4-4. The combined income statements of DIV1 and DIV2

5. With the pointer at cell A1, type /File Combine Add Entire-File **DIV3**, and press the ENTER key.

6. While the pointer is still at cell A1, type /File Combine Add Entire-File **DIV4**, and press the ENTER key.

The consolidation is now complete. Looking at the revenue and net income figures, we see that the corporation is not performing too poorly. It earns $9731 thousand in net income on $48000 thousand of revenues in Year 1, better than a 20% margin. In real life, the divisions of a corporation may not all fare as well as Divisions 1 through 4 of Rags-to-Riches. You may, of course, change the forecasts of the individual divisions before combining them, but the methodology for developing a consolidated income statement is the same: retrieve the first division, and then overlay the other divisions with the Combine Add command.

One important note: *The overlay method works because the divisional worksheets have identical layouts.* It is crucial that the incoming items line up exactly.

Numeric Column Headings And Combine Add

You may have noticed that the column headings 0 through 5 (cells C4 through H4) have been affected by the Combine Add command. That is because these column headings are numeric. To fix them, you will need to go to the column headings and reenter them—an inconvenience, but an important lesson. If you are going to use the Combine Add command, make sure that numeric headings and titles are entered with a label-prefix, so that they will be unaffected by the incoming file.

The RATE column also has been aggregated. However, the growth rate assumptions of the divisions are not important for this analysis, so we will ignore them. We could always erase them with the Range Erase command if we have to show this worksheet to someone else.

Clearing the Windows

Lotus 1-2-3 even cleans windows! The Worksheet Window Clear command returns the display to a single, full-screen window. Which of the split-screen windows is chosen for the full-screen display? To find out,

1. Type /Worksheet Window Clear.

In a screen split horizontally, the top window assumes full size. In a screen split vertically, the left window takes over.

Macros: The Typing Alternative

Spreadsheet applications often involve repetition. For example, it is rare that a financial forecast is correct the first time around. Even if the assumptions are correct, it is usually desirable to try out several sets of assumptions, or scenarios, before the forecast is put to rest. It is likely that the consolidation will have to be run several times as the divisional forecasts are revised. This becomes tedious for two reasons. First, repeatedly entering the same set of commands becomes monotonous. Second, if the model is not run frequently, it is easy to forget the commands involved, as well as the names of the worksheets that must be combined. Luckily, 1-2-3 offers its "typing alternative," the macro facility.

A *macro* is a column of cells that stores the keystrokes of 1-2-3 commands and data entries exactly as you would have typed them yourself. You assign the macro a unique name; when that name is invoked, the contents of the macro are executed. In other words, by storing a batch of 1-2-3 commands in a range of cells, you can instruct 1-2-3 to execute the batch by simply entering its name. An entire set of commands can be run automatically and repeatedly by using macros.

We will create a macro to run the entire consolidation. Once the macro is developed, we will not need to remember which commands and filenames to use and in what sequence to use them. Not only will the macro save typing time; once the macro functions correctly, there will be less opportunity to make mistakes.

Translating Keystrokes
To Macro Commands

The first step in developing a macro is to run through the procedure yourself—just what we have done up to this point in this chapter. It is a good idea to write down the commands and a description of what they do on a piece of paper as you go through your trial run. This has been done for you in Table 4-1 (the preliminary step of loading the TOT—COMP worksheet has

Command	*Description*
HOME	Move to cell A1 before combining the first division
/File Combine Copy Entire-file **DIV1** ENTER	Copy Division 1's worksheet onto the current worksheet
GOTO **C2** ENTER	Move pointer to the second title line of the income statement
CONSOLIDATED INCOME STATEMENT ENTER	Type the label
HOME	Move to cell A1 before adding the next division
/File Combine Add Entire-file **DIV2** ENTER	Add the second division
/File Combine Add Entire-file **DIV3** ENTER	Add the third division
/File Combine Add Entire-file **DIV4** ENTER	Add the fourth division
GOTO **C4** ENTER RIGHT **1** RIGHT **2** RIGHT **3** RIGHT **4** RIGHT **5** ENTER	Correct the column headings

Table 4-1. Commands used to consolidate worksheets

been left out because we will do this step ourselves before we execute the macro). If the commands are not fresh in your memory, you might want to review Table 4-1 before continuing.*

Once you know the commands to enter into the macro, the next step is to translate them into keystrokes—the keystrokes that you actually typed when you went through this procedure yourself. The keystrokes are summarized in Table 4-2.

---

*In this and later macro command summaries, we will represent an arrow key by the name of its direction (such as RIGHT) and special function keys by the names of the functions they perform (such as GOTO).

HOME
/FCCEDIV1 ENTER
GOTO C2 ENTER
CONSOLIDATED INCOME STATEMENT ENTER
HOME
/FCAEDIV2 ENTER
/FCAEDIV3 ENTER
/FCAEDIV4 ENTER
GOTO C4
RIGHT 1 RIGHT 2 RIGHT 3 RIGHT 4 RIGHT 5 ENTER

Table 4-2. Keystrokes used to consolidate worksheets

Key Name	Macro Code Name*
ENTER key	~
Up arrow key	{UP}
Down arrow key	{DOWN}
Right arrow key	{RIGHT}
Left arrow key	{LEFT}
HOME key	{HOME}
END key	{END}
PG UP key	{PGUP}
PG DN key	{PGDN}
ESC key	{ESC}
DEL key	{DEL}
BACKSPACE key	{BS}
F2 (Edit) key	{EDIT}
F3 (Name) key	{NAME}
F4 (Abs) key	{ABS}
F5 (GoTo) key	{GOTO}
F6 (Window) key	{WINDOW}
F7 (Query) key	{QUERY}
F8 (Table) key	{TABLE}
F9 (Calc) key	{CALC}
F10 (Graph) key	{GRAPH}
Pause for manual input until user presses ENTER	{?}

*Note: Macro code names may be entered in uppercase or lowercase.

Table 4-3. Macro codes for special key names

Before the keystrokes may be entered into the macro, there is still one more step in the translation process. There are a number of keystrokes that 1-2-3 will not interpret directly in a macro. These include such special keys as ENTER, HOME, the function keys F1 through F10, and the arrow keys, among others. These keys must be encoded in the macro according to Table 4-3, which can also be found in the Macro section of the 1-2-3 User's Manual.

The special keys that are embedded in our command sequence are ENTER, HOME, the right arrow key (RIGHT), and the F5 key (GOTO). The macro code for ENTER is ~ (a *tilde*); the codes for the HOME, RIGHT, and GOTO keys are {HOME}, {RIGHT}, and {GOTO}, respectively (the words must be enclosed in "squiggly" brackets). The following are the translated keystrokes that will constitute our consolidation macro:

```
{HOME}
/FCCEDIV1~
{GOTO}C2~
CONSOLIDATED INCOME STATEMENT~
{HOME}
/FCAEDIV2~
/FCAEDIV3~
/FCAEDIV4~
{GOTO}C4~{RIGHT}1{RIGHT}2{RIGHT}3{RIGHT}4{RIGHT}5~
```

These commands will be stored as labels in a column of cells somewhere on the worksheet. (Figure 4-5 shows what this macro looks like.) Actually, you can combine several commands in a single label if you wish. Here, we have separated the commands for explanatory purposes only.

Entering Commands Into a Macro

Recall that the first step in the consolidation was to retrieve the TOT—COMP file, which contains the total-company section of the income statement. We will do this first step manually ourselves. Then, in a section of the worksheet that will not interfere with the model, we will store our column of macro labels. It is important to choose a place that will not be inadvertently erased or deleted.

1. Type /File Retrieve TOT—COMP, and press the ENTER key.

2. Go to cell K1.

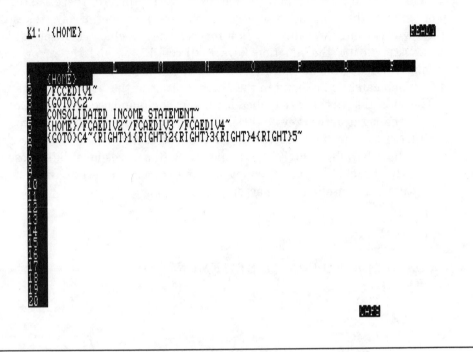

Figure 4-5. The \A macro on the worksheet

All cells of a macro are required to be labels. Be careful to begin a command label such as /FCCEDIV1~, with a label-prefix (apostrophe); otherwise, when you press the / character, 1-2-3 will think that you want to issue an immediate command. Our intent is not to execute /FCCEDIV1 immediately but to store the command for later use.

3. Type the label {**HOME**}. (No label-prefix is needed here because 1-2-3 recognizes the { character as the beginning of a label.)

Nothing dramatic happens yet. As far as 1-2-3 is concerned, we have simply fed another label into its stomach. Later we will instruct 1-2-3 to digest it.

4. Press the down arrow key to move to cell K2.

5. Type **'/FCCEDIV1~** and press the ENTER key.

6. Enter the label **{GOTO}C2~** in cell K3.

This macro label moves the pointer to the second line of the worksheet title. If you were doing things yourself, you would now proceed to type CONSOLI- DATED INCOME STATEMENT and press the ENTER key. A macro can enter data in the same way.

7. Move down to cell K4, type **CONSOLIDATED INCOME STATE- MENT~** and press the ENTER key.

Do not forget the tilde at the end of the label. In fact, make certain that your entries conform precisely to the steps described here, lest you be macro- zapped. If you forget the tilde between {GOTO}C2 and CONSOLIDATED, it would be as if you pressed the GOTO key and, responding to 1-2-3's inquiry of where it should go, you typed C2CONSOLIDATED. This error would cause the macro to malfunction.

There is no requirement to restrict each cell to a single command. Instead of storing the next four commands in four separate cells, string them together in a single cell.

8. Move to cell K5.

9. Type **{HOME}/FCAEDIV2~/FCAEDIV3~/FCAEDIV4~,** and press the ENTER key.

10. In cell K6, type **{GOTO}C4~{RIGHT}1{RIGHT}2{RIGHT}3{RIGHT}4{RIGHT}5~.**

If you do combine several commands, do not imbed any extra blanks in the label. After all, if you were typing yourself, you would not have pressed any extraneous blanks. Figure 4-5 shows the macro.

Naming and Invoking a Macro

Special names must be assigned to macros. A macro name consists of a \ (backward slash) followed by a single letter. Thus \A, \L, and \X are valid macro names. The reason for this special naming convention is to allow 1-2-3 to recognize your column of labels as a macro so that it can give this macro special treatment. The *Range Name Create* command is used to designate the first cell of the macro with the macro's name.

1. Move to the first cell of the consolidation macro (cell K1).

2. Type /Range Name Create.

The response of 1-2-3 is to display the names of any currently set ranges in the control panel. We do not want any of these names for our macro, so we will specify a new name.

3. Type \A and press the ENTER key to name the macro \A. Then press the ENTER key again to limit the range to one cell, K1..K1.

We are now ready to execute the macro. First, however, protect yourself by resaving the worksheet, just in case the macro fails to work:

4. Type /File Save; then press the ENTER key, and select R to replace the previous version of your file.

Invoking a macro involves pressing the ALT key and holding it down as you press the letter name (such as A) assigned to the macro. When 1-2-3 senses that you have pressed ALT and a letter, it searches its list of range names for the special macro name that consists of a \ and that same letter.

Then 1-2-3 turns its attention to the cell associated with the macro name. Beginning with this cell, 1-2-3 interprets and executes each consecutive macro command in the column. Execution ends if a blank cell is encountered as 1-2-3 moves down the column. As each command is executed, the keystrokes appear in the control panel as if you were typing them. But 1-2-3 is an extremely fast typist. Watch what happens when you invoke macro \A:

5. Hold down the ALT key and type the A key.

Lotus 1-2-3 zips through the procedure, as long as there are no errors. If there are any problems, see if the error message gives you a hint as to which command did not work. The most likely source of trouble is a typing error, so retrieve the TOT_COMP file and carefully compare your macro to Figure 4-5. After making corrections, invoke the macro again.

Consolidating the income statements of the corporation is now easily accomplished. Macro \A does all the work for you; you need not even memorize the names of the divisional worksheets. Macros have tremendous potential for simplifying applications. In later chapters, we will see that macros are far more than mere typing alternatives. For now, though, we will move on to one of the best features of 1-2-3: graphics.

Using Graphics to Show
The Revenue Forecast

With 1-2-3, it is remarkably easy to express worksheet data in graphic form. Charts with a professional appearance can be generated on the screen in a few minutes—often less—by employing commands that are similar in form to other worksheet commands. You can depict worksheet data in five types of graphs: *line, bar, XY, stacked-bar,* and *pie.* In this section, we will explore two of these graph types. The others are introduced later in this book.

The Parts of a Graph

Figure 4-6 shows a bar chart. Its components are similar to those of other types of graphs. A graph is mapped out by its horizontal and vertical *axes,* called the *X-axis* and *Y-axis* respectively. The Y-axis measures the values of the graphed data. The X-axis shows what the data points correspond to—in this case, the years 1982 through 1985.

The graph shows three sets of bars, distinguished by their shading patterns. The legend at the bottom of the graph tells you which set of bars belongs to which shading pattern. The three sets of bars correspond to three *data ranges,* called the *A-range, B-range,* and *C-range.* Actually, 1-2-3 allows you to graph up to six data ranges on one graph (the other three are called the D-range, E-range, and F-range). Each data range consists of values, one for each year shown on the chart. Another special range, the *X-range,* consists of the X-axis labels—in this case, 1982, 1983, 1984, and 1985.

A graph can have up to two *titles,* which appear centered above the chart. You can also give titles to the Y-axis (such as DOLLARS) and to the X-axis (such as YEARS).

Graphing the Consolidated
Revenue Row

Using our income-statement model as an example, we could designate the range of cells containing revenue for Years 0 through 5 in the pro forma income statement as one data range. Net income might be another data

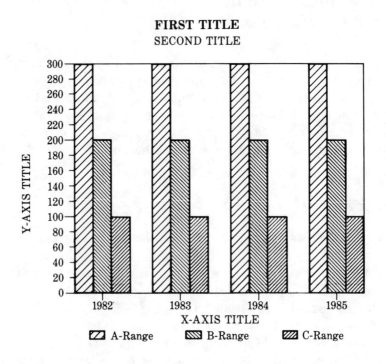

Figure 4-6. The parts of a graph

range. We could use the Graph command to assign a letter (A, B, C, D, E, or F) to the range that we would like to graph. Let us try this out by graphing consolidated revenue. With the TOT—COMP worksheet on your screen,

1. Type **/Graph** to invoke the Graph command menu.

The Graph menu looks like this:

Type X A B C D E F Reset View Save Options Name Quit

To specify a data range for graphing, choose one of the letter options, A through F:

2. Type **A** to designate a data range as the A range.

Now 1-2-3 will ask you for a range, which you specify exactly as you did in other instances when a range was requested. You may type a range name or type the coordinates of a range or use pointing to specify the range's boundaries.

3. Move the pointer to the Year 0 REVENUE cell (C6).

4. Type the . key to anchor the range.

5. Press the END key and then the right arrow key to move the pointer to the Year 5 REVENUE cell (H6).

The range is highlighted, as always.

6. Press the ENTER key.

Now that you've designated a data range, 1-2-3 has all the information it needs to generate a rudimentary graph. To see the graph,

7. Choose the View option of the Graph menu.

The graph on your screen should resemble Figure 4-7. In order to create this

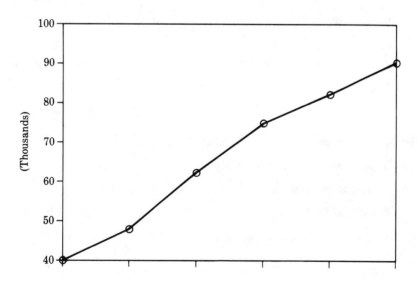

Figure 4-7. Preliminary consolidated revenue graph

graph, 1-2-3 had to make several assumptions.

First, because you did not specify a graph type, 1-2-3 drew a line graph. This selection will be chosen by default if no other graph type is designated.

Second, based on the values of the data range, 1-2-3 figured out its own scaling for the vertical (REVENUE) axis, using 40 as a minimum and 100 as a maximum with an interval of 10 between tick marks. The horizontal axis represents time, although 1-2-3 has no idea whether the frequency of the revenue values is years, months, or weeks.

Notice also that 1-2-3 scaled down the revenue values. Year 0, for instance, was converted from 40000 to 40. This is because there is not enough room on the left side of the screen for 1-2-3 to display more than three digit numbers along the vertical axis. If you ask 1-2-3 to graph values requiring more than three digits, it will scale the values as much as necessary to fit them in. The "(Thousands)" message along the vertical axis informs you that this has occurred.

This graph is nice, but 1-2-3 can do better—if we provide the right instructions. The first embellishment we will make is to put labels along the tick marks of the horizontal axis to help explain what is being graphed. Assuming that somewhere in the worksheet there is a range of cells containing appropriate labels or values to be used for the horizontal axis, we can choose the X option of the Graph menu to assign the X-range. However, we must first erase the graph from the screen.

8. Press any key to return to the Graph menu and the worksheet.

9. Type **X** to designate the X range.

The column labels, 0 through 5 in row 4, are perfect for the job.

10. Move the pointer to the 0 column label in cell C4.

11. Type the . key to anchor the range.

12. Move the pointer to the 5 column label in cell H4.

13. Press the ENTER key.

Now take another peek at the graph:

14. Type **V** to view the graph.

When you are finished looking,

15. Press any key to retrieve the Graph menu.

Using Graph Options

If a graph is to have an impact on the viewer, it should give an instant impression of the story it attempts to present. Graph and axis titles go a long way toward achieving this effect. The Options choice of the Graph menu includes commands to incorporate these titles into the graph. With the Graph menu in the control panel,

1. Type the letter **O** to choose Options.

2. Choose the Titles option by typing **T**.

You may elect to create four types of titles: First, Second, X-axis, Y-axis. First and Second are two lines of title that are centered above the graph, as shown in Figure 4-6. X-axis is the option to label the horizontal axis, and Y-axis is the option to label the vertical axis.

3. Type **F** to enter the first line of a graph title.

When 1-2-3 asks for the title line,

4. Type **FINANCIAL FORECAST**, and press the ENTER key.

The control panel now brings back the Options menu. Why does 1-2-3 remain in the Options menu instead of returning to the original graph menu? That is because the Options menu is a "sticky" menu. (You will be introduced to other such menus later in this book.) The reason 1-2-3 stays in the Options menu is that it assumes we will want to enter another option—and indeed we do. Although it isn't mandatory, we would like to enter a second title.

5. Choose the Titles option again.

6. Type **S** to enter the second title.

7. Type **CORPORATE CONSOLIDATION**, and press the ENTER key.

The sticky Options menu returns.

8. Choose Titles again, then the **X-Axis** option.

The horizontal axis represents years, so

9. Type **YEARS**, and press the ENTER key.

The vertical axis represents revenue, so

10. Type **T** and then **Y** to choose the Y-Axis option.

11. Type **REVENUE**, and press the ENTER key.

To get back to the main Graph menu, you must explicitly exit the Options menu:

12. Choose the **Q**uit option.

Review the results:

13. Type **V** to view the graph.

As Figure 4-8 shows, this graph is certainly more illustrative than the primitive one shown in Figure 4-7. The trend of revenue over the forecast period is quite clear from the line, and the titles describe succinctly what this graph is about.

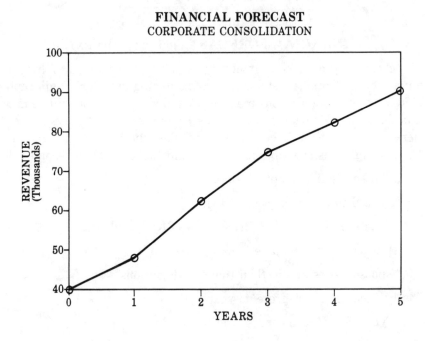

Figure 4-8. Revenue graph showing axis titles

Displaying Values Within the Graph

There is a problem with this graph, however. The revenue data taken from the worksheet was originally stated in thousands (for example, the value 10 really represented 10 thousand), but 1-2-3 has no way of knowing this. To 1-2-3, 10 means 10, not 10 thousand. Thus, when it scales down the data, 1-2-3 thinks that it has converted the values to thousands when in fact it has converted them to millions. Worse, there is no way to suppress the "(Thousands)" message that has been posted along the vertical axis.

One way around the problem is to go back into the worksheet and create a row of values equal to revenues divided by 1000 in order to convert the revenues to millions by ourselves. Then we could use the Graph command to graph these converted values. Because these values are less than four digits in magnitude, 1-2-3 will not try to convert them. We would then be free to provide our own rounding message, such as (REVENUES IN MILLIONS), as a Y-axis title. We will not implement this technique here, but you should be aware of it in case you meet this obstacle at some point.

Another way to make the graph clearer is to display the actual values being graphed directly above the corresponding data points. We will try this approach.

1. Press any key to get back to the worksheet; then type the letter **O** to return to the Options menu.

2. Choose the Data-labels option by pressing **D**.

The Data-labels option permits you to specify a range of label cells that will be assigned to a graph range. The labels will be placed in the area of the corresponding values of the graph range. We want to attach data labels to our A-range. Therefore, when 1-2-3 requests the data range you wish to label,

3. Type **A**.

Next tell 1-2-3 which range of cells in the worksheet contains the data labels. There are six data points in the A-range, so there should be six cells in the data-label range. If you specify value cells instead of label cells, the values will be used as labels for purposes of the graph, so we can use the revenue values as our data labels.

4. Move the pointer to the Year 0 REVENUE cell (C6).

5. Type the . key to anchor the range.

6. Press the END key, followed by the right arrow key, to shift the pointer to the Year 5 REVENUE cell (H6).

7. Press the ENTER key.

Now 1-2-3 asks where you wish to place the labels: "Centered Left Above Right Below."

8. Type **A** to position the labels above the data points.

9. Type **Q** to exit the Data-labels menu.

10. Type **Q** to exit the Options menu.

11. Type **V** to view the graph.

As Figure 4-9 shows, you can now see not only the trend but the data

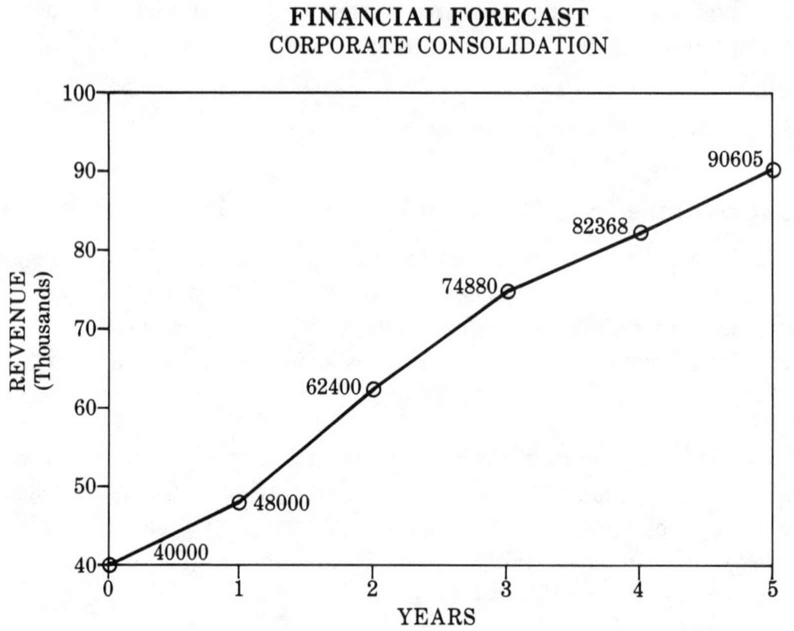

FINANCIAL FORECAST
CORPORATE CONSOLIDATION

Figure 4-9. Final consolidated revenue graph

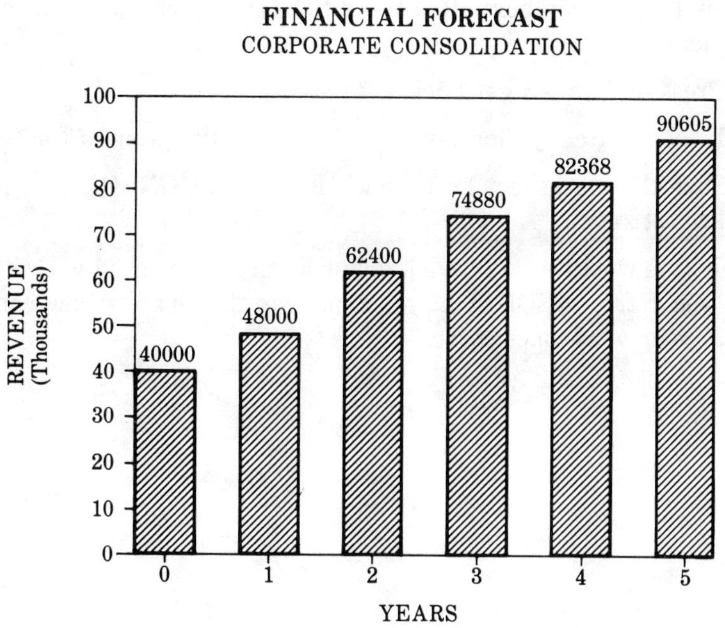

FINANCIAL FORECAST
CORPORATE CONSOLIDATION

Figure 4-10. Consolidated revenue shown in a bar chart

values as well. This provides a partial solution to the data-conversion problem because the viewer sees the data label unconverted, sees the "(Thousands)" message, and may guess that the vertical axis is actually in millions.

Other Graphing Options

If you are using a color monitor, you can take advantage of your screen by choosing another option in the Options menu, the Color option. Each of the six data ranges will then be shown in a different hue.

We will describe one more trick in this chapter. How hard do you think it would be to convert this line chart to the bar chart of Figure 4-10?

1. Press any key to get back to the Graph menu.

2. Select **Type**, then **Bar**, and then **View**.

Lotus 1-2-3 remembers all of the options that have been set thus far, and it uses them for this new graph.

3. Press any key to get back to the worksheet.

4. Exit into Ready Mode by choosing the **Q**uit option of the Graph menu.

5. Save the worksheet by typing **/** **F**ile **S**ave **CONSOL** and pressing the ENTER key.

When the worksheet is saved, graph settings are saved with it. Therefore, when you retrieve CONSOL, you can issue the Graph View command and admire your work once more.

Chapter 5
A Simulation Model

As you become familiar with the 1-2-3 program, you will continually discover that even the little enhancements of the language can open up entire new worlds of applications. In this chapter, the foundation of an entire model rests upon a simple, unheralded function named @RAND. The @RAND function merely generates a random decimal number between 0 and 1. Yet, combined with the ability of 1-2-3 to look up numbers in a table and to run through multiple iterations of a model automatically, the random number generator empowers the spreadsheet with an analytical capability previously reserved for more complicated and difficult programs: simulation.

Simulation is a technique that allows us to portray a real-life situation in mathematical terms. A *Monte Carlo simulation* is a special type of model used to predict situations based on random events. For example, one can simulate the random arrival of people at a bank in order to determine whether the bank employs enough tellers and to predict the average amount of time a person will need to wait in line before being served. In this chapter, we will use a simulation model to forecast the backlog of orders at a manufacturing firm and to measure how well the company's work force is utilized. Monte Carlo simulations are usually more complicated than the one we will develop, but this chapter will give you an idea of what you can do in this area with 1-2-3.

This chapter's application introduces us to two other functions besides the @RAND function. The @VLOOKUP function is used to look up a number in a table (such as a tax table on an income tax form). The @MIN function selects the minimum of a group of values. We also will introduce the Worksheet Titles command to fix rows and columns onto the screen window (so that they will not scroll with the rest of the window) and the Data Fill command to enter a number sequence.

The Purpose of the Simulation Model

The Modex Corporation manufactures intelligent communications modems. Modex has developed a new model, the Tote 'Em Modem, which the firm is about to launch into production. The production manager needs to hire enough workers to meet the projected demand for the modem, allowing for a reasonable level of delay in filling orders. Based on Modex's past manufacturing experience, the daily demand for modems will vary between 100 and

600 units, although 65% of the days will have a number of orders received that falls between 200 and 400.

If you were the production manager, you might want a model that would tell you whether the number of workers you plan to hire is enough to meet demand—or whether it is too much. This will depend on how many modems the firm must produce each day and on how many modems the factory can assemble in a day. If the production capacity is much larger than the number of modems demanded, then workers will be sitting idle at the company's expense. On the other hand, if demand far exceeds capacity, then a large backlog of orders will build up over time, and the company will eventually lose business.

If we know the assembly line's capacity, it should be easy enough to calculate the number of orders processed or backlogged, so long as we know how many new orders come in each day. But how do we predict new orders? Each day brings in a different number, randomly distributed between 100 and 600.

Somehow, we would like to simulate a typical manufacturing day. The workers arrive at the plant ready to produce X modems. The bell rings. The product manager gets on the public address system and announces the number of new orders received by the company and the accumulated number of orders that were not filled as of yesterday. As the day unfolds, modems are assembled and shipped, the backlog is depleted, the workers take a coffee break, resume production, and work feverishly until the daily capacity has been reached. The bell rings, the sun sets, and the workers return home to wash the backlog of dishes that occupy the kitchen sink from breakfast. Can Lotus mimic this daily routine? Lotus can do everything except make the coffee.

The Random Number Generator

The @RAND function is the key to the model. We will experiment with @RAND to see what it does and how to manipulate it to make it do what we want. Once we know how to use @RAND, we will employ it to project the daily demand for the Tote 'Em Modem.

When you enter @RAND into a cell, the cell will display a number between 0 and 1. The @RAND function may display any number; 1-2-3 decides what number to display. That is why @RAND is called a *random number generator*. Let us see exactly how @RAND works by trying it out on the worksheet.

Start with a blank worksheet. (Use **/Worksheet Erase Yes** if you currently have a worksheet on your screen, being careful to save it first if you want to return to it later.) Press the CAPS LOCK key, and then press the HOME key to move to cell A1.

1. Type **@RAND,** and press the ENTER key.

The result is a decimal number between 0 and 1. Lotus 1-2-3 shows as many decimal digits as it can within the limits of the cell width. The result might be a number such as 0.147506. If you examine the contents of the cell (as displayed in the control panel), you will see that the entry stored in cell A1 is a formula, @RAND, not the value that results from the formula.

Every time you load the 1-2-3 program and type @RAND as your first step, you will get the same number. Suppose that the result you just obtained was 0.147506. If you turn off your machine, turn it back on, load 1-2-3, and enter @RAND in A1, you will again obtain 0.147506. Perhaps you are thinking that this function is not so random after all. To prove that it is,

2. Move down to A2, type **@RAND,** and then press the ENTER key.

Two things happen. First, the @RAND function in cell A2 generates a random number (say, 0.690568) that is different from the one in cell A1. Each number generated by an @RAND function is likely to be different from the value of any other cell containing @RAND. This is the random nature of @RAND. In a single worksheet session, it is nearly impossible to generate the same number twice.

The second thing that happens when you make the @RAND entry into cell A2 is that the value of A1 changes. It now may read 0.414100. We have seen instances where an entry in one cell changes the value of others automatically. This occurs through automatic recalculation, which changes the values of cells containing formulas that depend on a newly revised cell. But why would automatic recalculation affect A1? The @RAND function contained in A1 makes no reference to A2, so changing A2 should not affect A1.

It is true that A1 and A2 are not related by their formulas. However, automatic recalculation causes the @RAND function—every @RAND function on the worksheet—to generate a new random value. The automatic recalculation caused by making an entry to A2 forces the value of cell A1 to change.

Every @RAND formula recalculates each time you press the ENTER key, so you may well end up with different values on your worksheet than those of someone else, even if you are both developing the identical model. In fact, the results you derive in the following application may well differ from the results depicted in the chapter's figures and examples. So do not worry if your results are not identical to those in this book. Just make sure that your formulas work correctly as described in the text.

Manual Recalculation

For this application, it will be best to suppress the automatic recalculation, so that cells containing @RAND and other cells containing formulas that depend on the @RAND cells do not change every time you press the ENTER key. Automatic recalculation is not always a blessing, and fortunately we can turn it off with the Worksheet Global Recalculation Manual command.

1. Type /Worksheet Global Recalculation Manual.

From now on, automatic recalculation is disabled, and changing formulas on the worksheet will not automatically update other cells. To update the worksheet now, you must press the *Calc* key, function key F9. Pressing the F9 (Calc) key causes the worksheet to recalculate. If you save the worksheet with manual recalculation in effect, manual recalculation is stored with it, so that it automatically goes into effect when the worksheet is retrieved.

If you make an entry onto the worksheet that is set for manual recalculation, a highlighted CALC indicator will appear on the bottom-right portion of the screen. This indicator informs you that an entry has been made that may affect the calculation of the model, reminding you to press the F9 (Calc) key at a point when you wish to see updated results. Manual recalculation need not be permanent. You can resume automatic recalculation by issuing the Worksheet Global Recalculation Automatic command.

With manual recalculation in effect, let us use Copy to create some more @RAND cells and see how the F9 (Calc) key works. Copy cell A2 down the A column as follows:

2. Type /Copy, and press the ENTER key.

3. Move down once to cell A3, and type the . key to anchor the target range.

4. Move the pointer to cell A8.

5. Press the ENTER key.

All eight cells contain the same formula, @RAND. However, as Figure 5-1 shows, each cell has a different value between 0 and 1. Also, because new entries were made onto the worksheet, the CALC indicator appears on the bottom right of the display. For our next trick,

6. Press the F9 (Calc) key, and watch the screen to see what happens.

The F9 (Calc) key causes 1-2-3 to recalculate any formulas that appear on the worksheet. The @RAND function, like all @ functions, qualifies as a formula. Therefore, Calc forces each @RAND to regenerate a random value. Press the F9 (Calc) key again, and the numbers will change once more.

Generating Random Numbers Larger Than One

Using @RAND, there is as much chance of obtaining any particular value as there is of obtaining any other value between the boundaries of 0 and 1.

But what if you want to generate random numbers beyond these boundaries? For instance, suppose you want to generate a number between 0 and 100, instead of one between 0 and 1. You can simply use the formula @RAND*100.

You may try this out by moving to cell A1 and entering **@RAND*100**. You will obtain a value between 0 and 100, with as many decimal digits as 1-2-3 can fit into the column width of nine characters. If you copy the formula down the column using the steps described above, you will obtain other

```
        A
1 0.414100
2 0.690568
3 0.895124
4 0.006453
5 0.454472
6 0.748348
7 0.655470
8 0.869768
```

Figure 5-1. Random numbers generated by the @RAND function

values between 0 and 100. The numbers are still randomized; you have merely changed the range of the random number generator.

Similarly, you can limit @RAND to numbers between 0 and 5 by using the formula @RAND*5. The @RAND term yields a value between 0 and 1, so multiplying by 5 will result in a value that is 5*0, or 0, at the least and 5*1, or 5, at the most.

Generating Random Integers Using @ROUND

Multiplying @RAND by some value yields a real number, one that has decimal digits. If you want to limit the results of @RAND to integer numbers (such as the integers 0, 1, 2, 3, 4, and 5), you use the @ROUND function in combination with @RAND.

The @ROUND function is entered as @ROUND(*value, number of digits*), where *value* may be either a number or a formula. Like some other 1-2-3 functions, @ROUND requires additional information in order to work. The function must know what number to round and how many digits to round to. The additional items that must be supplied to a function are called *arguments* of the function. The @ROUND function requires two arguments: *value* and *number of digits*. The @RAND function, on the other hand, does not require any arguments.

Converting the result of @RAND*5 to an integer is equivalent to rounding the value @RAND*5 to zero decimal places. In other words, we can apply the @ROUND function using @RAND*5 as the first argument and 0 as the second argument.

1. Move to cell A1, enter **@ROUND(@RAND*5,0)**, and press the ENTER key.

Cell A1 should now contain an integer between 0 and 5.

Generating Random Numbers Within Boundaries

The @RAND function can also be used to generate numbers within virtually any boundaries you wish. For instance, what if you want to generate a real number between 50 and 100? You can use (@RAND*50)+50. The formula @RAND*50 yields a number from the range 0 through 50. Adding 50 to this result changes the boundaries to 0+50, or 50, and 50+50, or 100.

Similarly, it is not difficult to develop a formula that generates numbers between −115 and 20. You can do this in three steps. First, determine the difference between the high and low boundaries: $20-(-115) = 135$. Second, generate a number between 0 and the result of the first step, using @RAND*135. And finally, add the desired low boundary to the result of the second step, using (@RAND*135)+(−115). The result will be a random number that can take on a minimum value of 0−115 (that is, −115) and a maximum value of 135−115 (that is, 20). The same method will work for any two boundaries.

With extensive control over the @RAND function, we are in a position to simulate the daily demand for Modex's product. Thus far, what we have been doing has been purely experimental. Now we will use what we have learned to project daily demand, as the initial step in finding a solution to the staffing problem. Then we will model the factory's ability to handle that demand on a day-to-day basis. First,

1. Type /Worksheet Erase Yes to clear the worksheet.

The Worksheet Erase command reinstitutes automatic recalculation, so

2. Type /Worksheet Global Recalculation Manual.

This command disables automatic recalculation once more.

Using @RAND to Project Demand

Figure 5-2 shows the worksheet that we are about to develop. We will simulate 50 days of the factory's operations. For each of these days, we will generate a random number, use it to predict the number of new orders received that day, and then calculate how many of the orders were filled.

Using Frequency Distribution
To Look Up Demand

Based on the company's past history of modem production, the number of orders received on any given day can be predicted by using a frequency distribution table.

	A	B	C	D	E	F	G	H	I
1									
2									
3	NUMBER OF WORKERS			8					
4	PRODUCTION RATE PER WORKER			28					
5						FREQUENCY	CUM FREQ.	AVERAGE DEMAND	
6						--------	--------	--------	
7						0.15	0	100	
8						0.25	0.15	200	
9						0.18	0.4	300	
10						0.22	0.58	400	
11						0.13	0.8	500	
12						0.07	0.93	600	
13									
14									
15					PRODUCTION SIMULATION				
16									DAILY
17			NO. OF	ORDERS		NO. OF	NO. OF	# OF DAYS	WORKER
18		RANDOM	ORDERS	TO BE		ORDERS	ORDERS	OF	UTILIZ.
19	DAY	NUMBER	REC'D	PROC'D	CAPACITY	PROC'D	UNPROC'D	BACKLOG	RATE
20									
21									
22	1	0.459880	300	300	224	224	76	0.3	100%
23	2	0.321959	200	276	224	224	52	0.2	100%
24	3	0.897648	500	552	224	224	328	1.5	100%
25	4	0.811128	500	828	224	224	604	2.7	100%
26	5	0.236483	200	804	224	224	580	2.6	100%
27	6	0.570748	300	880	224	224	656	2.9	100%
28	7	0.118072	100	756	224	224	532	2.4	100%
29	8	0.135086	100	632	224	224	408	1.8	100%
30	9	0.227641	200	608	224	224	384	1.7	100%
31	10	0.713402	400	784	224	224	560	2.5	100%
32	11	0.514642	300	860	224	224	636	2.8	100%
33	12	0.944803	600	1236	224	224	1012	4.5	100%
34	13	0.425352	300	1312	224	224	1088	4.9	100%
35	14	0.421181	300	1388	224	224	1164	5.2	100%
36	15	0.971492	600	1764	224	224	1540	6.9	100%
37	16	0.133882	100	1640	224	224	1416	6.3	100%
38	17	0.463840	300	1716	224	224	1492	6.7	100%
39	18	0.617881	400	1892	224	224	1668	7.4	100%
40	19	0.799380	400	2068	224	224	1844	8.2	100%
41	20	0.708907	400	2244	224	224	2020	9.0	100%
42	21	0.117307	100	2120	224	224	1896	8.5	100%
43	22	0.556431	300	2196	224	224	1972	8.8	100%
44	23	0.745636	400	2372	224	224	2148	9.6	100%
45	24	0.411452	300	2448	224	224	2224	9.9	100%
46	25	0.458797	300	2524	224	224	2300	10.3	100%
47	26	0.794914	400	2700	224	224	2476	11.1	100%
48	27	0.469932	300	2776	224	224	2552	11.4	100%
49	28	0.512940	300	2852	224	224	2628	11.7	100%
50	29	0.102088	100	2728	224	224	2504	11.2	100%
51	30	0.681360	400	2904	224	224	2680	12.0	100%
52	31	0.032747	100	2780	224	224	2556	11.4	100%
53	32	0.016731	100	2656	224	224	2432	10.9	100%
54	33	0.198450	200	2632	224	224	2408	10.8	100%
55	34	0.206720	200	2608	224	224	2384	10.6	100%
56	35	0.193402	200	2584	224	224	2360	10.5	100%
57	36	0.751813	400	2760	224	224	2536	11.3	100%
58	37	0.110170	100	2636	224	224	2412	10.8	100%
59	38	0.335365	200	2612	224	224	2388	10.7	100%
60	39	0.564537	300	2688	224	224	2464	11.0	100%
61	40	0.092463	100	2564	224	224	2340	10.4	100%
62	41	0.932711	600	2940	224	224	2716	12.1	100%
63	42	0.172510	200	2916	224	224	2692	12.0	100%
64	43	0.919915	500	3192	224	224	2968	13.3	100%
65	44	0.288270	200	3168	224	224	2944	13.1	100%
66	45	0.287371	200	3144	224	224	2920	13.0	100%
67	46	0.577921	300	3220	224	224	2996	13.4	100%
68	47	0.202415	200	3196	224	224	2972	13.3	100%
69	48	0.638874	400	3372	224	224	3148	14.1	100%
70	49	0.056332	100	3248	224	224	3024	13.5	100%
71	50	0.085287	100	3124	224	224	2900	12.9	100%

Figure 5-2. Simulation of Modex's factory operations

FREQUENCY	CUMULATIVE FREQUENCY	AVERAGE DEMAND
.15	.00	100
.25	.15	200
.18	.40	300
.22	.58	400
.13	.80	500
.07	.93	600

This means that on any given day there is a 15% chance that the company will receive 100 orders (on average), a 25% chance of 200 orders, and so on. This kind of frequency distribution is relatively simple for the production manager to glean from empirical records, and it corresponds rather well with the random way in which orders come in from day to day.

The cumulative frequency column is an accumulation of the frequency column. Beginning with the value 0, it is a running total of the frequency column to its left. We will use this cumulative frequency to "look up" the day's demand for modems.

To see how this works, try picking a random number—say, 0.43. If you look down the cumulative frequency column, you will find that our random number lies between the entries 0.40 and 0.58. Now suppose that we impose upon ourselves a rule stating that whenever we are given a number, we will look that number up in the cumulative frequency column, find the first number in the column that is greater than our number, move up to the previous number in the column, and then choose the corresponding demand from the next column over (the AVERAGE DEMAND column). Using 0.43 as an example, we look down the cumulative frequency column and find that 0.58 is the first number that exceeds 0.43. Our rule tells us to back up to the previous number in the column, 0.40, and then to choose 300, which is the corresponding demand.

What we have just done is to simulate a random receipt of orders for new modems for a day, according to the frequency table. The method is to generate a random number, look it up in the table, and select the corresponding demand figure as the number of new orders randomly received.

Let us try one more example just to clarify the mechanics. Using a random value of 0.85, we find that the first cumulative number greater than 0.85 is 0.93. We then back up to 0.80, and we find that the corresponding demand is 500 modems. The random number 0.3 would translate into 200 modems. What about a random number such as 0.98? We will use the value of 600 orders for anything greater than 0.93, the last value in the cumulative frequency column.

By generating 1000 random numbers and looking each one up in the table, we could derive the number of new orders received for each of 1000 days of production. Moreover, the order schedule would conform to the original frequency distribution of orders (the first column of the table), since there is a 15% chance that a particular random number will be less than 0.15, a 25% chance that it will be greater than 0.15 but less than 0.40, an 18% chance that it will fall between 0.40 and 0.58, and so on. If we simulate enough days in this way and then compute the number of times that our simulation predicts orders of 100, 200, and so on, we will find that the computed frequencies come close to the ones specified in the frequency table (assuming that the random numbers are truly random).

Going through this process manually would be tedious, but 1-2-3 can do the job quite handily. We will enter the frequency chart onto the worksheet, produce our random numbers, and then perform the table lookup procedure.

Building a Frequency Table

Figure 5-3 shows the frequency table as we are about to enter it onto the worksheet.

1. Move to cell F5, and type the label **FREQUENCY**.

2. Move down once, to cell F6, and enter an underscore by typing \- and pressing the ENTER key.

3. Enter the frequencies in column F, starting in position F7, as in the first column of Figure 5-3.

Next we enter the cumulative frequency column beginning at G4.

4. Move to cell G4, and type the centered label ^**CUM** (note the prefix ^ used to center the label within the cell).

5. Move down to cell G5, and type ^**FREQ**.

6. Move down to cell G6, and enter an underscore by typing \-.

7. Move down to cell G7, and type **0**, the first cumulative frequency percentage.

The next entry in the column should be 0.15, which is the sum of the previous cumulative percentage (0) and the previous row's frequency (0.15).

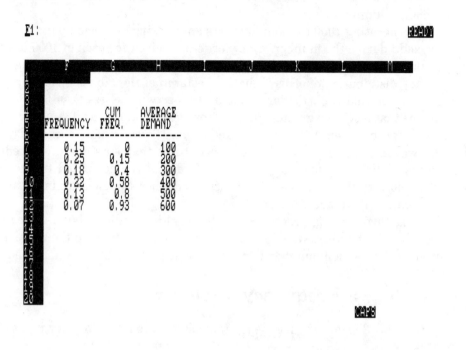

Figure 5-3. Frequency distribution table of demand for modems

Instead of typing in this value at G8, however, we will enter it as a formula. Then we will be able to copy the formula down the rest of the column.

8. Move down to cell G8, and type the + key.

9. Move up once to cell G7, and type + to put the previous cumulative frequency into the formula.

10. Move left and up to cell F7, and press the ENTER key to put the previous row's frequency into the formula.

Next copy the formula down to the rest of the column:

11. Type /C, and press the ENTER key.

12. Move down once to cell G9, and type the . key.

13. Move down to cell G12, and press the ENTER key.

Compare your results to Figure 5-3.

14. Enter the centered label ^**AVERAGE** in cell H4, and enter ^**DEMAND** in cell H5.

15. Then enter an underscore in cell H6, and copy the associated values in column H, as shown in the figure.

Simulating Orders, Day 1

Now that the frequency table exists, we can begin to simulate Day 1 of operations. We will start by entering worksheet titles.

1. Move to cell D15, and enter the label **PRODUCTION SIMULATION**.

We will simulate 50 days of manufacturing in this worksheet, so we begin by putting the day numbers, 1 through 50, down column A.

2. Move to cell A19, and enter the label **DAY**.

3. Move down to cell A20, and enter an underscore by typing \- and pressing the ENTER key.

4. Go to cell A22.

The rest of the column will store sequential numbers from 1 to 50.

Using Data Fill to Enter a Sequence

If you are annoyed at the prospect of entering 50 numbers into 50 cells, you can relax. We will utilize one of the small wonders of 1-2-3, the Data Fill command. *Data Fill* generates a sequence of numbers. It even allows you to skip an amount between numbers, as in the sequence 0, 3, 6, 9,..., which adds the increment, or step value, of 3 to each number to produce the next number.

1. With the pointer at A22, type /Data Fill.

Now 1-2-3 prompts you for the *Fill range*, the range of cells in which it will store the sequence.

2. Type the . key to indicate that the range will begin where the pointer is now located (cell A22).

The sequence will contain 50 numbers, and since it begins in row 22, it must end 50 rows later in row 71. Therefore, to designate the end of the Data Fill range,

3. Move the pointer down to cell A71 using the PG DN and down arrow keys, and then press the ENTER key.

Next 1-2-3 will prompt you for a starting value for the sequence, with a recommendation of 0. We want our sequence to start at 1, so

4. Type 1, and press the ENTER key.

Next 1-2-3 prompts for a *step* value. This is what you would use to skip numbers in the sequence, if you so desired. We do not want to skip; we want 1-2-3 to increment the sequence by 1, which is what 1-2-3 suggests in its prompt.

5. Press the ENTER key to accept 1 as the step value.

The next item that 1-2-3 requests is the *stop*, the maximum value that may be used in the sequence. The program's suggestion of 2047 is more than adequate for our purposes, so simply

6. Press the ENTER key to accept 2047 as the stop.

This completes the DAY column.

Using @RAND to Simulate Orders

The next item of business is to generate a random number with which to derive the number of orders received on Day 1. We begin by creating a random number column next to the DAY column.

1. Move to cell B18, and type ^**RANDOM**.

2. Move to cell B19, and type ^**NUMBER**.

3. Place an underscore at B20 by typing \- and pressing the ENTER key.

4. Now go to cell B22, and type the formula **@RAND**. Press the ENTER key.

Copy this formula down to the rest of the column:

5. Type /C, and press the ENTER key.

6. Move down once to cell B23, and type the . key to anchor the range.

7. Move down to the end of the column, cell B71, and press the ENTER key.

You have obtained a column of random numbers, one for each of 50 days, to be used for deriving demand for modems. Now you must look up the Day 1 random number in the frequency table. You need not do this manually. Lotus 1-2-3 has a function that will automatically look up a number in a table, a process aptly called *table lookup*.

Using @VLOOKUP
With The Frequency Table

Remember how we looked up the random number in the frequency table earlier in the chapter? Our rule was to find the first greater number in the cumulative frequency column, back up to the previous value in the column, and choose a corresponding value in the next column over. The @VLOOKUP function works in exactly the same way (but much faster).

When we did the manual lookup, we needed three pieces of information: the number to be looked up (the random value), where to look up the number (the cumulative frequency column), and where to find the corresponding value (the AVERAGE DEMAND column). These three items are the arguments of 1-2-3's lookup functions.

Lookup tables can be either vertical or horizontal. Vertical lookup applies when you search for a number in a column, and horizontal lookup applies when you search for a number in a row. In the case at hand, the random number will be looked up in the cumulative frequency column, and the corresponding number of orders will be retrieved from the AVERAGE DEMAND column. This is vertical lookup. The vertical lookup function is called @VLOOKUP, and it takes the form @VLOOKUP (*value to look up, range containing vertical lookup table, offset*).

In this case, the *value to look up* is each random number in cells B22 through B71. The *range* containing the vertical lookup table consists of two conceptual parts, as shown in Figure 5-4. The first part is the column containing the comparative values—the CUM FREQ. column, in which the random value is looked up. The second part is the column(s) to the right of the comparative values column, containing the values to be retrieved by the function—in this example, the AVERAGE DEMAND column. The range containing the lookup table therefore spans G7 through H12. Observe that

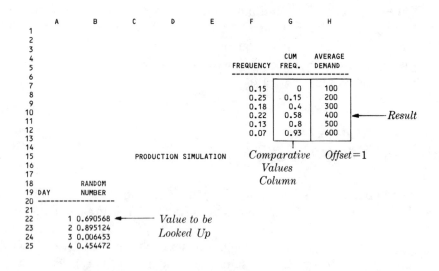

Figure 5-4. Lookup table for @VLOOKUP(B22, G7..H12,1) extends from cell G7 to cell H12

the first column of the frequency table is irrelevant to the @VLOOKUP function.

Remember that the first column of the vertical lookup table must be the column of comparative values, and that the remaining column(s) must include the values to be retrieved by the function. Another rule is that the column of comparative values (the first column of the lookup table) must be arranged in ascending order.

The third argument, *offset*, tells 1-2-3 where to find the corresponding values that must be retrieved by the function. Offset is a number representing a relative displacement from the first column of the lookup table. In this example, the offset of the DEMAND column is 1 because that column is one column to the right of the CUM FREQ. column. In other applications, there might be more columns to the right. These would have offsets of 2, 3, and so on.

The appropriate lookup formula for Day 1's orders received would be @VLOOKUP(B22,G7.H12,1). In English, this has the following meaning:

Look up, in the cumulative frequency table, the random number contained in cell B22. When you have located the group into which the random number falls, move over one column to the right and give me whatever number you find there.

Simulating the Number
Of Orders Received

Now that we understand the basic concepts, we can use @VLOOKUP to generate automatically the number of orders received in each of the 50 days. Start by entering the headings.

1. In cells C17, C18, and C19, enter the labels ^**NO. OF**, ^**ORDERS**, and ^**REC'D**, respectively.

2. Go to cell C20, and enter an underscore by typing \- and pressing the ENTER key.

3. Move down to cell C22.

4. Type **@VLOOKUP(** to begin the formula for orders received.

5. Move the pointer left to cell B22, and type the , key to enter the first argument of the function.

6. Move the pointer to cell G7, and type the . key to anchor the range containing the lookup table.

7. Move the pointer to cell H12, the end of the lookup table range.

Because we will be copying this formula down the column and because we will want the lookup table range to be copied in an absolute (not relative) manner,

8. Press the F4 (Abs) key.

This will place the necessary $ signs in the formula's coordinates and thus cause them to be absolute for purposes of future copy commands; do not neglect this step.

9. Now type the , key to continue the formula.

10. Type the **1** and **)** keys to supply the offset number to the function.

11. Press the ENTER key to end the formula.

For the first random number, 0.725215, the formula would fetch the value of 400 from the AVERAGE DEMAND column. That is because 0.725215 falls between 0.58 and 0.8, and this cumulative frequency corresponds to 400 orders.

The @RAND function may have given you a different random value for Day 1, but as long as your formula works properly, there is no problem. The same may apply to the rest of the results of this chapter. Do not be surprised if your results do not coincide exactly with the figures. The important thing is that the model works. Now copy the formula in cell C22 to the rest of the NO. OF ORDERS REC'D column:

12. Press /Copy, designating the source range as cell C22 and the target range as C23..C71. (One shortcut to pointing to the bottom of the target range is to move over to the RANDOM NUMBER column, press the END key and then the down arrow key, and then move back over to the NO. OF ORDERS PROC'D column and press the ENTER key.)

The worksheet now contains a complete 50-day simulation of the receipt of new orders by Modex, as shown in Figure 5-5. We can now concentrate on what happens during the rest of Day 1 of operations.

Simulating the Number of Orders Processed, Day 1

Column D will house the number of orders to be processed on each day. On Day 1, this number will be the same as the number of orders received. On subsequent days, however, there may be a backlog of orders to be processed in addition to the new orders received. We will worry about that later.

1. In cells D17, D18, and D19, enter the centered labels ^ORDERS, ^TO BE, and ^PROC'D, respectively.

2. Enter an underscore in cell D20 by typing \- and pressing the ENTER key.

3. Move to cell D22, and type the + key to begin the formula.

4. Move the pointer to the number of orders received (cell C22) and press the ENTER key to complete the formula.

Four hundred orders are ready to be processed on Day 1.

	A	B	C	D	E
15					PRODUCTION SIMULATION
16					
17			NO. OF		
18		RANDOM	ORDERS		
19	DAY	NUMBER	REC'D		
20	--------------------------				
21					
22	1	0.725215	400		
23	2	0.472762	300		
24	3	0.228899	200		
25	4	0.746051	400		
26	5	0.795880	400		
27	6	0.782893	400		
28	7	0.748695	400		
29	8	0.245416	200		
30	9	0.575570	300		
31	10	0.506222	300		
32	11	0.191429	200		
33	12	0.349525	200		
34	13	0.671893	400		
35	14	0.585499	400		
36	15	0.873207	500		
37	16	0.084085	100		
38	17	0.551273	300		
39	18	0.079198	100		
40	19	0.035327	100		
41	20	0.399945	200		
42	21	0.508859	300		
43	22	0.114586	100		
44	23	0.314674	200		
45	24	0.987978	600		
46	25	0.744876	400		
47	26	0.716758	400		
48	27	0.312753	200		
49	28	0.180878	200		
50	29	0.844306	500		
51	30	0.498035	300		
52	31	0.685224	400		
53	32	0.551240	300		
54	33	0.206753	200		
55	34	0.442077	300		
56	35	0.423829	300		
57	36	0.065308	100		
58	37	0.223390	200		
59	38	0.267109	200		
60	39	0.252564	200		
61	40	0.901766	500		
62	41	0.247839	200		
63	42	0.102613	100		
64	43	0.309997	200		
65	44	0.294933	200		
66	45	0.657881	400		
67	46	0.463877	300		
68	47	0.539586	300		
69	48	0.011755	100		
70	49	0.554860	300		
71	50	0.758772	400		

Figure 5-5. Simulation of new order receipts

Calculating Production Capacity

The maximum number of modems that the plant can produce in a single day depends on both the number of workers that are hired and the number of modems that each worker can produce in a day. We will store these latter two items in another location of the worksheet so that we can revise them easily if we change our minds later.

1. Go to cell A3, and enter the label **NUMBER OF WORKERS**.

2. Move to cell D3, and enter the value **8**.

3. Move to cell A4, and enter the label **PRODUCTION RATE PER WORKER**.

4. Move to cell D4, and enter the value **28**.

5. Go to cell E19, and enter the label ^**CAPACITY**.

6. Place an underscore at cell E20 by typing \- and then pressing the ENTER key.

Capacity is equal to the number of workers multiplied by the daily production rate per worker. We will want to copy the formula later to the rest of the column, so we must make the references in the capacity equation absolute.

7. Move to cell E22, and type the + key.

8. Move the pointer up to the NUMBER OF WORKERS cell (D3).

9. Press the F4 (Abs) key to make the formula reference absolute.

10. Type the * key.

11. Move the pointer up to the PRODUCTION RATE PER WORKER cell (D4).

12. Press the F4 (Abs) key to make the formula reference absolute.

13. With the formula complete, you can now press the ENTER key.

The production capacity of the plant is 224 modems per day.

Using @MIN to Determine
Orders Processed

We are now in a position to calculate the number of orders actually processed during Day 1. In general, the number of orders processed will equal the plant capacity, the maximum number of units that can be produced in a day. However, if the number of units necessary to fill current orders (in our worksheet, the ORDERS TO BE PROC'D column) is less than capacity and if the production manager does not desire any excess inventory, then the plant will produce only the number of orders to be processed in a given day. On the other hand, if the number of orders to be processed is greater than the capacity, then the plant will produce the daily capacity, and there will be some unfilled orders. The rule is that the number of orders actually processed will equal the minimum (the lesser of the values) of CAPACITY and ORDERS TO BE PROC'D. It should come as no surprise that your first-rate software has an *@MIN function* that determines the minimum of a set of values.

1. In cells F17, F18, and F19, enter the labels ^**NO. OF**, ^**ORDERS**, and ^**PROC'D**, respectively.

2. Place an underscore in cell F20 by typing \- ENTER.

3. Move to cell F22, and type **@MIN(** to begin the formula.

4. Move the pointer to Day 1's ORDERS TO BE PROC'D, cell D22.

5. Type the , key to continue the formula.

6. Move the pointer to the Day 1 CAPACITY cell (E22).

7. Type the **)** key, and press the ENTER key.

The plant produces its capacity of 224 modems on Day 1.

Determining Backlog, Day 1

Now that we have computed the number of orders processed, it is a simple matter to determine how many orders were *not* processed: subtract the number of orders actually processed in the day from the number of orders to be processed.

1. In cells G17, G18, and G19, enter the labels ^**NO. OF**, ^**ORDERS**, and ^**UNPROC'D**, respectively.

2. Place an underscore in cell G20.

3. Move to G22, and type the + key. Move the pointer to the ORDERS TO BE PROC'D cell (D22), and type the − key. Move the pointer to the NO. OF ORDERS PROC'D cell (F22), and press the ENTER key.

The result, 176, represents the backlog for the day. (Remember, your results could be different because we are using random numbers.)

Calculating Days To Deplete Backlog

It would be of interest to display the number of days that it would take to deplete the backlog of orders (assuming there is a backlog).

1. In cells H17, H18, and H19, enter the labels ^**# OF DAYS**, ^**OF**, and ^**BACKLOG**, respectively.

2. Place an underscore in cell H20.

3. Move to cell H22.

The number of days of backlog equals the number of unprocessed orders divided by the daily production capacity of the plant.

4. Type the + key, and move to the NO. OF ORDERS UNPROC'D cell (G22).

5. Type the / key to indicate division, and move to the CAPACITY cell (E22).

6. Press the ENTER key to complete the formula.

7. Type /**Range** Format **Fixed 1** to format the result to one decimal place and press the ENTER key two times.

In the example shown in Figure 5-6, it would require nearly an entire day of production just to catch up to demand.

	A	B	C	D	E	F	G	H
15			PRODUCTION SIMULATION					
16								
17			NO. OF	ORDERS		NO. OF	NO. OF	# OF DAYS
18		RANDOM	ORDERS	TO BE		ORDERS	ORDERS	OF
19	DAY	NUMBER	REC'D	PROC'D	CAPACITY	PROC'D	UNPROC'D	BACKLOG
20		-------	-------	-------	-------	-------	-------	-------
21								
22	1	0.725215	400	400	224	224	176	0.8
23	2	0.472762	300					
24	3	0.228899	200					
25	4	0.746051	400					
26	5	0.795880	400					
27	6	0.782893	400					
28	7	0.748695	400					
29	8	0.245416	200					
30	9	0.575570	300					
31	10	0.506222	300					
32	11	0.191429	200					
33	12	0.349525	200					
34	13	0.671893	400					
35	14	0.585499	400					
36	15	0.873207	500					
37	16	0.084085	100					
38	17	0.551273	300					
39	18	0.079198	100					
40	19	0.035327	100					
41	20	0.399945	200					
42	21	0.508859	300					
43	22	0.114586	100					
44	23	0.314674	200					
45	24	0.987978	600					
46	25	0.744876	400					
47	26	0.716758	400					
48	27	0.312753	200					
49	28	0.180878	200					
50	29	0.844306	500					
51	30	0.498035	300					
52	31	0.685224	400					
53	32	0.551240	300					
54	33	0.206753	200					
55	34	0.442077	300					
56	35	0.423829	300					
57	36	0.065308	100					
58	37	0.223390	200					
59	38	0.267109	200					
60	39	0.252564	200					
61	40	0.901766	500					
62	41	0.247839	200					
63	42	0.102613	100					
64	43	0.309997	200					
65	44	0.294933	200					
66	45	0.657881	400					
67	46	0.463877	300					
68	47	0.539586	300					
69	48	0.011755	100					
70	49	0.554860	300					
71	50	0.758772	400					

Figure 5-6. Worksheet showing days to process Day 1 backlog

Computing Worker Utilization Rate, Day 1

We may well want to add more workers at a later point. If we do (and even if we don't), it will be useful to know what percentage of time the workers are currently kept busy. If the capacity of the plant is 224 units, but the number of orders to be processed for the day is only 150, then the workers will be on the assembly line only 150/224 of the day, or 67%. The daily worker utilization rate is equal to the number of orders processed divided by the capacity.

1. In cells I16, I17, I18, and I19, enter the labels ^DAILY, ^WORKER, ^UTILIZ., and ^RATE, respectively.

2. Place an underscore in cell I20.

3. Move to cell I22.

4. Type the + key, and move to the Day 1 NO. OF ORDERS PROC'D cell (F22).

5. Type the / key, and move to the CAPACITY cell (E22).

6. Press the ENTER key.

7. Format the result as a percent by typing /Range Format Percent 0 and pressing the ENTER key twice.

As expected, the workers are utilized 100% of Day 1.

Finishing the Worksheet

Now we must complete the simulation for Days 2 through 50. We will begin by completing ORDERS TO BE PROC'D for Days 2 through 50. Then, in a single step, we can complete Days 2 through 50 for CAPACITY, NO. OF ORDERS PROC'D, NO. OF ORDERS UNPROC'D, # OF DAYS OF BACKLOG, and DAILY WORKER UTILIZ. RATE. Before we do that, however, we will carry out one short procedure that will make our oversized worksheet easier to read.

Fixing Worksheet Titles
On the Screen

It is inconvenient to use a worksheet that contains more rows and columns than the screen is capable of displaying. You want to refer to row and column titles as you examine or enter data, but as you scroll away from the top row or left column, the titles disappear. It is possible to fix row and column titles onto the screen so that scrolling the worksheet affects only the block of rows and columns that have not been fixed.

First, scroll the worksheet so that the row titles to be fixed appear as the top rows of the display and the column titles to be fixed appear as the columns farthest left:

1. Press the HOME key.

2. Press the down arrow key until row 16 is the top row on the screen.

The top rows of the display, rows 16 through 19, are occupied by the column headings that will be fixed. We will also fix the row headings (the DAY numbers of column A, which is the far-left column of the display).

3. Move the pointer to the first coordinate of the block of cells that will be "scrollable" (unfixed), cell B21.

If we choose cell B21, we can fix columns to the left of column B (that is, column A) and rows above row 21 (rows 17 through 20).

The command used to fix titles on the screen is the Worksheet Titles command.

4. Type / Worksheet Titles.

Our intention is to fix, or "set," both horizontal and vertical titles. It also is possible to set either horizontal or vertical titles exclusively, or to clear (that is, "unfix" so that they are no longer locked onto the screen) titles that have previously been set. The prompt asks you to choose among "Both Horizontal Vertical Clear."

5. Type **B** to choose Both.

Now try using the arrow keys to scroll the worksheet. The row and column headings are fixed. An attempt to scroll beyond the fixed boundaries evokes a beep. If you need to delve into the protected zone, you may either use the F5 (GoTo) key or issue the Worksheet Titles Clear command. Pressing the HOME key with titles set transfers the pointer to the first unfixed cell (B21).

Copying Formulas for Backlogged Orders

Recall that from Day 2 onward, the number of orders waiting to be processed during the day will equal the number of orders received plus any backlog that may remain from the previous day.

1. Move to the Day 2 ORDERS TO BE PROC'D cell (D23).

2. Type the + key, and move to the Day 2 NO. OF ORDERS REC'D cell (C23), which represents today's new orders.

3. Type the + key and move to the Day 1 NO. OF ORDERS UNPROC'D cell (G22), which represents yesterday's backlog.

4. Press the ENTER key.

We see that 176 backlogged units plus 300 new orders await production on Day 2. Copy the Day 2 formula to the rest of the column:

5. Type /Copy, and press the ENTER key.

6. Move the pointer to the Day 3 ORDERS TO BE PROC'D cell (D24).

7. Type the . key.

8. Point to the Day 50 ORDERS TO BE PROC'D cell (D71).

9. Press the ENTER key.

Copying the Remaining Formulas

The remainder of the 50-day simulation can be completed in a single step. The Day 1 formulas for CAPACITY, NO. OF ORDERS PROC'D, NO. OF ORDERS UNPROC'D, # OF DAYS OF BACKLOG, and DAILY WORKER UTILIZ. RATE can be copied directly to Days 2 through 50 as follows:

1. Go to the Day 1 CAPACITY cell (E22).

2. Type / Copy to begin copying a range.

3. Move the pointer to the last colunm in the row cell (I22) by pressing the END key and then the right arrow key.

4. Press the ENTER key to signal the end of the source range for the Copy command.

5. Move the pointer to the Day 2 CAPACITY cell (E23), and type the . key to anchor the target range.

6. Move the pointer to the end of the CAPACITY column (cell E71).

7. Press the ENTER key.

Remember that the results of the model are not updated until you press the F9 (Calc) key.

8. Press the F9 (Calc) key.

Pressing the F9 (Calc) key regenerates the RANDOM NUMBER column too, so that the entire simulation changes. You worksheet should be similar to the new results shown in Figure 5-7.

Can the Backlog Be Fixed?

It is clear that Modex Corporation has a backlog problem. With 100% utilization from Day 2 on, the NO. OF ORDERS UNPROC'D grows to 4424 on Day 50, a backlog of 19.8 days. If this situation is left unchanged, Modex will be unable to supply customers effectively, and the market share will surely decrease.

There are two options for improving the situation: either increase the number of employees or increase the daily rate of production per employee. Increasing the rate of production might be difficult, if not impossible. It might involve further automation of the production process, and this may not be feasible. We therefore resort to increasing the number of employees.

Fortunately, this is easy to do. We simply change the number of workers in cell D3. Fifteen employees should move production along much more quickly.

1. Go to cell D3, the NUMBER OF WORKERS cell. (The display will look confusing because you are moving the pointer into the fixed titles area.)*

---

*Thus, the fixed title rows (16 through 19) appear above the section that we scrolled to (beginning in row 3), and the rows appear to be out of order. Moreover, the labels in column A are truncated because column D "crowds them out" of the worksheet.

	A	B	C	D	E	F	G	H	I
15				PRODUCTION SIMULATION					
16									DAILY
17			NO. OF	ORDERS		NO. OF	NO. OF	# OF DAYS	WORKER
18		RANDOM	ORDERS	TO BE		ORDERS	ORDERS	OF	UTILIZ.
19	DAY	NUMBER	REC'D	PROC'D	CAPACITY	PROC'D	UNPROC'D	BACKLOG	RATE
20	----	----	----	----	----	----	----	----	----
21									
22	1	0.147506	100	100	224	100	0	0.0	45%
23	2	0.414100	300	300	224	224	76	0.3	100%
24	3	0.690568	400	476	224	224	252	1.1	100%
25	4	0.895124	500	752	224	224	528	2.4	100%
26	5	0.006453	100	628	224	224	404	1.8	100%
27	6	0.454472	300	704	224	224	480	2.1	100%
28	7	0.748348	400	880	224	224	656	2.9	100%
29	8	0.655470	400	1056	224	224	832	3.7	100%
30	9	0.869768	500	1332	224	224	1108	4.9	100%
31	10	0.130148	100	1208	224	224	984	4.4	100%
32	11	0.375249	200	1184	224	224	960	4.3	100%
33	12	0.688185	400	1360	224	224	1136	5.1	100%
34	13	0.062679	100	1236	224	224	1012	4.5	100%
35	14	0.178575	200	1212	224	224	988	4.4	100%
36	15	0.704439	400	1388	224	224	1164	5.2	100%
37	16	0.937345	600	1764	224	224	1540	6.9	100%
38	17	0.697482	400	1940	224	224	1716	7.7	100%
39	18	0.663530	400	2116	224	224	1892	8.4	100%
40	19	0.725215	400	2292	224	224	2068	9.2	100%
41	20	0.472762	300	2368	224	224	2144	9.6	100%
42	21	0.228899	200	2344	224	224	2120	9.5	100%
43	22	0.746051	400	2520	224	224	2296	10.3	100%
44	23	0.795880	400	2696	224	224	2472	11.0	100%
45	24	0.782893	400	2872	224	224	2648	11.8	100%
46	25	0.748695	400	3048	224	224	2824	12.6	100%
47	26	0.245416	200	3024	224	224	2800	12.5	100%
48	27	0.575570	300	3100	224	224	2876	12.8	100%
49	28	0.506222	300	3176	224	224	2952	13.2	100%
50	29	0.191429	200	3152	224	224	2928	13.1	100%
51	30	0.349525	200	3128	224	224	2904	13.0	100%
52	31	0.671893	400	3304	224	224	3080	13.8	100%
53	32	0.585499	400	3480	224	224	3256	14.5	100%
54	33	0.873207	500	3756	224	224	3532	15.8	100%
55	34	0.084085	100	3632	224	224	3408	15.2	100%
56	35	0.551273	300	3708	224	224	3484	15.6	100%
57	36	0.079198	100	3584	224	224	3360	15.0	100%
58	37	0.035327	100	3460	224	224	3236	14.4	100%
59	38	0.399945	200	3436	224	224	3212	14.3	100%
60	39	0.508859	300	3512	224	224	3288	14.7	100%
61	40	0.114586	100	3388	224	224	3164	14.1	100%
62	41	0.314674	200	3364	224	224	3140	14.0	100%
63	42	0.987978	600	3740	224	224	3516	15.7	100%
64	43	0.744876	400	3916	224	224	3692	16.5	100%
65	44	0.716758	400	4092	224	224	3868	17.3	100%
66	45	0.312753	200	4068	224	224	3844	17.2	100%
67	46	0.180878	200	4044	224	224	3820	17.1	100%
68	47	0.844306	500	4320	224	224	4096	18.3	100%
69	48	0.498035	300	4396	224	224	4172	18.6	100%
70	49	0.685224	400	4572	224	224	4348	19.4	100%
71	50	0.551240	300	4648	224	224	4424	19.8	100%

Figure 5-7. Worksheet simulation with completed formulas

2. Enter the value **15**.

3. Press the END and HOME keys to move the pointer to the lower-right corner of the worksheet.

4. Press the HOME key to return to the top-left corner of the unfixed portion of the worksheet. (Moving to a distant cell and pressing HOME removes the confusing display effect that occurred in Step 1.)

5. Press the F9 (Calc) key.

Now check the NO. OF ORDERS UNPROC'D column. The situation has improved. In fact, there may even be some underutilization of employees, as registered in the last column of Figure 5-8.

Extending the Formula: Beyond Day 50

You can see how a spreadsheet like this can be used to help decide how many workers to hire, how much backlog to expect, and whether production is feasible and affordable for the projected demand.

Fifty days is not a very long period of time to simulate. In fact, the results for only 50 days may disguise possible negative effects that would not accumulate or surface until a longer time has elapsed. It would be preferable to simulate over a period of at least 1000 days. Although you could use the Data Fill and Copy commands to simulate a time span longer than 50 days, you would need quite a lot of memory to store a simulation of 1000 days or more. However, there is another way.

Using a Circular Reference For Iteration

The formula for ORDERS TO BE PROCESSED from Days 2 through 50 was set to the day's new orders received plus the previous day's backlog. However, Day 1 ORDERS TO BE PROCESSED was set exclusively to new orders because there is no backlog on Day 1. But now that we have run the first 50 days of production, what would happen if we revised the Day 1 formula to equal the new orders plus the backlog from Day 50, the end of the

	A	B	C	D	E	F	G	H	I
15				PRODUCTION SIMULATION					
16									DAILY
17			NO. OF	ORDERS		NO. OF	NO. OF	# OF DAYS	WORKER
18		RANDOM	ORDERS	TO BE		ORDERS	ORDERS	OF	UTILIZ.
19	DAY	NUMBER	REC'D	PROC'D	CAPACITY	PROC'D	UNPROC'D	BACKLOG	RATE
20	---								
21									
22	1	0.029100	100	100	420	100	0	0.0	24%
23	2	0.997813	600	600	420	420	180	0.4	100%
24	3	0.981963	600	780	420	420	360	0.9	100%
25	4	0.236633	200	560	420	420	140	0.3	100%
26	5	0.740226	400	540	420	420	120	0.3	100%
27	6	0.339845	200	320	420	320	0	0.0	76%
28	7	0.302259	200	200	420	200	0	0.0	48%
29	8	0.691144	400	400	420	400	0	0.0	95%
30	9	0.289075	200	200	420	200	0	0.0	48%
31	10	0.376122	200	200	420	200	0	0.0	48%
32	11	0.844283	500	500	420	420	80	0.2	100%
33	12	0.717781	400	480	420	420	60	0.1	100%
34	13	0.519482	300	360	420	360	0	0.0	86%
35	14	0.451587	300	300	420	300	0	0.0	71%
36	15	0.247494	200	200	420	200	0	0.0	48%
37	16	0.931058	600	600	420	420	180	0.4	100%
38	17	0.627931	400	580	420	420	160	0.4	100%
39	18	0.208978	200	360	420	360	0	0.0	86%
40	19	0.238836	200	200	420	200	0	0.0	48%
41	20	0.379363	200	200	420	200	0	0.0	48%
42	21	0.857099	500	500	420	420	80	0.2	100%
43	22	0.753805	400	480	420	420	60	0.1	100%
44	23	0.131453	100	160	420	160	0	0.0	38%
45	24	0.345188	200	200	420	200	0	0.0	48%
46	25	0.717717	400	400	420	400	0	0.0	95%
47	26	0.304681	200	200	420	200	0	0.0	48%
48	27	0.968914	600	600	420	420	180	0.4	100%
49	28	0.466648	300	480	420	420	60	0.1	100%
50	29	0.285629	200	260	420	260	0	0.0	62%
51	30	0.563376	300	300	420	300	0	0.0	71%
52	31	0.986826	600	600	420	420	180	0.4	100%
53	32	0.039671	100	280	420	280	0	0.0	67%
54	33	0.370923	200	200	420	200	0	0.0	48%
55	34	0.288978	200	200	420	200	0	0.0	48%
56	35	0.313696	200	200	420	200	0	0.0	48%
57	36	0.610218	400	400	420	400	0	0.0	95%
58	37	0.605998	400	400	420	400	0	0.0	95%
59	38	0.810522	500	500	420	420	80	0.2	100%
60	39	0.082936	100	180	420	180	0	0.0	43%
61	40	0.215923	200	200	420	200	0	0.0	48%
62	41	0.749465	400	400	420	400	0	0.0	95%
63	42	0.462480	300	300	420	300	0	0.0	71%
64	43	0.377864	200	200	420	200	0	0.0	48%
65	44	0.886519	500	500	420	420	80	0.2	100%
66	45	0.752735	400	480	420	420	60	0.1	100%
67	46	0.177474	200	260	420	260	0	0.0	62%
68	47	0.681599	400	400	420	400	0	0.0	95%
69	48	0.262430	200	200	420	200	0	0.0	48%
70	49	0.386173	200	200	420	200	0	0.0	48%
71	50	0.720587	400	400	420	400	0	0.0	95%

Figure 5-8. Simulation results with 15 workers

simulation we just ran? Day 1 would then be the 51st day of simulation, carrying the backlog that accumulated during the previous 50 days. Let us try it.

1. Move to cell D22, and type the + key.

2. Move left to the NO. OF ORDERS REC'D cell (C22).

3. Type the + key, and move to the Day 50 NO. OF ORDERS UNPROC'D cell (G71).

4. Press the ENTER key.

5. Press the F9 (Calc) key.

After you press the ENTER key, the word CIRC appears in inverse video on the bottom right of the screen. This indicates that you have entered a circular reference in a formula. A *circular reference* occurs when a formula in a cell depends on the cell itself, either directly or indirectly. For example, if the pointer were at cell A1 and you entered the formula +A1, then cell A1 depends on its own value—it contains a direct circular reference. An *indirect* circular reference occurs when, for example, cell A1 is set equal to +B1 and cell B1 is set equal to +A1. In such a case, cell A1 depends on another cell, but that other cell depends on cell A1. Thus, A1 ultimately depends on itself.

Circular reference is rare. In most cases when the CIRC indicator appears, you have made a mistake in the formula. In the current situation, however, the circular reference was quite deliberate.

What has changed to cause the CIRC indicator to appear suddenly? We reset Day 1's ORDERS TO BE PROC'D to equal Day 1's NO. OF ORDERS REC'D plus Day 50's NO. OF ORDERS UNPROC'D. But the NO. OF ORDERS UNPROC'D equals ORDERS TO BE PROC'D minus the NO. OF ORDERS PROC'D. Thus, the new Day 1 ORDERS TO BE PROC'D ultimately depends on a cell that depends on ORDERS TO BE PROC'D itself. This is an indirect circular reference. It is not an error, but 1-2-3 is warning us to be aware of what we have done.

Pressing the F9 (Calc) key ripples the effect through Days 2 through 50, which now actually represent Days 52 through 100. By pressing the F9 (Calc) key once more, we can cause Day 1 to pick up the backlog of the 100th day so that the model simulates Days 101 through 150. Thus, each push of the F9 (Calc) key will simulate the next 50 days. Some simple math reveals that simulation of 1000 days requires 19 recalculations of the model, in addition to the original 50-day run, because 20*50 equals 1000.

We have already pressed the F9 (Calc) key twice. If you were to press this key 17 more times, you would have simulated 1000 days. That would take some time. But, as so often happens with 1-2-3, there is a better way.

Automatic Recalculation With Iteration

The good news is that 1-2-3 does not require you repeatedly to press the F9 (Calc) key and wait for the model to run. You can tell 1-2-3 how many times to recalculate a model by using the Worksheet Global Recalculation Iteration command.

1. Type /Worksheet Global Recalculation Iteration.

You are asked to enter the iteration count (the number of times you want 1-2-3 to repeat the recalculation).

2. Type 17, and press the ENTER key.

The model will recalculate 17 times, but not until you tell it to do so by pressing the F9 (Calc) key.

3. Press the F9 (Calc) key.

This will take a few minutes, so you may want to take a break. Then come back to the machine and marvel at the results of 1000 simulations. Check the Day 50 NO. OF ORDERS UNPROC'D and # OF DAYS OF BACKLOG. It will look something like Figure 5-9.

The company is still doing well on holding down the backlog—perhaps too well. Some savings may be feasible by cutting down on the number of workers. Try it yourself.

From now on, you must press the F9 (Calc) key to recalculate the model. Each time you press the Calc key, the model will reiterate 17 times. If you want to go back to one iteration for each depression of the F9 (Calc) key, simply

9. Type /Worksheet Global Recalculation Iteration.

10. Type 1 and press the ENTER key when 1-2-3 asks you how many times to iterate.

Remember also that global recalculation was set to manual, which turns off

	A	B	C	D	E	F	G	H	I
15				PRODUCTION SIMULATION					
16									DAILY
17			NO. OF	ORDERS		NO. OF	NO. OF	# OF DAYS	WORKER
18		RANDOM	ORDERS	TO BE		ORDERS	ORDERS	OF	UTILIZ.
19	DAY	NUMBER	REC'D	PROC'D	CAPACITY	PROC'D	UNPROC'D	BACKLOG	RATE
20	------	------	------	------	------	------	------	------	------
21									
22	1	0.037462	100	100	420	100	0	0.0	24%
23	2	0.467745	300	300	420	300	0	0.0	71%
24	3	0.724938	400	400	420	400	0	0.0	95%
25	4	0.470611	300	300	420	300	0	0.0	71%
26	5	0.776671	400	400	420	400	0	0.0	95%
27	6	0.150193	200	200	420	200	0	0.0	48%
28	7	0.552363	300	300	420	300	0	0.0	71%
29	8	0.482597	300	300	420	300	0	0.0	71%
30	9	0.038726	100	100	420	100	0	0.0	24%
31	10	0.266611	200	200	420	200	0	0.0	48%
32	11	0.412053	300	300	420	300	0	0.0	71%
33	12	0.342892	200	200	420	200	0	0.0	48%
34	13	0.960610	600	600	420	420	180	0.4	100%
35	14	0.375415	200	380	420	380	0	0.0	90%
36	15	0.337428	200	200	420	200	0	0.0	48%
37	16	0.895764	500	500	420	420	80	0.2	100%
38	17	0.759582	400	480	420	420	60	0.1	100%
39	18	0.632100	400	460	420	420	40	0.1	100%
40	19	0.845236	500	540	420	420	120	0.3	100%
41	20	0.864391	500	620	420	420	200	0.5	100%
42	21	0.097137	100	300	420	300	0	0.0	71%
43	22	0.728147	400	400	420	400	0	0.0	95%
44	23	0.913273	500	500	420	420	80	0.2	100%
45	24	0.592990	400	480	420	420	60	0.1	100%
46	25	0.244712	200	260	420	260	0	0.0	62%
47	26	0.932463	600	600	420	420	180	0.4	100%
48	27	0.939549	600	780	420	420	360	0.9	100%
49	28	0.039914	100	460	420	420	40	0.1	100%
50	29	0.223032	200	240	420	240	0	0.0	57%
51	30	0.594740	400	400	420	400	0	0.0	95%
52	31	0.979778	600	600	420	420	180	0.4	100%
53	32	0.006113	100	280	420	280	0	0.0	67%
54	33	0.336958	200	200	420	200	0	0.0	48%
55	34	0.720098	400	400	420	400	0	0.0	95%
56	35	0.810062	500	500	420	420	80	0.2	100%
57	36	0.833310	500	580	420	420	160	0.4	100%
58	37	0.777723	400	560	420	420	140	0.3	100%
59	38	0.474399	300	440	420	420	20	.0	100%
60	39	0.611641	400	420	420	420	0	0.0	100%
61	40	0.056288	100	100	420	100	0	0.0	24%
62	41	0.214425	200	200	420	200	0	0.0	48%
63	42	0.729592	400	400	420	400	0	0.0	95%
64	43	0.324595	200	200	420	200	0	0.0	48%
65	44	0.743647	400	400	420	400	0	0.0	95%
66	45	0.546647	300	300	420	300	0	0.0	71%
67	46	0.008480	100	100	420	100	0	0.0	24%
68	47	0.967361	600	600	420	420	180	0.4	100%
69	48	0.511413	300	480	420	420	60	0.1	100%
70	49	0.240095	200	260	420	260	0	0.0	62%
71	50	0.438268	300	300	420	300	0	0.0	71%

Figure 5-9. Worksheet after 1000 simulation

automatic recalculation; the model will recalculate formulas now only when you press the F9 (Calc) key. To resume automatic recalculation, issue the Worksheet Global Recalculation Automatic command.

Another important point to bear in mind when using this model is that if you want to start the simulation from Day 1, you must go back to Day 1 ORDERS TO BE PROC'D and set it equal to NO. OF ORDERS REC'D exclusively. Then to simulate more than 50 days, go back to Day 1 and reset it to new orders plus the Day 50 backlog, as shown previously.

Displaying Cell Contents
For Trouble-Shooting

In the last few chapters, you have begun to work with complex worksheets that involve large numbers of formulas. You have also seen that 1-2-3 has its own warning system to let you know when formulas do not adhere to what it considers to be a logical structure.

When you are not sure why 1-2-3 is giving you a CIRC message or why a model is not giving you the results you expect, it helps to examine the underlying formulas of the model. One way of doing this is to move the pointer to each of the cells you want to examine and then to review the contents of the cell in the control panel. If you want to look at all or most of the cells, however, this is a very inconvenient way of doing so.

Using Text Format to Display
Cell Contents

Lotus 1-2-3 gives you the option of seeing the contents of cells right on the worksheet by assigning the *Text* format to the cells. The Text format displays the contents of a cell instead of its value. If you use Text format, the display shows a formula as it was entered (for instance, @RAND in cell B23) rather than its resulting value.

To assign Text format to an entire worksheet, you can issue the Worksheet Global Format command, choosing the Text option. We used the Worksheet Global Format command in Chapter 3 to set the default worksheet format to integer. All cells are displayed according to the default format, except those that have been assigned formats with the Range Format command.

1. Type /Worksheet Global Format Text.

As soon as you select Text, all cells that have not been formatted explicitly by Range Format are assigned the Text format. For example, Days 1 to 50 of the RANDOM NUMBER column are displayed as @RAND.

What happened to column C, NO. OF ORDERS REC'D? Because the width of column C is nine characters, you see only the first nine characters of the formulas stored there. If you want to see the entire formula, you can issue a Worksheet Column-Width Set command and use the right arrow key to expand the column-width until the column is wide enough to display the entire formula. We won't do this now, however.

Notice that # OF DAYS OF BACKLOG and DAILY WORKER UTILIZ. RATE have not been assigned a Text format. This is because we previously set the display of these columns to Fixed format, using the Range Format command.

Once your worksheet displays the formulas the way you want them, you can use the Print command to get a hard copy of the re-formatted worksheet. This is not only convenient for verifying cell contents; it is also an excellent device for documenting your models.

To change the default worksheet format from Text back to General,

2. Type /Worksheet Global Format General.

Printing Cell Contents
With the Print Command

Formatting the entire worksheet with the Text format can take some time. If you are in a hurry, 1-2-3 provides a shortcut with the Print command. Without having to reformat any cells, you can use the *Other Cell-Formulas* option of the Print command. The result is a report of the cell contents of the Print range that you designate. However, the report prints one line per cell. If you have a worksheet with many cells, your printout will be quite long. Each line prints the same information that you would see on the first line of the control panel if you had placed the pointer on a cell (that is, cell address, format, and contents).

To print out such a listing, you would turn on your printer with the paper aligned to the top of the page and (from Ready Mode) type /Print Printer Options Other Cell-Formulas. You would also have to enter a Print range and any other Print options you would want. This method of reporting cell contents is easier to use than the Text formatting method, but the latter provides a nicer format on the report.

By the way, if you begin to print and you want to interrupt the printout before it is completed, you may press the CTRL and BREAK keys to stop printing and return to Ready Mode. This will work for virtually any printing you do with 1-2-3.

PART 2
Database Functions

Part 2 explores 1-2-3's database management capabilities and the Data command. The invoice tracking system in Chapter 6 shows you how to use the Data Sort command to reorder a worksheet alphabetically and numerically. You will also learn 1-2-3's special date functions and the Data Distribution command, which summarizes frequency distributions in table and graph forms.

Chapter 7 explains another option of the Data command, Query. You will use the Data Query command to locate specific information in a database, copy selected data from a database to another section of the worksheet, and delete records from a database.

The same types of procedures are often repeated in a database application. Chapter 8 uses a sales ranking example to explain how you can automate such procedures. By building macros and presenting them as options on a user-defined menu, you can create a database tool that can be used by persons with little knowledge of 1-2-3.

Chapter 9 wraps up Part 2 with a market survey example. This application shows how you can use 1-2-3's database statistical functions and the Data Table command, which allows you to summarize database statistics in a table.

Chapter 6
Database Management: Sorting and Data Distribution

Database management and spreadsheet analysis are two of the primary uses of microcomputers. Until recently, these two areas of application were quite distinct, because the software that was developed for database management was not adapted to spreadsheet analysis, and calculation programs were incapable of manipulating spreadsheets in the same way as databases. Although each genre of software became increasingly more manageable and easier to use, it was not possible for the user to combine the features of both in a single application within a single software package. The novelty of Lotus 1-2-3 is that it permits a merger of the database and the spreadsheet.

This chapter provides an initial view of 1-2-3 as a database management system. After defining what database management is, we will use the Data command to develop an invoice tracking system. Numerous commands and concepts are involved in database management, so we will cover sorting in this chapter and will illustrate other Data command options in the next chapter, where we will continue the invoice tracking example.

This chapter also introduces date arithmetic (using the @DATE function) and the Data Distribution command, a useful tool for summarizing information contained in a database. In addition, we will use graphics to show how database information can be extracted and illustrated in a graph.

About Database Management

A database is nothing more than a file of information. It is a collection of *records*, individual items of information grouped together in some meaningful way. The card catalog in your neighborhood library is an example of a database. Every card in the catalog is a record of information pertaining to a particular book. The individual records of a database are further broken down into *fields* of information. On a library catalog card, the fields include the catalog number, the title of the book, and the name of the author.

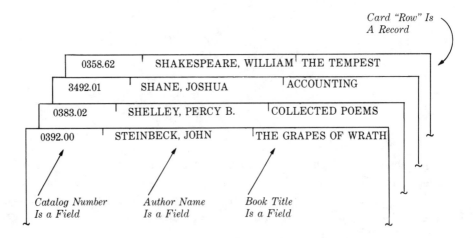

Suppose you take the catalog cards out of the drawer and lay them out on a countertop. As the illustration shows, the collection of cards can be viewed as a series of rows and the data items as a series of columns. Looking at the illustration, you can see how a database might be viewed as a table of rows and columns. Each row of the table corresponds to a record (a single card), and each column of the table corresponds to a field (such as the catalog number).

If a database is a table of rows and columns, then it can also be regarded as a type of spreadsheet—a point that did not elude the developers of 1-2-3. They observed that the terminology of database management is not sacred. A database is simply a table of information, just as a spreadsheet is a table of information. A field is nothing more than a spreadsheet column, and a record is another name for a row. The matrix of rows and columns that forms a spreadsheet translates into the network of records and fields that form a database.

If a database is so familiar a concept, then why has there been so much celebration of an innovation that has been around since the list of animals that sailed in Noah's Ark? The reason for all the fuss is database *management*, not the database itself.

Database management is the manipulation of the information contained in a file. It includes reorganizing the file's structure, updating the file, deleting old records, and printing the file in a particular format.

An essential function of database management is sorting information. *Sorting* is one of the most tedious tasks of manual file maintenance. One wonders whether Noah would have made his journey if he had been asked to alphabetize his passenger list. With 1-2-3, Noah would have been able to sort 2000 records in a matter of seconds.

Another facet of database management is data retrieval, the ability to search for and select particular items of the data file. Data retrieval, or *querying*, encompasses several tasks. The database query might consist merely of finding a particular record and making a mental note of it—exactly what you do when you look up a book in a library's catalog to determine whether the library owns it or to find out the author's name.

A database query also might consist of extracting records—choosing particular records from a file and putting them in another place. In a library, you might wish to put down on a piece of scratch paper the titles and catalog numbers of the books you want to borrow. In doing so, you are extracting records from the card-catalog database.

The rules that dictate which records should be located or extracted from the file are called *criteria*. A criterion can be a simple match, which is what occurs when you select the library catalog card that contains a book title that coincides with the one you want to borrow. Alternatively, a criterion can be a condition such as "Select all records that have catalog numbers greater than 500."

Lotus 1-2-3 has the capacity for all of these database management functions, and each will be illustrated in the next three chapters. The 1-2-3 database is capable of managing 8191 records (2047 in Version 1A) of 256 fields each. However, you will not have enough memory in your computer to utilize the complete potential database (spreadsheet). Nonetheless, even the minimum RAM requirement of 256K will accommodate a variety of applications, including the one that follows.*

Think of how many files and catalogs a company, service organization, or individual maintains. Lists of names, telephone numbers, and addresses of clients, friends, customers, and employees; accounting records; inventories and supplies; payroll information; stock and bond holdings; daily schedules; and weekly golf scores. These are some of the many databases used by professionals and managers. Although this chapter deals with a specific database application, the database functions of sorting, extracting, deleting, editing, and updating apply to databases in general.

Dr. DoMuch's Database Application

A database application that is commonly found in businesses and organizations is invoicing. The invoice file is simply a catalog of invoices, with each invoice corresponding to a single transaction. In a doctor's office, an invoice might represent charges associated with a medical examination. In a store, it would represent a specific sale of merchandise. Although an invoice file might be used as a database to control the entire billing process, we will begin with a simple worksheet whose purpose is merely to determine the age of receivables—that is, the number of days that have elapsed for each unpaid invoice since the date of the services rendered.

Dr. R.X. DoMuch maintains a catalog of patient invoices. Each day, copies of patients' bills are added to the box, and the bills of patients who have paid

---

*The minimum requirement is only 192K for Version 1A.

in full are removed from the box. The outstanding bills must be sorted each month in chronological order, and notices are then sent to the patients whose payments are overdue by a month or more. Bills that are more than four months past due are referred to a collection agency. Then the bills must be reordered alphabetically to facilitate finding the invoices for particular patients during the month. Lotus 1-2-3 is well suited to such an application.

Figure 6-1 identifies records and fields in Dr. DoMuch's file. As it shows, each invoice record includes seven fields: NAME, SERVICES RENDERED, MONTH, DAY, YEAR, AMOUNT, and DAYS PAST DUE. The NAME column contains the patient's name—last name first, so that the doctor can easily locate the record of a patient by name. The second field contains a description of the services rendered by the doctor, such as an examination or a blood test. Lotus 1-2-3 internally holds up to 256 characters in a cell, even if

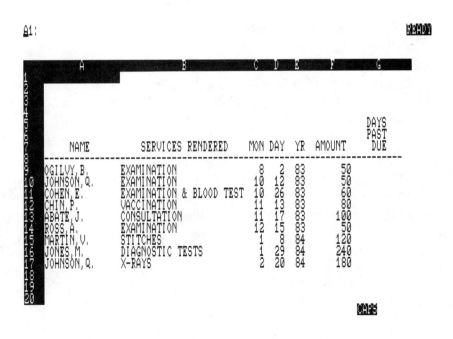

Figure 6-1. Dr. DoMuch's invoice record

fewer characters are displayed, so there is ample space to store a lengthy description of services.

The date of services rendered (or purchase date) occupies three consecutive columns: MONTH, DAY, and YEAR. Each of these is a numeric value. For example, a date of March 16, 1984 would be represented by three entries (3, 16, and 84) in the MONTH, DAY, and YEAR columns. We will soon see how to use 1-2-3's date functions in order to do arithmetic with the purchase date.

The goal of this worksheet will be the DAYS PAST DUE calculation. On any given day, the user will enter the day's date, and 1-2-3 will figure out the number of days that have elapsed between the entered date and the date of services rendered. Before we calculate DAYS PAST DUE, however, we are going to build Dr. DoMuch's worksheet and put the names in order by using the Sort command.

Setting Up the Worksheet

You should begin this exercise by entering the titles for the worksheet columns.

1. Enter the column headings exactly as shown in Figure 6-1, beginning with row 5.

Note that the spreadsheet begins in row 5, not in row 1. Press the CAPS LOCK key first to make cell headings and entries in capital letters. The heading underscores in row 8 were made by using the \- command in cell A8, and then using the Copy command to replicate the underscore to cells B8 through G8. Do not forget to use the Range Label-Prefix Center command to center all labels in the range A5..G7.

2. Set the column widths for each column, or field, according to the following chart. For each field, place the pointer in the appropriate column and issue the Worksheet Column Set command.

FIELD NAME	COLUMN-WIDTH
NAME	15
SERVICES RENDERED	25
DATE: MON	4
DAY	4
YR	4
AMOUNT	9
DAYS PAST DUE	9

Note that the total of all of these columns is 70 characters.

3. Next move to row 9, and enter the nine records shown in Figure 6-1.

If you make any mistakes, use the same correction methods you would have used on a normal worksheet. The worksheet has not turned into a database yet — and even when it does, you will still be able to use the same spreadsheet commands to make changes to cells.

Sorting Data

The records we have entered are not in any particular order. However, Dr. DoMuch would like an alphabetized list of the patients in the billing file so that it will be easy to find the bill of a particular patient.

If you were 1-2-3, what information would you require before being able to sort a worksheet? For one thing, you would need to know exactly where the records to be sorted are located in the worksheet. In the present case, the first record, for B. Ogilvy, begins at cell A9. The information pertaining to Ogilvy ends with the DAYS PAST DUE field (which is blank for now) in cell G9. The last record pertains to Q. Johnson, and it spans cells A17 through G17.

You would also need to know which field in this worksheet sector should be sorted. The current request will be for column A. Knowing *where* the records are and *what* fields to sort is not sufficient. You also need to know *how* to sort: whether in ascending order or in descending order. An alphabetized list would be in ascending (A to Z) order. Lastly, 1-2-3 will need to know *when* to sort. It will wait until you have entered or revised your responses to the What, Where, and How queries before it proceeds to execute a sort.

To initiate a sort operation,

1. Type /Data.

The control panel now displays the list of topics that we will cover in this and the following chapters (although this was probably not the original intent of the authors of 1-2-3). The Data menu looks like this:

Fill Table Sort Query Distribution Matrix Regression Parse

(Version 1A does not include the last three items of this menu.)

2. Select the Sort option, and press the ENTER key.

This brings us to the Sort menu, and it looks like this:

Data-Range Primary-Key Secondary-Key Reset Go Quit

The first option, *Data-Range*, refers to the section of the worksheet that contains the records to be ordered. The two keys, *Primary* and *Secondary*, refer to the columns to be sorted; we will discuss them shortly. *Reset* makes 1-2-3 "forget" previous settings for the data range and sort keys. *Go* is the trigger that executes the sort according to the data range and sort keys specified.

Assigning the Data Range

You can enter the sort specifications in any order. We will start with the data range.

1. Choose the **Data-Range** option.

In response to the "Enter Data Range" prompt,

2. Move the pointer to the top left of the range, cell A9.

Notice that the data range of the Sort command does *not* include the field headings —it begins with the first record to be sorted.

3. Type the . key to anchor the range, and move the pointer to the bottom right of the range, cell G17. (You may use the END and HOME keys to move the pointer quickly to the bottom right of the data range.)

4. Press the ENTER key.

The pointer will return to where it was before you entered the range, and the Sort menu will reappear in the control panel.

Assigning the Sort Keys

The term *sort key* refers to the field that is to be sorted. A library might use the "author's name" field as the sort key to alphabetize its card catalog; alternatively, it might use the "book title" field.

Sometimes you need multiple sort keys. For example, if a single author wrote ten books, then a catalog that is sorted primarily by author name should be sorted secondarily by book title. Ten books written by a single author would then be ordered alphabetically. Without a second sort key, the authors would be alphabetized, but the arrangement of titles for each author would be haphazard.

Lotus 1-2-3 allows you to specify two sort keys for a single sort operation.

The *Primary key* refers to the primary field to be sorted, such as the author's name in the catalog example. The *Secondary key* is sorted within each classification of the Primary key, just as book titles would be sorted for each author in the catalog.

There are even situations in which you might want to sort on more than two keys. However, 1-2-3 has a limit of two keys. You do not have to use a Secondary key if you do not need to. For Dr. DoMuch's request, we do not need a Secondary key, so we will proceed by alphabetizing the invoice file using the NAME field as the Primary key.

1. Choose the **Primary-Key** option.

You will be prompted with "Enter Primary sort key address:". All you have to do is move the pointer to *any* cell in the column to be sorted, which is the Primary-key column. For Dr. DoMuch's current purposes, the Primary key is the NAME field in column A.

2. Move the pointer to a cell in column A.

3. Press the ENTER key.

Now you are asked to "Enter Sort order (A or D):".

4. Press **A** to specify ascending alphabetical order.

5. Press the ENTER key.

Once more you are returned to the Sort menu, but you have finished entering the requirements for an alphabetized listing of the file. Before you tell 1-2-3 to go ahead, reflect for a moment on how long it would take you to sort these nine records manually.

Now choose the Go option. Do not blink, because 1-2-3 will sort the records in less time than it took you to reflect about doing it by hand. In the sorted list, shown in Figure 6-2, observe that Ogilvy, which was the first record (row 9), is now the eighth record (row 16) and that all the items pertaining to Ogilvy were moved together to row 16. This is because the data range extends to column G. If we had mistakenly restricted the data range to the NAME field alone without including the other fields, then only the NAME field would have been reordered. The other fields would have stayed in place. Mistakes like this one can happen—one good reason that you should always protect yourself by saving the spreadsheet before manipulating it.

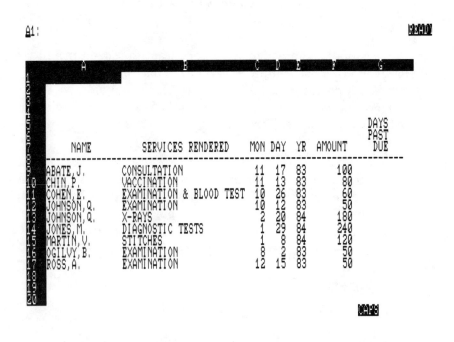

Figure 6-2. Dr. DoMuch's invoice record after alphabetical sort

Blank Spaces in the Database

Another important point about the data range is that it should not extend past the last record of the database (row 17 in this instance). To see why, we will try an experiment and observe what happens when this rule is violated.

1. Type **/Data Sort** to get into the Sort menu.

2. Select the **Data-Range** option.

Lotus 1-2-3 remembers what you last entered as the data range, and it highlights the data-range section. If you were to press the down arrow key, the highlighted range would encompass an additional row (row 18).

3. Press the down arrow key once, and press the ENTER key.

The data range now spans A9..G18. It includes a blank row at the bottom of the database.

Recall that the Primary key was the NAME field, and the sort order was ascending. We need not respecify these because 1-2-3 remembers them from the last time. If we choose Go at this point, 1-2-3 will resort the data range, but it will include the empty row 18 in the sorting process.

4. Type **G** to select the Go option.

As Figure 6-3 shows, the blank row is inserted above ABATE as the first entry. This is because *1-2-3 considers a blank to be ahead of the letter A in the*

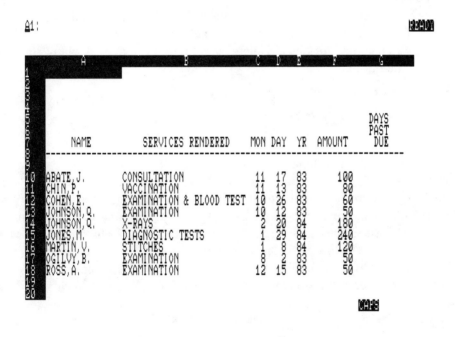

Figure 6-3. Results of sort showing blank row first

alphabet. A blank cell in the sort key field would therefore be ordered above cells that contain labels or values.

Acknowledging our blunder, we would like to get rid of that blank row, now positioned at row 9. We do not need a special database command to remove a row. We will use a worksheet command to delete a row — for after all, the database is a worksheet.

The Worksheet Delete Command

Do you recall inserting a column into the worksheet using the Worksheet Insert command in Chapter 2? The Worksheet Insert command inserts either columns or rows into the worksheet. The reverse of insertion — deletion — is also possible with the *Worksheet Delete* command.

To use Worksheet Delete, first position the pointer at any cell in the first row or column you want to delete. Then issue the Worksheet Delete command. Now 1-2-3 will ask you whether you want to delete columns or rows; then it asks which columns or rows you want to delete. When you respond, 1-2-3 removes the unwanted columns or rows, shifts whatever is to the right of or below the deleted section to replace the deletions, and adjusts the worksheet formulas to account for the relocated cells.

We will use the Worksheet Delete command to remove the blank row at the top of the database.

1. Move the pointer to any cell in row 9.

2. Type **/W**orksheet **D**elete **R**ow.

3. Press the ENTER key.

The blank record is gone.

Incidentally, because we deleted the first row of the data range, 1-2-3 will no longer be able to remember the data range. Why does this happen? Whenever 1-2-3 asks for a range, we always specify the range by indicating the first and last coordinates. 1-2-3 uses these coordinates to remember where the range is. If we delete the first row of the data range, we remove the "placeholder" for remembering the beginning of the range. Thus, we will need to reenter the data range the next time we do a sort.

Blank Characters in a Cell

Just as blank rows in a database can cause unexpected results, blank characters in a cell also produce similar surprises. For example, if our database had contained the name ABATE,J. and another name ABATE, J. (space after the comma), the second name would appear first in the sorted list because *space*-J comes before J. Similarly, suppose that a space were inadvertently inserted before the name JONES,M., as in the following list of names:

ABATE,J.
CHIN,P.
  JONES,M.
ROSS,A.

The sorted list would put JONES on top, because *space*-JONES comes before ABATE in the alphabet of 1-2-3. Spaces count in terms of both blank cells and blank characters within cells, and you should be aware of this whenever you use the Data commands.

Date Arithmetic

Now that we have responded to Dr. DoMuch's request to alphabetize the file, let us proceed with determining the number of days past due for each invoice.

For this task, we will need two pieces of information: the invoice date and the current date. Then we must compute the number of days between these two dates. In other words, we must "subtract" the invoice date from the current date. Subtracting dates is a *date arithmetic* operation, and 1-2-3 has several unique functions designed to handle date arithmetic.

Using @DATE to Convert
To Integer Dates

Here we meet another @ function, similar in form to the @SUM, @MIN, and @VLOOKUP functions that we have seen in previous chapters. The *@DATE function* converts a date into an integer number, the number of days that have elapsed between December 31, 1899, and the specified date. There is nothing sacred about December 31, 1899, except that it serves as a reference point for converting dates to numbers. Once a date is converted, we can derive the number of days between two dates by subtracting the earlier date from the later one.

Testing the @DATE Function

Recall that certain @ functions require some additional items of information, called arguments, in order to work. The @DATE function, whose structure is @DATE (*Year*, *Month*, *Day*), requires three arguments, each of which can be a value or a cell reference. Try the function in an unused portion of the worksheet. We will use @DATE to convert November 17, 1983, into an integer.

1. Move to cell A1.

2. Type **@DATE(83,11,17)**, and press the ENTER key.

The result, 30637, means that 11/17/83 is 30,637 days after December 31, 1899. So what, you say. But let us continue.

3. Move to cell A2, and type **@DATE(84,2,28)**. Then press the ENTER key.

You have now derived the integer conversion of February 28, 1984. Next we move to cell A3 and subtract the earlier date from the later one.

4. At cell A3, type **+A2−A1**, and press the ENTER key.

The difference between the two dates is 103.

The numeric conversions may have little meaning to us on their own, but they do allow us to determine the number of days between November 17, 1983, and February 28, 1984. In Dr. DoMuch's case, 103 represents the number of days J. Abate's invoice is past due as of 2/28/84.

Formatting Dates in Cells

Those numeric date conversions you have just completed are useful, but they are also unsightly. They need not be; Lotus 1-2-3 allows you to disguise them with a special feature of the Range Format command. When you enter the Range Format command, the control panel displays *Date* as one of the format options. There are three date formats: Day-Month-Year, Day-Month, and Month-Year. To improve the appearance of the date number in cell A1,

1. Press the HOME key to move to cell A1.

2. Type **/Range Format Date**.

Now 1-2-3 will prompt you to choose between "1 (DD-MMM-YY) 2 (DD-MMM) 3 (MMM-YY)". We are interested in the entire date, so

3. Type the **1** key.

Next 1-2-3 asks for the range of cells to format.

4. Move the pointer down once to cell A2.

5. Press the ENTER key.

The results you see (17-Nov-83 and 28-Feb-84) represent a marked improvement over 30637 and 30740. But keep in mind that with formats, what you see is not necessarily what you have. As far as 1-2-3 is concerned, the contents of A1 and A2 are numbers, not dates.

6. Get rid of the scratch area by typing **/Range Erase A1.A3**, and press the ENTER key.

We now are ready to move on to Dr. DoMuch's second request, calculating days past due.

The @TODAY Function

Deriving the number of days overdue requires a current date. With this information, the procedure is quite straightforward. On any given day, Dr. DoMuch would load the invoice database and type in today's date, and then the days past due would be updated. (If global recalculation were set to manual with the Worksheet Global Recalculation Manual command, then the doctor would have to press the F9 (Calc) key to update the formulas.) Let us enter the current date into the model.

Lotus 1-2-3 has a function named @*NOW* (@*TODAY* in Version 1A) that yields today's date. However, 1-2-3's version of today's date may differ from yours. The result of the @NOW function is a numeric conversion of the kind used in the @DATE function. Unless you routinely think of dates as days elapsed since December 31, 1899, you will not know whether the date obtained from @NOW is correct. The result of @NOW is the system date—that is, the date you entered in response to the "Enter new date:" prompt when you first switched on your machine. If you did not enter the correct date at that time, then you will know the answer to the riddle "When is today not today?" for the system date will not be the correct date.

1. Move to cell A2, and enter the label **CURRENT DATE:**.

2. Move right once to cell B2.

3. Type **@NOW**, and press the ENTER key. (For Version 1A, type **@TODAY** instead of @NOW.)

You can improve the appearance of the cell contents using the Range Format Date command.

4. Type **/Range Format Date 1**, and press the ENTER key.

If the date you see is not today's date, then you can enter today's date with the @DATE function. In order to make the results of this book comparable to your results, use a date of March 2, 1984, which is what the text's figures are based on. With the pointer still on B2,

5. Type **@DATE(84,3,2)**, and press the ENTER key.

If you previously formatted this cell with a Date format, you need not repeat the format command, because the format stays in the cell until you erase the cell or assign it a different format.

Calculating Days Past Due

We are now ready to calculate the DAYS PAST DUE column. To derive the number of days elapsed since the invoice date, we must convert the invoice date to a number (using the @DATE function) and subtract it from the current date (which has already been converted, though the format disguises the number).

1. Move the pointer to cell G9, the first entry in the DAYS PAST DUE column.

2. Type the + key, and move the pointer to the CURRENT DATE cell (B2).

3. Type the − key.

Now convert the year, month, and day of the invoice date to a numeric value.

4. Type **@DATE(**.

5. Move the pointer to the invoice date YR cell (E9).

6. Type the , key, and move the pointer to the invoice date MON cell (C9).

7. Type the , key, and move the pointer to the invoice date DAY cell (D9).

8. Type the) key, and press the ENTER key.

Using a current date of 02-Mar-84, J.Abate is 106 days overdue on the first invoice.

To determine the other days past due, we would simply copy the formula down the column. But remember, unless you make special arrangements, 1-2-3 copies formula addresses *relatively*. Thus, if we were to copy the formula +B2− @DATE(E9,C9,D9) to cells in other rows, the cell references would change. However, we don't want the reference to CURRENT DATE (cell B2) to change, because CURRENT DATE will always be found in cell B2. The reference to cell B2 must therefore be absolute.

Although we neglected to make the reference to B2 absolute when we originally entered the formula, we can easily make up for the oversight by entering Edit Mode and inserting the necessary $ signs.

9. Press the F2 (Edit) key to enter Edit Mode.

10. Move the pointer to the first term in the formula, and change it from +B2 to +$B$2.

11. Press the ENTER key to store the formula.

Now copy the formula down the column.

12. Type these keystrokes: **/C** ENTER **G10.G17** ENTER.

A quick inspection of Figure 6-4 reveals that the most recent invoice belongs to Q. Johnson, and a negligible 11 days have passed since that invoice

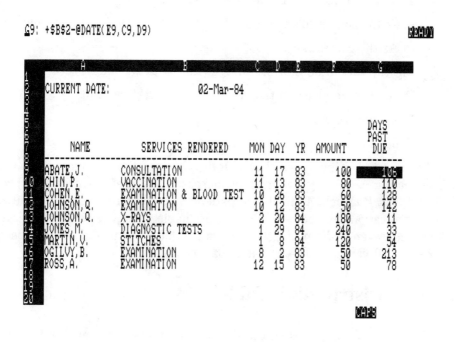

Figure 6-4. Results of days-past-due calculation

date. On the other end of the spectrum, B. Ogilvy is almost seven months past due. Dr. DoMuch will be calling the collection agency about that one.

Sorting Days-Past-Due Records

A list of invoice records sorted in descending order of days past due would be most convenient, because it would identify the oldest receivables by placing them on top. This is easy to do with the Data Sort command.

1. Type /Data Sort Data-Range.

To enter the data range,

2. Move the pointer to cell A9, the top left of the data range.
3. Type the . key, and move the pointer to cell G17, the bottom right of the data range.
4. Press the ENTER key.

The Primary key is the DAYS PAST DUE column, so

5. Type **P** to select the Primary-Key option.
6. Move the pointer to any cell in the DAYS PAST DUE column (column G).
7. Press the ENTER key.

We want the sort to be in descending order, with the oldest records first, so

8. Type **D** in response to the "Enter Sort Order" prompt.
9. Press the ENTER key.
10. Type **G** to select the Go option.

As expected, Figure 6-5 shows Ogilvy first on the list and Johnson last. The sorting capability has greatly increased the usefulness of the spreadsheet to Dr. DoMuch. As the list of patients increases, the simple flexibility of this application will become more appreciable. And you will be pleased to know that even if the billing file grows to 2000 records, the sorting speed of 1-2-3 is still remarkable—a matter of seconds.

The Data Distribution Table

The list of nine names in the doctor's database represents only a small portion of the doctor's invoice file. As the database grows, it becomes more important and more difficult to identify the distribution of invoices by age.

```
C9: +$B$2-@DATE(E9,C9,D9)                                    READY

        A              B              C   D   E     F       G
                                                          DAYS
                                                          PAST
      NAME          SERVICES RENDERED  MON DAY YR AMOUNT   DUE
    ------------------------------------------------------------
  9 OGILVY,B.       EXAMINATION          8   2  83     50    213
 10 JOHNSON,Q.      EXAMINATION         10  12  83     50    142
 11 COHEN,E.        EXAMINATION & BLOOD TEST 10 26 83   60    128
 12 CHIN,P.         VACCINATION         11  13  83     80    110
 13 ABATE,J.        CONSULTATION        11  17  83    100    106
 14 ROSS,A.         EXAMINATION         12  15  83     50     78
 15 MARTIN,V.       STITCHES             1   8  84    120     54
 16 JONES,M.        DIAGNOSTIC TESTS     1  29  84    240     33
 17 JOHNSON,Q.      X-RAYS               2  20  84    180     11

CURRENT DATE:                 02-Mar-84
```

Figure 6-5. Results of days-past-due sort, descending order

What portion of overdue invoices are significantly past due? Do most of the overdue payments relate to services rendered in the past two months, or is there an abundance of invoices older than six months? How much of the payment backlog should be sent to a collection agency? Is the collection agency doing its job?

Why Use Data Distribution Tables?

The DAYS PAST DUE column is the key to answering these questions. But as the file becomes unwieldy, the detailed information becomes less useful for analyzing the data, and it becomes necessary to summarize or group the data in a more meaningful fashion. One method for categorizing the file is by tallying *frequency distribution*, enumerating the data records that fall within given value ranges. For example, how many patients are 0 to 30 days overdue in their payments, how many are 31 to 60 days overdue, and so on?

If you were calculating such a distribution manually, you would take the invoice file, lay it on a table top, and begin sorting the invoice slips into piles, perhaps placing each pile in a separate container or *bin*. When you were done sorting, you would design a frequency table on a piece of paper. The table would consist of two columns. The first column would specify the groupings or categories into which the invoices will be divided (for example, 0 to 30 days, 31 to 60 days). The second column would store the number of records that fall into each category.

The Data Distribution command works the same way except that instead of sorting the invoice slips on a table top, 1-2-3 sorts them *in* a table. Although 1-2-3 does the actual counting and categorizing of the data, it is your job to choose appropriate groupings and to designate the portion of the worksheet into which 1-2-3 will deposit its results.

Building a Data Distribution Table

In terms of billing, the invoices that are less than 30 days old are not yet worrisome, so we will separate them into the first category range: 0 to 30 days. The frequency distribution of two- and three-month overdue bills is important, so we make bins for 31 to 60 days and 61 to 90 days. Invoices that are 91 to 120 days old are highly suspect, and they deserve a category of their own. The last category, 121 days and more, includes the freeloaders who will be delegated to the collection agency.

Figure 6-6 illustrates the design of the data distribution table. Each cell in the *bin-range column* contains the upper limit of one grouping of the data. If the first interval is 0 to 30 days, the first cell in the bin range should be 30. The second cell should be 60, the third 90, and the fourth 120. The *results* column will contain the frequency corresponding to each bin interval. However, the results column extends one cell below the bin range. The extra cell in the results column will contain the number of data values greater than the last interval specified in the bin range. In this example, the extra cell will contain the number of invoices more than 120 days old.

The groupings need not be intervals of equal size. If there were no reason to distinguish two-month-old accounts from three-month-old accounts, we could have assigned interval ranges of 1 to 30, 31 to 90, 90 to 120, and more than 120.

To enter the ranges, choose an empty section of the spreadsheet for the distribution table. We will use column I to house the bin range, which means that the corresponding cells in column J will contain the distribution results (as shown in Figure 6-6).

```
        A                    B               C   D   E     F        G        H          I      J
 1
 2 CURRENT DATE:                      02-Mar-84
 3                                                                                     ┌──30──┬──1──┐
 4                                                                                     │  60  │  2  │
 5                                                              DAYS                   │  90  │  1  │
 6                                                              PAST    Unused         │ 120  │  2  │
 7    NAME             SERVICES RENDERED     MON DAY  YR  AMOUNT  DUE    Cell  →        └──────┼──3──┤
 8 ---------------------------------------------------------------------                      └─────┘
 9 OGILVY,B.        EXAMINATION              8   2   83      50     213
10 JOHNSON,Q.       EXAMINATION             10  12   83      50     142          Bin        Results
11 COHEN,E.         EXAMINATION & BLOOD TEST 10  26   83      60     128          Range      Column
12 CHIN,P.          VACCINATION             11  13   83      80     110          Column
13 ABATE,J.         CONSULTATION            11  17   83     100     106
14 ROSS,A.          EXAMINATION             12  15   83      50      78
15 MARTIN,V.        STITCHES                 1   8   84     120      54
16 JONES,M.         DIAGNOSTIC TESTS         1  29   84     240      33
17 JOHNSON,Q.       X-RAYS                   2  20   84     180      11
```

Figure 6-6. Data distribution table on worksheet

1. In cell I1, enter the label **DISTRIBUTION OF PAST DUE INVOICES**.

2. Move to cell I3, and enter the upper limit of the first interval, **30**.

3. Next enter the other limits (**60**, **90**, and **120**) in cells I4 through I6.

Cells I3..I6 form the bin range. Cell J3 will contain the number of invoices with a DAYS PAST DUE value less than or equal to 30 days. Cell J4 will count the invoices that are more than 30 but less than or equal to 60 days overdue. Cell J5 will tally the 61 to 90 range, and cell J6 will count the 91 to 120 range. Cell J7, the extra result cell, will tally the number of invoices older than 120 days (not including 120).

4. Type **/Data Distribution**.

Now 1-2-3 prompts you for the *values range*, which is the range of database cells that you would like to distribute.

5. Move the pointer to the beginning of the DAYS PAST DUE column (cell G9).

6. Type the . key, then press the END key and the down arrow key to expand the pointer to cell G17, the end of the DAYS PAST DUE column.

7. Press the ENTER key.

8. Move the pointer to cell I3, the beginning of the bin range.

9. Type the . key, the END key, and the down arrow key to expand the pointer to cell I6, the end of the bin range.

There is no need to specify a results column because it is determined by the bin range. Now watch as you

10. Press the ENTER key.

The frequencies instantly dart into the results column. Notice that three of the nine invoices fall in the last category of over 120. This is not a significant statistic because the database is intentionally miniscule at this point. But it is important to point out that the process of categorizing the database would be just as easy with 2000 records as it is with 9, and the proportion of old accounts would be as easy to identify. The frequency data can be more clearly seen by using the graphics capabilities of 1-2-3.

Showing Data Distribution With Graphics

Graphics can help you quickly identify a disproportionately high frequency of accounts in any particular category. In this section, we will create a bar chart based on the data in the frequency distribution table to show at a glance how the groupings compare to one another. We will also develop a pie chart to depict the proportion of each age grouping to the database as a whole.

Designing a Histogram (Bar Chart)

A *histogram* is simply a bar chart pertaining to a distribution. To obtain a histogram of the frequency distribution shown in Figure 6-6, we will designate the distribution table's results column as the range to be graphed.

To begin the histogram,

1. Type /Graph.

We will represent the distribution with a bar chart:

2. Select Type, then select Bar.

The Graph menu reappears. The horizontal axis (X-axis) of the graph will represent the graph intervals. The vertical axis (Y-axis) will measure the frequencies. Recall from Chapter 4 that 1-2-3 can graph up to six sets of data (ranges), which are named A, B, C, D, E, and F. The range of values that we want to plot is the results column, which we will assign to graph range A. To specify the A-range,

3. Select **A** from the Graph menu.

If the A-range had been used previously during the current 1-2-3 session, 1-2-3 would display the previous A-range. If not, you would specify the beginning of the range yourself.

4. Move the pointer to the first cell in the results column (cell J3).

5. Type the . key, press the END key, then the down arrow key, and finally the ENTER key to define the range.

6. Select **V** to view the graph.

What you see is a picture of the distribution table, as shown in Figure 6-7.

Adding Labels and Titles

So far, the graph is not very descriptive, but it only needs some labels and titles. You may press any key to return from the graph to the worksheet. (Using the ESC key is a good habit, because ESC works in other instances to bring you back to where you were.)

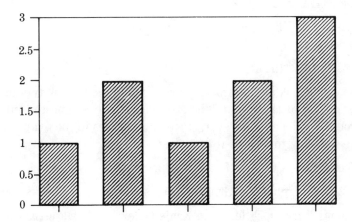

Figure 6-7. Histogram of Figure 6-6 results column

1. Press the ESC key.

Once more, the Graph menu appears.

Let us first enter labels for the horizontal axis. Each label should correspond to a value in the A-range (results range), so there should be five labels that will be made members of the X-range for the graph command. We could indicate the bin range as the X-range, because the bin range contains the intervals that went into grouping the data. However, because the Data Distribution command required using only the upper limit of each grouping to represent the bin intervals, these would not serve well as labels for a graph. The label 60 would be inadequate to represent the range 31 to 60. Therefore, let us create five labels from scratch, to be used as data labels for the X-range of the Data command.

2. Select the **Q**uit option of the Graph menu.

3. Go to cell K3.

The first label is for the interval 1 to 30. Remember that if a label begins with a number, you must precede the label with a label-prefix character, such as '.

4. Type **'1-30**, and press the ENTER key.

5. In cells K4 through K7 enter the labels **'31-60**, **'61-90**, **'91-120**, and **OVER-120** respectively.

Now specify the X-range for the graph:

6. Type /Graph **X**.

7. Move to cell K3, type the . key, and then press the END key followed by the down arrow key.

8. Press the ENTER key.

Take another look at the graph, shown in Figure 6-8, by typing **V** to select the View option of the menu. The X-labels now describe the intervals. The graph would be clearer, however, if we added titles to the graph and its axes. Press the ESC key to return to the Graph menu.

9. Select **O**ptions to specify graph options.

Now 1-2-3 will display the Graph Options menu, which looks like this:

Legend Format Titles Grid Scale Color B&W Data-Labels Quit

To enter a graph title,

10. Select the **T**itles option.

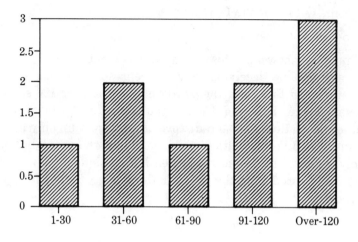

Figure 6-8. Histogram with X-axis labels added

In response, 1-2-3 will display the Graph Options Titles menu:

First Second X-Axis Y-Axis

"Distribution of Invoices" is the first line of the title for this chart.

11. Select First.

You will be asked to enter the title.

12. Type **DISTRIBUTION OF INVOICES**, and press the ENTER key.

The Graph Options menu returns. A second title line is unnecessary, but headings for the horizontal and vertical axes would enhance the graph. To enter these,

13. Select Titles again.

14. Type **X** to select the X-Axis title option.

15. Enter the label **DAYS PAST DUE**, and press the ENTER key.

16. Again, either type **T** or press the ENTER key to get back the Titles menu.

17. Type **Y** to select the Y-Axis title option.

18. Enter the heading **FREQUENCY**, and press the ENTER key.

19. Type **Q** to quit the Options menu.

20. Select **V** to view the graph.

As Figure 6-9 shows, the histogram is now complete.

A graph can be deceiving when it represents such a small number of observations. In this case, the graph makes the over-120 section of the file seem very large. This might cause you some unwarranted alarm until you examine the vertical axis and discover that it goes up only to a frequency of three invoices. Like the data distribution table, the graph becomes meaningful only when it represents a larger base of information. But again, the procedure for producing the graph is the same, whether for 9 records or for 2000 records.

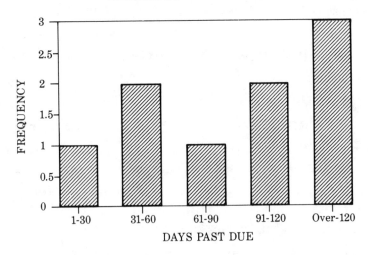

Figure 6-9. The finished histogram

The F10 (Graph) Key

Suppose Dr. DoMuch wanted us to add another 50 invoices to the database and then regenerate the graph to see how the data distribution would be affected. We would have to exit into Ready Mode, add the 50 records, reissue the Data Distribution command to update the distribution table, and then regenerate the graph.

Would we have to go through the entire Graph command again? As long as we do not turn off our machine or erase the worksheet after generating the previous histogram, we need not reenter the graph settings and options. In fact, we need not even issue a Graph command.

From within Ready Mode, you may press the F10 (Graph) key, and 1-2-3 will instantly display the last graph that it produced, which was our histogram. It doesn't matter that we changed the *contents* of the distribution table, because 1-2-3 graphs whatever it finds in the range(s) that it was told to draw. We will not enter the 50 invoices or recalculate the distribution table, but let us return to Ready Mode to see how F10 works.

1. Press the ESC key to return to the Graph menu.

2. Select the Quit option to return to Ready Mode.

3. Press the F10 (Graph) key.

Our histogram has returned. If you now press any key, you will return to Ready Mode.

4. Press the ESC key to return to Ready Mode.

One of the great advantages of the F10 (Graph) key is that it allows you to change some numbers on the worksheet and still get an updated graph at the mere touch of a key.

Using the Graph Name Command

Now that you have created a graph for this worksheet, will the graph settings and options still be there if you erase the worksheet and subsequently retrieve it from disk? Graph settings are stored with the worksheet only if you save the worksheet *after* you generate the graph. If we save the worksheet now, after generating the histogram, 1-2-3 will also store the graph and its settings with the file. We could then retrieve the file, press the F10 (Graph) key, and obtain the graph. You may wish to try this for yourself.

1. Type /File Save **INVOICE**, and press the ENTER key.

2. Now type /File Retrieve **INVOICE**, and press the ENTER key.

3. Press the F10 (Graph) key.

As promised, the graph appears on the monitor.

4. Press the ESC key to return to Ready Mode.

We will soon be developing a different graph. Unless we take special precautions, 1-2-3 will forget the previous graph, and we will not be able to retrieve it again. If you want to save multiple graphs with the worksheet, you must use the *Graph Name* command.

The Graph Name command assigns a name to the current graph (the one you developed most recently). This name consists of up to 15 characters. Assigning a name to a graph is similar to assigning a name to a range. Lotus 1-2-3 will remember the graph and its settings and will allow you to retrieve the graph by the name you assigned. Like a range name, a graph name is made permanent only if you save the worksheet after you have assigned the graph name.

The Graph Name command allows you to retrieve a named graph, assign a name to the current graph, delete a graph name, or delete all graph names. We will use Graph Name to identify our histogram.

5. Type /Graph Name to choose the Name option.

Now 1-2-3 responds with the Graph Name menu:

Use Create Delete Reset

6. Type **C** to select the Create option.

We will assign the name INVBAR to the invoice bar graph. Therefore, respond to the "Enter graph name:" prompt by typing in the name.

7. Type **INVBAR**, and press the ENTER key.

You are now returned to the main Graph menu. The next step is to test the new graph name.

8. Type **R** to enter the Reset menu.

9. Type **G** to reset all graph settings.

Choosing Graph Reset Graph has the effect of making 1-2-3 forget all graph settings. If you now choose the View option, the spreadsheet will disappear, and a blank screen will attest to the effect of this command. Press any key to get back the menu. If you now want to review the histogram, you must either reenter its settings from scratch or use the Graph Name Use command.

10. Type **N** to invoke the Name menu.

11. Type **U** to use a named graph.

In the same way that 1-2-3 displays the ranges when you issue a Range Name Create command, the control panel now exhibits the names of any graphs previously defined with the Graph Name command. Because INVBAR is the only graph named so far, you just need to

12. Press the ENTER key.

The graph now materializes with all titles and other options intact. Now

13. Press the ESC key to return the worksheet.

Generating a Pie Chart

Now that we have defined our bar chart, it is an easy matter to produce another graph that shows the same range. We will generate a pie chart whose slices represent the proportion of invoices belonging to each of the five age categories. Unlike a histogram, a pie chart is restricted in that it can portray only a single range of values, which must be range A. Ranges B through F may not be used for a pie chart.

To create a pie chart from scratch, you would have to define data range A and any other desired options. But we have already defined the A-range, titles, and labels for the INVBAR histogram (X and Y labels will not be used, because there are no axes in a pie chart). By invoking INVBAR with the Graph Name command, you made these settings active again. Lotus 1-2-3 remembers the settings for purposes of the next graph.

To convert the histogram to a pie chart, simply

1. Type **T** to choose the Type option.

2. Press **P** to specify a pie chart.

3. Enter **V** to view the graph.

The resulting pie chart, shown in Figure 6-10, is sliced to represent each interval's frequency as a fraction of the total. The pie labels (such as 1-30 for the first clockwise slice) were specified by the Data-labels option. The numbers in parentheses represent percentages corresponding to each pie slice. According to the distribution table, the 1-30 category includes 1 of the 9

DISTRIBUTION OF INVOICES

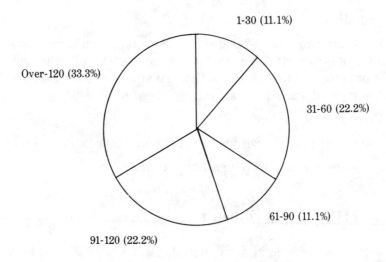

Figure 6-10. Pie chart generated from histogram settings

invoices in the invoice file, or 11.1%. Lotus 1-2-3 automatically calculates the percentage for each of the slices of a pie chart. At a glance, we can see that the OVER-120 category occupies the largest slice, 33% of the whole pie.

For a large database, a pie chart would quickly highlight those categories that might warrant further inspection. If more detail is required, the underlying distribution table is available. And if necessary, the database spreadsheet itself can be examined, without leaving the 1-2-3 environment.

Do not forget to name this graph so that if the data changes or the graph settings are altered, the pie chart will be only a few keystrokes away. If the graph is still present on the screen, you should now press any key to return to the Graph menu. Then

4. Press **N** to invoke the Name menu.

5. Press **C** to assign a new name.

6. Type the name, **INVPIE**, and press the ENTER key.

Exit from the graph environment by selecting the Quit option of the menu, and you will return to Ready Mode. If you long for another look at the last graph generated, just press the F10 (Graph) key to retrieve it.

Save Your Worksheet

Remember, graph names and their associated settings are made permanent only by resaving the worksheet after the graphs and names have been defined. From Ready Mode,

1. Type /File Save **INVOICE**, and press the ENTER key. Then type **R** to select the Replace option.

The invoice database is now saved, allowing you to invoke the INVPIE graph at a later time simply by retrieving the INVOICE file and pressing the F10 (Graph) key.

Save Your Graph Before Making A Hard Copy

Although naming a graph allows you to retrieve it for display on the monitor, the Graph Name command does not allow you to make a hard copy of the graph. Before you can produce a hard copy of a graph, you must go through a separate operation.

The Graph Save command stores the current graph in a special *graph file* that later can be used to print the graph. Graph Save is similar to the File Save command. Lotus 1-2-3 will ask you under what file name you would like to save the graph file. A graph file name, like a worksheet file name, can be up to eight characters long (letters and numbers only—no spaces or special characters).

For our purposes here, we will demonstrate the Graph Save command by making a graph file for the pie chart, INVPIE, which is the current graph.

1. Type /Graph Name Use **INVPIE** to make the pie chart current.

2. Press the ESC key to get back to the Graph menu.

3. Select the Save option.

4. Type **INVPIE** as the file name, and press the ENTER key.

Notice that you can use a graph name as your file name, if you choose.

Only after you have saved the graph file can you make a hard copy of it. To make the hard copy, you must first exit the worksheet environment (type /Quit Yes) to get into the Lotus Access System. Then you must select Print-Graph (GRAPH for Version 1.0). You will be asked to replace the system diskette with the PrintGraph diskette.

Each graphics device (printer or plotter) has its own special setup options, and you must configure your PrintGraph diskette to let 1-2-3 know how you plan to print graphs. For instance, you may use the IBM printer to print your worksheets but use a pen-plotter device to produce hard copy for graphs; or you may use the Graphic Matrix printer for both. Or you may use a different type of printer or plotter. Remember that not all printers can be used to print 1-2-3 graphs. Consult your 1-2-3 User's Manual to find out which graphics devices are supported.

Because so many different options are available, we will not attempt to provide printing instructions here. Once you have named your graph and saved both it and the worksheet, you should refer to your 1-2-3 User's Manual and follow the instructions it provides for using the particular type of graphics device you have.

We have now completed the initial phase of Dr. DoMuch's invoice application. Sorting is only one of the database functions that 1-2-3 can execute, and the frequency distribution is only one of 1-2-3's statistical capabilities. In the following chapter we continue with the invoice example in order to illustrate the querying features of the Data command.

Chapter 7
The Data Query Command

Within the universe of Data commands, Query occupies a galaxy unto itself. The *Data Query command* lets you locate specific records, extract portions of the database, delete parts of the file, and compile a list that omits duplicate entries. The scope of each of these procedures depends upon *selection criteria*, user-defined rules that dictate which records will be subjected to the query and which will be excluded.

In this chapter, we extend the invoice tracking example of Chapter 6 to encompass the Data Query command. The *Find option* of Data Query will permit us to locate invoices according to the selection criteria that we will define. We also will use the *Extract option* to copy selected records and fields from the database to a different section of the worksheet, and the *Delete option* to remove records.

Although this is the database section of this book, we can never quite divorce ourselves from the spreadsheet. Many of the commands that we used in the worksheet section are well suited to database management. We will discuss how to apply some familiar commands to manipulate a database, and we also will introduce a new worksheet command, *Move*, which transfers a range of cells from one location of the worksheet to another.

To begin this exercise, you will need the INVOICE model developed in Chapter 6. If it is not yet on your screen,

1. Type /File Retrieve **INVOICE**, and press the ENTER key.

(If you do not have a copy of the model, you can produce it by following the numbered steps in Chapter 6.)

If the CAPS indicator does not appear on the bottom right of your screen, press the CAPS LOCK key.

Now let us see how much 1-2-3 can do for Dr. DoMuch.

Using the Query Find Command

Locating a particular record in a file can be a formidable, tedious, time-consuming task if the database is a large one—especially if the database is not arranged in any particular order. Imagine trying to find a catalog card in a public library where the card file is not sorted in any manner. Or suppose our own Dr. DoMuch needs to obtain a particular patient's bill from a file containing 1500 invoices that are arranged chronologically in order of the patient's appearance at the doctor's office. The Find command addresses these needs.

To find one or several records, 1-2-3 requires two items of information: where it should look, and what it should look for. The first item is the input range, which is the portion of the worksheet that makes up the database. The second item needed is the criterion, the rule that defines which records are searched for.

The Input Range

The *input range* is a rectangle of cells composed of two sections. The first section, the top row of the input range, consists of *field names*. These are the headings above the columns of data that make up the database. In the invoice database, shown in Figure 7-1, the field names are located in row 7 of the worksheet.

For purposes of the Query input range, only one row may contain field names. This is why the last field in the invoice input range is DUE, rather than DAYS PAST DUE. When we get to defining the input range, only row 7 (cells A7 through G7) will contain field names.

All of the records (rows) beneath the field-names row form the remainder of the input range. These are the records that will be searched according to the selection criterion discussed in the next section. The last record in the database occupies row 16. We therefore designate the input range as A7...G16. Within this range, rows 8 through 16 contain the records that will be searched.

There is a difference between the file you retrieved and the one that appears in Figure 7-1. Your file includes a row of underscores in row 8.

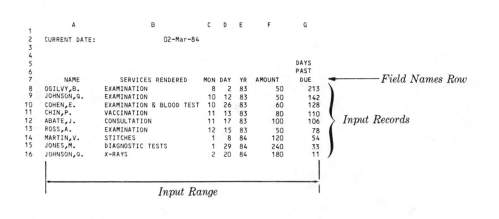

Figure 7-1. Invoice database showing Query input range

Because 1-2-3 considers the row beneath the field names to be the first record of the database, it is inconvenient, and occasionally problematic, to have a row between the field names and the first actual record. Therefore, we will delete the row of underscores, using the Worksheet Delete Row command.

1. Press the F5 (GoTo) key to move the pointer to cell A8.

2. Type /**W**orksheet **D**elete **R**ow, and press the ENTER key.

Now your worksheet should be identical to Figure 7-1.

Using the Criterion Range With a Label Match

Like the input range, the *criterion range* is a block of cells. It consists of a row of field names just above the cells that contain selection criteria for the Query command. The simplest kind of criterion is the match of a label or value with a field in the database, and we will begin by using the Query command with a label criterion. (We will soon look at two other kinds of criteria, the number match and the formula criterion. We will use several other types of criterion matches later in this chapter.)

An example of a label match is the selection of the record containing the label CHIN,P. in its NAME field. The top cell in the criterion range, as shown in Figure 7-2, would contain the field name NAME. The next cell

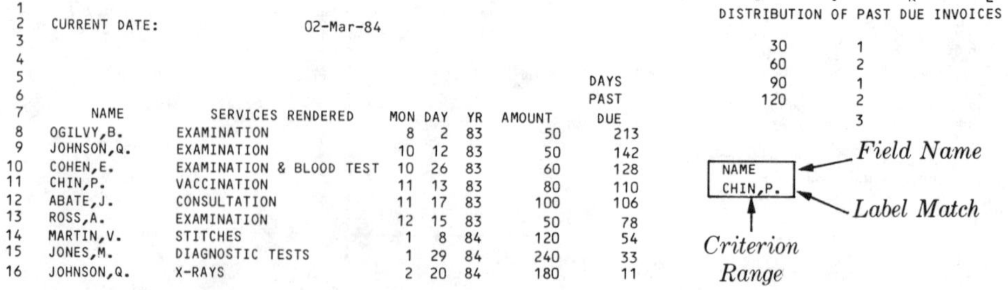

Figure 7-2. Invoice database showing criterion range

below would contain the label CHIN,P. When we give 1-2-3 the go-ahead, it will interpret this criterion range as a directive: "Search the input range for the first record that contains CHIN,P. in its NAME field."

The criterion range may be situated in any unused portion of the worksheet. We will place it on the right side of the worksheet.

1. Go to cell I10.

The field name must be spelled exactly as it appears in the input range, because 1-2-3 uses this label to identify the field in the input range to which it should apply the selection criterion.

2. Type **NAME**, and then press the ENTER key to enter the field name of the criterion.

The criterion itself, CHIN,P., must be entered *exactly* as it was entered in the database—no spaces before, within, or after the name. Capital and lowercase letters in the criterion and input entries also must coincide exactly. The slightest deviation from the database entry will prevent 1-2-3 from matching the database record with the criterion. For this reason, instead of inviting a typing error by typing CHIN,P. into the criterion cell, it is a good habit to copy the label from its location in the input range to the criterion cell.

3. Press the F5 (GoTo) key to move the pointer to A11, the cell containing the label CHIN,P.

4. Type /Copy, and press the ENTER key; then move the pointer to cell I11, and press the ENTER key.

Defining the Input and Criterion Ranges

Although we now have the *contents* of the input range and criterion range on the worksheet, we have not yet informed 1-2-3 where these ranges reside. To do this, we must enter the Query menu.

1. Type /Data Query to enter the Query environment.

The Query menu looks like this:

Input Criterion Output Find Extract Unique Delete Reset Quit

To execute any of the selection options (Find, Extract, Unique, or Delete), you must first specify at least the input range and the selection criterion. Enter the input range according to the following steps:

2. Select the Input option.

The control panel displays "Enter Input Range:", and 1-2-3 guesses that the range begins at the pointer's location when you issued the Data command. We have seen that 1-2-3 makes many assumptions in an effort to be helpful, and here is another example. Lotus 1-2-3 assumes that most people will go to the area of the worksheet on which they want to work before they begin the Data command. Because we are not at the beginning of the input range, we must show 1-2-3 where we want the input range to be.

3. Move the pointer to cell A7, the beginning of the row of field names.

4. Type the . key to anchor the range.

5. Move the pointer to the end of the last record of the database, cell G16.

6. Press the ENTER key.

With the input range identified, 1-2-3 returns to the Query menu. We may now designate the criterion range.

7. Select Criterion.

You are prompted to "Enter Criterion range:".

8. Move the pointer to cell I10, the beginning of the criterion range.

9. Type the . key to anchor the range.

10. Move the pointer to cell I11, the end of the range.

11. Press the ENTER key.

The Query menu reappears. With the input and criterion ranges identified, 1-2-3 now has the information it needs to execute the Find command.

12. Select the Find option of the menu.

It takes only a moment for 1-2-3 to locate the matching record. The speed with which 1-2-3 executes its Data commands is as fast as, if not faster than, that of the best database management systems on the market.

When 1-2-3 finds the matching record, it highlights the portion of the record that lies within the input range. When you are finished examining the record that has been located, you can bring back the Query menu by pressing any key. For consistency, we will press the ESC key:

13. Press the ESC key.

Repeating Find: the F7 (Query) Key

At this point, you may want to locate another name in the file. This would involve changing the contents of the criterion cell (I11) and then repeating the Data Query Find command. But to make an entry into cell I11, we must exit from the Data Query menu into Ready Mode by selecting Quit.

1. Select the **Q**uit option of the Query menu.

Let us find the invoice for JONES,M. To create the label-match criterion, we will copy the label in cell A15 to the criterion cell (I11).

2. Press the F5 (GoTo) key to go to cell A15.

3. Type /Copy, and press the ENTER key. Then move to cell I11, and press the ENTER key to replace the original label criterion with the new one, JONES,M.

Here 1-2-3 makes another assumption, an astute one. It assumes that you might want to repeat a Data Query command using the same locations for the input and criterion ranges, but using different contents within these ranges. Therefore, once an input and criterion range have been defined, 1-2-3 commits their locations to memory. There is no need to respecify the input range and criterion range once they have been defined, unless you want to change their addresses.

From Ready Mode, you may repeat the Find command the long way, by typing /**D**ata **Q**uery **F**ind ENTER. Better yet, 1-2-3 allows you to reissue the last Data Query you executed by simply pressing one key, the F7 (Query) key. Pressing F7 (Query) in Ready Mode right now would locate the record in the current input range that matches the current criterion range.

4. Press the F7 (Query) key to find the JONES invoice.

Pressing any key after a Find procedure gets you back to where you came from. If you execute the Find command using the F7 (Query) key from Ready Mode, then you will return to Ready Mode. If you execute Find from the Data Query menu, you are returned to the menu.

5. Press the ESC key to return to Ready Mode.

The Find command begins its search from the top of the database and continues down until it finds the first matching record. But what if there were more than one matching record and you wanted to see all of them? Specifically, if you were interested in reviewing all of Q. Johnson's records, how could you use Find to highlight both of Johnson's invoices? Try it:

6. Copy the label JOHNSON,Q. to the criterion cell by going to cell A16 and typing /Copy ENTER I11 ENTER.

7. Press the F7 (Query) key.

The expanded pointer falls upon the second record in the file, showing

Johnson's examination on 10/12/83. However, there is also a second record for this patient on the bottom of the file, in row 16. You can move the highlight to the next matching record by using the down arrow key:

8. Press the down arrow key.

The expanded pointer skips to Johnson's x-ray invoice. Pressing the down arrow key again produces a beep because there are no more matches in the file. However, pressing the up arrow key returns the highlight to the preceding match.

9. Press the ESC key to resume Ready Mode.

You have seen that a repeated Query works even if you change the contents of a criterion range. It also works if you change any part of an input range. Lotus 1-2-3 does its best to make things easier for you.

Criteria can assume many forms, simple and complex. This chapter will give you the ability to use 1-2-3 to develop whatever selection rules you need. For now, though, we will discuss only two more criterion examples, and we will then proceed to other features of the Query command.

Using Query With Number Criteria

The label match used in the preceding example has a numeric counterpart. A *number match* works in the same way as a label match, except that the field name in the criterion range must belong to a numeric field, not an alphabetic one. Thus, a search for all invoices that were created in January would involve a field name of MON and a criterion cell containing the number 1.

Again, merely putting MON and 1 into two cells of the worksheet will not create a criterion range; 1-2-3 must know where the criterion range is. If you replace the existing field name and criterion in the previously indicated criterion range, the match will work because 1-2-3 remembers the previous criterion range. Alternatively, you may choose to place the new criterion range in a different location on the worksheet. If so, you must redefine the criterion range of the Query command. We will use the former method.

1. Copy the label MON (located in cell C7) to the field-name portion of the criterion range (I10) by typing the following keystrokes: /Copy C7 ENTER I10 ENTER.

2. Go to cell I11, and enter the value 1 (be sure to press the ENTER key after entering the value).

3. Press the F7 (Query) key.

The pointer shifts to the MARTIN,V. invoice, the first invoice appearing for January. To locate the next January invoice, press the down arrow key. When you are done,

4. Press the ESC key to resume Ready Mode.

Remember: For a criterion to be effective, the first cell beneath the field name must refer to an entry belonging to the corresponding field in the input range. For a match to occur, the actual contents of the criterion cell must also be contained in at least one cell in the associated database field.

About Formula Criteria

There is a third species of criterion, and it differs in some respects from its label and number counterparts. The *formula criterion* is a conditional test that is applied to each record. For example, the criterion might be to select records that have a DAYS PAST DUE value greater than 90 days. Each record in the input range is evaluated for this condition. The result for each record is either *true* or *false*. An invoice that is 128 days past due is true, and it is selected for the Query. A 10-day-old invoice is excluded because it is false.

True and False Conditions

Lotus 1-2-3 has a convention for coding true and false conditions numerically. False is equivalent to 0, and true is equivalent to 1. To see how this works,

1. Position the pointer at cell H1, an unused cell.

2. Enter the statement **1=5**, and press the ENTER key.

This statement 1=5 may look strange, but it is a logical formula that asks the question, "Does 1=5?" The answer to this question is no, so the resulting value displayed in the cell is 0. Now replace the formula with the condition 5=5.

3. Type **5=5**, and press the ENTER key.

This formula yields the value 1 because it is true.

A cell containing a logical formula represents an answer to a question. Does 1=5? Does 5=5? Is cell C5 greater than 50 and less than 100? The answer or result displayed in the cell is either 1 (true) or 0 (false).

4. Erase the contents of cell H1 by typing **/ R**ange Erase and pressing the ENTER key.

You have just been introduced to one type of logical formula: the formula that uses = as a logical operator. In addition to testing the = condition, 1-2-3 uses other logical operators to test other conditions. Table 7-1 defines most of the logical operators used by 1-2-3. We will be referring to these occasionally through the remainder of this book.

The @MAX Function

Suppose you would like to select the invoice that is longest overdue. The DUE field, located in column G, contains the number of days that each invoice is overdue. The condition that we would like to apply to each and every record is whether the DUE field of the particular record is the maximum of the DUE fields of all records in the database.

The DUE column, in addition to being a field, is also a range of cells. To find the maximum of a range of cells in a worksheet, you can use a worksheet function called *@MAX*. The @MAX function is the opposite of the @MIN function, which we used in Chapter 5 to find the minimum of a group of values. The structure of the function is @MAX(*list*), where *list* can be a single cell, a range of cells, or a list of cells, ranges, or numbers separated by commas. @MAX(*list*) results in the maximum value of *list*.

In our case, the desired *list* is the range containing the DUE field, which currently extends from cells G8 to G16. Therefore, the record representing

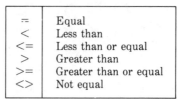

=	Equal
<	Less than
<=	Less than or equal
>	Greater than
>=	Greater than or equal
<>	Not equal

Table 7-1. Logical operators used in formulas

the most overdue invoice has a DUE field equal to @MAX(G8..G16). This is the condition that 1-2-3 must apply to each record. Thus, for the first record, the condition is G8=@MAX(G8..G16). If the condition is true for cell G8, we have found our maximum. Otherwise, 1-2-3 must proceed to the next record to see whether its DUE field, G9, equals @MAX(G8..G16).

Using @MAX in a Formula Criterion

To apply a formula criterion to the entire input range, compose the formula as if it applied strictly to the first data record, the second row of the input range. Lotus 1-2-3 recognizes a formula criterion when it sees one, and it knows to apply the formula to the other records as well as the first. In our example, the formula we should enter into the criterion range is G8=@MAX ($G$8.$G$16).

Why do we put the $ signs in the cell references to the right of the equation? Because 1-2-3 applies formula criteria to records in a way that is similar to its method of processing a Copy command. If you copied the formula to the next row (row 9), then any cell references that did not contain $ signs would be changed in a relative way. If the formula for the first record were entered as G8=@MAX (G8..G16), without $ signs, then the formula applied to the next record would be G9=@MAX(G9..G17). The left side of the formula is correct for the record in row 9, but the range referenced in the @MAX function has been changed, whereas we want it to remain unchanged. In other words, we want the @MAX range to be absolute, whereas the DUE field should be left relative (it *should* change with each successive record).

What field name is required for this criterion range? You might assume that you must use the label DUE because the formula refers to cells in the DUE field. However, unlike other criteria, the field name is only a formality in using formula criteria. The criterion need not have a direct relationship with the field name, so you can use any valid field name that appears in the input range. Therefore, in this example we retained the previous field name of MON, although the condition itself has no direct connection with the month column.

1. Go to I11, the criterion cell.

2. Type **+G8=@MAX(** to begin the formula.

3. Move to the first cell of DAYS PAST DUE, cell G8.

4. Press the F4 (Abs) key to make the range references absolute.

5. Type the . key, then press the END key and the down arrow key to move to the end of the DAYS PAST DUE column (cell G16).

6. Type the) key, and press ENTER.

The result refers to the first record, so the criterion cell displays 1, indicating that the condition is true for OGILVY. To find the record, simply

7. Press the F7 (Query) key.

The expanded pointer highlights the OGILVY record, which has the maximum DAYS PAST DUE of 213 (see Figure 7-3). To find the minimum DAYS PAST DUE,

8. Press ESC to get to Ready Mode.

9. With the pointer at cell I11, press the F2 (Edit) key, change @MAX to @MIN, and press the ENTER key.

10. Now press the F7 (Query) key.

The most recent invoice belongs to JOHNSON,Q.

11. Press ESC to return to Ready Mode.

Thus far we have discussed three types of criteria. These three can be mixed and matched to design more complicated selection rules, as we will see later. But first, let us examine another feature of Data Query, the Extract command.

	A	B	C	D	E	F	G	H	I	J	K	L
1									DISTRIBUTION OF PAST DUE INVOICES			
2	CURRENT DATE:		02-Mar-84									
3									30	1		
4									60	2		
5							DAYS		90	1		
6							PAST		120	2		
7	NAME	SERVICES RENDERED	MON	DAY	YR	AMOUNT	DUE				3	
8	OGILVY,B.	EXAMINATION	8	2	83	50	213					
9	JOHNSON,Q.	EXAMINATION	10	12	83	50	142					
10	COHEN,E.	EXAMINATION & BLOOD TEST	10	26	83	60	128		MON			
11	CHIN,P.	VACCINATION	11	13	83	80	110		1			
12	ABATE,J.	CONSULTATION	11	17	83	100	106					
13	ROSS,A.	EXAMINATION	12	15	83	50	78					
14	MARTIN,V.	STITCHES	1	8	84	120	54					
15	JONES,M.	DIAGNOSTIC TESTS	1	29	84	240	33					
16	JOHNSON,Q.	X-RAYS	2	20	84	180	11					

$+G8 = @MAX(\$G\$8.\$G\$16)$

Figure 7-3. Formula criterion match showing underlying formula

Using the Extract Command

The Find command merely locates a record for your viewing pleasure. You cannot alter the contents of the selected record. The Extract command, however, allows you not only to find selected records, but also to copy them into another section of the worksheet. Once copied, they may be altered, printed, graphed, or manipulated in the same way as the rest of the worksheet.

As with the Find command, you must define an input range and a criterion range before 1-2-3 can perform an Extract command. But 1-2-3 also needs more information to execute Extract: it must be told where to place the copy of the desired record(s). And because you have the option of duplicating only particular fields of the selected records, you must specify which fields should be copied into the output section. This is accomplished by designating an *output range*.

Defining the Output Range

The output range has the same two components as the input and criterion ranges. The first row of the output range contains the field names of the columns that will be copied for the selected records. You need not include all of the field names in the output range—only those you want copied. Also, the output range's field names need not be in the same order as they appear in the input range. But whatever field names you use, they must be spelled and entered exactly as they appear in the input range. As was true with designating criterion field names, the surest way of duplicating field names accurately is to use the Copy command.

The second component of the output range is a block of rows beneath the field names to contain the extracted records. There must be at least as many rows in your output range as there are selected records. Otherwise, the Extract operation will not be completed.

With a large database, sometimes it is hard to know how many records you will be extracting. In this situation, there is a way to tell 1-2-3 to make the output range a "bottomless pit." If you designate only one row—the row of field names—as the output range, 1-2-3 will use up as much space as it needs to put the extracted records into the output range.

You should be careful in using this "bottomless pit" method. If there are entries below the output range's field names before the Extract command is issued, these entries will be erased, even if the extracted records do not extend to the row in which these entries are stored. Therefore, you should always make sure that no important entries are stored in the columns below the output-range field names.

Suppose you want to extract the January invoices from the database. The input range has already been entered for the Find command. Both Find and Extract are options of the Query command, so the same input range is used for both, and 1-2-3 remembers it from the last use of Query. Similarly, there is no need to reiterate the location of the criterion range. However, we will have to change the contents of the criterion cell, I11.

1. With the pointer at cell I11, type the number **1** and press the ENTER key to select January invoices.

Now for the output range. We will place the output range in an unused sector below the database, beginning in row 30. We will also copy all of the fields for each record. This means that the top of the output range will be an exact duplicate of the first row of the input range. Before we designate the coordinates of the output range, we will create its row of field names. We could type them in, but the Copy command ensures that our duplicate is exact.

2. Move to the first field name of the input range, cell A7.

3. Type /Copy, press the END key, and then press the right arrow key to expand the pointer to the last field name, DUE.

4. Press the ENTER key, move to cell A30 (the beginning of the target range), and press the ENTER key to complete the command.

Using Range Name
For the Output Range

Several blank rows have been left between the input range and the output range, as Figure 7-4 shows. These blank rows allow for additions to the invoice file. Eventually, though, more room will be needed to expand the database, and the output range will have to be moved down. In anticipation of this problem, it will be convenient (though it is not required) to assign a name to the output range, using the Range Name command.

1. Move the pointer to cell A30.

2. Type /Range Name Create.

In response to the "Enter name" prompt,

3. Type **OUTRECS** ENTER.

```
              A                 B          C    D    E      F         G       H     I         J         K         L
                                                                                       DISTRIBUTION OF PAST DUE INVOICES
 1
 2   CURRENT DATE:             02-Mar-84                                                          30        1
 3                                                                                                60        2
 4                                                                                      DAYS      90        1
 5                                                                                      PAST     120        2
 6
 7     NAME            SERVICES RENDERED   MON  DAY  YR   AMOUNT      DUE                           3
 8   OGILVY,B.         EXAMINATION          8    2   83      50      213
 9   JOHNSON,Q.        EXAMINATION         10   12   83      50      142
10   COHEN,E.          EXAMINATION & BLOOD TEST  10  26  83  60      128               MON
11   CHIN,P.           VACCINATION         11   13   83      80      110                 1
12   ABATE,J.          CONSULTATION        11   17   83     100      106
13   ROSS,A.           EXAMINATION         12   15   83      50       78
14   MARTIN,V.         STITCHES             1    8   84     120       54
15   JONES,M.          DIAGNOSTIC TESTS     1   29   84     240       33
16   JOHNSON,Q.        X-RAYS               2   20   84     180       11
17
18
19
20
21
22
23
24
25
26
27
28
29
30     NAME            SERVICES RENDERED   MON  DAY  YR  AMOUNT      DUE
```

Figure 7-4. A one-row "bottomless" output range

You are now asked to enter the range coordinates, and 1-2-3 recommends A30..A30. Because we will use the "bottomless" output range, we will be specifying the range of cells containing the field names as our output range. To include the field names in the range named OUTRECS,

4. Press the END key, then the right arrow key to expand the pointer to the last field name of the output range (cell G30).

5. Press the ENTER key.

The output area has been set up, but 1-2-3 will not know where the output range is until we issue a Data Query Output command.

6. Type /Data Query Output.

Lotus 1-2-3 recommends cell A30, the current position of the pointer, as the output range. Instead of entering the endpoints, however, we can override the recommendation and use the range name, OUTRECS.

7. Enter **OUTRECS**, and press the ENTER key.

Now the Query menu reappears.

8. Type **Q** to exit.

Viewing Extracted Data
With a Window

In Chapter 4, we created a split-screen effect using 1-2-3's ability to make windows. A split screen will now allow us to watch the input range and the output range simultaneously as we issue the Extract command.

1. Press the HOME key.

2. Press the F5 (GoTo) key to move the pointer to cell A11, the location where we want the windows to be divided.

3. Type /Worksheet Window Horizontal.

To allow the two windows to be scrolled independently,

4. Type /Worksheet Window Unsynchronized.

The pointer is located in the top window, but we want to move it to the bottom window so that we can bring the output range into view.

5. Press the F6 (Window) key to shift the pointer to the bottom window.

To display the output range in the bottom window,

6. Press the F5 (GoTo) key, type **OUTRECS**, and press the ENTER key.

Notice that when you press F5 to go to a range that consists of several cells, the pointer moves to the first cell in the range.

When the Extract command is executed, the bottom window will receive the January invoices.

7. Type /Data Query Extract.

In the blink of an eye, the MARTIN and JONES invoices have been copied to the output range. Figure 7-5 shows how the entire worksheet would look if you could view it all at once, without using windows. The extracted records have not been deleted from the database, only replicated. This procedure is a convenient way to report a given month's credit activity for Dr. DoMuch's practice or for any other business that tracks billing in a similar manner.

8. Choose the **Q**uit option to resume Ready Mode.

Obtaining a November report is a cinch. Just change I11, the criterion cell, from 1 to 11, and press the F7 (Query) key. With 1-2-3, unlike dentistry, extracting is not as hard as pulling teeth.

```
                A                  B           C   D   E     F       G    H      I      J      K       L
 1                                                                             DISTRIBUTION OF PAST DUE INVOICES
 2   CURRENT DATE:            02-Mar-84                                          30      1
 3                                                                               60      2
 4                                                                               90      1
 5                                                             DAYS             120      2
 6                                                             PAST                      3
 7     NAME             SERVICES RENDERED    MON DAY  YR  AMOUNT     DUE
 8   OGILVY,B.        EXAMINATION              8   2  83      50     213
 9   JOHNSON,Q.       EXAMINATION             10  12  83      50     142
10   COHEN,E.         EXAMINATION & BLOOD TEST 10 26  83      60     128        MON
11   CHIN,P.          VACCINATION             11  13  83      80     110         1  ←——— Number
12   ABATE,J.         CONSULTATION            11  17  83     100     106                  Criterion
13   ROSS,A.          EXAMINATION             12  15  83      50      78                  Cell
14   MARTIN,V.        STITCHES                 1   8  84     120      54
15   JONES,M.         DIAGNOSTIC TESTS         1  29  84     240      33
16   JOHNSON,Q.       X-RAYS                   2  20  84     180      11
17
18
19
20
21
22
23
24
25
26
27
28
29
30     NAME             SERVICES RENDERED    MON DAY  YR  AMOUNT     DUE
31   MARTIN,V.        STITCHES                 1   8  84     120      54  ←——— Output Records
32   JONES,M.         DIAGNOSTIC TESTS         1  29  84     240      33
```

Figure 7-5. Query Extract selects records with 1 in MON column

More Criteria

There is much more to selection criteria than the simple label-match, number-match, and formula criteria that we have used thus far. In the next few pages, we will extend our use of match criteria to include the blank criterion, which selects *all* records, and to include special label-match characters that greatly increase the flexibility of label-match criteria. Then we will see how to make selection criteria even more powerful and discriminating, using multiple criteria.

The Blank Criterion

Sometimes you may need to copy some, but not necessarily all, of the fields of the input range to another part of the worksheet. The *blank criterion* is a special criterion that selects all of the records of the database. It is as if there were no special requirements for selection at all.

At first thought, it would seem that a Data Query Extract using a blank criterion range has no advantage over a simple Worksheet Copy command. However, you can use the blank criterion to copy only select fields of the input range—a procedure that would require multiple Copy commands. By specifying only the names of fields that you want in the output range, in any order you desire, you have greater control and flexibility using Extract than you do using Copy.

For example, to obtain only the NAME, AMOUNT, and DAYS PAST DUE columns for the entire file, you could define an output range consisting of only the three columns desired and then perform a single extraction. The alternative of using the Copy command would require two separate steps: copying the NAME column and then copying the block containing the AMOUNT and DAYS PAST DUE columns.

We will not revise the field headings of our output range right now, because we will be needing them as they are. But to illustrate the effect of a blank criterion, let us erase the criterion in cell I11 and see what happens when we reissue Data Query Extract by pressing the F7 (Query) key. We will use the existing field name, MON, in the first cell of the criterion range. Erasing the cell beneath the field name establishes a blank criterion.

1. If the pointer is in the bottom window, move it to the top window with the F6 (Window) key.

Then

2. Move the pointer to cell I11.

3. Type / Range Erase ENTER to erase the cell.

Now watch the lower window as you

4. Press the F7 (Query) key.

Notice that 1-2-3 erases the output range before extracting the new selected records.

As Figure 7-6 shows, all nine records are duplicated. It is as if you had used the Copy command to copy the entire database. Because we designated a bottomless output range, there was no space limitation for the output records; there was enough room to store the entire input range.

Multiple Matches

So far, we have discussed only the smallest possible criterion ranges. Actually, criteria can extend down a column and across a row in order to achieve multiple conditions for selection. Extending criteria to subsequent cells

```
         A                  B              C  D  E     F       G     H   I       J       K      L
  1                                                                    DISTRIBUTION OF PAST DUE INVOICES
  2   CURRENT DATE:              02-Mar-84                                 30      1
  3                                                                        60      2
  4                                                                        90      1
  5                                                       DAYS            120      2
  6                                                       PAST                     3
  7     NAME          SERVICES RENDERED   MON DAY  YR  AMOUNT  DUE
  8   OGILVY,B.     EXAMINATION             8   2  83     50   213
  9   JOHNSON,Q.    EXAMINATION            10  12  83     50   142
 10   COHEN,E.      EXAMINATION & BLOOD TEST 10 26 83     60   128          MON
 11   CHIN,P.       VACCINATION            11  13  83     80   110                     ←——— Blank
 12   ABATE,J.      CONSULTATION           11  17  83    100   106                          Criterion
 13   ROSS,A.       EXAMINATION            12  15  83     50    78                          Cell
 14   MARTIN,V.     STITCHES                1   8  84    120    54
 15   JONES,M.      DIAGNOSTIC TESTS        1  29  84    240    33
 16   JOHNSON,Q.    X-RAYS                  2  20  84    180    11
 17
 18
 19
 20
 21
 22
 23
 24
 25
 26
 27
 28
 29
 30     NAME          SERVICES RENDERED   MON DAY  YR  AMOUNT  DUE
 31   OGILVY,B.     EXAMINATION             8   2  83     50   213   ⎫
 32   JOHNSON,Q.    EXAMINATION            10  12  83     50   142   ⎪
 33   COHEN,E.      EXAMINATION & BLOOD TEST 10 26 83     60   128   ⎪
 34   CHIN,P.       VACCINATION            11  13  83     80   110   ⎬  Output Records
 35   ABATE,J.      CONSULTATION           11  17  83    100   106   ⎪
 36   ROSS,A.       EXAMINATION            12  15  83     50    78   ⎪
 37   MARTIN,V.     STITCHES                1   8  84    120    54   ⎪
 38   JONES,M.      DIAGNOSTIC TESTS        1  29  84    240    33   ⎪
 39   JOHNSON,Q.    X-RAYS                  2  20  84    180    11   ⎭
```

Figure 7-6. Blank criterion extract selects all records

within the column instructs 1-2-3 to select records that match any of the cells in the column. Thus, if Dr. DoMuch wanted to extract the invoices of ROSS,A. and JONES,M., the criterion range in cells I10 through I12 would consist of

NAME	(*field name*)
ROSS,A.	(*first match*)
JONES,M.	(*second match*)

The matching criteria must be in contiguous cells, one after the other in the same column.

   1. Go to cell I10, and change the criterion range on the worksheet to select **ROSS,A.** and **JONES,M.**, as we have just illustrated.

These criteria should now extend from I10 to I12.

2. Press the F7 (Query) key to extract the records.

If you followed that instruction precisely, you will have only one record in the output range, ROSS,A. What happened to the second match? There must be a mistake in the criterion range.

3. Move to cell I10, and check for typing errors in the names.

4. Type /Data Query Criterion to tell 1-2-3 to highlight what it considers to be the criterion range.

We forgot to inform 1-2-3 about our intention to extend the criterion range downward one more cell. There is a blinking dash at the bottom of the range, which means that pressing the down arrow key will extend the highlighted range downward.

5. Press the down arrow key once, and then press ENTER to lock in the new criterion range.

6. Select the Extract option.

The two records will appear in the lower window. Figure 7-7 illustrates their placement on the worksheet.

```
          A               B            C   D   E    F        G      H      I          J      K       L
 1                                                                       DISTRIBUTION OF PAST DUE INVOICES
 2   CURRENT DATE:              02-Mar-84
 3                                                                          30       1
 4                                                                          60       2
 5                                                            DAYS          90       1
 6                                                            PAST         120       2
 7      NAME           SERVICES RENDERED   MON DAY  YR  AMOUNT  DUE                   3
 8   OGILVY,B.        EXAMINATION           8    2  83     50    213
 9   JOHNSON,Q.       EXAMINATION          10   12  83     50    142
10   COHEN,E.         EXAMINATION & BLOOD TEST 10 26 83    60    128       NAME
11   CHIN,P.          VACCINATION          11   13  83     80    110       ROSS,A.  ◄──────── Multiple
12   ABATE,J.         CONSULTATION         11   17  83    100    106       JONES,M. ◄──────── Criterion
13   ROSS,A.          EXAMINATION          12   15  83     50     78                           Cells
14   MARTIN,V.        STITCHES              1    8  84    120     54
15   JONES,M.         DIAGNOSTIC TESTS      1   29  84    240     33
16   JOHNSON,Q.       X-RAYS                2   20  84    180     11
17
18
19
20
21
22
23
24
25
26
27
28
29
30      NAME           SERVICES RENDERED   MON DAY  YR  AMOUNT  DUE
31   ROSS,A.          EXAMINATION          12   15  83     50     78   ◄──────────── Output Records
32   JONES,M.         DIAGNOSTIC TESTS      1   29  84    240     33
```

Figure 7-7. Results of multiple label match

7. Select the **Q**uit option to exit from the Data Query menu and return to Ready Mode.

Most often, the problems that occur with the Query command are due to errors in the input, criterion, and output ranges.

The * Label-Match Character

The precision that 1-2-3 requires for entering label criteria can be rather tedious. A desired match can be spoiled not only by a misspelling, but also by an unintentional blank or even by a difference between uppercase and lowercase letters. The longer the label, the greater the risk of error.

Fortunately, 1-2-3 relaxes this restriction by providing some special characters for use in label matches. The asterisk, *, when placed at the end of some characters in a label criterion, instructs 1-2-3 to search for any records that begin with the characters preceding the *. For example, to retrieve the JOHNSON,Q. records, it would be sufficient to use JOHN* as the criterion because only the two Johnson records begin with the four letters JOHN. Only the letters before the * are compared to the database records.

Be careful not to insert any blanks between the * and the characters preceding it (unless you wish to require a space there). Also, be sure to include enough characters to distinguish the particular record you want. JO* instead of JOHN* retrieves not only JOHNSON,Q., but also JONES,M.

As long as you use it carefully, the * feature is a distinct advantage. Suppose you want every invoice that begins with the letter C. Without the * feature, you would have to create a criterion column containing each and every name beginning with C, spelled fully and flawlessly. If the database were large, it could be a substantial and error-prone job. But with the * feature, all you have to do is the following:

1. Erase cells I11 and I12 by typing **/Range Erase I11.I12** ENTER.

2. In cell I11, type **C***.

3. Use **/Data Query Criterion** to set the criterion range to I10..I11, and press the ENTER key to lock in the new range.

4. Type **E** to extract the records.

5. Select **Q**uit.

The COHEN,E. and CHIN,P. records have been selected and copied to the output range.

Other special characters are described in the Lotus User's Manual under the Label-Match Criteria section of the Data Query command.

AND and OR Criteria

It is not always enough to apply a single condition to a Data Query operation. ometimes you need to be more exclusive by selecting records that meet not one but several conditions. Lotus 1-2-3 allows you to establish multiple criteria for selecting such records from the input range.

One type of multiple criteria occurs when a record must meet two or more criteria *simultaneously* in order to be selected. For example, if you wanted to select only those invoices pertaining to medical examinations that were conducted in 1983, you would need two criteria. The first test is whether the SERVICES RENDERED field contains the word EXAMINATION. The second test is whether the YR field contains the value 83. A record should be selected only if *both* conditions are simultaneously fulfilled: SERVICES RENDERED contains EXAMINATION, and YR equals 83. Such a set of simultaneous criteria is called an *AND condition*.

Another type of multiple criteria occurs when a record must meet any one of several conditions. Suppose you wanted to choose invoices having an AMOUNT exceeding $99 *or* a DAYS PAST DUE greater than or equal to 90 days. This is called an *OR condition*. If a record meets either one of these two conditions (but not necessarily both), it passes the test for selection. We will examine both types of conditions, AND and OR, using the two examples just cited.

AND Criteria

To create multiple criteria, we put the individual ranges next to each other in the criterion range. Lotus 1-2-3 interprets the criteria based on their arrangement within the criterion range. If the criterion formulas of the individual criterion ranges are located in the *same* row, then the conditions are related by an AND condition; they must *all* be true in order for the record to be chosen. The illustration shows the criterion range for selecting all 1983 examination invoices.

Columns

		I	J
Rows	10	SERVICES RENDERED	YR
	11	EXAM*	83

The two criterion formulas are lined up in the same row, row 11. You can think of this AND condition as an obstacle course. The course is set up with a few obstacles (conditions), and the runners (Ogilvy, Johnson, et al.) who can overcome *all* of the barriers are the ones who successfully complete the course.

An obstacle course can have only a few barriers, as in the illustration, or it may have many. You can have as few as one criterion in a multiple criterion range, or as many as 32.

In the illustration, the first column of the criterion range that we are about to enter has a field name of SERVICES RENDERED. Beneath the field name is a cell containing EXAM*, the criterion for this field. Here is an example of using the special label-match character, *. This criterion selects records containing a SERVICES RENDERED field beginning with the letters EXAM. Next to the SERVICES RENDERED field name, in the next column over, is the second criterion. It consists of the field name YR, with the number 83 as the criterion in the cell below the field name. Enter these criteria as follows:

1. Move to cell I10.

2. Type the field name **SERVICES RENDERED**. (We have not used the Copy command, so be sure to type accurately.)

3. Move down once to cell I11, and type **EXAM***.

4. Move to cell J10, and enter the second field name, **YR**.

5. Move down once to cell J11, and type **83**.

When we entered the label SERVICES RENDERED in I10, it spilled over into column J because column I is only nine characters wide. However, when we made the entry in J10, the display of SERVICES RENDERED was "interrupted" by YR. To remedy the problem, we must widen column I.

6. Move left to cell I11, and type **/Worksheet Column-Set Width**.

7. Press the right arrow key several times until the column width is sufficient to show the entire SERVICES RENDERED label in cell I10.

8. Press the ENTER key.

Now the criterion cells are set up, but we must inform 1-2-3 that the criterion range should encompass both sets of criteria.

9. Type **/Data Query Criterion**.

The previous criterion began at I10, which is still valid. Just expand the pointer to the new bottom right of the range.

10. Press the right arrow key, and press the ENTER key.

11. Select the **Extract** option, and select **Q**uit.

As Figure 7-8 shows, four records were accepted: OGILVY, JOHNSON, COHEN, and ROSS. Notice that COHEN had a blood test in addition to an examination. Because the criterion was EXAM* rather than EXAMINA-TION, a precise match was not imposed. The label EXAMINATION & BLOOD TEST begins with EXAM, so Cohen was accepted. Note that a record containing the label BLOOD TEST & EXAMINATION would *not* have been selected by this criterion because this label does not begin with EXAM.

OR Criteria

The preceding example involved an AND condition. Now let us try multiple criteria with an OR condition. Dr. DoMuch might want to attend to invoices that are either for relatively large amounts *or* significantly overdue.

	A	B	C	D	E	F	G	H	I	J	K
1									DISTRIBUTION OF PAST DUE INVOICES		
2	CURRENT DATE:	02-Mar-84									
3									30	1	
4									60	2	
5							DAYS		90	1	
6							PAST		120	2	
7	NAME	SERVICES RENDERED	MON	DAY	YR	AMOUNT	DUE			3	
8	OGILVY,B.	EXAMINATION	8	2	83	50	213				
9	JOHNSON,Q.	EXAMINATION	10	12	83	50	142				
10	COHEN,E.	EXAMINATION & BLOOD TEST	10	26	83	60	128		SERVICES RENDERED YR		
11	CHIN,P.	VACCINATION	11	13	83	80	110		EXAM*		83
12	ABATE,J.	CONSULTATION	11	17	83	100	106				
13	ROSS,A.	EXAMINATION	12	15	83	50	78				
14	MARTIN,V.	STITCHES	1	8	84	120	54				
15	JONES,M.	DIAGNOSTIC TESTS	1	29	84	240	33		*Criterion Cells*		
16	JOHNSON,Q.	X-RAYS	2	20	84	180	11				
17											
18											
19											
20											
21											
22											
23											
24											
25											
26											
27											
28											
29											
30	NAME	SERVICES RENDERED	MON	DAY	YR	AMOUNT	DUE				
31	OGILVY,B.	EXAMINATION	8	2	83	50	213				
32	JOHNSON,Q.	EXAMINATION	10	12	83	50	142		*Output Records*		
33	COHEN,E.	EXAMINATION & BLOOD TEST	10	26	83	60	128				
34	ROSS,A.	EXAMINATION	12	15	83	50	78				

Figure 7-8. Multiple criteria match, AND condition

The first applicable criterion for a record to be accepted is that the AMOUNT field must exceed a given value—say, $99. The second condition requires that the DAYS PAST DUE be at least as great as some minimum number, such as 90 days.

Neither of these criteria are simple label or number matches. They are conditional formulas, so special rules apply. Recall that a conditional formula is constructed as if it refers only to the first record of the input range. The first condition is AMOUNT>=100 (that is, AMOUNT is greater than or equal to 100). The first data record is, by definition, the second row of the input range, row 8. The AMOUNT field is in column F. Therefore, the correct criterion is +F8>=100. The DAYS PAST DUE field is in column G, so the second criterion is +G8>=90.

Where should these criteria be placed on the worksheet? Because this example involves two criteria, the criterion range will span two columns, one for each criterion. However, unlike the AND condition, an OR condition requires that the criterion cells must be in different rows of the criterion range, as follows:

Columns

	I	J
10	AMOUNT	DUE
11	+F8>=100	
12		+G8>=90

Rows { 10 11 12

The first criterion range has its conditional formula in row 11, directly beneath the field name. In order for 1-2-3 to understand that we want an OR relationship between the two criteria, the conditional formula of the second criterion range must be placed in the next row down, row 12. (If we had placed the second formula in J11 instead of J12, then 1-2-3 would infer that we want only records that satisfy *both* conditions, not those that satisfy only one or the other.)

Imagine that you are a spectator at the Criterion Derby, an obstacle raceway housing two parallel obstacle courses. The entrants in the race line up in front of Course 1 and run the race. Those who overcome all of the obstacles are winners. But because this is a dual raceway, the unsuccessful runners get a second chance. They get to run on Course 2, which has a different set of barriers. Those who complete the second course get to join those who completed the first course in the winner's circle.

As you look across the second row of the criterion range, row 11, it is as if you are looking at the first obstacle course. There is only one obstacle in this course, located in column I. Records that cannot meet the condition stored in I11 get to run the second course in the third row of the criterion range, row 12. Here, too, there is only one obstacle, in column J. Records that meet this second criterion are selected along with those that satisfy the first criterion.

In this example, only two fields are being tested in the criteria, joined by a single OR condition. However, it is possible to be more complex. A criterion range can have numerous rows, each row having a criterion entry in one or more of the columns of the criterion range. Selected records are those that satisfy all of the criteria specified across any one of the rows. (By way of analogy, winners in the Criterion Derby are those who overcome all of the barriers *in any one* of the several obstacle courses of the raceway.)

To enter the criterion range shown in the figure, erase any previous criteria from columns I and J. Now

1. Move to cell I10.

2. Type **AMOUNT**.

3. Move down once, to cell I11, and type **+F8>=100** ENTER.

4. Move up to cell J10, and type **DUE**.

5. Move to cell J12, and type **+G8>=90** ENTER.

The coordinates of the criterion range must be redefined to include the additional row.

6. Type **/Data Query Criterion**.

7. Expand the pointer to the bottom right of the new criterion range, cell J12.

8. Press the ENTER key.

Incidentally, the formulas show as 0 in I11 and 1 in J12. Remember, they are logical formulas. The first record has an AMOUNT that fails the first criterion but passes the second. Next retrieve the invoices:

9. Choose the Extract option.

When you are finished,

10. Select Quit.

As Figure 7-9 shows, eight records passed the test. The first one is

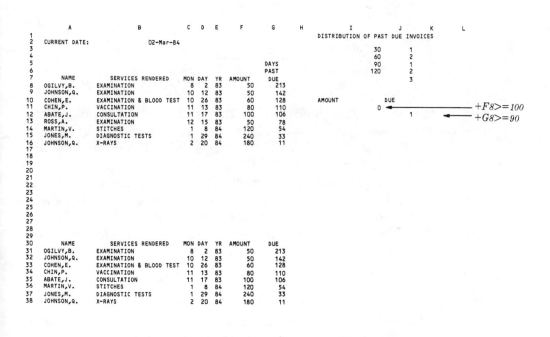

Figure 7-9. OR condition match showing underlying formulas

OGILVY, in which AMOUNT is equal to 50 (so the first criterion failed). The DAYS PAST DUE cell, however, contains 213, which does exceed 90. Look at ABATE. Both AMOUNT and DUE are greater than the minimum amounts stipulated in the criteria. JONES, who owes the most money with an amount of $240, is only 33 days overdue. Nonetheless, seeing the Jones information alerts Dr. DoMuch to the status of an invoice that represents a significant part of the future receivables.

Using Move to Convert OR to AND

We have extracted invoices that are excessive in either amount or lateness. To be even more selective, we can choose invoices that are both excessive *and* late. In other words, we will convert the OR condition to an AND condition. To accept records with both AMOUNT>=100 *and* DAYS PAST DUE>=90, the criterion range should look like this:

	I	J
10	AMOUNT	DUE
11	+F8>=100	+G8>=90

Whereas the OR condition applies when the two formulas are in separate rows, the AND condition applies whenever they are in the same row. Instead of retyping the criteria, we will use the Worksheet Move command to lift the DUE formula one cell up.

The *Move command* transfers a range of cells from one area of the worksheet to another. Lotus 1-2-3 moves a range of cells as you would slide a stack of papers from one side of your desk to another. The area where the papers originally lay is left empty. The area to which they were transferred is now occupied by the papers, and whatever used to be there has been lost. Similarly, 1-2-3 leaves the source range of the Move command empty, and it overwrites any entries that were previously in the target range.

Move is doubly convenient because it automatically adjusts formulas on the worksheet that refer to the moved cells. Even named ranges and command ranges, such as the Query input range and the Data Fill range, are automatically revised. However, you must be careful not to inadvertently move the top-left or bottom-right cells of a range. Recall that 1-2-3 uses these endpoints to map out the range, so if you move an endpoint, you have redefined the range.

1. Move the pointer to cell J12, the current location of the DUE formula.

2. Type /**Move** ENTER.

3. Move up once to cell J11, and press the ENTER key.

What happens to the criterion range coordinates?

4. Type /**Data Query Criterion**.

Notice the highlighted block. The bottom-right cell of the range was automatically shifted from row 12 to row 11, thanks to the Move command.

5. Press the ENTER key.

6. Choose the **Extract** option, and then **Quit**.

Only the ABATE record is both greater than $100 and older than 90 days. This would indicate to Dr. DoMuch that if there is one bill to try to collect, it is Abate's.

Deleting Records From a Database

The invoice file contains only unpaid invoices. Once an invoice has been paid, that invoice should be removed from the file. Because all worksheet commands may be applied to a database — after all, a database is a worksheet — the Worksheet Delete Row command will remove a row, or record, from the database.

When using the Worksheet Delete Row command in a database, however, you must be cautious. First you must move the pointer to each row that you want to eliminate. Second, you must be careful about how the deletion affects the input range of the Query command. If you delete the first or last record of the input range, you must reenter the range, because an endpoint of the range will have been removed. If there is information stored to the right of the database, you must take care not to erase it inadvertently by deleting an entire row with the Worksheet Delete Row command. Thus, although this command can be used on database worksheets, it is not without risks.

A more efficient method is the Data Query Delete command. Query Delete has the same requisites as Find, an input range and a criterion range. Based on the criterion, records are removed from the file, and the database is compacted to close the gap created by the deleted record. Naturally, all references to formulas and ranges that have been moved are adjusted.

If JONES,M. paid for services rendered on 1/29/84, then the criterion range to remove the invoice from the active file would be

	I	J	K	L
	I	J	K	L
10	NAME	MON	DAY	YR
11	JONES*	1	29	84

This criterion stipulates that records with names that begin with JONES will be removed from the file, but only if the associated MON is 1 and the DAY is 29 and the YR is 84. These are AND conditions, so the criteria are all on the same row. The reason that the date was included in the criteria is that there could be more than one invoice outstanding for Jones; the date is a reasonable way to distinguish between several bills pertaining to a single patient. To enter the criterion range,

1. Move to cell I10, the beginning of the criterion range, and enter all criteria exactly as they were just shown.

2. Type /Data **Q**uery Criterion.

3. Expand the pointer to cell L11, the bottom right of the new criterion range.

4. Press the ENTER key.

5. Choose the **D**elete option of the Query menu.

As a precaution against inadvertent deletions, 1-2-3 makes you think twice about deleting the records by prompting "Cancel Delete."

6. Choose the **D**elete option.

7. Type **Q** to quit.

8. Press the HOME key.

Check the input range. You should have only eight invoices left, as shown in Figure 7-10. JONES has paid up, the invoice has been pulled out of the file, and the record below JONES has been moved up.

The Unique Command

The invoice file has been set up to contain all outstanding invoices. If a particular patient has more than one bill outstanding, that patient will be represented by more than one record. JOHNSON,Q., for instance, has two unpaid invoices. Dr. DoMuch, however, may want a list of patient names that contains no duplicate entries. We can use the Unique command to obtain such a list.

The Unique command is similar to Extract. It requires input, criterion, and output ranges in order to work. Selected fields for selected records are copied into the output range. The criterion range should consist of the field name NAME, followed by a blank criterion cell underneath. The reason for using a blank criterion is that all records of the database should be considered as valid candidates for the list of unduplicated names. The Unique command itself will take care of weeding out duplicates, so there is no need to use any selection criteria at all.

Using Unique to Prepare
A List of Patients

Cell I10 should contain NAME, the field name of the column that the Unique command will examine for duplicates, but before we try out the Unique com-

	A	B	C	D	E	F	G	H	I	J	K	L
1												
2	CURRENT DATE:	02-Mar-84										
3												
4										DISTRIBUTION OF PAST DUE INVOICES		
5												
6							DAYS					
7	NAME	SERVICES RENDERED	MON	DAY	YR	AMOUNT	PAST DUE				INVOICES	
8	OGILVY,B.	EXAMINATION	8	2	83	50	213			30	1	
9	JOHNSON,Q.	EXAMINATION	10	12	83	50	142			60	2	
10	COHEN,E.	EXAMINATION & BLOOD TEST	10	26	83	60	128			90	1	
11	CHIN,P.	VACCINATION	11	13	83	80	110			120	3	
12	ABATE,J.	CONSULTATION	11	17	83	100	106					
13	ROSS,A.	EXAMINATION	12	15	83	50	78		NAME			
14	MARTIN,V.	STITCHES	1	8	84	120	54		JONES*	MON	DAY	YR
15	JOHNSON,Q.	X-RAYS	2	20	84	180	11			1	29	84

Figure 7-10. Query Delete removes records that match criterion range

mand we will erase the rest of the previous criterion range.

1. Type /**Range Erase J10.L11** ENTER, **and type** /Range Erase **I11** ENTER to create the blank criterion.

Before invoking the Data menu, set up the output range. For this list, only the NAME field name is required; the others are unnecessary. Therefore, erase them:

2. Go to cell B30.

3. Type /**Range Erase**.

4. Press the END key and then the right arrow key.

If there are any records in the output range, move the pointer down until the highlighted area encompasses them.

5. Press the ENTER key.

The NAME field of the output range will remain, but the other field names are erased. Now it is time to inform 1-2-3 of the new addresses of the criterion and output ranges.

6. Type /**Data Query Criterion**.

7. Shrink the criterion range to include only cells I10 and I11 by pressing the left arrow key until only those two cells are highlighted. Check the control panel to make sure that the criterion range reads I10..I11.

8. Press the ENTER key.

9. Select the **Output** option.

10. Press the F6 (Window) key to transfer the pointer to the bottom window; only the NAME field name (A30) should be highlighted.

11. Press the ENTER key.

12. Select the Unique option of the Query menu.

13. Type **Q** to quit.

Inspect the results in the output range. The names are the unique names of the file. Because JOHNSON,Q. is listed just once, only seven names are included in the output shown in Figure 7-11.

```
       A              B                    C   D   E   F       G       H    I
                                                                            DISTRIBUTION OF PAST DUE INVOICES
 1
 2   CURRENT DATE:                    02-Mar-84                                            30      1
 3                                                                                         60      2
 4                                                                               DAYS      90      1
 5                                                                               PAST     120     2
 6
 7        NAME         SERVICES RENDERED   MON DAY  YR  AMOUNT   DUE                                3
 8   OGILVY,B.         EXAMINATION          8   2   83    50     213
 9   JOHNSON,Q.        EXAMINATION         10  12   83    50     142
10   COHEN,E.          EXAMINATION & BLOOD TEST 10 26 83   60    128   NAME
11   CHIN,P.           VACCINATION         11  13   83    80     110
12   ABATE,J.          CONSULTATION        11  17   83   100     106
13   ROSS,A.           EXAMINATION         12  15   83    50      78
14   MARTIN,V.         STITCHES             1   8   84   120      54
15   JOHNSON,Q.        X-RAYS               2  20   84   180      11
16
17
18
19
20
21
22
23
24
25
26
27
28
29
30        NAME
31   OGILVY,B.
32   JOHNSON,Q.
33   COHEN,E.
34   CHIN,P.
35   ABATE,J.
36   ROSS,A.
37   MARTIN,V.
```

Figure 7-11. Output records showing listing of unique names

Clearing the Windows
And Saving the File

We are finished for now, so let us clear the windows and save the file.

1. Type **/**Worksheet Window Clear to return to a full-screen display.

2. Press the HOME key.

Save the worksheet for future use.

3. Type **/**File Save **INVOICE2** ENTER.

Using Worksheet Commands to Maintain the Database

Although the Data command performs various database management tasks, it does not represent the entire capability of 1-2-3 in this area. The worksheet commands complement the Data command in permitting you to update and maintain your database. Any worksheet command can be applied to a database as well as to a worksheet, because the database is a part of the worksheet.

Thus, if you wanted to insert a new field into the database, you could use the Worksheet Insert column command to insert the field. The other fields would be moved over to make room for the insertion, and any formula references to cells in the moved section would be automatically adjusted. The addresses of the input, output, and criterion ranges will also be adjusted automatically by 1-2-3.

Be careful, though, when you issue a worksheet command that causes the boundaries of the input, output, criterion, or other ranges to change. For example, suppose your input range were A7.G15 and you wanted to insert a new field at the far left of the database. If you place the pointer in column A and issue a Worksheet Insert Column command, the new column causes the input range to move to the right (to B7..H15). Because the insertion was made outside of the input range, the new field will not be included in the input range, so you must use a Data Query Input command and revise the range's coordinates.

A field may be deleted using Worksheet Delete Column, but be careful not to delete information above or below the database that you do not want to delete. You can widen or trim a field's width using Worksheet Column-Width Set, and you can rearrange the order of fields using the Move command. The Copy command is handy for entering repetitive values or labels in a field or for copying records from one area of the input range to another.

You have now learned the basic techniques of database management using Lotus 1-2-3. The maneuverability and flexibility of the 1-2-3 database, however, do not solve all problems of database applications. Specifically, applications that involve databases exceeding the record and column limits are not appropriate for 1-2-3. In addition, it can be difficult to handle multiple databases using the program. Nonetheless, the number of applications that can be handled capably by 1-2-3 far exceeds the limits of the previous generation of spreadsheet programs, and few programs can match 1-2-3 for speed.

Chapter 8
Sorting, Macros, And Menus

The Data command is a very powerful tool, but implementing a database application can entail quite a few steps. This is particularly true for an application that is used frequently. Moreover, the user must be acutely aware of the 1-2-3 database management commands and of the structure of the spreadsheet. Imagine trying to teach a novice how to sort and query.

217

If the database will be used often or if it will be used by a person uninitiated in the software, then it may be beneficial to invest some extra time in developing the project in order to make later use of the worksheet easier and quicker. The object is to try to streamline, or package, the application as much as is practical and reasonable.

The macro facility, introduced in Chapter 4, is one way of making the finished product easier for yourself or someone else to operate. But 1-2-3 lets you go even further. It allows you to create your own customized menu, similar to the menus that you have used to issue 1-2-3 commands. A user-defined menu lets a user select and execute a macro from a menu of macros. Together, macros and menus can reduce a complicated, time-consuming task to a few keystrokes.

This chapter develops a marketing measurement tool to sort and rank the salespeople of an organization. It makes use of the Data Sort command discussed in Chapter 5 and focuses on macros and menus, capabilities that will prove invaluable to the 1-2-3 owner who wants to get the most out of the Lotus software.

Ranking Sales Staff With Data Sort

The Play-Rite Merriment Company, a toy manufacturer, employs a marketing force of 200 individuals. The company wishes us to rank the sales of each person on a quarterly basis and to identify the top salespeople in each quarter for incentive awards. For development purposes, we will use a sample database of six people.

Setting Up the Worksheet

Make sure that the CAPS indicator is visible on the lower right of the monitor. If not, press the CAPS LOCK key.

1. Set column A's width to 10 characters by pressing HOME and typing / Worksheet Column Set-Width **10** ENTER.

2. Move to cell B1, and set the column-width for column B to 15 by typing / Worksheet Column Set-Width **15** ENTER.

3. Enter the column headings and salespeople's data as shown in Figure 8-1.

4. Type **/Range Label Center** to center the column titles.

5. Type the titles **PLAY-RITE MERRIMENT COMPANY** in cell C2 and **SALES RANKING SYSTEM** in cell C3. Press the ENTER key.

The second title is not centered beneath the main title. Shifting it over three spaces will do the trick.

6. With your pointer on cell C3, enter Edit Mode by pressing the F2 (Edit) key.

To displace the label toward the right, you must insert spaces on the left of the label. The spaces must be placed between the label-prefix (apostrophe) and the first character of the label, the initial S in SALES.

7. Press the HOME key to transport the edit pointer to the left side of the label, the apostrophe.

8. Press the right arrow key once, press the space bar three times, and press ENTER.

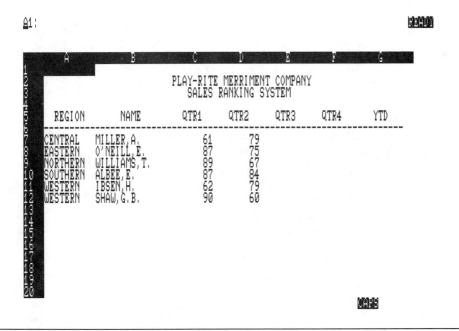

Figure 8-1. Worksheet showing column headings and sales data

The control panel should now show the cell's contents as SALES RANKING SYSTEM, with the label centered below the title. Because the sales figures in this worksheet will be in thousands of dollars,

9. Go to cell F1, and type the label '($ IN THOUSANDS).

The last column, YTD sales, is the sum of the quarterly amounts. At the beginning of the year, the worksheet is blank. As each quarter passes, the quarterly data is input. Thus, after any given quarter, the YTD column equals the year-to-date sales for each Play-Rite salesperson. We will use the @SUM function to set YTD equal to the sum of the four quarters contained in columns C through F.

10. Go to cell G7 to enter the equation for year-to-date sales for A. Miller.

11. Type @SUM(to begin the formula.

12. Move the pointer to fourth-quarter sales at cell F7.

Why do we point to the fourth quarter as the beginning of the range? Doesn't 1-2-3 require us to specify the range as first quarter (C7) through fourth quarter, not the other way around? Fortunately, 1-2-3 is very flexible when it comes to ranges. It even lets us point "backward."

13. Type the . key to anchor the range.

14. Move to first-quarter sales at cell C7.

Notice that the pointer expands normally, encompassing the range that we want.

15. Type the) key, and press the ENTER key.

Lotus 1-2-3 uses the endpoints of the range to figure out where the range is. It makes no difference to 1-2-3 in what order the endpoints are specified, as long as they are endpoints.

Copy the YTD formula to the rest of the data records:

16. Type /Copy ENTER G8.G12 ENTER.

Your results should look like the YTD column in Figure 8-2.

Sorting by Primary and Secondary Keys

Now that we have set up the worksheet, we can begin to manipulate its contents. The first step in organizing the data is to sort it in descending order of year-to-date sales. This is easily accomplished with the Sort command.

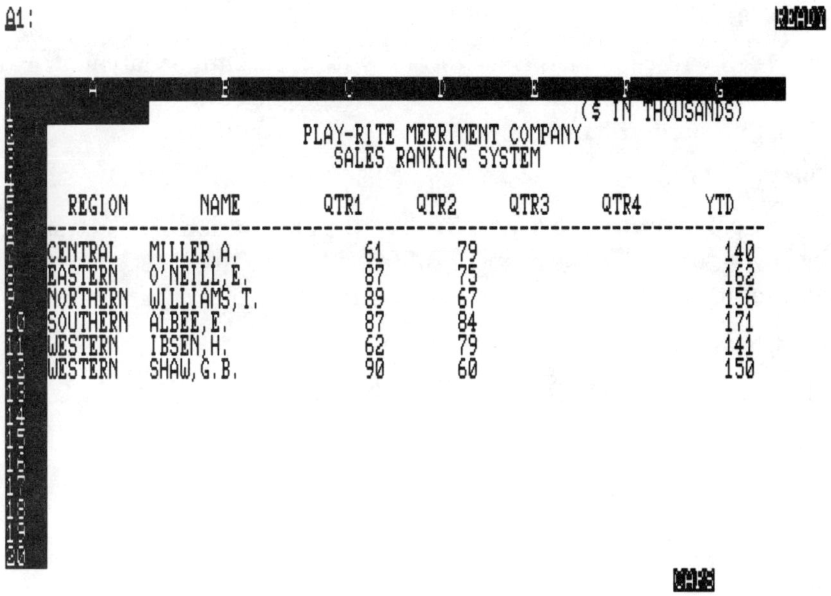

A1:
REDY

```
                A            B         C       D       E       F        G
                                                                ($ IN THOUSANDS)
                              PLAY-RITE MERRIMENT COMPANY
                                  SALES RANKING SYSTEM

        REGION        NAME        QTR1    QTR2    QTR3    QTR4     YTD
        ---------------------------------------------------------------
        CENTRAL     MILLER,A.       61      79                    140
        EASTERN     O'NEILL,E.      87      75                    162
        NORTHERN    WILLIAMS,T.     89      67                    156
        SOUTHERN    ALBEE,E.        87      84                    171
        WESTERN     IBSEN,H.        62      79                    141
        WESTERN     SHAW,G.B.       90      60                    150
```

CAPS

Figure 8-2. The YTD column resulting from @SUM calculations

1. Type /Data Sort.

2. Choose the **Data-Range** option in order to tell 1-2-3 where to find the records to be sorted.

3. Move the pointer to cell A7, the first field of the first record.

Remember: You do not include the field names in a **Data Sort** range because you do not want them involved in the sort. You want them to stay at the top.

4. Type the . key, and press the END and HOME keys to move to the bottom right of the database, cell G12.

5. Press ENTER.

The range of records to be sorted is thus A7..G12. The Sort menu reappears.

6. Choose the **Primary-Key** option by typing **P**.

You must now indicate which column should be the basis of the sort and in what order the sort is to be arranged.

7. Move the pointer to any cell in the YTD field (column G).

8. Press ENTER.

Now 1-2-3 will request the sort order, with a recommendation of A (ascending). Our interest is in seeing the top salespeople on top of the list, so we will reject this suggestion.

9. Type **D** to choose descending order; then press ENTER.

The Sort menu returns, and we are given the option of selecting a Secondary key to sort on. If two or more salespeople have the exact same year-to-date sales total, you can sort those people in alphabetical order:

10. Choose the Secondary-Key option.

11. Move the pointer to any cell in the NAME field (column B).

12. Press ENTER.

In response to the sort-order prompt,

13. Type **A** to choose ascending (alphabetical) order; then press ENTER.

Now begin the sort:

14. Choose the Go option of the Sort menu.

As Figure 8-3 shows, E. Albee is the top Play-Rite Merriperson, with midyear sales of $171,000.

Assigning Rankings With Data Fill

One of the primary reasons for developing this worksheet is to rank salespeople, so it would be useful to add a column that numbers the year-to-date sales performances from top (1) to bottom (6). Later when we resort the file, we can use this column to compare other types of ranking to the year-to-date ranking.

We can assign rankings to the sales force by entering a sequence of numbers, starting with 1, in the column to the right of YTD.

1. Move to cell H4, and enter the label ^**YTD**; then move to cell H5, and enter ^**RANK**. (The label-prefix ^ serves to center the label.)

2. Fill cell H6 with a line of hyphens, using \\- ENTER.

Rankings can be attached to the sorted records using the Data Fill command, introduced in Chapter 5. Data Fill creates a sequential list of numbers in a range of consecutive cells. In this instance, the sequence of numbers

A1:

```
              A           B          C        D        E        F         G
                                                            ($ IN THOUSANDS)
                                  PLAY-RITE MERRIMENT COMPANY
                                    SALES RANKING SYSTEM

         REGION       NAME       QTR1     QTR2     QTR3     QTR4      YTD
        --------------------------------------------------------------------
         SOUTHERN    ALBEE,E,      87       84                         171
         EASTERN     O'NEILL,E,    87       75                         162
         NORTHERN    WILLIAMS,T,   89       67                         156
         WESTERN     SHAW,G,B,     90       60                         150
         WESTERN     IBSEN,H,      62       79                         141
         CENTRAL     MILLER,A,     61       79                         140
```

Figure 8-3.   Records sorted in descending order for YTD sales

would be placed in column H, beginning with 1 in row 7 and increasing in steps of 1 through the rest of the range.

   3. Move to cell H7.

   4. Type /Data Fill.

Now 1-2-3 will ask for the fill range, the range of cells that will contain the sequence. It suggests the current position, H7, as the beginning of the range. This is desired, so

   5. Type the . key to anchor the range.

   6. Move down to the end of the field, to the cell corresponding to the record of A. Miller (cell H12).

   7. Press the ENTER key.

Now you are asked to supply the beginning of the sequence. In response to the "Start" prompt,

   8. Type 1.

This will give Albee a ranking of 1.

9. Now press the ENTER key.

The next prompt asks for "Step," the value of the increment. Because this sequence should increase by 1, accept 1-2-3's recommendation:

10. Press the ENTER key.

The "Stop" prompt gives you the opportunity to specify a maximum value for the sequence. If the fill range were so long that it exceeded the maximum value that could be filled, then the sequence would be abbreviated before reaching the end of the fill range. For the current example, the suggested 2047 is more than enough.

11. Press ENTER to accept the recommended stop value.

Instantly, the sequential rankings of 1 through 6 will fill the RANK column of the worksheet.

Before we forget, it is necessary to update the addresses of the Sort data range to include the RANK column.

12. Type /Data Sort Data-Range.

The control panel displays the active data range of A7..G12, the corners of the highlighted area.

13. Press the right arrow key once to expand the data range toward the right to include column H.

14. Press the ENTER key.

Sorting by Second-Quarter Sales

Although the company's quarterly incentives are based on year-to-date sales, it is also of interest to sort the salespeople by the sales of the most recent period, the second quarter. This simply means changing the Primary key and resorting.

1. Select the **Primary-Key** option.

The pointer will move to the current Primary key in the YTD column. To use the second quarter as the basis for sorting,

2. Move the pointer to any cell in the QTR2 column (column D).

3. Press the ENTER key.

The suggestion of descending sort order is acceptable, so

4. Press ENTER again.

The Secondary key, which is the NAME field, can remain in effect, so

5. Select the Go option.

Notice that the old year-to-date rankings were rearranged when the file was resorted. Albee is still in first place, but Ibsen, who ranked fifth for YTD, is runner-up for the quarter.

Translating the Sort Tasks To Macros

Now that the data range has been established, it need not be repeated until it changes. Sorting on a different sort key requires specifying the new Primary key and the new Secondary key (if desired) and issuing the Go command. Play-Rite will be doing a lot of sorting with this worksheet, so it will be worthwhile to develop macros that automate and simplify the sorting task.

Recall from Chapter 4 that a macro is a vertical range of cells containing 1-2-3 keystrokes that can either invoke commands or enter information. The keystrokes are stored as labels—that is, each is preceded by a label-prefix, such as an apostrophe. The first cell of a macro is given a special range name consisting of a backward slash followed by a single letter (for instance, \A). You invoke the macro by typing its name. This is done by pressing the ALT key in combination with the letter assigned to the macro's name. The macro \A would be invoked by pressing the ALT key while typing the A key.

A Summary of Keystrokes

Here is a list of the commands and responses to prompts that we used to rearrange our file in order of year-to-date sales:

/Data Sort Primary-Key G1 ENTER Descending ENTER
Secondary-Key B1 ENTER Ascending ENTER Go

(We will present the macro translation shortly.)

If we re-sort the file by year-to-date sales, it must be ranked again with the Data Fill command. Data Fill requires four pieces of information: the fill range, the starting value of the sequence, the step (increment), and the stop, or maximum, value. If, during the current session, you have already issued a

Data Fill, 1-2-3 will remember all four of these settings and will recommend them the next time you issue the command.

Note, however, that if you save the worksheet and retrieve it later, 1-2-3 will remember only the fill range. *The start, step, and stop will revert back to their initial default values of 0, 1, and 2047 respectively.* For our purposes, the step and stop can assume the default values. But the starting value of the sequence must be set to 1, not 0, in order to assign the highest ranking salesperson a rating of 1, not 0. Therefore, when the Data Fill command is issued, the entries should be as follows:

/Data Fill	to initiate the command and invoke the Fill range prompt
ENTER	to accept the previous range (H7..H12)
1 ENTER	to begin the sequence with 1
ENTER	to accept the "Step" recommendation of 1
ENTER	to accept the "Stop" recommendation of 2047.

In summary, then, the commands and responses to prompts that are necessary to sort and rank the file on the basis of year-to-date sales are

/Data Sort Primary-Key G1 ENTER Descending ENTER
Secondary-Key B1 ENTER Ascending ENTER Go
/Data Fill ENTER 1 ENTER ENTER ENTER

Storing Macro \A

To translate these steps into a macro, you must convert the commands and prompts to labels, and then you must convert any special keystrokes (virtually every nontypewriter keystroke) to the special macro keystroke indicators. The only special key used in the sequence above is the ENTER key. Recall from Chapter 4 that any reference to ENTER in a macro must be replaced by the ~ (tilde) character. Thus, the sequence of keystrokes that actually goes into the macro would be

/DSPG1~D~SB1~A~G/DF~1~~~

A macro need not reside entirely in one cell. In fact, creating long macro labels by chaining keystrokes together is not a good idea. In the first place, macros are difficult enough to understand by looking at them. If you do not remember exactly what a macro label does, it is hard to figure out the macro by looking at a long, coded label. (It is a good idea to document your macros in plain English, storing this documentation either on the worksheet or on paper.) Shorter macro labels are more easily deciphered.

In addition, macros are extremely susceptible to error. Even a misplaced comma can cause ruin. Finding an error in a long macro label can be as frustrating as searching for a needle in a haystack.

Therefore, we will divide the commands of the macro into segments, stored in cells J5 through J7, as shown in Figure 8-4. Lotus 1-2-3 will read the first segment and then examine the next cell below. If that cell contains a label, it is interpreted as a continuation of the macro. Lotus 1-2-3 will interpret and execute any labels it sees as if they were together in a single cell. *Processing stops when the next cell in the macro is a blank or when a macro is explicitly ended by a command.*

Follow these steps to store the macro:

1. Move to J5, an unused cell.

2. Type '/DSPG1~D~, and press ENTER.

3. In cell J6, enter the label **SB1~A~G**.

4. In cell J7, enter the label '/DF~1~~~.

Merely entering a label into the cell does not tell 1-2-3 that cell J5 is a macro. We must assign the macro a name and, in the process, let 1-2-3 know where to find the macro when we invoke it.

5. With the pointer on the first cell of the macro, J5, type /**R**ange **N**ame Create.

Assign a special name to the cell:

6. Type \A, and press ENTER.

```
        A          B          C        D       E        F         G        H      I       J
 1                                                   ($ IN THOUSANDS)
 2                              PLAY-RITE MERRIMENT COMPANY
 3                                SALES RANKING SYSTEM
 4                                                                       YTD
 5      REGION     NAME       QTR1     QTR2    QTR3     QTR4      YTD     RANK           /DSPG1~D~
 6      -----------------------------------------------------------------------         SB1~A~G
 7      SOUTHERN   ALBEE,E.     87       84                       171      1            /DF~1~~~
 8      WESTERN    IBSEN,H.     62       79                       141      5
 9      CENTRAL    MILLER,A.    61       79                       140      6
10      EASTERN    O'NEILL,E.   87       75                       162      2
11      NORTHERN   WILLIAMS,T.  89       67                       156      3
12      WESTERN    SHAW,G.B.    90       60                       150      4
```

Figure 8-4. Macro \A sorts records by YTD column

Now 1-2-3 will recommend the current cell, J5, as the named range. This is acceptable, so

7. Press ENTER.

Before trying out the macro, protect yourself against zapping by saving the worksheet:

8. Type /File Save **PLAYRITE**, and press the ENTER key.

Now test the macro. Press the ALT key, holding it down as you type **A**. Very swiftly, 1-2-3 will execute the macro as if you were actually typing the keystrokes. When READY appears in the mode indicator of the control panel, check the results. The names and ranks should be rearranged as they were when we first sorted them according to YTD sales.

If there is an error in the macro, 1-2-3 will sound a beep. Depending on the problem, the macro may be interrupted or it may execute completely but erroneously. If the results of the macro are not what they should be, or if a beep was emitted, there is probably a typing error in the macro.

How Inserting a Column
Affects the Macro

How would the operation of \A be affected if we decided, at some point, to insert a column on the left side of the worksheet? Recall that the Primary and Secondary keys, YTD and NAME, were given as cells G1 and B1 in the command

/Data Sort Primary-Key G1 ENTER Descending ENTER
Secondary-Key B1 ENTER Ascending ENTER Go

If a column is inserted to the left of column B, then the fields to the right of the inserted column are displaced to the right. The YTD column will be shifted from column G to column H, while the NAME column will move from column B to column C. The Sort command would have to be adjusted to

/Data Sort Primary-Key H1 ENTER Descending ENTER
Secondary-Key C1 ENTER Ascending ENTER Go

But the macro is not aware of the inserted column. It knows only to refer to cells G1 and B1, no matter what, because a macro is comprised of labels, and labels are not altered by rearranging cells in the worksheet. The inserted column renders the macro useless until it is corrected.

Range Names to the Rescue

This is an instance where the range-naming capability is a blessing, for a named range of cells is automatically adjusted when the worksheet is altered. No matter where a named range is moved to, its name is still assigned to it at its new location. By assigning range names to the G1 and B1 cells, and by referring to those range names rather than to the cell coordinates, the macro will use the new addresses for the ranking procedure. Because this chapter will ultimately involve macros that refer to all of the columns, we will give range names to all of them at this point.

When 1-2-3 prompts for the location of a sort key, it requests the address of a cell within the column that is to be sorted. To be able to sort any column in the worksheet, we should assign a unique name to one cell in each of the eight columns. The eight names could be assigned with eight Range Name Create commands. However, it is possible to assign all eight names in one fell swoop with the Range Name Labels command.

Suppose that there is a range of cells, containing unique labels, in the worksheet. The range of field names in cells A5..H5 is an example. With the Range Name Labels command, it is possible to use these labels as names to be assigned to cells bordering the range of labels. To see how this applies,

1. Move the pointer to cell A5.

2. Type /Range Name Labels.

The control panel displays a menu:

Right Down Left Up

If you choose Down, then the cells below the range of labels (which you will soon specify) will be given names.

3. Choose the Down option.

Next 1-2-3 wants to know the label range, the range of coordinates containing labels that will be used as names. Because the pointer is on A5, 1-2-3 recommends the range A5..H5.

4. Move the pointer to the right, to H5, to expand the label range to A5..H5.

5. Press the ENTER key.

The READY mode indicator returns. To find out whether the cells were named, we could use the F5 (GoTo) key to move to the named cells and see if the GoTo works. To do this, it would be convenient to see a list of all the names currently active in the worksheet.

6. Press the F5 (GoTo) key.

Now 1-2-3 enters Point Mode, and it wants you to tell it where to go. If you press the F3 (Name) key in Point Mode, you will retrieve a list of active range names.

7. Press the F3 (Name) key.

The names are alphabetized. The list includes NAME, QTR1, QTR2, QTR3, QTR4, RANK, REGION, YTD, and \A (the name of our macro). There is not enough room in the control panel to display all of the names, but you can move the menu pointer across with the right arrow key to view the rest of the list. Placing the menu pointer on a particular range name and pressing ENTER will select that name for the current command, which is GoTo.

8. Move the menu pointer to YTD.

9. Press the ENTER key.

The pointer jumps to cell G6, the cell below the YTD field name. If you test the GoTo command using one of the other field names, the pointer will move to the cell beneath that field name. That is because the Range Name Labels Down command uses the contents of the labels range to name the row of cells immediately below the labels range, as illustrated here:

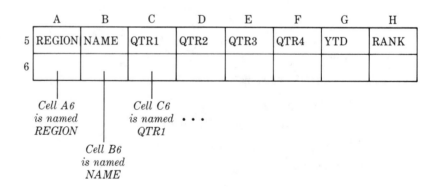

The other Range Name Label commands work in a like manner. The Range Name Labels Up command names the bordering cells above the labels. If the labels were contained in a vertical range of cells, you could use the Right or Left options to name the bordering cells on the left or right of the labels.

Incidentally, the F3 (Name) key can be used to obtain a list of range names whenever 1-2-3 is in Point Mode. Thus, it can be used with the Move, Copy, Data, Print, File, and Graph commands and in a formula entry, whenever a range name is called for. The F3 (Name) key is especially convenient if you have forgotten the name of a range while you are entering a command or formula.

Revising \A With Range Names

Now that the Range Name Labels command has been issued, let us return to the \A macro. Instead of using Data Sort Primary-Key G1 to sort the records in order of year-to-date sales, we will use the named cell, entering Data Sort Primary-Key YTD. This command not only is more descriptive, it is more flexible. If the YTD column is moved for any reason, the name YTD will be automatically reassigned to the new address, and the macro will function correctly.

1. Press the F5 (GoTo) key, and type \A ENTER to move the pointer to the \A macro.

2. Press the F2 (Edit) key to enter Edit Mode.

The current macro label will appear in the control panel as '/DSPG1~D~.

3. Replace the characters G1 with **YTD**, and press ENTER.

4. Similarly, in cell J6, replace the characters B1 with **NAME**, so that the Secondary key will refer to the NAME cell, not the B1 coordinate.

5. Press ENTER.

Make certain that you entered the macro label correctly, then hold down ALT while typing A to see if the macro works. The results should be the same as before.

Creating a Second Macro: \B

Now we will create a second macro, \B, to sort the second-quarter sales records in decreasing order. Observe that the commands to reorder the file should be identical, except that the Primary key should be designated as QTR2. Therefore, as a shortcut to entering the macro, we will copy the sorting commands (the first two cells) of \A to another column and change the Primary key from YTD to QTR2.

We will put this new macro right next to \A in column K. This location for the new macro is not chosen haphazardly. As we soon will see, the two macros must be "neighbors" in order to be part of a user-defined menu. Otherwise, we could have put the second macro somewhere else. (We could even have put it beneath macro \A in column J, leaving at least one blank cell between the two macros.)

1. Use the F5 (GoTo) key to go to the named range \A (press F5, and type \A ENTER).

2. Type /Copy, type the . key, and then press the down arrow key to move to the last cell of \A. Press the ENTER key.

3. Move to cell K5, the target cell for the copy.

4. Press the ENTER key.

5. Move to cell K5.

6. Press the F2 (Edit) key to edit the cell's contents.

7. Replace the characters YTD in the label with the characters **QTR2**.

8. Press the ENTER key.

Next name the macro.

9. Type /**R**ange Name Create \B ENTER ENTER.

You have probably noticed that the width of column J is not sufficient to display the macros clearly. We will take care of this by widening column J:

10. Move to cell J5, and type / **W**orksheet Column Set-Width **12** ENTER.

Macro \B should be located directly next to the revised macro \A, like this:

```
            J              K
  5    /DSPYTD~D~    /DSPQTR2~D~
  6    SNAME~A~G     SNAME~A~G
  7    /DF~1~~~      /DF~1~~~
                          ↑
                      Macro \B
```

Scroll the display so that you can see the QTR2 column; then invoke the macro by holding down ALT and typing **B**. The results should be the same as those we saw when we did the same sort operation without a macro earlier in this chapter.

Making Macros More Flexible

The \B macro is adequate for sorting the second quarter, but what about sorting the other quarters? One possibility is to create a macro for each of the other three quarters, but this would take quite a bit of effort. A better method is to make \B more flexible by enabling it to handle any quarter. In the revised procedure, the user will have to tell 1-2-3 which quarter's sales should be the sort key. Once 1-2-3 has this information, it can be instructed to set the Primary key to the associated column. The sequence of operations is outlined in the box, *Steps for Creating a Flexible Macro.*

Controlling Macro Execution: Advanced Macro Commands

Before you create a flexible macro, you must know how to endow a macro with the intelligence needed to distinguish between quarters, and how to instruct a macro to issue sequences of keystrokes conditionally, depending on which quarter is the current quarter.

The macros developed up to this point have been exact duplicates of keystrokes that could have been typed manually by the user. These keystroke macros contained no internal intelligence or logic, just plain 1-2-3 keystrokes. However, there exists a class of commands unique to the macro environment, commands that cannot be used outside of a macro. These are the *advanced macro commands.** The advanced macro commands control the sequence of execution of a macro. With the advanced macro commands, the macro becomes far more than a mere typing alternative: it becomes an intelligent "automatic pilot."

Version 2.0 adds a significant number of advanced macro commands to 1-2-3's repertoire. In this book you will learn about the macro commands that Version 2.0 and Version 1A have in common. Additional commands, as well as more advanced techniques, are covered in the advanced 1-2-3 book, by the same author (Osborne/McGraw-Hill, 1986).

---

*Version 1A includes a subset of advanced macro commands, called \X *commands.*

234 GUIDE TO USING LOTUS 1-2-3

STEPS FOR CREATING A FLEXIBLE MACRO

In this chapter, the macro \B sorts the worksheet according to second-quarter sales. If you wish to perform the same sort operation for first-, third-, or fourth-quarter sales, it is not necessary to write three additional macros. Instead, \B can be revised to make it more flexible. The following steps show how to revise the macro in this chapter, but the same technique can be applied to any similar macro.

STEP 1: Store the value of the current quarter (1, 2, 3, or 4) in a cell that is separate from the macro. In this case, we will name the cell QTRX.

STEP 2: If QTRX contains a 1, then the first-quarter sales should be sorted. The macro will assign the cell named QTR1 to the Primary key, assign NAME to the Secondary key, execute the sort, and then skip to STEP 6. If QTRX does not contain a 1, the macro will proceed to STEP 3.

STEP 3: If QTRX contains a 2, the macro will assign QTR2 to the Primary key and NAME to the Secondary key, then execute the sort and skip to STEP 6. If QTRX does not contain a 2, the macro will proceed to STEP 4.

STEP 4: If QTRX contains a 3, the macro will assign QTR3 to the Primary key and NAME to the Secondary key, then execute the sort and skip to STEP 6. If QTRX does not contain a 3, the macro will proceed to STEP 5.

STEP 5: If QTRX contains a 4, the macro will assign QTR4 to the Primary key and NAME to the Secondary key, then execute the sort and proceed to STEP 6.

STEP 6: Stop.

In Version 1A, the advanced macro commands are called */X commands*, because they each begin with /X. Version 2.0 includes the /X commands, but also includes command *keywords* that are equivalent to /X commands. In this chapter, as well as in the remainder of the book, we present both the Version 2.0 keywords and the /X formats for the advanced macro commands. In the steps to follow, Version 2.0 instructions are labeled "V 2.0," and the equivalent /X-format instructions are labeled "/X." If you are using Version 1A, you must restrict yourself to the /X syntax, whereas if you are using Version 2.0 you may employ either keyword or /X syntax.

Keyword Syntax (Version 2.0 Only)

Just as rules of grammar dictate the form of English-language statements, rules of syntax dictate how 1-2-3 advanced macro command statements must be put together. Advanced macro keywords are enclosed in curly braces {keywords}. The macro statement within these braces can consist of one or more parts. The first part is the keyword. Depending on the keyword, it may be followed by one or more *arguments*, variables that affect the keyword operation. You may not split a statement into two different cells; each statement enclosed in its set of curly braces must be within a single cell. (You may, however, store several statements in one cell.)

It makes no difference whether you type a keyword in upper- or lowercase letters; they are the same to 1-2-3. However, this book will use uppercase letters to distinguish keywords from other command keystrokes in 1-2-3 macros.

The IF(/XI) Command

The *IF(/XI) command* directs 1-2-3 to perform certain tasks only if a certain condition has been fulfilled. The format of the command is

V 2.0: {IF *conditional formula*}...*keystrokes*
/X: /XI *conditional formula* ~...*keystrokes*...

The conditional formula is like the one used in the Data Query criteria discussed in the previous chapter. The IF(/XI) command has the following meaning: If the result of the conditional formula is true, then read any keystrokes that follow the } (or the ~ for the /X format) in this cell; otherwise, skip to the next macro cell below this and continue execution. (The I in /XI stands for *if*, and the ~ represents *then*, so that the anglicized version of the command is, "IF the condition is satisfied, THEN execute the keystrokes that follow.")

Whatever comes between the IF (or the I of /XI) and the end brace (or the tilde in the /X format) is the conditional formula. For example, consider the macro label

V 2.0:   {IF QTRX = 1}/DSPQTR1~
/X: /XIQTRX=1~/DSPQTR1~

The condition is QTRX=1. If this condition is true (that is, if the cell named QTRX contains a 1), then the macro will execute the remaining keystrokes in the cell, which represent the following command:

/Data Sort Primary-Key QTR1 ENTER

In other words, if the current quarter is the first quarter, then the macro sets the Primary key to QTR1 and then continues with the next macro label. Otherwise, 1-2-3 skips to the next macro label without executing the /DSPQTR1~ keystrokes.

In the /X format, observe that the tilde following the conditional formula stands for *then*, but the tilde at the end of the Data command represents an ENTER keystroke. Whatever follows that first tilde, whether a single command or several commands, will be performed only if QTRX=1 is true. Otherwise, the flow of command proceeds to the next cell down.

The BRANCH (/XG) Command

Another useful command is *BRANCH* (/XG in the /X format), which instructs 1-2-3 to skip to some other macro cell to obtain the next macro command. The format of the command is

V 2.0:   {BRANCH *location*}
/X: /XG*location*~

For example, {BRANCH J9} (/XGJ9~) would direct 1-2-3 to stop whatever it is doing, go to cell J9 (a macro cell), and follow whatever instructions are contained there. The destination of the BRANCH command can be an actual cell reference or a cell name. In /X format, the tilde following the coordinate is essential. If the destination coordinate is not followed by a tilde, the macro will not work.

Together, IF (/XI) and BRANCH (/XG) permit us to translate Steps 2 through 6 of the box into the language of macros. Assume that cell QTRX already contains the value of the current quarter. Begin entering macro \B with the following steps:

1. Name the QTRX cell by moving to J1 and typing **/R**ange **N**ame Create **QTRX** ENTER ENTER.

2. Move to \B (cell K5).

The first task for the macro is to examine the contents of QTRX to see whether the file should be sorted by first-quarter sales. If so, we want it to issue the appropriate Sort command. The macro label to do this would be

V 2.0: {IF QTRX = 1}/DSPQTR1~D~SNAME~A~G
/X: /XI(QTRX=1)~/DSPQTR1~D~SNAME~A~G

In the /X format version we have enclosed the condition in parentheses, which contributes to clarity. To the right of the conditional formula are the keystrokes to be executed for the first quarter, which translate to

/Data Sort Primary-Key QTR1 ENTER Descending ENTER
Secondary-Key NAME ENTER Ascending ENTER Go

In this case, we must violate our convention of keeping the labels short. There is a good reason for this. All keystrokes that are subject to the IF (/XI) condition *must* be stored in the same label as the IF (/XI) command itself.

Begin by entering the label in cell K5. (We will be replacing the old contents of K5 with a new entry.) In this and the following steps, the keystrokes for both keyword and /X formats are given. Choose the appropriate format.

3. Type the following:

V 2.0: **{IF QTRX=1}/DSPQTR1~D~SNAME~A~G**
/X: **'/XI(QTRX=1)~/DSPQTR1~DSPQTR1~D~SNAME~A~G**

Do not press ENTER yet. If you did, press the F2 (Edit) key to continue entry. So far, we have entered only part of Step 2 of our planned procedure, which was to sort the file based on QTR1. If we were to end the label here and if QTRX were 1, then 1-2-3 would execute the keystrokes of the rest of the cell and then proceed to the next cell of the macro.

Instead of proceeding to the next label, however, we want 1-2-3 to stop processing the macro. One way of stopping macro execution is to instruct 1-2-3 to go to a blank cell. When 1-2-3 goes to the blank cell, it stops processing the macro because only nonblank labels are valid macro cells.

To which cell should we tell 1-2-3 to go? We will use a cell at the end of the macro we are currently developing, but we have not yet finished the macro, so we do not know where the end is—we know only that we want to skip to that location. Wherever that cell may be, let us plan now to give it the name CONTINUE1. We will create CONTINUE1 with the Range Name Create command later—as soon as we can ascertain the address of CONTINUE1. For now, we need to tell the macro that, if QTRX=1 is true, it should assign the Primary key and skip to CONTINUE1. We use the BRANCH (/XG) command:

4. Type the following:

> *V 2.0:* **{BRANCH CONTINUE1}**
> */X:* **/XGCONTINUE1~**

The first \B cell, cell K5, should now contain the label

> *V 2.0:* {IF QTRX=1}/DSPQTR1~D~SNAME~A~G{BRANCH CONTINUE1}
> */X:* /XI(QTRX=1)~/DSPQTR1~D~SNAME~A~G /XGCONTINUE1~

The next cell will represent Step 3 of the planned procedure. It is almost exactly like Step 2, except that QTRX=1 is replaced by QTRX=2, and QTR1 is replaced by QTR2. Instead of typing the entire label again into the next cell, K6, we will just copy K5 and edit its contents.

5. With the pointer on cell K5, type /Copy ENTER.

6. Move down once, to cell K6.

7. Press the ENTER key.

8. Move down to cell K6.

Now enter Edit Mode:

9. Press the F2 (Edit) key.

10. Change the characters QTRX=1 to QTRX=2, and change QTR1 to QTR2.

11. Press ENTER.

The next cell, K7, will perform Step 4 of the plan.

12. Repeat the procedure of instructions 5 through 11, but substitute QTRX=3 for QTRX=2 and QTR3 for QTR2. Do the same for the next cell, K8, replacing QTRX=3 with QTRX=4 and QTR3 with QTR4.

Now Steps 2 through 5 of the plan are done.

The next macro cell, K9, represents Step 6. It is the blank cell that ends the macro, the elusive CONTINUE1 that we have been waiting to define. Before continuing, we will name cell K9 CONTINUE1.

13. With the pointer at cell K9, type **/** Range Name Create **CONTINUE1**
ENTER ENTER.

When the macro is done, 1-2-3 will resume the Ready Mode. The updated version of macro \B is shown below.

V 2.0:	K	L	M	N	O	P
5	{IF QTRX=1}/DSPQTR1~D~SNAME~A~G{BRANCH CONTINUE1}					
6	{IF QTRX=2}/DSPQTR2~D~SNAME~A~G{BRANCH CONTINUE1}					
7	{IF QTRX=3}/DSPQTR3~D~SNAME~A~G{BRANCH CONTINUE1}					
8	{IF QTRX=4}/DSPQTR4~D~SNAME~A~G{BRANCH CONTINUE1}					

/X:	K	L	M	N	O	P
5	/XI(QTRX=1)~/DSPQTR1~D~SNAME~A~G/XGCONTINUE1~					
6	/XI(QTRX=2)~/DSPQTR2~D~SNAME~A~G/XGCONTINUE1~					
7	/XI(QTRX=3)~/DSPQTR3~D~SNAME~A~G/XGCONTINUE1~					
8	/XI(QTRX=4)~/DSPQTR4~D~SNAME~A~G/XGCONTINUE1~					

To put \B to the test, we will load **QTRX** with the value for the second quarter.

14. Go to QTRX (cell J1), and set it equal to 2.

Then invoke the macro.

15. Say your favorite prayer.

16. Hold down the ALT key while typing **B**.

Your results should coincide with those of the second-quarter sort that we did previously.

Identifying Macro Errors

With a macro such as \B, it is very easy to make logical or typographical errors. If you heard a beep or if your results are wrong, then you probably have made a typographical error. Under normal conditions, 1-2-3 executes a macro as fast as it can, often faster than the user can follow. It is difficult to detect exactly which command the macro is executing when an error occurs. How can you find the error?

A very useful facility for testing macros is the *Single-Step Mode* of macro execution. Whether or not you were successful with macro \B, it is important to know how to use this facility.

By holding down the ALT key while pressing the F1 (Help) key, you will cause 1-2-3 to enter Single-Step Mode.

1. Hold down ALT while pressing the F1 (Help) key.

The word STEP is displayed in the lower-right portion of the screen; from here on, the macro will execute only one "step" at a time. A *step* is defined as a single keystroke or a single macro command. Before each step, 1-2-3 waits until you press any key; then it will execute the step. It is possible to speed up the process by holding a key down—in effect, repeating the keystroke. Release the key when you reach the steps that you would like to follow closely.

Begin the single-step execution of \B:

2. Hold down ALT while typing **B**.

Notice that an SST (Single-Step) indicator appears at the top right, a signal to press any key. Press a key several times and watch the control panel. As 1-2-3 executes each keystroke or macro command, the control panel displays what is being "typed," or performed by 1-2-3. Hold the key down, and the macro will execute quickly. Because QTRX=2 is true, the macro ends after it does the processing for the second quarter. You will not see the keystrokes related to the third and fourth quarters; these keystrokes were skipped over, thanks to the BRANCH (/XG) command.

To disable single-step mode:

3. Press ALT while pressing the F1 (Help) key.

The STEP indicator will disappear from the lower-right portion of the screen.

Single-Step Mode is very useful, especially in long or complicated macros. Another technique, more preventive in nature, is *verbal coaxing*. If you talk to your macro, encourage it, and praise it, your macro may respond positively. This technique is rumored to work in all versions of 1-2-3.

Including Prompts With GETNUMBER (/XN)

The quarterly sort can be automated even more. As it stands, the user must remember to put the value of the quarter into QTRX; otherwise, the macro will malfunction.

There is another macro command called *GETNUMBER (/XN)*, which prompts the user for a number, retrieves the user's responses, and stores the response in a designated cell. The format of the command is

V 2.0: {GETNUMBER *message,location*}

/X: /XN*message~location~*

Here *message* is the prompt that will be displayed to the user in the control panel, and *location* is the cell address or name where the number is stored. If the \B macro began with the command/label

> *V 2.0:* {GETNUMBER "I BESEECH THEE, ENTER THE
> QUARTER:", QTRX~}
>
> */X:* /XNI BESEECH THEE, ENTER THE QUARTER:~QTRX~

then as soon as ALT-B was pressed, the user would be asked to enter the quarter. If the user then pressed 2 followed by ENTER, the number 2 would be stored in QTRX (cell J1). Cordial, courteous prompts can make the worksheet much more pleasant to use.

Note that in keyword format the message argument of the GETNUMBER statement may be (1) a string of characters contained in quotation marks, (2) an address of a cell containing a label or character-string to be used for the message, or (3) a range name assigned to a cell containing the message. The message may contain up to 80 characters.

Note that in /X format the message may contain up to 39 characters.

The \B macro currently begins in cell K5. When inserting a command into a macro, you can manipulate the macro's cells just like any other cells in the worksheet. However, after any changes to the positions of the cells, it is essential that the range name for the macro (in this case, \B) be attached to the first cell. For future purposes, it is necessary to have this macro begin in cell K5. Therefore, to insert the GETNUMBER (/XN) command at the beginning of \B, the rest of the macro must be moved down one cell as follows:

1. Press the F5 (GoTo) key; then type **\B** ENTER to move to the cell named \B.

2. Type **/M**ove to invoke the Move command.

3. Press the END key, and then press the down arrow key *twice* to highlight the entire macro, including the blank cell CONTINUE1.

4. Press the ENTER key.

The pointer returns to its original position, and 1-2-3 requests the destination of the move.

5. Move down one cell to K6.

6. Press the ENTER key.

The macro is shifted down, and the pointer returns to the blank cell above the macro. Enter the GETNUMBER (/XN) command, beginning with a label prefix.

7. Type the following:

> *V 2.0:* {GETNUMBER "I BESEECH THEE, ENTER THE QUARTER:", QTRX~}
>
> */X:* '/XNI BESEECH THEE, ENTER THE QUARTER:~ QTRX~.

8. Press the ENTER key.

Next check on the location of \B using the F5 (GoTo) key. Type F5 \B ENTER. You will find that \B is attached to its old assignment, which is now the second cell of the macro, so it must be reassigned.

9. Type /Range Name Create \B ENTER.

Now 1-2-3 will recommend K6, the current assignment of the \B name.

10. Move the pointer up once to cell K5.

11. Press the ENTER key.

We are back in business.

12. Test the macro by holding down ALT while typing **B**.

In the control panel, 1-2-3 will beseech you to tell it which quarter you wish to use for the sort.

13. Respond with a **1** to sort according to first-quarter sales.

Remember to press ENTER after the 1. Your results should match the portion of the worksheet shown in Figure 8-5.

	A	B	C	D	E	F	G	H
1						($ IN THOUSANDS)		
2			PLAY-RITE MERRIMENT COMPANY					
3			SALES RANKING SYSTEM					
4								YTD
5	REGION	NAME	QTR1	QTR2	QTR3	QTR4	YTD	RANK
6	---------	----------	----	----	----	----	----	----
7	WESTERN	SHAW,G.B.	90	60			150	4
8	NORTHERN	WILLIAMS,T.	89	67			156	3
9	SOUTHERN	ALBEE,E.	87	84			171	1
10	EASTERN	O'NEILL,E.	87	75			162	2
11	WESTERN	IBSEN,H.	62	79			141	5
12	CENTRAL	MILLER,A.	61	79			140	6

Figure 8-5. Results of macro \B showing sort by QTR1 sales

Adding More Macros

Thus far, we have built macros to sort and rank by year-to-date sales and to sort by quarterly sales. Next we will create three more macros to sort by name, sort by region, and print the worksheet.

Sort by Name: Macro \C

When the entire sales force of 200 is eventually incorporated into the database, it would be easier to locate particular individuals in the file if it were sorted alphabetically. All that is required is to point the Primary key to the NAME field and Go. The data range is already in 1-2-3's memory. The command would look like this:

Data Sort Primary-Key NAME ENTER Ascending ENTER Go

If we put this into a macro called \C, the procedure will be that much easier in the future.

1. Move to cell L5.

2. Type /Range Name Create \C ENTER ENTER to name the macro.

3. Enter the label '/DSPNAME~A~G, and press ENTER.

Hold down ALT and press C to execute the macro. To rank the file on YTD sales and then alphabetize it, invoke macro \A and then invoke macro \C.

Because the label in the previous column (beginning in cell K5) was so long, the \C label interrupts it. Let us move back to column K and widen the column so that we can see the entire macro.

4. Move to cell K5, and type /Worksheet Column Set-Width 48 ENTER.

Before we continue, let us also widen the columns for the other macros in advance.

5. Move to cell L5, and type /Worksheet Column Set-Width 14 ENTER.

6. Move to cell M5, and type /Worksheet Column Set-Width 24 ENTER.

7. Move to cell N5, and type /Worksheet Column Set-Width 50 ENTER.

Sort by Region: Macro \D

Another useful arrangement would be one with records alphabetized by region and, within each region, by name. This is accomplished by the following commands.

Data Sort Primary-Key REGION ENTER Ascending ENTER
Secondary-Key NAME ENTER Ascending ENTER Go

Hence, to enter macro \D,

1. Move to cell M5.

2. Type /Range Name Create \D ENTER ENTER to name the macro.

3. Type '/DSPREGION~A~SNAME~A~G.

4. Press the ENTER key.

Invoke the \D macro. Observe that the two records of the Western region,
Ibsen and Shaw, are arranged alphabetically within their region.

Print the File: Macro \E

Now that the macros have been developed to sort the file in various ways, a
macro should be written to output the file to a printer.

When developing a macro, the initial step is to figure out how the task
might be accomplished interactively, without a macro. Implement the steps
to report the file, record the steps as they are executed, and then translate
them into a macro.

The report should start from the top-left corner of the worksheet, which is
where you should transfer the pointer:

1. Press the HOME key.

Enter the Print menu:

2. Type /Print.

3. Select the Printer option.

Clear any previous print ranges:

4. Select Clear Range.

To enter a print range,

5. Select the Range option.

6. Type the . key to anchor the range.

Now 1-2-3 requests the lower-right corner of the range to be printed. Normally, it would be sufficient to use the down arrow and right arrow keys to
move the pointer to the bottom right. However, we are going through this

exercise for the sake of writing a macro, and a macro executes automatically — it is not aware of the bottom right of the worksheet. It must be instructed exactly how many times to move right and how many times to move down, which is not readily available information. By using the END key, we can cleverly circumvent the problem.

If the pointer is on a blank cell, then pressing END followed by an arrow key transplants the pointer to the next nonblank cell in the direction of the arrow. If the pointer is on a nonblank cell, then pressing END and an arrow key moves the pointer to the last contiguous nonblank cell before a blank cell.

With the proper combination of keys, the pointer can be shifted down to the REGION field name (cell A5), over to the RANK field name (H5), and down to the bottom-right corner of the worksheet.

7. Press the END key, followed by the down arrow key.

The range A1..A5 will be highlighted, but this is not yet the entire range desired.

8. Press the END key again, followed by the right arrow key.

Now the range A1..H5 is highlighted.

9. Press END and then the down arrow key again.

Right on the money! The entire range, A1..H12, is now designated in the control panel, so

10. Press the ENTER key to accept this range.

If you were to add the column widths of the print range, you would find that our report will be 79 characters wide. Because 1-2-3's defaults are a left margin at 5 and a right margin at 76 (75 in Version 1.0), the report will be too wide to print. This can be fixed by changing the left and right margins to 0 and 79, respectively.

11. Type **Options Margins Left 0**, and press the ENTER key.

12. Type **Margins Right 79**, and press the ENTER key.

13. Select **Q**uit to return to the Print menu.

Make sure the paper in the printer is aligned and that the printer is on, and then

14. Type **G** to select the Go option.

The report should print out. To skip to the next page and exit the print menu,

15. Select **P**age and **Q**uit.

Here is a recapitulation of the commands used to print the report:

HOME /Print Printer Clear Range
Range . END DOWN END RIGHT END DOWN ENTER
Options Margins Left 0 ENTER Margins Right 79 ENTER Quit
Go Page Quit

The special keys that must be translated to the macro are HOME, END, down arrow, right arrow, and ENTER. Using the special key code listing provided in Table 4-3 to translate these keystrokes, we create the macro to print the report:

{HOME}/PPCRR.{END}{DOWN}{END}{RIGHT}{END}{DOWN}~
OML0~MR79~Q
GPQ

We will split this macro into two labels:

16. In cell N5, enter the label

    {HOME}/ PPCRR.{END}{DOWN}{END}{RIGHT}{END}{DOWN}~

17. In cell N6, enter the label

    OML0~MR79~QGPQ

18. Press the ENTER key.

Name the macro \E:

19. Move to cell N5, the beginning of the macro, and type

    / Range Name Create \E ENTER ENTER.

Now align the printer paper, and invoke macro \E.

Creating a Menu
For Easy-To-Use Macros

The worksheet now has a collection of five macros. To invoke them, the user must know how to execute a macro and must also remember which macro is which. The names that the macros have been given are not particularly descriptive. Wouldn't it be nice to turn on the machine, and—without having to be aware of macros, databases, or range names—see the screen display in English a choice of procedures that are available for use with the Sales Ranking System?

The *MENUBRANCH (/XM) command* lets you create your own 1-2-3 menus. You can choose your own command names and assign these names to macros that you have created. Each menu can contain up to eight commands. Like regular 1-2-3 menus, the user-defined menu displays the command names on the second line of the control panel. The menu pointer highlights one of these commands, and it can be moved to another command by using the pointer movement keys. On the third line of the control panel, a descriptive phrase, (designed by the user) explains what will occur if the command highlighted by the menu pointer is selected.

Setting Up the Menu Range

Figure 8-6 portrays the specific way in which a menu must be constructed. A user-defined menu consists of up to eight commands, which are incorporated into a *menu range*. The menu range includes one column for each of the menu commands and at least three rows for each. The first column of the menu range relates to the first command of the menu. Its uppermost cell contains the command name, which should begin with an uppercase letter.

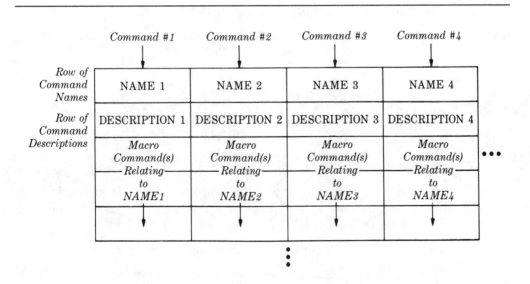

Figure 8-6. Format of a user-defined menu range

The second cell in the column is a label containing an explanation of the command. The third cell, and any cells below it, store a macro that is executed when the associated command is chosen.

Now it is clear why all of the macros of this chapter are located side by side in consecutive columns and why they all start in row 5. We plan to integrate the macros into a menu. We can use row 3 for command names and row 4 for command descriptions, thus completing the menu range. With the menu range constructed, we need only inform 1-2-3 that a menu exists and tell 1-2-3 where it is located in the worksheet.

To review, the macros that have been defined for the ranking system are:

MACRO	COLUMN	DESCRIPTION
\A	J	Rank salespeople by year-to-date sales
\B	K	Rank salespeople by quarter sales
\C	L	Sort database alphabetically by name
\D	M	Sort database alphabetically by region and name
\E	N	Send file to printer

In choosing command names for a menu, make sure that no two commands begin with the same letter. Then there will be no ambiguity when a command is chosen by typing the first letter of its name. Here are names for the five commands that will invoke macros \A through \E:

MACRO	COMMAND NAME
\A	YTD
\B	QTR
\C	NAME
\D	REGION
\E	PRINT

With this information, we can enter the menu.

1. Use the command names just given to complete the row of command names (row 3) for the menu range. For example, the label **YTD** should be entered into cell J3, **QTR** into cell K3, and so on.

2. Next press the CAPS LOCK key to allow for lowercase typing.

3. Use the table of macro descriptions to enter descriptive labels into row 4 of the worksheet. For example, "Rank salespeople by year-to-date sales"

is the label that should be entered into J4. "Rank salespeople by quarter sales" into K4, and so on

The completed menu range should resemble Figure 8-7 (except that the mid-section of the menu range has been omitted from the figure because of space limitations).

4. Press CAPS LOCK again to return to uppercase typing.

The Menu Macro: \M

Figure 8-7 also shows a new macro in cell I1. This macro contains another advanced macro command, MENUBRANCH (/XM). The *MENUBRANCH (/XM) command* informs 1-2-3 of a menu's existence and location. The structure of the command is

> *V 2.0:* {MENUBRANCH *location*}
> */X:* /XM*location*

where *location* is the top-left corner of the menu range—in this case, cell J3. All 1-2-3 needs is the location of the top-left cell. It can deduce where the rest of the menu is, because it knows that the macros that form the menu must be next to each other.

Instead of referring to cell J3 in the MENUBRANCH (/XM) command, let us give J3 the name of MENUPLACE, just in case the menu gets moved away from cell J3.

1. Move to cell J3.

2. Type /Range Name Create **MENUPLACE** ENTER ENTER.

The MENUBRANCH (/XM) command will be:

> *V 2.0:* {MENUBRANCH MENUPLACE}
> */X:* /XMMENUPLACE~

Like other advanced macro commands, MENUBRANCH (/XM) may be used only within a macro. Therefore, we must create a new macro whose only entry is

> *V 2.0:* {MENUBRANCH MENUPLACE}
> */X:* '/XMMENUPLACE~

For example, a macro \M could be defined, containing the MENUBRANCH

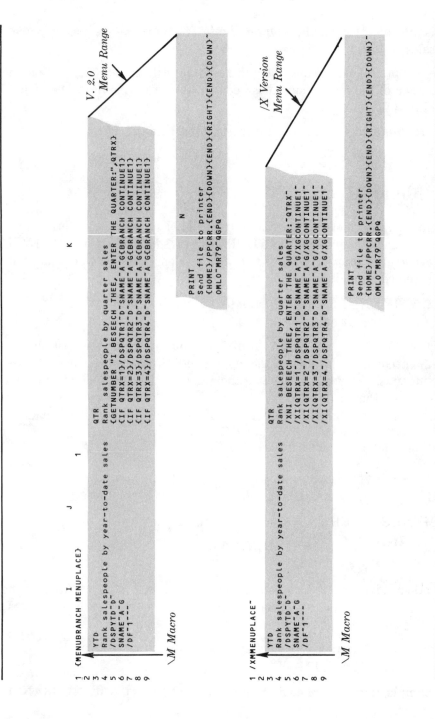

Figure 8-7. The menu macro and the menu range (midsection not shown)

(/XM) command. Invoking the \M macro will activate the user-defined menu.

3. Move to cell I1 and enter

V 2.0: {MENUBRANCH MENUPLACE}
/X: '/XMMENUPLACE~

Then press the ENTER key.

4. Type /Range Name Create \M ENTER ENTER.

The label was cut off by the entry in cell J1, so widen column I:

5. With the pointer on cell I1, type Worksheet Column Set-Width **13** ENTER.

Now hold down the ALT key while typing **M** to invoke the macro. The moment M is pressed, the user-defined menu appears on the second line of the control panel:

YTD QTR NAME REGION PRINT

and the menu pointer highlights the first option, YTD. The mode indicator on the top right shows CMD MENU, because 1-2-3 is executing a menu under the command of a macro. The bottom line of the control panel displays the description for the YTD command, which is stored in cell J4.

When we move the pointer to the right, another command is highlighted, and its associated description appears below it. Pressing ENTER will execute the macro pertaining to whatever command is highlighted by the menu pointer, and typing the first letter of a menu option has the same effect. Pressing the HOME key transfers the pointer to the first command in the menu, whereas END shifts it to the last command.

Select the QTR command. In an instant, the prompt for the quarter appears. Respond by entering **1** and pressing ENTER. The file is now in descending order of first-quarter sales. The menu disappears, the macro is completed, and Ready Mode is resumed. To invoke the menu again, just invoke the \M macro.

If you invoke the menu but then decide you do not want to use the macro, how do you abort the menu? There are three ways to do this. One method is to press the ESC key; another is to hold the CTRL key down while pressing SCROLL LOCK; a third method is to mimic other 1-2-3 menus by including an Exit command within the menu.

Adding a Command
To a User-Defined Menu

We can add a command to the menu range simply by entering it into the next column of the menu.

1. Move to cell O3.

2. Enter the label **EXIT**, which serves as the command name.

3. Move down once to cell O4.

4. Enter the description **Exit from the menu.**

How can you make the Exit command work? There is no way of instructing the macro to press CTRL SCROLL LOCK because these two special keys have no macro translations. However, there is another advanced macro statement, *QUIT (/XQ)*, that has precisely the same function as this keystroke sequence.

5. Move down once to cell O5.

6. Enter
   V 2.0: {**QUIT**}
   /X: '/**XQ**

7. Press the ENTER key.

Now see if it works. Invoke the macro \M, and choose the Exit option.

A Homemade User Interface

Let us step back for a moment and consider the design of our menu. Whenever a user selects one of the options we have provided, 1-2-3 will execute the appropriate macro and then relinquish control to Ready Mode. It is likely, though, that the user would rather be returned to the user-defined menu than to Ready Mode. For example, the user might want to sort the worksheet and then print it—two separate commands of our menu.

Can we instruct each command of the menu (except for Exit) to return to the menu when it is done? We certainly can, using the QUIT (/XG) command. In the last cell of each of macros \A, \B, \C, \D, and \E, we will enter the label
   V 2.0: {BRANCH \M}
   /X: '/XG\M~
This will send 1-2-3 to the menu macro, which invokes the menu anew.

1. In each of cells J8, K10, L6, M6, and N7, enter the following:

    V 2.0: {BRANCH \M}

    /X: '/XG\M~

Invoke the menu by holding down the ALT key while typing **M**, and then execute a command. You will be returned to the menu when the selected macro finishes executing. We have succeeded in creating a fairly closed environment, one that a nonexperienced person could learn quickly. In fancy terms, this is called a *user interface*.

Why Use Macros and Menus?

In this chapter, we have automated five of the principal tasks of Play-Rite Merriment's ranking system by incorporating them into macros. Moreover, we made the macros themselves easier to use by integrating them into a menu. Now to execute any of the principal tasks, a user need only hold down the ALT key while typing **M**. From that point on, the system almost runs itself.

Training a nontechnical person to utilize this menu system will be much simpler, and much faster, than trying to teach someone to use the more complex operations of the Data Sort, Data Fill, and Print commands. The user only needs to know how to use the menu pointer and how to respond to prompts. This can be taught in a matter of minutes.

The macros used in this application are not particularly sophisticated in relation to what is available. You can make the macros as intricate as the 1-2-3 command set will permit, but the complexity can be made totally transparent—that is, invisible to the user.

There is much more to say about macros and menus, and we will revisit them in the third section of this book, which discusses more advanced techniques. But they were used in this chapter because they are extremely important features of 1-2-3, greatly enhancing its flexibility and versatility. Use these features, and you will go much further with your applications.

And by the way, welcome to the world of programming.

Chapter 9
Database Statistics
And Data Tables

Constructing the Survey
Worksheet

Using Database Statistical
Functions

Data Tables

In the last three chapters we used the Data command of 1-2-3 to analyze and manipulate the records of a database. In general, our goal has been to examine detailed information rather than to summarize the data in some way. But a database can grow too large or too detailed to be useful by itself. When this happens, a numerical summary of the database becomes much more informative and valuable than the individual records it contains.

Lotus 1-2-3 has a set of functions, such as @SUM and @AVG, that is useful for summarizing data on a worksheet. However, when you need to apply numerical analysis to groups of records selected from a database, you will be glad to have the database functions of 1-2-3.

One area in which database statistical functions are particularly useful is survey analysis. When you are analyzing the results of a political poll or a marketing survey, your interest is not in the individual responses that make up the database. Rather, you want to glean from the database information that tells you something about the survey population as a whole or about specific groups within the survey population.

In this chapter, we use a marketing survey to illustrate the statistical functions of 1-2-3: @DCOUNT, @DSUM, @DMIN, @DMAX, @DAVG, @DVAR, and @DSTD. We also expand our coverage of criteria, which control the scope of the database functions. We round off the chapter with a discussion of data tables. Combined with the database functions, data tables provide an astonishingly simple way to summarize a vast amount of information with minimal effort.

Constructing the Survey Worksheet

We use as our example a marketing survey conducted by Too Bee or Not Too Bee, Inc., a manufacturer of natural and artificial honey. Too Bee or Not Too Bee has polled 100 consumers to determine the market's reaction to one of its products that has been commercially available for a year. The survey asks its respondents to rate the product's quality and price on a scale of 1 to 10. In addition, it asks respondents how many jars they purchased during the last 12 months.

Figure 9-1 shows a worksheet that records the survey responses of 100 participants. It would be very cumbersome to key the entire survey into your own worksheet for this exercise. However, it is possible to generate a quick random-but-rigged survey by using the @RAND function.

We introduced @RAND in Chapter 5 as a random number generator, a function that yields a number between 0 and 1. We can quickly create 100 "questionnaires" by manipulating @RAND so that it generates survey ratings between 1 and 10 and then by copying the formula containing @RAND to 100 rows.

Creating Data With @RAND And @ROUND

Begin the exercise by typing the column headings of the survey.

1. Enter the worksheet headings in rows 1 through 5, exactly as shown in Figure 9-1.

	A	B	C		A	B	C
1		TOO BEE		51	6	8	4
2		SURVEY		52	5	4	2
3				53	6	5	3
4			ANNUAL	54	6	9	4
5	QUALITY	PRICE	PURCHASES	55	6	6	3
6	9	8	4	56	8	5	3
7	9	5	4	57	10	5	4
8	7	8	4	58	10	6	4
9	5	5	3	59	6	7	3
10	9	10	5	60	6	8	4
11	8	8	4	61	5	5	3
12	9	7	4	62	5	10	4
13	6	8	4	63	10	5	4
14	9	9	5	64	9	6	4
15	9	5	4	65	7	8	4
16	8	7	4	66	6	6	3
17	6	6	3	67	9	8	4
18	8	8	4	68	8	7	4
19	9	5	4	69	6	10	4
20	8	4	3	70	8	5	3
21	5	6	3	71	6	6	3
22	8	5	3	72	9	9	5
23	7	10	4	73	6	6	3
24	9	8	4	74	9	6	4
25	7	5	3	75	10	7	4
26	9	7	4	76	6	7	3
27	8	7	4	77	10	4	4
28	6	7	3	78	7	6	3
29	7	4	3	79	7	8	4
30	6	6	3	80	8	9	4
31	6	9	4	81	5	5	3
32	6	5	3	82	9	7	4
33	7	6	3	83	7	9	4
34	8	7	4	84	9	5	4
35	8	4	3	85	8	6	4
36	8	9	4	86	7	8	4
37	7	6	3	87	9	7	4
38	9	9	5	88	7	6	3
39	6	7	3	89	6	6	3
40	6	5	3	90	5	7	3
41	6	8	4	91	7	8	4
42	8	10	5	92	9	4	3
43	7	7	4	93	6	10	4
44	10	5	4	94	6	4	3
45	7	8	4	95	7	10	4
46	9	8	4	96	7	9	4
47	6	7	3	97	8	10	5
48	9	6	4	98	10	10	5
49	7	9	4	99	8	5	3
50	7	7	4	100	8	9	4

Figure 9-1. Survey responses for 100 participants

2. Move the pointer to cell A6, and type **@RAND**. The result is some decimal number between 0 and 1.

Pressing the F9 (Calc) key causes the @RAND formula to recalculate, producing a different random number. To load up the column of quality ratings, we will be slightly dishonest and generate random ratings between 5 and 10.

A random value between 0 and 5 can be derived by using the formula @RAND*5. This is so because @RAND yields a number between 0 and 1. Multiply that number by 5, and the result is at least 0*5=0 and at most 1*5=5. By adding 5 to @RAND*5, we get a random number between 5 and 10, because the minimum that (@RAND*5)+5 can be is 0+5=5 and the maximum is 5+5=10.

3. With the pointer still at cell A6, type **(@RAND*5)+5** and press ENTER.

We enclose @RAND*5 in parentheses in order to avoid ambiguity. The formula works without parentheses, but parentheses clarify the intention to multiply @RAND by 5 *before* adding 5, as opposed to adding 5+5 and then multiplying by @RAND.

The cell now contains a number between 5 and 10 that includes some decimal digits. Because it is very unlikely that a respondent will give quality a rating of 7.326786, it would be best to round off the number by truncating digits with the @ROUND function. The formula should have the form @ROUND(*value*,0), where the second argument (the 0) specifies no digits after the decimal place. For the quality rating, the formula should be changed to @ROUND((@RAND*5)+5,0). With the pointer stationed at cell A6, either edit the formula to include the @ROUND function or

4. Type **@ROUND((@RAND*5)+5,0)**.

5. Press the ENTER key.

Although we are already in a position to "fill out" all 100 questionnaires for the quality rating, we will proceed instead to the other two fields, completing the first questionnaire before we copy its formulas to the rest of the database.

Too Bee's honey costs about as much as any other brand, so it would be modestly realistic to rig its price ratings to fall between 4 and 10. We will use the @ROUND function again to convert the numbers to integers. Begin with @RAND, the value between 0 and 1. Multiply @RAND by 6 to produce a number between 0 and 6. Add 4 to the result to derive a value between 4 and 10. The correct formula is, therefore, @ROUND((@RAND*6)+4,0).

6. Move to cell B6.

7. Enter **@ROUND((@RAND*6)+4,0)**.

8. Press the ENTER key.

The last question of the survey, the number of units purchased by the respondent during the year, is probably a function of how favorably the customer felt toward the quality and price of the item. For this example, we make the simplifying assumption that the number of units purchased equals the sum of the quality and price ratings, divided by 4. Thus, a consumer who awards the value 10 for both quality and price will have purchased $(10+10)/4$, or 5 jars in the past year. One who thinks highly of the price (9) but does not care for the quality (5) will have bought $(9+5)/4$, or 3 jars (after the result is rounded). To enter this assumption into the worksheet,

9. Move to cell C6.

10. Enter **@ROUND((** to begin the formula.

11. Move the pointer to the QUALITY column, cell A6.

12. Type the **+** key.

13. Move the pointer to the PRICE column, cell B6.

14. Type **)/4,0)**.

15. Press the ENTER key.

Cell C6 should contain @ROUND((A6+B6)/4,0). Now the other 99 questionnaires can be "filled out" with the Copy command:

16. Move to cell A6.

17. Type **/**Copy END, and press the right arrow key.

18. Press the ENTER key.

19. Move down once to cell A7, the beginning of the target for the Copy command.

20. Type the **.** key to anchor the range.

21. Use the PG DN and down arrow keys to move to cell A105.

22. Press the ENTER key.

The result is a worksheet of 100 fabricated surveys. It is possible that your results will differ from Figure 9-1 because of the nature of the @RAND function. For this exercise, the exact values are unimportant, except that QUALITY should always be between 5 and 10, PRICE should always be between 4 and 10, and PURCHASES should be equal to (QUALITY+PRICE)/4.

This worksheet is larger than some of the ones we have been using. To speed things up, deactivate automatic recalculation.

23. Type **/W**orksheet **G**lobal **R**ecalculation **M**anual.

From now on, we must press the F9 (Calc) key in order to recalculate the model.

Converting Formulas to Values With File Xtract

Pressing the F9 (Calc) key will cause all the numbers of the worksheet to change. This is of no consequence now, but later it will be beneficial to have constant numbers to refer to. We would like to convert the underlying formulas in a range to their currently visible values. This can be accomplished by using the File Xtract command to save the values of the indicated cells in a data file.

1. Press the HOME key.

2. Type /File Xtract.

Now 1-2-3 asks whether to save the file with its formulas or to save only the values that are displayed in the cells.

3. Type V to choose values.

In response to the "Enter xtract file name" prompt,

4. Type **SURVEY**, and press the ENTER key.

Next, 1-2-3 must know the lower-right corner of the section of the range that is to be saved. To save the entire active area of the worksheet,

5. Press END and HOME to move to the lower-right corner of the worksheet.

6. Press the ENTER key.

After the file is recorded onto the diskette, retrieve it and examine the contents of the cells:

7. Type /File Retrieve **SURVEY** ENTER.

Use the arrow keys to examine the contents of the cells. Where there previously were @RANDs and @ROUNDs, there are now only values. So switch gears — forget everything that you have done until now, and pretend that the 100 responses on your worksheet are legitimate inputs that were keyed in by one of Too Bee's market analysts.

Using Database Statistical Functions

Now that you have a database, there are many questions you may want to answer about it. You may want to find out how many respondents gave a rating of 10 for quality or how many awarded 10 to both quality and price.

Or, of the people who rated quality above 8, how many also rated price above 8? What percentage of sales are being purchased by people who rated price favorably? How many jars were purchased by consumers who bought the honey only because of its price? What was the average quality rating for those who bought more than three jars during the year? For this same group, what was the maximum price rating? The minimum?

These are the types of questions addressed by the database statistical functions, and we will answer them in this chapter. We will be using all seven of the database statistical functions: @DCOUNT, @DSUM, @DAVG, @DMAX, @DMIN, @DVAR, and @DSTD. They all have a common structure, which is rendered as @D*function* (*input range, offset, criterion range*).

The *input range* and *criterion range* in this formula should be familiar to you—they are similar to those used with the Data Query command in Chapter 7. The input range begins with a row of field names, followed by the records that pertain to the database. The criterion range also begins with a row of field names, followed by one or more rows of criteria.

You may recall using an *offset* argument for the @VLOOKUP function in Chapter 5. Offset tells 1-2-3 which column the @D function should be applied to—for example, which field (or column of figures) to average.

In specifying the offset, you do not designate a column letter or a coordinate. Rather, you give 1-2-3 a number—the number of fields to move over until it reaches the field you want. The idea is similar to the relative address concept of the Copy command. Specifying the offset tells 1-2-3 to locate the field that is *offset* a certain number of columns to the right of the first column of the input range (the range that we specified as the first argument of the @D function). In other words, an offset of X points to a field X columns to the right of the beginning of the input range.

Counting Responses: @DCOUNT
With One Criterion

The @DCOUNT function tallies the number of records that conform to a given criterion. Before entering the @DCOUNT formula, it is important to identify the input range, the offset, and the criterion range. In this case, the input range is the database itself, including the row of field names. The top left of the input range is cell A5; the bottom right is cell C105. Because we will be employing this range throughout the chapter, it is a good idea to give the range a name. We will name it SAMPLE.

1. Go to cell A5.

2. Type /Range Name Create **SAMPLE** ENTER.

3. Press END, then HOME, and then ENTER.

For this example, the field to be tested by the criterion is PRICE. The records that store 10 in the PRICE field will be candidates for the @DCOUNT function. Therefore, the criterion range should contain a cell storing the field name PRICE, followed below it by a criterion cell containing the number 10. To construct the criterion range,

4. Move to cell E1.

5. Enter the label **PRICE** (or use the Copy command to be sure that the criterion label matches the input range label exactly).

6. Move down once, to cell E2.

7. Enter the number **10**.

We now have the input range and the criterion range. What about the offset? Offset points to the field from which we want @DCOUNT to count records selected by the criterion. Offset begins counting at 0. Thus, the first column of the input range, QUALITY, has the offset value of 0. PRICE is one column to the right of QUALITY, so it has an offset value of 1. PURCHASE is two columns to the right, so its offset value is 2.

The formula entry @DCOUNT(SAMPLE,1,E1..E2) directs 1-2-3 to consider the database contained in the range SAMPLE. Specifically, it tells 1-2-3 to select those records that comply with the criterion stipulated in the range E1..E2 and, for the records selected, to count those that have a non-blank field in the PRICE column (which has an offset of 1). In plain English, 1-2-3 will count how many respondents awarded a rating of 10 to PRICE.

The @DCOUNT formula, like any other formula, can be entered anywhere on the spreadsheet.

8. Move to cell E10.

9. Enter the label **COUNT OF PRICE=10:** and press ENTER.

10. Move to cell H10.

11. Type **@DCOUNT(SAMPLE,1,** to begin the formula.

Now enter the coordinates of the criterion range as follows:

12. Move the pointer to cell E1.

13. Type the . key to anchor the range.

14. Move the pointer to cell E2.

15. Type **)** and press the ENTER key.

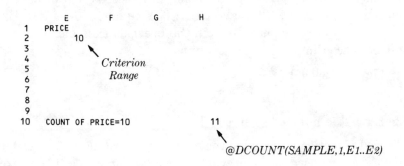

Figure 9-2. Cell H10 yields result of @DCOUNT tally for price rating of 10

The formula in H10 should now be displayed in the control panel as @DCOUNT(SAMPLE,1,E1..E2). The result of this function will depend on the random sampling on your own worksheet. Based on the sample of Figure 9-1, 1-2-3 produces a count of 11, as shown in Figure 9-2.

Because this worksheet is based on random numbers, the results on your screen may not always match the figures in this chapter. If your sample differs from Figure 9-1, you may expect your results to differ somewhat from the text. Check your results manually to make sure that your formulas work as you expect them to.

Using @DCOUNT With More Than One Criterion

Of the group that gave Too Bee's price a rating of 10, some also gave it a 10 for quality. To find out how many answered 10 on both ratings, we will need to use multiple criteria with the @DCOUNT function. Recall from Chapter 7 that, for an AND condition, two or more criteria must be placed on the same row of the criterion range. The criterion range for the present example would look like this:

PRICE	QUALITY
10	10

The two criteria, PRICE = 10 and QUALITY = 10, are number-match criteria. Because they are on the same row, records will be considered for counting only if both PRICE and QUALITY equal 10. Cells E1..E2 already contain the first selection rule from the previous example. The second rule must be placed in an adjacent column.

1. Move to cell F1.

2. Enter the label **QUALITY**.

3. Enter the number **10** in cell F2.

The @D function for tallying the database according to these criteria is the same as the one used in the previous example, stored in cell H10, except that the criterion range must be revised.

The formula for counting the number of people who assigned a 10 to price was @DCOUNT(SAMPLE,1,E1..E2). The formula to count how many gave both price and quality a rating of 10 is @DCOUNT(SAMPLE,1,E1..F2).

4. Move to cell E12.

5. Enter the label **COUNT OF PRICE = 10, QUALITY = 10**.

6. Move to cell H12.

7. Type **@DCOUNT(SAMPLE,1,E1.F2)**.

8. Press ENTER.

To avoid overlap, enlarge the width of column E:

9. Move to cell E12, and type **/ Worksheet Column-Width Set 20** ENTER.

For the data in Figure 9-1, the result of the formula is 1. (You can look ahead to Figure 9-3 to find this tally in cell H12.) As expected, fewer people gave the highest ratings to both price and quality. Do not be surprised if, in your own sampling, you find no one who was utterly excited about both aspects of the product.

Using # AND # With @DCOUNT

It would be nice if more people gave 10 ratings to both price and quality, but Too Bee's marketing group feels that any rating of 8 or above is quite favorable. Therefore, the number of people who rated both price and quality as 8 or more is an important statistic to report. Testing for a rating equaling or exceeding 8 requires more than merely matching a criterion with a database record. It requires comparing a *condition* with the records of the database and then applying the database function only to those records that satisfy the condition. As explained in Chapter 7, a condition is called a *formula* criterion. Formula criteria evaluate to one of two results, *true* or *false*. In 1-2-3, *true* is encoded as the number 1 and *false* as the number 0. A formula such as +A6>=8 would be *true* (1) if A6 is greater than or equal to 8, and it would be *false* (0) if A6 is less than 8.

Compound Logical Formulas

Until now, the formula criteria that we have used have been simple logical comparisons, such as +A6>=8. In addition to simple logical operators such as =, >, and the other operators listed in Table 7-1, 1-2-3 provides logical operators that permit you to join two or more conditions in a single formula. These operators are called #AND# and #OR#.

For example, to test whether two cells, A6 and B6, are *both* greater than 1, you could use the formula +A6>1#AND#B6>1. To test whether one or the other is greater than 1, use +A6>1#OR#B6>1.

You create the compound logical formula by taking the #AND# or #OR# and sandwiching it between the two conditions that it applies to. You are not restricted to two conditions, however. You can string several #AND# and #OR# comparisons together. You can even have #AND#s and #OR#s in the same formula. Thus, (A6=1#AND#B6=1)#OR#C6<5 is *true* in two instances: (a) if *both* A6 and B6 equal 1, or (b) if C6 is less than 5.

Compound logical formulas using #AND# and #OR# are very similar to multiple criteria, but they do not work in quite the same way. Multiple criteria depend upon their placement within the criterion range. (Recall that criteria in the same row of a criterion range indicate an AND condition, whereas placement in different rows establishes an OR condition.)

In practice, you can often use compound logical formulas and multiple criteria interchangeably. Here we will use a compound formula criterion to choose records that have both PRICE and QUALITY ratings greater than or equal to 8. But you could also accomplish the same record selection by using multiple criteria.

Recall from Chapter 7 that a formula criterion should be constructed as if it referred exclusively to the first record of the input range, which is the first row beneath the field names. Also, as always, the criterion range for a formula begins with a row of field names followed by one or more rows of criteria. And remember, the unique aspect of a formula criterion is that it does not care which field name appears above it. Thus, the field name of the criterion need not relate to the formula itself—any valid field name of the input range is adequate.

We will use the field name PURCHASES. It has nothing to do with the formula, but since it is a valid field name, it will do.

1. In cell E4, enter the label **PURCHASES**.

2. Move to cell E5, and enter the formula **+A6>=8#AND#B6>=8**; then press ENTER.

Using Text Format to Display Cell Contents

The criterion cell, E5, displays a 0 or 1 depending on whether the first record of the input range failed or passed the formula criterion. This can be confusing, because it disguises the underlying selection criterion. It would be clearer if 1-2-3 displayed the formula, +A6>=8#AND#B6>=8, rather than its value, 0 or 1.

In Chapter 5 we saw a way to instruct 1-2-3 to display the contents of a cell (as it would appear in the control panel) rather than its result. You can format the cell with the text format so that the formula will be displayed. This is an easy and automatic way to document a formula criterion on a worksheet.

With the pointer still at cell E5,

1. Type **/Range** Format **Text** ENTER.

Now you can tell what this criterion is supposed to do.

The input range and the offset of the @DCOUNT function are the same as the ones used previously, but the criterion range is now E4..E5.

2. Move to cell E14, and enter the following label: **COUNT OF PRICE >= 8, QUALITY>= 8**.

3. Move to cell H14, and type **@DCOUNT(SAMPLE,1,E4.E5)**.

4. Press the ENTER key.

Based on the Figure 9-1 sample, Figure 9-3 shows that 20 respondents were favorable about both price and quality. This represents 20% of the consumers surveyed, a respectable achievement (ignoring the fact that the numbers were fabricated).

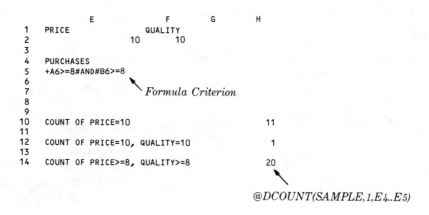

```
           E              F        G        H
1    PRICE           QUALITY
2                    10       10
3
4    PURCHASES
5    +A6>=8#AND#B6>=8
6                              Formula Criterion
7
8
9
10   COUNT OF PRICE=10                          11
11
12   COUNT OF PRICE=10, QUALITY=10               1
13
14   COUNT OF PRICE>=8, QUALITY>=8              20
```

@DCOUNT(SAMPLE,1,E4..E5)

Figure 9-3. Cell H14 yields tally for price and purchase ratings >=8

Tallying Purhases by Criterion Group: @DSUM

One would expect that the 20% of the surveyed consumers who approved of both price and quality would have purchased more than 20% of the year's sales. To find out exactly what percent of sales were purchased by the 8-and-above group, we will use the same selection criteria as in the previous case. However, instead of tallying the selected records using @DCOUNT, we will add their ANNUAL PURCHASES by using the @DSUM function.

The @DSUM function adds the values of a particular field, designated by the offset, for records selected by the criteria. Like @DCOUNT, the structure of the function is @DSUM(*input range, offset, criterion range*). The *input range* and *criterion range* are still SAMPLE and E4..E5 in this instance. However, in order to add the ANNUAL PURCHASES for the selected records, the offset must point to ANNUAL PURCHASES, which is the third column of the survey—an offset of 2 from the first column of the input range.

1. Move to cell E16.

2. Enter the label **SUM OF PURCHASES BY FAVORABLE GROUP.**

3. Move to cell H16.

4. Type **@DSUM(SAMPLE,2,E4.E5)**.

5. Press ENTER.

According to our sample, 89 jars of honey were bought by 20 admirers of Too Bee or Not Too Bee.

More Calculations

Over the next few pages, we present several more operations as we investigate the survey more thoroughly. If you wish to check either the worksheet format or the results as you go through the steps that follow, turn ahead to Figure 9-4. (Figure 9-4 displays only the calculations area of the worksheet. The database is shown in Figure 9-1.)

Percent of Total Respondents

What percentage of total units sold is the 89 jars? To find out, use the regular @SUM (not @DSUM) function to derive total units sold, and then divide these purchases by the total, as follows:

1. Move to cell E18, and enter the label **PERCENT OF TOTAL**.

2. Move to cell H18.

3. Type the + key to begin the formula.

4. Move the pointer to cell H16 to point to the sum of purchases by the admirers.

5. Type / to indicate division.

6. Type **@SUM(** to begin the sum function.

7. Move the pointer to the first entry under ANNUAL PURCHASES (cell C6).

8. Type the . key to anchor the range.

9. Press END and the down arrow key to move to the bottom of the field (cell C105).

10. Type the) key and then press ENTER to end the formula.

11. Type **/Range Format Percent 1** ENTER ENTER.

Based on the sample of Figure 9-1, 23.9% of the units sold went to the 20% of the respondents who rated price and quality as 8 or above.

Significance of Price

How many jars were purchased by customers who bought the honey only because of its price? To answer this question, we must distinguish those who favored price exclusively from those who were enthused by both price and quality. The selection rule will be to choose those records for which price is greater than or equal to 8 and for which quality is less than 8. Hence the formula criterion +B6>=8#AND#A6<8, where B6 is the first PRICE entry and A6 is the first QUALITY entry, as shown in Figure 9-1.

1. Move to cell E7, and enter the label **PRICE.**

2. Move to cell E8, enter the formula +B6>=8#AND#A6<8, and press ENTER.

3. Give this cell a Text format by typing /**R**ange **F**ormat **T**ext ENTER.

4. Move to cell E20, and enter the following label:
   PURCHASES OF PRICE>=8, QUALITY<8.

The three arguments of the @DSUM function are unchanged, so

5. Move to cell H20, and type **@DSUM(SAMPLE,2,E7.E8)** ENTER.

Eighty jars were sold to people who were unimpressed by the quality but liked Too Bee's price (based on the Figure 9-1 sample).

Average Quality Rating: @DAVG

The database equivalent to the worksheet @*AVG* function is @DAVG, which computes the average of records selected from a specified field by the user-defined criteria. Suppose we are interested in the average quality rating provided by respondents who purchased more than three jars during the year. The criterion would be +C6>3, cell C6 being the first ANNUAL PURCHASES entry shown in Figure 9-1.

1. Go to cell G1, and enter the label **PRICE.** (Remember, for a formula criterion, any valid field name will do.)

2. Move down to cell G2, enter the formula +C6>3, and press ENTER.

3. Assign the cell a Text format by typing /**R**ange **F**ormat **T**ext ENTER.

The field to be averaged is QUALITY. Its offset value is 0 because it is the leftmost column of the input range. Thus, @DAVG(*input range, offset, criterion range*) assumes the form @DAVG(SAMPLE,0,G1.G2).

4. Go to cell E29, and enter the label **AVERAGE.**

```
              E              F      G        H        I        J
 1   PRICE                QUALITY PRICE            PRICE    QUALITY
 2                     10      10 +C6>3            +B6>=8
 3                                                         +A6>=8
 4   PURCHASES
 5   +A6>=8#AND#B6>=8
 6
 7   PRICE
 8   +B6>=8#AND#A6<8
 9
10   COUNT OF PRICE=10                            11
11
12   COUNT OF PRICE=10, QUALITY=10                1
13
14   COUNT OF PRICE>=8, QUALITY>=8                20
15
16   SUM OF PURCHASES BY FAVORABLE GROUP          89
17
18   PERCENT OF TOTAL                          23.9%
19
20   PURCHASES OF PRICE>=8, QUALITY<8             80
21
22
23
24
25
26
27
28
29   AVERAGE
30   --------------------
31   QUALITY RATING FOR
32   PURCHASES>3                                 8.0
33
34
35
36   MINIMUM
37   --------------------
38   PRICE RATING FOR
39   QUALITY=10                                   4
40
41
42
43   MAXIMUM
44   --------------------
45   PURCHASES
46   PRICE>=8 OR QUALITY>=8                        5
47
48
49
50   PRICE>=8 AND QUALITY>=8
51   --------------------------------------
52   AVERAGE PURCHASES                          4.45
```

Figure 9-4. Worksheet displaying "More Calculations" results

5. In cell E30, type \- ENTER to underscore the label.

6. In cell E31, enter the label **QUALITY RATING FOR** to begin the title.

7. In cell E32, type **PURCHASES>3** ENTER.

8. Move to cell H32, enter the formula **@DAVG(SAMPLE,0,G1.G2)**, and press ENTER.

9. Type **/**Range Format Fixed **1** ENTER ENTER.

The average quality rating of the respondents who purchased more than three jars of honey is 8.0, as shown in Figure 9-4. More than three purchases is a considerable amount of honey in a year's time, and it is not surprising that the people who bought that much rated quality highly.

Minimum Price Rating: @DMIN

You can also calculate minima and maxima for groups of records by using the @DMIN and @DMAX functions. What is the minimum price rating of the records that contain a quality rating of 10? To obtain the correct group of records, the criterion must be a number-match for the value 10 in the field QUALITY. This is a criterion range that already exists on the worksheet (in cells F1.F2); reentering the criterion is unnecessary.

1. Move to cell E36.

2. Enter the label **MINIMUM**.

3. Enter an underscore at cell E37 by typing **\-** ENTER.

4. In cells E38 and E39, type the labels **PRICE RATING FOR** and **QUALITY=10**, respectively.

5. Move to cell H39.

The formula should come as no surprise:

6. Type **@DMIN(SAMPLE,1,F1.F2)** ENTER.

The offset of 1 corresponds to the PRICE field in the database.

The lowest price rating of the QUALITY=10 group is 4. Because we used the @RAND function to rig the price rating to a range of 4 to 10, this minimum value is predictable.

Highest Consumption Using
The OR Condition: @DMAX

To illustrate the use of @DMAX, we will derive the highest annual consumption of honey by an individual who rated either price or quality greater than or equal to 8. Because the criteria involve an OR condition, we can store multiple criteria in different rows of the criterion range. (We could also select the records using a compound formula with #OR#, but we will not do that now.) The criterion range should appear as follows:

PRICE	QUALITY
+B6>=8	
	+A6>=8

We will place this range in cells I1.J3.

1. Enter the criterion range in cells I1.J3 as shown in the preceding illustration.

2. Assign a format of Text to the range I2.J3.

3. Move to cell E43, and enter the label **MAXIMUM**.

4. Store an underscore in cell E44 by using the \- command.

5. In cell E45, enter the label **PURCHASES**; in cell E46, enter the label **PRICE>=8 OR QUALITY>=8**.

6. Move to cell H46, and enter the formula **@DMAX(SAMPLE,2,I1.J3)**.

Because the formula refers to PURCHASES, which is two columns to the right of the leftmost column of the SAMPLE database shown in Figure 9-1, the offset value is 2.

7. Press the ENTER key.

According to Figure 9-4, the maximum of five jars was purchased by a person who rated either price or quality (or both) favorably. This result comes as no surprise, because we set purchases equal to (PRICE+QUALITY)/4. Since several respondents rated both price and quality as 10, the maximum purchase should indeed be (10+10)/4=5.

Average Annual Purchases

The Too Bee analysts are curious about the group that rated both price and quality as 8 or more. We have already learned that this group accounts for 20% of the individuals surveyed and for 23.9% of annual purchases. Let us determine the average annual consumption of the >=8 group. The requisite criteria are already stored in cells E4..E5, and the offset value is 2. Develop the formula yourself; then follow these steps to obtain the result:

1. Move to cell E50, and enter the label **PRICE>=8 AND QUALITY >=8.**

2. Move to cell E51, and use \- to enter underscoring; then copy this underscore cell to cells F51 through G51.

3. Enter the label **AVERAGE PURCHASES** in cell E52.

4. Move to cell H52.

5. Enter the formula **@DAVG(SAMPLE,2,E4.E5)**, and press ENTER.

6. Type **/Range** Format Fixed **2** ENTER ENTER.

Based on the Figure 9-1 sample, Figure 9-4 shows that the average annual purchase by an individual of the >=8 group is 4.45 jars of honey.

However, just because 4.45 is the average, we cannot necessarily conclude that most members of the group bought 4.45 jars—or 4 jars, or even 5 jars. We know only that the sum of the group's purchases (89) divided by the number of people in the group (20) is 4.45. It is possible that 11 people bought 4 jars and 9 people bought 5 jars. However, it is also conceivable that 19 people bought no jars while one person bought 89 jars. Under such circumstances, the dispersion from the average of 4.45 jars is considerable. Thus, the average can be a deceptive statistic.

Variance and Standard Deviation

How deceptive is the average we just calculated? How could you find out? One possibility might be to measure the difference between individual purchases and the group average for each person in the group, sum all of these differences, and see if the total is significant. But this method will not work. The variations for purchases above the average will cancel out those below it, so that the total of all variations will be near zero.

We can get around this problem by counteracting the effect of the negative deviations. This can be done by taking the square of each difference. The square of any number is a positive number. Thus, if an individual purchases three jars, the deviation would be $3-4.45$, or -1.45, below the mean. The square of the result is -1.45^2, or 2.1025. The sum of these squared deviations for all individuals in the group, divided by the number of people in the group, yields the average of the squared deviations, and this value is called the *variance*. The higher the variance, the greater the general dispersion from the mean.

The *standard deviation* is defined as the square root of the variance. Because the variance is an average of the *squared* deviations from the average, measured in jars-squared, taking the square root removes the "squared" nature of the result, which may therefore seem more natural. A more detailed explanation of variance and standard deviation may be found in any introductory statistics text. For the purpose of this exercise, it is sufficient to know that both measure the disparity of a group of findings from the average, and that the standard deviation is the square root of the variance.

Calculating Variance With @DVAR

The *@DVAR* function computes the variance of a single field of values for those records chosen by the criteria. To find the variance of the purchases of respondents in the $>=8$ class, apply @DVAR to the SAMPLE range shown in Figure 9-1. The offset should be 2, and the criterion range is E4..E5.

1. In cell E54, enter the label **VARIANCE**.

2. Move to cell H54.

3. Type **@DVAR(SAMPLE,2,E4.E5)** ENTER.

The variance, the average of the squared deviations from the mean purchase of 4.45, is 0.2475 for the Figure 9-1 sample. On the average, then, the purchases of the group are within one jar of the group mean.

Calculating Standard Deviation With @DSTD

The standard deviation involves the same formula as the variance, except that *@DSTD* is used instead of @DVAR.

1. In cell E56, enter the label **STANDARD DEVIATION**.

2. Move to cell H56.

3. Type **@DSTD(SAMPLE,2,E4.E5)** ENTER.

The result is 0.497493. If you multiply this result by itself, you will obtain the variance.

Data Tables

The database functions @DCOUNT, @DSUM, @DAVG, @DMAX, @DMIN, @DVAR, and @DSTD have provided valuable insights into the statistical nature of the marketing survey. Once you have mastered the art of developing criteria, these database functions can go a long way toward making statistical analysis simple and fast. Still, the power of the Data command, which begins with Sort and Query, does not end with database functions. We now turn to the *data table* facility, which adds new dimensions (literally) to the database functions.

Data tables allow you to put temporary substitution values into a worksheet and to determine the results of formulas affected by the substitutions. You can use data tables with the database statistical functions to derive a table of values that shows many different ways to summarize the information contained in a database. There are two types of data tables, called *Data Table 1* and *Data Table 2*. We will examine both of these and see how they can be applied to our survey analysis.

Data Table 1

The preceding examples used database functions to address specific questions. (For instance, how many people rated price at 10? How many jars were sold to people who rated quality and price higher than 7?) Consider what would be required to report the average of the quality ratings submitted by respondents who gave price ratings of 1, 2, 3, 4,...10. You would have to develop a table that would look like the one shown.

AVERAGE QUALITY RATING

```
            1 )
        R   2 )
    P A     3 )
    R T     4 )
    I I     5 )
    C N     6 )
    E G     7 )
        S   8 )
            9 )
           10 )
```

We can make the example a bit more complicated by insisting on an additional column representing the annual purchases of each of the ten groups that rated price 1 through 10. With this second dimension, the table would look like this:

AVERAGE QUALITY RATING   TOTAL ANNUAL PURCHASES

```
           1 )
     R     2 )
 P   A     3 )
 R   T     4 )
 I   I     5 )
 C   N     6 )
 E   G     7 )
     S     8 )
           9 )
          10 )
```

To fill in the results section of this table, we would have to enter @DAVG and @DSUM formulas in each cell and also prepare criterion ranges for each of the 10 price-rating categories. Entering the 10 criteria and 20 formulas would be quite a drudgery were it not for the Data Table 1 command. To use Data Table 1, you need enter only one criterion, one @DAVG formula, and one @DSUM formula.

Look at the criterion in the range E1.E2. It was used to select records whose price rating is 10. We could use this criterion to compute the last entry of the first column of the table we just illustrated (the average quality rating of the group that gave price a rating of 10) with the formula @DAVG (SAMPLE,0,E1..E2).

Wouldn't it be wonderful if 1-2-3 could substitute each of the price ratings, 1 through 10, into the criterion cell and, for each successive substitution, calculate the @DAVG for the criterion and enter the result into the appropriate cell of the AVERAGE QUALITY RATING column? For that matter, it would be nice if 1-2-3 could do the same for the @DSUM formulas of the second column of the table. In other words, we would like 1-2-3 to automatically complete the results section of the table by using the price ratings as substitutions for the number-match criterion contained in cell E2.

It may seem too good Too Bee true, but this is precisely the capability of Data Table 1. Data Table 1 will use the price ratings column as substitution values, which it will sequentially place in any designated "input" cell of the worksheet — in this case the criterion cell, E2. Then 1-2-3 will recalculate the worksheet and place the formula result in the appropriate cell, repeating the process using each successive value in the substitution column.

Blank Cell					Formula Row
		Results	Area		

Substitution Entries

Figure 9-5. Diagram of Data Table 1

Figure 9-5 illustrates the generic form of Data Table 1, and Figure 9-6 shows its structure for our particular example. Conceptually, Data Table 1 comprises four items, shown in Figure 9-6:

- A column of values that will be used as substitution entries for the input cell.

- The input cell, the cell replaced by the substitution entries.

- A row of formulas whose result depends on the criterion input cell.

- A range of results, containing the results of the formulas specified in the formula row that were evaluated by using the substitution values defined in the leftmost column of the table.

We will evaluate two formulas in the table, one to compute the average quality rating for each of the price-rating categories, and one to compute total annual purchases for these same categories. The first formula, @DAVG (SAMPLE,0,E1.E2), calculates the average of the QUALITY field (offset of 0 in the Figure 9-1 database) for records that match the criterion in cell E2. Because E2 is the input cell, 1-2-3 will begin filling out the table by replacing E2 with the first substitution entry, 1. The criterion would then be

PRICE
1

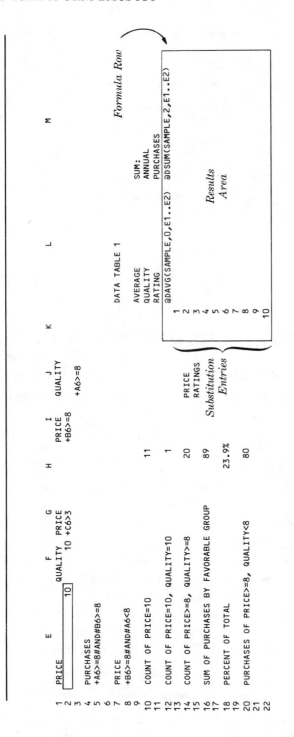

```
        E        F          G         H      I         J         K          L             M

 1   PRICE    QUALITY    PRICE              PRICE    QUALITY                           Formula Row
 2    10        10      +c6>3              +B6>=8
 3                                                  +A6>=8
 4   PURCHASES
 5   +A6>=8#AND#B6>=8
 6
 7   PRICE
 8   +B6>=8#AND#A6<8
 9
10   COUNT OF PRICE=10                      11                     DATA TABLE 1
11
12   COUNT OF PRICE=10, QUALITY=10           1                            AVERAGE         SUM:
13                                                                        QUALITY         ANNUAL
14   COUNT OF PRICE>=8, QUALITY>=8          20                            RATING          PURCHASES
15                                                                  @DAVG(SAMPLE,0,E1..E2)  @DSUM(SAMPLE,2,E1..E2)
16   SUM OF PURCHASES BY FAVORABLE GROUP    89                      1
17                                                   PRICE          2
18   PERCENT OF TOTAL                      23.9%     RATINGS        3
19                                                   Substitution   4                            Results
20   PURCHASES OF PRICE>=8, QUALITY<8      80        Entries        5                            Area
21                                                                  6
22                                                                  7
                                                                    8
                                                                    9
                                                                   10
```

Figure 9-6. Data Table 1 in K12..M22; criterion input cell is E2

which selects records with a price rating of 1. The @DAVG function is evaluated for the records selected, and the result is placed in cell L13.

The second formula, @DSUM(SAMPLE,2,E1.E2), computes the total of the purchase field for the same group of selected records. Its result for the price rating of 1 is reported in cell M13.

Next 1-2-3 replaces the input cell with 2, the next substitution entry (cell K14). The @DAVG and @DSUM functions are reevaluated for the new criterion, and their results are stored in cells L14 and M14, the second row of the table. These steps are repeated until the entire table has been filled.

Constructing Data Table 1

Begin constructing Data Table 1 by entering the row and column headings of the table, as follows:

1. At cell L7, enter the label **DATA TABLE 1**.

2. Move to cell L9.

3. Enter the labels **AVERAGE**, **QUALITY**, and **RATING** in cells L9, L10, and L11 respectively.

4. Move to cell M9.

5. Enter the labels **SUM:**, **ANNUAL**, and **PURCHASES** in cells M9, M10, and M11 respectively.

6. Move to cell J14.

7. Enter the labels **PRICE** and **RATINGS** in cells J14 and J15 respectively.

8. Move to cell K13.

9. Enter the numbers **1, 2, 3, . . . 10** in cells K13..K22. You may use **/Data Fill** to do this in one step. To enter the formula row,

10. Move to cell L12.

11. Enter the formula **@DAVG(SAMPLE,0,E1.E2)**.

12. Go to M12.

13. Enter the formula **@DSUM(SAMPLE,2,E1.E2)**, and press ENTER.

Both formulas will result in numbers. It would be clearer to show the formulas that are being used to derive the table by assigning a Text format to the formula row of the data table:

14. Move to cell L12, and type **/ Range Format Text**.

15. Move to cell ,M12 to expand the range, and press ENTER.

We need to extend the column width of columns L and M to make the formulas visible. Leaving the pointer on L12,

16. Type **/ Worksheet Column Set-Width 24** ENTER.

17. Now move to cell M12, and type **/ Worksheet Column Set-Width 24** ENTER.

Getting (and Explaining) Results

Data Table 1 is now complete — except for the results. To invoke the Data Table 1 command, it is necessary to tell 1-2-3 where the data table and input cell are located. The data table is specified as a range. The top-left cell of the range is the empty cell above the substitution column and to the left of the formulas row — in this instance, cell K12. The bottom right of the table is at cell M22.

1. Move to cell K12, the beginning of the table range.

2. Type **/Data Table**.

Now 1-2-3 will ask whether you desire Table 1 or Table 2.

3. Type **1** to choose Data Table 1.

Now you are prompted for the table range. Note that 1-2-3 recommends the current cell as the beginning of the range. This is acceptable. To indicate the end of the range,

4. Type the . key, then move to cell M22.

5. Press the ENTER key.

In response to the prompt for the input cell's address,

6. Move the pointer to cell E2.

7. Press the ENTER key.

It will take a minute or two before 1-2-3 returns with a completed table, because the worksheet is being recalculated several times.

When 1-2-3 has completed its task, the results should look like Figure 9-7 (with allowances, of course, for the difference between our @RAND-operated database and yours). The figure shows that the average quality rating of each price group above 3 lies consistently between 7 and 8. Do not be disturbed by

	J	K	L	M
7			DATA TABLE 1	
8				
9			AVERAGE	SUM:
10			QUALITY	ANNUAL
11			RATING	PURCHASES
12			@DAVG(SAMPLE,0,E1..E2)	@DSUM(SAMPLE,2,E1..E2)
13		1	ERR	0
14	PRICE	2	ERR	0
15	RATINGS	3	ERR	0
16		4	7.5714285714	21
17		5	7.6842105263	64
18		6	7.0588235294	56
19		7	7.4705882353	62
20		8	7.375	64
21		9	7.6923076923	55
22		10	7.5454545455	50

Figure 9-7. Data Table 1 completed

the appearance of ERR and 0 in the first three rows of the result column. There are no surveys that contain a price rating of 3 or less, so the average for these groups is incalculable (yielding ERR), and the purchases total 0 for each group.

The table makes one confusing statement. Even though the average quality rating was somewhat stable for the existing groups, the number of jars purchased by each group did not rise as the price rating went up. If the respondents consistently feel that quality rates about 7.5, we would normally expect that the groups with higher price ratings would have higher annual purchases. In other words, if all respondents are about equally satisfied with the quality, we would expect those who are happier about the price to buy more honey. Yet Figure 9-7 shows purchases to be rather random—and indeed they are, because of the @RAND function. When we fabricated the survey, we made no attempt to relate price and quality. They were left totally independent, and the data table shows the result.

Data Table 2

In Data Table 1, a single cell (the input cell) is replaced by substitution entries, and the results of formulas that depend on that cell are registered in the table. In contrast, Data Table 2 involves *two* input cells. The first input cell is varied by using one set of substitution entries. A second input cell is replaced by another set of substitution entries.

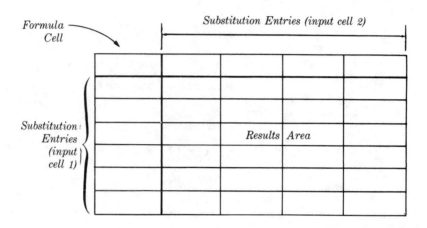

Figure 9-8. Diagram of Data Table 2

Structure of Data Table 2

Figure 9-8 diagrams Data Table 2's structure. The first set of substitution entries is placed along the leftmost column of the table, as in Data Table 1. The second set of substitutions is stored on the top row of the table, where formulas are stored in Data Table 1. A single formula, dependent on both input cells, is evaluated and stored in the upper-left corner of this table. The difference between Data Table 1 and Data Table 2 is that Data Table 1 evaluates several formulas that are functions of a single variable, whereas Data Table 2 evaluates one formula that depends on two variables.

For example, suppose you want to know the number of responses associated with every possible combination of quality and price ratings. How many people rated quality 1 and price 1? How many rated quality 1 and price 2? For each of the ten quality ratings (1 through 10), there are ten possible ratings for price. Actually, we know that there are no quality ratings less than 5 and no price ratings less than 4, so we will restrict this discussion to combinations of quality ratings between 5 and 10 and price ratings between 4 and 10.

Constructing Data Table 2

Figure 9-9 shows how Data Table 2 appears on the worksheet. In the steps that follow, we will duplicate the figure on the worksheet and then invoke Data Table 2. Prepare the table using these steps:

1. Go to cell L26, and enter the label **DATA TABLE 2**.

2. In cell J28, enter the label **FREQUENCY OF COMBINATIONS OF PRICE AND QUALITY RATINGS**.

3. In cell M31, enter the label **QUALITY RATINGS --->** (the arrow is made up of three dashes and a >).

4. In cells J34 and J35, enter the labels **PRICE** and **RATINGS** respectively.

Now the price ratings must be stored in the column of substitution entries for input cell 1:

5. Go to cell K33, and enter the values **4, 5, 6,...10**, respectively, in cells K33..K39.

The substitutions for input cell 2, the quality ratings, belong in row 32 of the spreadsheet:

6. Enter the values **5, 6, 7,...10** in cells L32 through Q32 respectively.

The formula to tally the responses for each combination of price and quality rating is @DCOUNT(*input range, offset, criterion range*). The input range is, as always, SAMPLE. The offset, pointing to the database field to be tallied, will be 0 (1 or 2 would serve as well in this instance, because @DCOUNT counts nonblank entries, and all three columns of the input range are nonblank).

There are two criteria to be reckoned with. One criterion is a number-match on the QUALITY field. If you turn back to Figure 9-6 and examine the first two criterion ranges developed in this chapter, stored in the range E1..F2, you will observe that these two ranges can be utilized for the purposes of this table. The criterion cells, E2 and F2, will be defined as input cell 1 and input cell 2 respectively. During the first iteration of the data table, cell E2 will be replaced with the value 4, the first PRICE substitution. Cell F2 will be replaced with the value 5. The fact that both criteria are on the same row dictates an AND condition. Therefore, the formula @DCOUNT

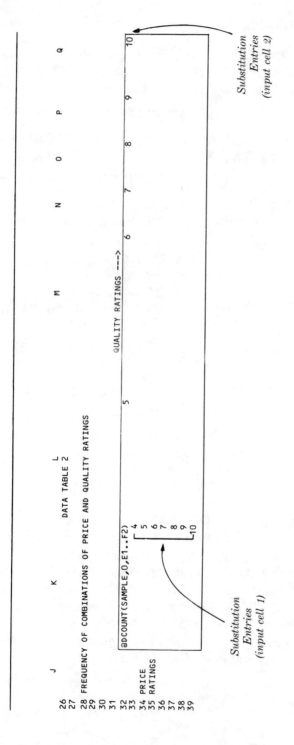

Figure 9-9. Data Table 2 on worksheet, with formula cell in K32

(SAMPLE,0,E1.F2) totals the number of surveys that have a price rating of 4 and a quality rating of 5. Lotus 1-2-3 uses this same technique to iterate through the other rating combinations.

The Data Table 2 formula must reside in the top-left corner of the table range, cell K32.

7. Move to cell K32.

8. Type **@DCOUNT(SAMPLE,0,E1.F2)** ENTER.

9. Give this cell a Text format by typing **/Range Format Text** ENTER.

10. Widen the column so that the entire formula is visible on the worksheet by typing **/Worksheet Column Set-Width 25** ENTER.

To fill out the table,

11. Type **/Data Table.**

Before selecting Data Table 2, consider the fact that 1-2-3 has committed to memory the table range and input cell addresses of Table 1. As you enter the Data Table menu, 1-2-3 will continually suggest the old settings, and you must press ESC to undo the suggestions. To avoid this slight nuisance,

12. Type **R** to choose the Reset option.

With the previous settings released,

13. Type **/Data Table 2.**

You are asked for the Table range.

14. Move the pointer to cell K32, the top left of the table.

15. Type the . key to anchor a range.

16. Point to the bottom right of the table, cell Q39, and press ENTER.

In response to the request for the address of input cell 1,

17. Move the pointer to cell E2, and press ENTER.

In response to the prompt for input cell 2,

18. Move the pointer to cell F2, and press ENTER.

Now, take a break—perhaps get a cup of coffee. Because of the required number of recalculations, it takes 1-2-3 about 3 1/2 minutes to finish the table, but it is still a lot faster than doing it by hand. The results, as Figure 9-10 shows, are rather haphazard. But this was expected because we used @RAND to generate random ratings in the first place.

	J	K	L	M	N	O	P	Q
26								
27			DATA TABLE 2					
28	FREQUENCY OF COMBINATIONS OF PRICE AND QUALITY RATINGS							
29								
30								
31				QUALITY RATINGS --->				
32			@DCOUNT(SAMPLE,0,E1..F2)	5	6	7	8	9	10
33		4	1	1	1	2	1	1
34		PRICE 5	3	3	1	5	4	3
35		RATINGS 6	1	5	4	1	3	1
36		7	1	4	2	4	4	1
37		8	0	2	6	2	4	0
38		9	0	2	3	5	3	0
39		10	1	2	2	3	2	1

Figure 9-10. Data Table 2 completed

Verifying Results

If you are interested in checking the results, it is possible to do this with 1-2-3. An easy way to test the veracity of the table is to add up all of the entries in the results range. Because the table covers all possible combinations of survey responses, the total count should equal the total number of surveys, 100.

1. Go to cell L43.

You may use the @SUM function to compute the sum of an entire rectangular range.

2. Type **@SUM(** to begin the formula.

3. Move the pointer to the top-left corner of the response range, cell L33.

4. Type the . key to anchor the range.

5. Move the pointer to the bottom right of the results range (Q39) by pressing END and the right arrow key, then END and the down arrow key.

6. Type **)** ENTER.

The result is indeed 100.

With the spreadsheet statistical functions, the database statistical functions, the Data Distribution command, and the data tables, 1-2-3 provides a wide variety of tools for summarizing vast amounts of data. The utility of data tables specifically is not limited to database statistics. Data tables can be used to great advantage in "what if" and sensitivity analysis, as you will be able to see in the acquisition model of Chapter 12.

Although the term "database statistical function" may distance some users from the subject of this chapter, the ability to count, add, and average selected portions of a worksheet is basic to many applications. Even as a 1-2-3 graph is worth a thousand words, a statistic is worth a thousand records.

PART 3
Advanced
Methods
And Applications

Parts 1 and 2 of this book introduced you to the 1-2-3 program. By now you should be familiar with the worksheet and its spreadsheet, database, and graphics capabilities. Part 3 deals with topics of a more advanced nature. You should not proceed with Part 3 until you are comfortable with the material presented in the previous chapters.

The first two chapters of Part 3 focus on the use of macros to facilitate database management procedures. In Chapter 10 the invoice file developed in Chapters 6 and 7 illustrates forms-oriented processing—the ability to enter and retrieve data on an electronic form. This project makes use of 1-2-3's ability to protect areas of the worksheet from inadvertent changes. Chapter 11 demonstrates additional macro techniques by applying the forms-oriented method to stock portfolio tracking.

Chapter 12 describes an advanced spreadsheet model that evaluates the profitability of acquiring an asset like a company or a piece of equip-

ment. 1-2-3's financial functions produce a cash flow analysis that is used to compute a purchase price for the asset. The ability to do what-if and sensitivity analysis with its Data Table feature demonstrates 1-2-3's talent for spreadsheet analysis.

Chapter 13 concentrates exclusively on Version 2.0. It uses a purchase-order tracking system to introduce text-manipulation functions and demonstrates using the System command to suspend a 1-2-3 session in order to perform DOS functions.

Chapter 10
Forms-Oriented Database Management

_____
_____
_____

The Goal: An Automated
Billing System

Cell Protection

Transferring Records
To the Database

Printing Invoices From
The Database

Finishing the Invoice
System: Two Ideas

In Part II we saw the various ways in which 1-2-3 functions as a database management system. Chapters 6 and 7 were concerned with a billing system for a medical practice, Chapter 8 showed how macros can extend and simplify the database capabilities of 1-2-3, and Chapter 9 explored database statistical functions. But there is so much more that can be done with databases and macros.

One very useful application is electronic forms management. Many people who use manual systems to manage such functions as billing, inventory control, and payroll are accustomed to filling out forms to enter and display information that is part of the record-keeping system. In billing, for example, the form is the invoice. The process of filling out the invoice and putting it into a file cabinet is called *forms entry*.

With 1-2-3, you can imitate a forms-oriented system electronically by creating a screen that looks like a printed form. Even better, you can construct a macro that automatically copies information from the completed form into a database. Users need not know anything about the complex 1-2-3 commands they are using—they simply enter the information that is called for. Forms entry is a great enhancement to invoicing systems, such as the one used by Dr. R.X. DoMuch, whom we met in Chapters 6 and 7. In this chapter, we will create a forms-oriented database management system to streamline Dr. DoMuch's billing system.

One of the primary concerns of database management is that the user might accidentally clobber the database. It is so simple to delete important data inadvertently. A Range Erase here, a Delete Column there, a data entry misplaced, a Copy to the wrong row, a Move to the wrong range, and the worksheet is unusable. However, in this chapter we will see that there is a way to protect the worksheet from such mishaps. In fact, it is possible to prevent the user from even moving the cursor to a cell that must be protected.

Forms-oriented database management with 1-2-3 is a two-way street. Not only can you input information onto forms, but you can report the information quite handsomely as well. At the end of this chapter we will print a formal invoice from the information contained in the database.

Before proceeding with this chapter, you should be familiar with the content and concepts of Chapters 6, 7, and 8. (However, you will not need the models created in those chapters.) In particular, you should know how a 1-2-3 database is structured; what input ranges, criterion ranges, and output ranges are; how to use the Data Query command; how the date functions work; and how to create and use a macro. Some of this material is reviewed in this chapter.

The Goal: An Automated Billing System

Dr. R.X. DoMuch has been billing his patients in the same way for years. As a patient exits the office, the doctor's administrative assistant fills out by hand an invoice form that indicates the amount due and requests the patient's full remittance. A duplicate of the invoice is typed and placed in a file box marked RECEIVABLES.

The invoices are supposed to be kept in alphabetical order so that the invoice of a particular patient can be easily found. However, the overdue bills are periodically removed, copied, and sent to the patients with a polite note requesting immediate payment. This frequent usage often leaves the file box in disarray.

Lotus 1-2-3's mission is to automate the forms-entry and forms-output aspects of this billing process. Bear in mind that both the doctor and the administrative assistant are inexperienced at computing. The system must be user-friendly and mistake-proof.

Setting Up the Database

We will start by setting up the fields of the database. Then we will create an input form that will be used to enter records (invoices) into the database. Using macros, we will create a data-entry procedure that accepts data onto the input form and transfers the input to the database section of the worksheet. Finally, we will create an output form to report the information contained in the database.

The following table lists the names and column widths of fields that make up the patient-invoice database:

COLUMN	FIELD NAME	COLUMN WIDTH
A	NAME	20
B	STREET ADDRESS	25
C	CITY,STATE,ZIP	25
D	SERVICES	15
E	AMOUNT	8
F	MON	4
G	DAY	4
H	YR	3
I	DAYS PAST DUE	5
	Total	109

The first eight items will make up the input form. They will be input by the record keeper at Dr. DoMuch's office in a special area of the worksheet set aside for data entry. The last item, DAYS PAST DUE, is a computation that the system will automatically supply. If CAPS is not indicated on the lower right of the screen, press the CAPS LOCK key.

1. Enter the title ^**INVOICE DATABASE** in cell A1.

2. Enter the first eight field names listed in the table into columns A through H of row 4, as shown in Figure 10-1. Assign the corresponding column widths shown in the table, using /Worksheet Column Set-Width.

3. The ninth field name, DAYS PAST DUE, should be split into three cells: enter **DAYS** in cell I2, **PAST** in cell I3, and **DUE** in cell I4. Assign this field a column width of 5, as shown in the table, using /Worksheet Column Set-Width.

4. Move to cell A1; center all of the column headings at once by issuing /Range Label-Prefix Center; expand the pointer to I4, and press ENTER.

5. Move down to cell A5, and enter an underscore by using \-.

6. Copy this underscore across the row, below the remaining field names (cells B5..I5).

Your worksheet should now look like Figure 10-1.

The Invoice Input Form

The invoice input form should be on an otherwise blank screen. Because of the need to link the input form with the database, the form should not be saved on a separate worksheet. Instead, we move to a clear portion of the current worksheet, someplace where the form will not be in the way of the database. Anywhere to the right of the database fields will do.

1. Move to cell M1, and enter **INVOICE INPUT FORM**.

2. Move down once to cell M2 and enter an underscore.

The underscore extends beneath only half of the label. That is because the label INVOICE INPUT FORM, although stored in M1, spills over into the empty cell next to it, N1. The \- command fills up only one cell, M2.

3. Put another underscore in cell N2.

The input form that the record keeper will use for the invoice system is shown in Figure 10-2. We will translate this figure into a worksheet.

```
A
1 INVOICE DATABASE
2
3 --------------------------------------------------------------------
4 NAME            STREET ADDRESS      CITY,STATE,ZIP      SERVICES    AMOUNT MON DAY YR  DAYS
5 --------------------------------------------------------------------                  PAST
                                                                                        DUE
        B                   C                      D            E    F   G   H   I
```

Figure 10-1. Headings for invoice database

```
              K        L        M        N        O        P        Q        R
     1                          INVOICE INPUT FORM
     2                          ------------------
     3
     4      NAME
     5                          ---------------------------<--LAST NAME FIRST
     6      STREET ADDRESS
     7                          --------------------------<--BEGIN WITH APOSTROPHE
     8      CITY,STATE,ZIP
     9                          --------------------------
    10      AMOUNT
    11                          ---------
    12      SERVICES
    13                          --------------------------
    14      DATE:     MONTH          [NUMERIC]
    15                          ---------
    16                DAY            [NUMERIC]
    17                          ---------
    18                YEAR           [NUMERIC, 2 DIGITS]
    19                          ---------
```

Figure 10-2. The invoice input form

4. Enter the following labels:

IN CELL	ENTER
K4	**NAME**
K6	**STREET ADDRESS**
K8	**CITY,STATE,ZIP**
K10	**AMOUNT**
K12	**SERVICES**
K14	**DATE:**
L14	**MONTH**
L16	**DAY**
L18	**YEAR**

Splitting the date into three parts (month, day, year) will make it easier to later develop the formula for DAYS PAST DUE.

The next step is to put underscores in the right places. This will help clearly identify which cells will house the input.

5. Use \- and the Copy command to place underscores in the following cells: M5, N5, O5; M7, N7, O7; M9, N9, O9; M11; M13, N13, O13; M15; M17; M19.

Next we can annotate the form to make it easier to use. The NAME cell should be entered last name first so that the file can be sorted by last names. We will put a reminder next to the NAME input cell.

6. At cell P4, type <-- **LAST NAME FIRST**.

The <-- is constructed by typing a < (the shift and comma key, located on the lower right of the keyboard) and two dashes.

A second annotation will be helpful on the STREET ADDRESS line. Most addresses begin with a number, as in 22 Lovers Lane. But entering 22 Lovers Lane into the STREET ADDRESS cell would cause an error. As soon as the first 2 of 22 is pressed, 1-2-3 assumes Value Mode. It will accept the second 2, but when you try to save this number together with the Lovers Lane portion of the entry, you will be beeped. Lotus 1-2-3 thinks that you are trying to stuff label characters into a numeric cell. To avoid this problem, you must begin the STREET ADDRESS label with an apostrophe, the label-prefix that left-justifies the label within the cell. Here is another occasion when a reminder would be helpful on the input form.

7. Enter the label <-- **BEGIN WITH APOSTROPHE** at cell P6.

The month, day, and year must be entered as numbers (for instance, 11, 2, 83 for November 2, 1983).

8. Store the labels **[NUMERIC]** in cells N14 and N16 and store the label **[NUMERIC, 2 DIGITS]** in cell N18.

Your worksheet should now resemble Figure 10-2. Before proceeding, save the invoice and database headings in a file named BILLING.

9. Type /File Save **BILLING** ENTER.

Cell Protection

When you first boot up the 1-2-3 worksheet, each cell is invisibly surrounded by what the 1-2-3 User's Manual calls an "electronic fence," whose power is initially off. If you turn the "fence" on, however, it will protect the cell contents from alteration. The contents of a protected cell cannot be replaced or even edited.

Cell protection is used to safeguard data that should not be altered. It is also useful for protecting titles, headings, and macros. Cell protection helps prevent a careless, inexperienced, or malicious person from ruining your worksheet. Obviously, you would not want to protect each and every cell when you first boot up 1-2-3 because this would prevent you from doing anything with the worksheet. Once your application is set up, however, protection is a useful feature. To protect the invoice input form you have just developed,

1. Type /Worksheet Global Protection Enable.

The Worksheet Global Protection command can be issued at any time from Ready Mode. It is the switch that turns on the protective "fences" around the cells. To test it, try entering data in any cell. Try to copy one cell to another. Try a Move command. Nothing will work. The worksheet is protected from virtually all harm. There is such a thing as overprotection, however. Inasmuch as no data has been entered into the database yet, it was a bit premature to turn on the juice.

2. Type /Worksheet Global Protection Disable.

This brings us back to where we began.

Withdrawing Protection With Range Unprotect

There is no benefit in protecting the entire worksheet. Protection is an advantage only if it can coexist with "unprotection." That is, we need to be able to protect certain ranges of cells and to unprotect others. Perhaps you have noticed the Protect and Unprotect options of the Range command. Range Unprotect dismantles the "fence" around one or more cells so that even when global protection is enabled, cells that have been explicitly unprotected with Range Unprotect remain accessible. (The Range Protect command can be used, however, to replace the fence.)

1. Move to the NAME input cell, M4.

2. Type /Range Unprotect.

At this point you may either expand the range to be unprotected or press ENTER to unprotect the single-cell range, M4..M4.

3. Press ENTER to unprotect the NAME input cell only.

There is no functional difference between this cell and any others until you switch worksheet protection back on.

4. Type /Worksheet Global Protection Enable.

With protection enabled, the NAME input cell is the only cell on the entire worksheet that can be altered. You should prove this to yourself, then return to cell M4 and examine the first line of the control panel. The U indicates that this cell has been Unprotected with the Range Unprotect command.

While data is being entered into the input form, we can temporarily protect all but the input cells by having protection on and unprotecting only the eight input cells of the input form.

5. Move the cursor to the following input cells, and type /Range Unprotect ENTER at each: M6, M8, M10, M12, M14, M16, and M18.

Notice that the Range Unprotect command can take effect even while global protection is on. If you should ever need to enter data into a protected cell while protection is enabled, there is no need to use Worksheet Global Protection Disable. Instead, you may use Range Unprotect, then make the entry. Protection is entirely under your control—it is not permanent.

The Range Input Command

While the Worksheet Global Protection command prevents protected cells from being altered, it is still possible to move the pointer to a protected cell. However, in some situations (forms entry is an example), you might not want the record keeper to move freely around the worksheet. The Range Input command can be used to restrict movement. When you issue Range Input, 1-2-3 asks for a range, which must include at least one unprotected cell. Protection need not be turned on prior to using the Range Input command. The top-left corner of the range will become the top-left corner of the screen.

You should choose the top-left corner carefully so that the entire input form fits cleanly on the screen. To make sure you pick the correct spot, first go to a distant cell:

1. Press HOME.

Then,

2. Use the right arrow key to scroll the screen toward the right until the entire input form appears in the window. This would mean moving to cell R1.

Looking at the top-left cell of the display, we see that cell K1 should be the top-left corner of the input range.

3. Go to cell K1.

4. Type /Range Input.

5. Type the . key to anchor the input range, then expand the pointer to P20, and press ENTER. (Cell M20 or N20 would do just as well, because

they also would cause the unprotected cells to be within the input range.)

Notice that the input form now takes up the entire display. The screen is uncluttered and pleasing to the eye. The pointer migrates to the first unprotected cell of the input range, M4.

The pointer movement keys work differently while Range Input is in effect. The arrow keys still move the pointer in the direction of the arrow, but the pointer skips any cells that are protected. Similarly, the HOME and END keys are functional, but only to move the pointer within the input range. It is as if the worksheet were restricted to the input range alone. Now we can test the input form.

6. Enter the following data onto the invoice form (remember the apostrophe preceding the street address):

> NAME: **SMITH, JOHN**
> STREET ADDRESS: **'123 SOFTWARE STREET**
> CITY,STATE,ZIP: **SILICON VALLEY, CA 19829**
> AMOUNT: **10**
> SERVICES: **EXAMINATION**
> MONTH: **2**
> DAY: **1**
> YEAR: **84**

Your completed form should look like Figure 10-3. You can move the pointer, enter data, edit a cell, and use the Help facility. But you cannot issue a 1-2-3 command beginning with /, nor can you use any of the function keys other than the F1 (Help) key or the F2 (Edit) key. Range Input, along with its restrictions, remains in effect even after you make an entry in the last input cell. It is as if you have entered an entirely separate data-entry mode.

To disengage the Range Input command, you may press either ESC or ENTER *before* you have done anything else, such as beginning a cell entry or an edit. (Pressing ESC in the middle of an entry cancels the entry, and pressing ESC a second time cancels Range Input.) Also, that ultimate weapon, the combination of the CTRL key and the BREAK key, restores Ready Mode as always.

7. Press ESC to exit Range Input.

Try moving the pointer around. Pointer movement is back to normal, and you can issue commands as usual, subject to protection. You will have more opportunity to practice with Range Input shortly.

```
            K       L       M       N        O       P       Q       R
    1                       INVOICE INPUT FORM
    2                       ------------------
    3
    4 NAME                  SMITH, JOHN
    5                       ------------------------<--LAST NAME FIRST
    6 STREET ADDRESS        123 SOFTWARE STREET
    7                       ------------------------<--BEGIN WITH APOSTROPHE
    8 CITY,STATE,ZIP        SILICON VALLEY, CA 19829
    9                       ---------------------------
   10 AMOUNT                       10
   11                       ---------
   12 SERVICES              EXAMINATION
   13                       ---------------------------
   14 DATE:   MONTH               2 [NUMERIC]
   15                       ---------
   16         DAY                 1 [NUMERIC]
   17                       ---------
   18         YEAR               84 [NUMERIC, 2 DIGITS]
   19                       ---------
   20
```

Figure 10-3.   Completed invoice input form

Transferring Records
To the Database

Transferring the input from the form to the database is a job for the Copy command. It is not a one-step process, though. Each entry must be copied, one at a time, into the next available row of the database. The eight data entries necessitate eight Copy commands. There is no way out of this one — except, perhaps, to develop a macro to do all eight copies in one fell swoop. Meanwhile, let's see how it is done manually. (It is funny how, with 1-2-3, you begin to think of certain steps as "manual" even though they are highly automated by most standards.)

1. Turn off protection by typing /Worksheet Global Protection Disable.

If you neglect the preceding step, the Copy command will not function, because you cannot copy into a protected cell.

2. Move to the first input cell, the NAME cell (M4), and type /Copy ENTER to make NAME the source.

3. Move to the first cell of the next available record in the database, cell A6, and press ENTER to complete the Copy operation.

So eight times we must initiate a Copy, move here, move there, and so on. We can, however, make the process a little less tedious. For starters, we can assign range names to each of the input cells. With the pointer on the NAME input cell, M4,

4. Type /Range Name Create **NAME** ENTER ENTER.

5. Repeat Step 4 for the other seven input cells, using the following range names:

CELL	RANGE NAME
M6	**STREET**
M8	**CITY**
M10	**AMOUNT**
M12	**SERVICES**
M14	**MONTH**
M16	**DAY**
M18	**YEAR**

Back to the task of copying. This time we will deviate from the routine by placing the pointer at the target cell (instead of the source) before initiating the copy.

6. Go to cell B6, and type /Copy.

Now 1-2-3 suggests the current pointer position as the source. The suggestion can be overridden by explicitly typing the source coordinates or a range name.

7. Type **STREET** and press ENTER.

With the source accepted, 1-2-3 prompts for the target, suggesting the current cell position. This is fine, so

8. Press ENTER.

9. Move right once, and type /Copy **CITY** ENTER ENTER.

10. Repeat Step 9 for the other input cells, substituting their names in the command. Remember that if you forget a range name, you may press the F3 (Name) key to invoke a list of active range names.

Using the range names in the Copy command obviates the need to move all over the worksheet. Nonetheless, this is not what you would call an easy system to use.

Forms-Oriented Data Entry:
The Procedure

Let us review the steps taken to fill out the invoice form and store it in the database:

. Invoke /Range Input, and enter the input range.

. Fill out the invoice form.

. Escape from Range Input.

. Disable global protection.

. Move the pointer to the next available record of the database.

. Copy the input items to the database.

Three more steps should be appended to the procedure in order to complete the data entry:

. Compute DAYS PAST DUE.

. If another form is to be processed, repeat the preceding steps.

. Turn global protection back on.

This procedure can be represented as a macro.

A Macro for Forms-Oriented
Data Entry

The input range of the Range Input command was entered as K1..P20, using the ability to point. Within a macro, though, it is far better to use a range name than to use the pointing facility or to type the cell addresses. The pointing facility would be a problem because the macro, during execution, cannot "see" where to position the cursor in order to specify a range. Using the explicit coordinates K1..P20 is not a good idea either; if you need to change the location of these cells, the macro will not automatically be aware of it. The optimal strategy is to use range names whenever possible in a macro. Assign the name INPUTFORM to the input range:

1. Go to cell K1, and type /Range Name Create **INPUTFORM** ENTER. Then type the . key, expand the pointer to cell P20, and press ENTER.

Now we can begin building a macro, incorporating the range names that we have assigned. The first step of the macro procedure will be to invoke Range Input for the INPUTFORM range. The command keystrokes used to do this are /Range Input INPUTFORM ENTER, which translates into the macro label /RIINPUTFORM~. Recall that the ~ (tilde) is the macro substitution code for the ENTER key.

When the macro is executed, 1-2-3 will read the Range Input command, prompt for the input range, and see the letters INPUTFORM. Because 1-2-3 interprets the ~ character as an ENTER, it knows that the word INPUT-FORM refers to a range name.

Remember that the macro keystrokes must be preceded by an apostrophe. Otherwise, when you type the first character of the sequence (the /), 1-2-3 assumes that you are about to enter a command, not a macro label. We will name this macro \A and store its first step in cell M75:

2. Go to cell M75, and type '/**RIINPUTFORM**~ ENTER.

3. Name the macro by typing /**Range Name Create \A** ENTER ENTER.

As always, it is a good idea to document your macro. You can do this by going to cell T75 and typing a concise explanation that will remind you of what this first step of \A does, then providing similar documentation next to each succeeding line of the macro.

Now try this macro out: invoke it by holding the ALT key down while pressing the A key. The CMD indicator appears beside the mode indicator, suggesting that a macro is in effect. Enter a record onto the invoice form, and when the record is correct, press either ESC or ENTER to exit Input Mode. Not only is Ready Mode restored, but the CMD indicator disappears. When you pressed ESC, you returned processing control to the \A macro. But there are no other commands stored in the macro, so control is returned to Ready Mode.

The next enhancement to this macro is the ability to copy the input-form data to the database. If global protection will be on at the time other users invoke the macro, the Copy commands will not work. Therefore, we must turn off global protection with the Worksheet Global Protection Disable command:

4. At cell M76, enter '/**WGPD**.

There is no need for the ~ at the end of this label. If you were typing this command "live," it would not have been necessary to press ENTER after the command sequence, because 1-2-3 would proceed directly to Ready Mode as soon as you pressed the D of Disable.

Locating the Next Record In the Database

When we copied a record manually, we first positioned the cell pointer at the next available blank record of the database. If we always made our entries in this way, it would be simple enough to find the right target for the input record by scrolling to the database and using our eyes to find the next blank cell in the first data field, column A. But 1-2-3 does not have the human trait of visual recognition (at least, not in the current version of the software). When it is executing a macro, how will it be able to locate the next available record?

Actually, this is an easy problem to solve, although it requires a bit of imagination. In confronting this kind of problem, try to discover a means of pointing, using steps that a macro can emulate. Start by pressing the HOME key to move the pointer to the database area. Press END and then the down arrow key to transfer the pointer to the next nonblank cell (which is the field heading, NAME). Press END and then the down arrow key once more to skip to the next nonblank cell bordering a blank. Then press the down arrow key once to rest the pointer on the next available record. We are now there. A bit of clever fingerwork, combined with an intimate knowledge of how the database is structured, yields a procedure easily rendered into macro keystrokes. The keystrokes are HOME, END, down arrow, END, down arrow, and down arrow.

1. At cell M77, enter the label

   {HOME}{END}{DOWN}{END}{DOWN}{DOWN}

So far, our macro looks like this:

```
'/RIINPUTFORM~
'/WGPD
{HOME}{END}{DOWN}{END}{DOWN}{DOWN}
```

This sequence will work, no matter how many records we store in the database, as long as there are no blank entries in the NAME field—and there will not be any.

Copying the Data Fields

Now that the cell pointer is in the proper place, the Copy commands proceed exactly as we typed them when we plodded through the manual process. In each Copy operation, we used the range name of the input cell to designate the source. Because the pointer was already positioned at the target, pressing ENTER sufficed to complete the Copy. With the pointer on the NAME cell of the database record, typing /Copy NAME ENTER ENTER copied the NAME of the input form to the NAME field of the database. Pressing the right arrow key moves the pointer to the next data field in preparation for the next Copy. '/Crangename~~{RIGHT} is thus the macro label for each Copy command. It is permissible to combine several steps in a single macro, as follows:

1. At cell M78, enter '/CNAME~~{RIGHT}/CSTREET~~{RIGHT}.

2. At cell M79, enter '/CCITY~~{RIGHT}/CSERVICES~~{RIGHT}.

3. At cell M80, enter '/CAMOUNT~~{RIGHT}/CMONTH~~{RIGHT}.

4. At cell M81, enter '/CDAY~~{RIGHT}/CYEAR~~{RIGHT}.

The expanded macro \A now extends through cells M75..M81, and it looks like this:

```
'/RIINPUTFORM~
'/WGPD
{HOME}{END}{DOWN}{END}{DOWN}{DOWN}
'/CNAME~~{RIGHT}/CSTREET~~{RIGHT}
'/CCITY~~{RIGHT}/CSERVICES~~{RIGHT}
'/CAMOUNT~~{RIGHT}/CMONTH~~{RIGHT}
'/CDAY~~{RIGHT}/CYEAR~~{RIGHT}
```

Before you try out the new macro, protect yourself from needless loss by saving the worksheet file.

5. Type /File Save ENTER Replace.

Now if a typographical error causes the macro to malfunction, you will be able to retrieve it for cross-examination and correction.

We can now safely try out macro \A. Try the macro by holding down the ALT key while typing A. Range Input is the first command processed. Fill out the invoice form with new input. You are probably thinking that the procedure could be improved if 1-2-3 would automatically erase the contents of the form from the previous entry. Let us make a mental note of this possible enhancement and return to it later. Meanwhile, press the ESC key when you have completed the form.

Do not take your eyes off the screen. You'll see how 1-2-3 speeds through those eight Copy commands. This is a big improvement over the manual method. Enter another invoice by invoking the \A macro once more. Then move to the home position to check the database. Were the new records copied correctly?

Calculating DAYS PAST DUE

When macro \A has run its course, the pointer rests on the DAYS PAST DUE cell, which still remains empty. We can program the macro to calculate this field automatically after it has finished copying the input form. DAYS PAST DUE is the number of days elapsed since the date that services were provided. It equals the difference between the date we run the model minus the invoice date.

When you boot up 1-2-3 by inserting the System Disk and turning on the computer, the system prompts you for the current date. Your response to this prompt can be retrieved within 1-2-3 by using the @NOW function. (See Chapter 6 for a complete discussion of date functions, date arithmetic, and date formats.) The @NOW function (@TODAY for Version 1A) yields a value representing the number of days elapsed between December 31, 1899, and the current date.

The invoice date can also be converted to a number with the @DATE function. The formula @DATE *(year, month, day)* converts the date associated with the arguments *year, month,* and *day* to the number of days elapsed since December 31, 1899. With the current date and invoice date expressed on the same basis, a simple subtraction provides the desired result.

1. Move the pointer to cell D1, and type **@NOW** ENTER. (Type **@TODAY** instead for Version 1A.)

If you did not enter the correct date when you turned on your computer, then replace the previous step by using the @DATE function to store today's date. (For instance, for March 28, 1984, enter **@DATE(84,3,28)**.)

You may use the Range Format Date command to display the resulting current date in conventional date format:

2. Type **/Range Format Date**.

3. Select **1**, the Day-Month-Year format, and press ENTER to apply the format to the present location of the pointer (cell D1).

Assign a range name, TODAY, to this coordinate:

4. Type **/Range Name Create TODAY** ENTER ENTER.

The formula for DAYS PAST DUE can be expressed as

+TODAY−@DATE(YEAR,MONTH,DAY)

where @DATE's arguments represent the date of a given invoice record. However, we will be copying this formula down the column, and the TODAY cell should be copied absolutely, not relatively. Thus, we will use the formula $TODAY−@DATE(YEAR,MONTH,DAY). The $ changes any cells referenced by a range name to absolute addresses (in this case, $D$1).

5. Place the pointer on the DAYS PAST DUE cell of the first record of the database (cell I6).

6. Type **$TODAY−@DATE(** to begin the formula.

7. Move the pointer left once, to the YEAR field (cell H6), and type the , key to continue the formula.

8. Move the pointer left three times, to point to the MONTH (cell F6), and type the , key to continue.

9. Move left twice, to DAY (cell G6).

10. Type the **)** key ENTER to conclude the formula.

11. Copy this formula down the column to the other records currently stored in the file.

Invoices that were entered on the same day as the current date will have DAYS PAST DUE of 0 for this day. But when the system is run at a later date, DAYS PAST DUE will be recalculated and will yield a positive result.

The computation of DAYS PAST DUE translates into the following macro keystrokes:

$TODAY−@DATE({LEFT},{LEFT}{LEFT}{LEFT},{LEFT}{LEFT})~

You may want to verify this sequence of keystrokes by moving to one of the DAYS PAST DUE cells (for instance, cell I6) and reentering the above formula yourself, using pointing to fill in the arguments of the @DATE function.

The DAYS PAST DUE calculation becomes the next macro label. Because the command begins with a $, which would normally cause 1-2-3 to assume Value Mode, we must precede the macro keystrokes by a label-prefix.

12. At cell M82, type

'$TODAY−@DATE({LEFT},{LEFT}{LEFT}{LEFT},{LEFT}{LEFT})~.

Now when macro \A executes, it will copy the input form to the data record, put the pointer on DAYS PAST DUE, and automatically calculate the formula.

Erasing the Previous Form

Do a /Mental Note Retrieve (on your own cranial software, not on 1-2-3) to recall that enhancement to which we intended to return. Once the invoice has been copied to the database, we wish to blank out the input cells of the form before beginning the next entry.

Actually, we do not want to erase all of the inputs. Suppose there are ten invoices awaiting entry on a given day. The name, address, amount, and services rendered may be unique to each invoice, but the invoice month, day, and year will be the same for each. Therefore, only the first five inputs should be deleted.

To erase any input cell, we may apply the Range Erase command to the cell's range name. For example, the keystroke sequence /Range Erase NAME ENTER erases the NAME field from the input form.

1. Move to cell M83, the next cell of the macro.

Here is the macro label to erase the first five inputs of the invoice form:

2. Type '/RENAME~/RESTREET~/RECITY~/RESERVICES~ /REAMOUNT~ and press the ENTER key.

Now try the macro again. Invoke macro \A, fill out a form, and press ESC. If your eye can follow the movements on the screen, you will see the DAYS PAST DUE formula stored and the input form erased. Macro \A performs quickly and accurately. It can be speeded up a bit, however, if we turn off automatic recalculation.

3. Type /Worksheet Global Recalculation Manual.

From now on, we must remember to press the F9 (Calc) key whenever we want formulas to be updated (especially when the current date changes).

Closing the Loop

As it stands, you must invoke macro \A once for each invoice entered. We can further automate the process, though, by instructing 1-2-3 to go back and repeat the macro until the user tells it to stop. This kind of repetition of steps is called *looping*, and it is accomplished with the BRANCH (/XG) macro command, introduced in chapter 8. The format of the command is

V 2.0: {BRANCH *location*}
/X: /XG*location*~

The command instructs 1-2-3 to go to *location* and to continue reading macro commands there.

Thus, to tell 1-2-3 to repeat the \A macro when it has completed its execution, we can add a final step,

V 2.0: {BRANCH \A}
/X: /XG\A~

which means to go to the cell attached to the range name \A (cell M75) and execute whatever is there.

1. In the next macro cell, M84, enter

V 2.0: {BRANCH \A}
/X: '/XG\A~

Now invoke the macro, enter a record, and press ESC to get out of Range Input. Control reverts to the macro, which copies the form to the file, blanks out the input form, and automatically reenters Range Input in anticipation of another invoice. The process will go on and on. The macro will forever loop to the input sequence.

That's terrific, but what happens after you have entered all the invoices you have? Are you doomed to an endless loop? All this toil, only to be imprisoned in the Input Mode? You may be muttering to yourself, "Gimme a break!"

Actually, a break is exactly what is needed in this instance. When you have finished entering and storing the last invoice (at the point where the macro erases the form and awaits the next invoice), issue a break by holding down the CTRL key while pressing the BREAK key. This will usher you directly into Ready Mode. In a fix (especially within a macro), a break functions as the ultimate Houdini.

A break is not a particularly polished way to exit the macro, however, for it wrests control away from the macro. After we have entered data, global protection (which was turned off) should be reactivated. Unfortunately, a break does not give the macro a chance to do this.

Instead of breaking, we will leave the loop in the macro with a conditional instruction. When a form has been filled out and the user presses the ESC key, the macro will store the input and blank out the form, as before. Instead of immediately looping back to Range Input, however, it can ask the user whether data entry should be continued. If the user replies yes, the macro will run through the Range Input sequence. If the user replies no, however, the macro will reactivate global worksheet protection and exit into Ready Mode.

Controlling the Looping Process

In order to make the loop conditional, we must add one more step to our macro. *Before* the BRANCH (/XG) command, we need to tell 1-2-3 to ask users whether or not they want to continue the loop. This can be done with the GETNUMBER (/XN) command, which was introduced in Chapter 8.

The macro command

> *V 2.0:* {GETNUMBER "CONTINUE ENTRY? (0=CONTINUE,
> 1=STOP):", H1}
> *X:* /XNCONTINUE ENTRY? (0=CONTINUE, 1=STOP):~H1~

displays a message

CONTINUE ENTRY? (0=CONTINUE, 1=STOP):

in the control panel. Processing is deferred until the user responds. The response, either 0 or 1, is stored in cell H1.

Once a response is given, the macro IF (/XI) can be used to determine how to proceed (the IF, or /XI, command was explained in Chapter 8). If the condition imbedded in the command is true, then 1-2-3 continues executing the keystrokes following the end bracket (or the tilde in /X format). For example,

> *V 2.0:* IF H1=1}/WGPE
> *X:* /XIH1=1~/WGPE

means, "If cell H1 contains the value 1, execute the Worksheet Global Protection Enable command; otherwise, skip to the next line and continue reading keystrokes."

If the user's response is 1 (that is, "stop data entry"), then protection should be reactivated, and 1-2-3 should stop processing the macro. The macro QUIT (/XQ) command terminates the macro and restores Ready Mode. The IF (/XI) statement should thus be

> *V 2.0:* {IF H1=1}/WGPE{QUIT}
> *X:* /XIH1=1~/WGPE/XQ

In other words, if H1 contains a 1, then enable protection and quit; otherwise, proceed to the BRANCH (/XG) command and loop through the macro again.

The two revisions to the macro may be combined into one label:

> *V 2.0:* {GETNUMBER "CONTINUE ENTRY? (0=CONTINUE,
> 1=STOP):", H1}{IF H1=1}/WGPE{QUIT}
> *X:* '/XNCONTINUE ENTRY? (0=CONTINUE, 1=STOP):~
> H1}/XIH1=1~/WGPE/XQ

To make room for this label, move the BRANCH \A (/XG\A~) command down one cell:

1. Place the pointer on the label in cell M84.

2. Type **/Move** ENTER, point to the next cell below (cell M85), and press ENTER.

3. Insert the new label in cell M84 as specified previously.

Now invoke the macro. Fill out an invoice, and press ESC. After a short moment, the "CONTINUE ENTRY?" prompt appears. Continue entry by pressing **0** and ENTER. Fill out another form, and then exit the macro by pressing **1** and ENTER. Now move to the home position and try to make an entry. Has global protection been activated?

This macro is not merely a substitute for some Copy commands. It is a finished data-entry environment. Simultaneously pressing the ALT and A keys and then entering data are the only steps that the data clerk needs to know. The environment is closely controlled, so there is very little chance of destroying data accidentally. The macro is quick, and it even computes and stores the DAYS PAST DUE.

So much for forms-oriented input. Save your worksheet again, and take a coffee break if you wish. The next step will be an invoice-printing system based on the database.

Printing Invoices From the Database

Dr. DoMuch is pleased with this data-entry system, but desires enhancements. An automated invoice printing system would save time and money. We will use *forms-oriented reporting*—the process of copying individual fields of a record from a database to a report form—to print out invoices from Dr. DoMuch's invoice database. Although 1-2-3 is not a full-fledged word processor, it does have enough capability to allow us to incorporate text into the invoice.

Transferring the Data
Onto a Form

Dr. DoMuch's invoice form is shown in Figure 10-4. We will begin automating the invoice-printing procedure by creating the electronic output form. First, if global worksheet protection is still in effect, disable it by typing **/Worksheet Global Protection Disable**. Then

1. Go to cell K50.

```
R.X. DOMUCH, MD  777 Disk Drive, Portland, Maine 17392

PATIENT NAME
STREET ADDRESS
CITY,STATE,ZIP

SERVICES RENDERED: _____

AMOUNT DUE: --->      _____

The amount shown above is due for services rendered. If you fail
to remit payment immediately, your next medical treatment may be
your last.
```

Figure 10-4. Dr. DoMuch's invoice form

This is the location where the patient name will be stored. For later purposes, we will assign a name, ONAME, to this cell. (The O of ONAME signifies *output*.)

2. Type **/Range Name Create ONAME** ENTER ENTER.

3. Assign the name **OSTREET** to cell K51 and the name **OCITY** to cell K52.

The label SERVICES RENDERED is stored two rows down:

4. Store the label (not range name) **SERVICES RENDERED:** in cell K54.

5. Assign the name **OSERVICES** to cell M54.

6. Put underscores in cells M55 and N55, using \-.

The AMOUNT DUE is highlighted using dashes and an arrowhead:

7. In cell K56, type **AMOUNT DUE: --->**.

8. Assign the name **OAMOUNT** to cell M56.

9. Put an underscore in cell M57.

Copying Fields From the Database

Now that each of the items to be filled in has a name attached to it, the Copy command can easily be carried out. We will go through the manual process of copying the first record to the output form, then use these steps to develop a macro.

1. Move the pointer to the first record of the database (cell A6).

2. Copy the current cell to ONAME by typing /Copy ENTER **ONAME** ENTER.

The other four items may be copied similarly.

3. Move right to the STREET ADDRESS field, and copy it to OSTREET.

4. Move right to the CITY,STATE,ZIP field, and copy it to OCITY.

5. Move right to the SERVICES field, and copy it to OSERVICES.

6. Move right to the AMOUNT field, and copy it to OAMOUNT.

Now return to the output form, press the F5 (GoTo) key, and type **ONAME** ENTER to inspect the results. Add a bit of explanatory text, and we will have a report.

Adding Text to the Invoice

Dr. DoMuch wants the following text added to the invoice:

The amount shown above is due for services rendered. If you fail to remit payment immediately, your next medical treatment may be your last.

These three lines of text can simply be entered as three labels:

1. Press the CAPS LOCK key to allow uppercase and lowercase typing.

2. In cell K60, enter the first line of the text. Enter the second line in cell K61, and the third line in cell K62.

3. Press CAPS LOCK again to restore uppercase typing.

A label cell can store up to 240 characters. If there are more characters in the label than there is room in the cell, then characters spill over into succeeding blank cells.

Printing the Invoice

Now that the invoice form contains all the information it needs, the next step is to print it. The first requirement in printing is to designate a print range. The print range must encompass the entire output form, which begins with the cell named ONAME and ends with the last line of text. Assign the output form a range name of OUTPUTFORM.

1. Press the F5 (GoTo) key, and type **ONAME** ENTER.

2. Type **/Range Name Create OUTPUTFORM.**

3. Move the cell pointer to the last text line and then over to cell M62 to expand the range over the entire form, and press ENTER.

4. Turn on the printer. If the paper is not at the top of the page, adjust it.

5. Type **/Print Printer Range OUTPUTFORM** ENTER.

If you have to adjust the paper manually to get to the top of the page, select the **A**lign option.

6. Select **G**o.

The output looks good, but it does not include the top line of the invoice:

R.X. DOMUCH, MD 777 Disk Drive, Portland, Maine 17392

Instead of storing this line as part of the output form, we will print it with an option of the Print command.

The Header and Footer Print Options

A *header* is a line of text placed just below the top margin of the page. It may consist of three parts: a left-justified segment, a centered segment, and a right-justified segment. These segments must be separated by the ¦ character (split vertical bar). While within the Print menu,

1. Select Options, and then select **H**eader.

The header will consist of the doctor's name and address. To center this on the line, it must be designated as the second (centered) segment of the header. Because there is no first segment, begin entering the header by typing the ¦ key:

2. In response to the "Enter Header Line" prompt, type ¦**R.X. DOMUCH, MD 777 Disk Drive, Portland, Maine 17392** and press the ENTER key.

A footer, like a header, is an additional line of text, but it appears above the bottom margin of the page. It too has three segments divided by ¦ characters. There are two characters that have special meaning with regard to headers and footers. The @ symbol is replaced by the current date. The #

symbol is replaced by sequential page numbers for use on multiple-page printouts.

To right-justify the current date on the bottom of the invoice,

3. Select the **F**ooter option and type ¦¦@ ENTER.

4. Select **Q**uit to exit the Options menu.

5. Select **P**age to skip to the top of the next page.

6. Select **G**o to print the invoice, which now includes both the header and the footer.

The footer will not print until you get to the bottom of the current page. To do this,

7. Select **P**age to position the paper at the top of the next page, and then select **Q**uit to restore Ready Mode.

If you use paper that is shorter or longer than the 11-inch paper length (66 lines per page) that 1-2-3 assumes, you will need to select Print Option Page-Length and select the correct number of lines per page.

During this session, 1-2-3 remembers the Print options selected, using them until they are explicitly altered in another Print command. Saving the worksheet saves the currently active options, which will be reactivated when the file is retrieved.

A Macro for Printing the Invoice

It is quite simple to build a macro to copy the fields of a record into the fields of the output form, once the pointer is positioned on the first field of the record to be output. Here are the macro commands, transcribed and translated from the manual commands issued previously:

```
/C~ONAME~{RIGHT}
/C~OSTREET~{RIGHT}
/C~OCITY~{RIGHT}
/C~OSERVICES~{RIGHT}
/C~OAMOUNT~
/PPGPQ
```

The last command presumes that the print range (OUTPUTFORM) is left unchanged, as well as the header and footer options. We will call this macro \B.

1. Move the cell pointer to cell M90, and assign this cell the name **B**.

2. Enter the macro labels just listed in cells M90 through M95. *Be sure to use the apostrophe label-prefix* to prevent 1-2-3 from executing the commands immediately. Add documentation in a column to the right if you wish.

Now move the pointer to the first field of the first record of the database (cell A6), and invoke macro \B. The invoice is filled out and printed automatically. Move the pointer down to the next invoice (cell A7), and invoke \B once more.

Looping Through the Invoices Automatically

Can this macro be changed so that the process of moving the pointer down to the next record can be automated? Certainly. The methodology behind such a macro can be summarized in five steps:

- First, point to the first record.
- Second, copy data to the output form.
- Third, print the output form.
- Fourth, point to the next record.
- Finally, look back at the second step.

Macro \B already incorporates the second and third steps of this procedure. We need only add keystrokes to move the pointer to the first record, to point to the next record, and to loop back and copy the data to the output form.

Moving the pointer to the first cell is easy. Press HOME, then press END, and then press the down arrow key three times. These keystrokes will move the pointer to the first field of the first record, no matter how many records are in the database.

Once this record has been copied to the output form and printed, the pointer will rest on the last field from which we copied, the AMOUNT field. We need to move the pointer to the first field of the next record. This can be accomplished by pressing END and then the left arrow key to get to column A, and then pressing the down arrow key to move to the next record.

Finally, looping back to the Copy commands of the macro involves using the BRANCH (/XG) command to instruct 1-2-3 to continue reading keystrokes at the appropriate cell. Which cell? We will get to that later. First we must deal with a problem.

There is an error in this scheme. What happens when the macro finishes processing the last record? It moves the pointer down (to a blank row), then loops back to the copying steps. The process goes on, ad infinitum, until the error of trying to move beyond the last row causes an interruption. Somewhere in the loop we must check whether the last record has been processed, and if so, issue a QUIT (/XQ) command to stop the macro.

Our inclination is to use the IF (/XI) command to test whether the record being pointed to is a valid record. One way of determining whether the end of the file has been reached is to check whether the OAMOUNT field of the input form contains a 0. The OAMOUNT field cannot contain a 0 if the record that the macro is processing is a valid invoice. If OAMOUNT=0, the OAMOUNT output field is blank, which means that we have finished processing the database and 1-2-3 should terminate the macro. If OAMOUNT contains a nonzero value, then the macro is processing a valid record and should continue reading keystrokes to process the next record. The macro command to apply the end-of-file condition is

V 2.0: {IF OAMOUNT=0}{QUIT}
/X: /XIOAMOUNT=0~/XQ

We now have the tools necessary to develop the macro to print invoices for the entire database. We will name the macro \C and store it in cells M100..M108. Table 10-1 shows how the macro loops back to repeat the printing operation until the ONAME cell (K49) is blank.

1. Move to cell M100 and enter the macro command labels as follows:

IN CELL	ENTER
M100	{HOME}{END}{DOWN}{DOWN}{DOWN}
M101	'/C~ONAME~{RIGHT}
M102	'/C~OSTREET~{RIGHT}
M103	'/C~OCITY~{RIGHT}
M104	'/C~OSERVICES~{RIGHT}
M105	'/C~OAMOUNT~

2. Move to cell M106 and make the following entry:

V 2.0: {IF OAMOUNT=0}{QUIT}
/X: '/XIOAMOUNT=0~/XQ

3. In cell M107 type '/PPGPQ.

MACRO CELL
CONTENTS

EXPLANATION

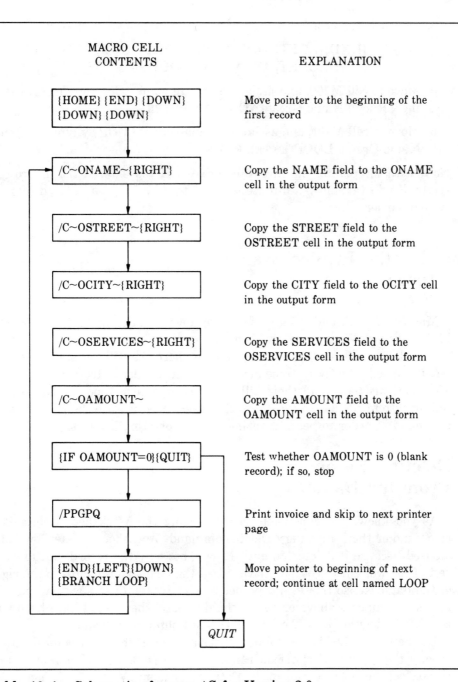

Macro Cell Contents	Explanation
{HOME} {END} {DOWN} {DOWN} {DOWN}	Move pointer to the beginning of the first record
/C~ONAME~{RIGHT}	Copy the NAME field to the ONAME cell in the output form
/C~OSTREET~{RIGHT}	Copy the STREET field to the OSTREET cell in the output form
/C~OCITY~{RIGHT}	Copy the CITY field to the OCITY cell in the output form
/C~OSERVICES~{RIGHT}	Copy the SERVICES field to the OSERVICES cell in the output form
/C~OAMOUNT~	Copy the AMOUNT field to the OAMOUNT cell in the output form
{IF OAMOUNT=0}{QUIT}	Test whether OAMOUNT is 0 (blank record); if so, stop
/PPGPQ	Print invoice and skip to next printer page
{END}{LEFT}{DOWN} {BRANCH LOOP}	Move pointer to beginning of next record; continue at cell named LOOP

QUIT

Table 10-1. Schematic of macro \C for Version 2.0

4. In cell M108 type

   V 2.0: {END}{LEFT}{DOWN}{BRANCH LOOP}
      /X: {END}{LEFT}{DOWN}/XGLOOP~

5. Move to cell M100, and assign the range name \C to the macro by typing **/R**ange Name Create **\C** ENTER ENTER.

6. Move to cell M101, and assign the range name LOOP by typing **/R**ange Name Create **LOOP** ENTER ENTER.

Now, with the printer on, invoke macro \C. If you entered the macro correctly, it will take only a minute to print the invoices you entered into the system earlier.

Finishing the Invoice System:
Two Ideas

Macros \A, \B, and \C go a long way toward automating Dr. DoMuch's billing system. What more could the doctor want?

Complete as our new system seems to be, there are still two stones we have left unturned. One is a procedure that deletes records from the database after patients have paid their bills. The other is a method for booting the billing-system file automatically so that users need not use the File Retrieve command in order to begin entering data or printing invoices.

Deleting Records
From the Database

As you know, you can delete records using the Worksheet Delete Row command or the Data Query Delete command. Worksheet Delete Row is ill-advised because it deletes an entire row — not only the record, but also the rest of the worksheet row. We have stored the forms and macros to the right of the database, so they could be deleted inadvertently. (If we had put the forms and macros above or below the database, they would have been susceptible to deletion by a Worksheet Delete Column command.)

The better method is to establish criteria to select the records for deletion, specify the input and criterion ranges for the Data Query command, and then select the Delete option of the Data Query menu. We used this method in Chapter 7 to delete records from an invoice file similar to the one used in this chapter. We will not repeat the steps here.

There are a few points about deleting records that you should bear in mind. First, global protection must be disabled in order to execute a deletion. Second, because you want to make sure that deletions are deliberate, you probably should *not* create a macro to delete entries. Without a macro, the user will have to know how to disable global protection and how to issue the Data Query Delete command. This should prevent novices from making costly errors.

The Delete option depends on the criterion range. Suppose that your criterion range were the following:

NAME
SMITH*

The record for SMITH, JOHN would be deleted (remember that * is a "wildcard" character that allows selection of any records that begin with the five letters SMITH).

However, if there were several SMITHs in the file, or if John Smith had several invoices outstanding, all SMITH records would be deleted, even if you intended to delete only John Smith's invoice for the examination on February 1, 1984. Therefore, to be explicit, you should use multiple criteria to delete. The following criteria ensure that only the record you want is deleted:

NAME	SERVICES	MONTH	DAY	YR
SMITH*	EXAM*	2	1	84

Another pitfall is issuing the Data Query Delete command using a blank criterion. Recall that a blank criterion such as the following selects *all* records:

NAME

Using a blank criterion with the Delete option would delete *all* records. *The best protection against this error is to save a backup copy of your file on disk before making any changes to the file.*

Automatic Worksheet Retrieval

Speaking of saving the file, there is one special file name that will add the finishing touch to our invoice system. If you save a worksheet under the name AUTO123, then 1-2-3 will automatically retrieve this file whenever you load up the 1-2-3 program (provided that the data diskette containing the AUTO123 file is in the second disk drive when you load the program). With an AUTO123 file, you need not even issue the File Retrieve command to bring the worksheet to the screen.

1. Type /File Save **AUTO123** ENTER.

2. Type /Quit to exit from 1-2-3 into the Lotus Access System.

To reenter the 1-2-3 program,

3. Select the **1-2-3** option of the Access System menu.

Without any further ado, Dr. DoMuch's invoice file automatically loads itself and appears on the display.

In the next chapter, we will discover additional ways to make 1-2-3 easy for almost anyone to use.

Chapter 11
Stock Portfolio Tracking

Capabilities of the System

Information to Be Stored
In the Portfolio Database

The Buy Transaction

The Sell Transaction

Reporting Gains and
Losses at Year End

The invoicing example of Chapter 10 introduced the technique of forms-oriented database management. In this chapter, we use a stock portfolio worksheet to illustrate additional methods for forms input and output. The portfolio worksheet keeps track of stock purchases, sales, and holdings. It also computes short- and long-term gains.

The techniques we will use to develop this worksheet apply to many types of database applications that resemble the purchase and sale of stock—such as inventory management, accounts receivable, accounts payable, and checkbook registering.

Note that most of the macros in this chapter make use of both the Version 2.0 macro commands and the /X commands that work for Version 1A.

Because the macros developed in this chapter are fairly long, you may want to begin by telling 1-2-3 to activate Single-Step Mode: hold down the ALT key while pressing the F1 (Help) key. As you may recall from Chapter 8, Single-Step Mode causes 1-2-3 to execute a macro one keystroke at a time. Pressing any key causes the macro to execute the next step. Single-Step Mode helps you catch any errors that might have crept into your macros. (Holding ALT down while pressing the F1 (Help) key again turns off Single-Step Mode.)

Capabilities of the System

Personal financial management has become a popular applications area for spreadsheet programs. Investments are an important part of personal finances, but until recently, spreadsheets did not offer the capabilities required to help individuals comprehensively manage their investment portfolios. This is one reason that investment management packages have found a comfortable niche in the personal software market. With a bit of effort, however, you can develop a 1-2-3 model that performs quite capably, even when compared to dedicated investment packages.

One of the purposes of the stock-tracking system is to manage the inventory of stocks in the portfolio. The system must record how many shares of each stock are owned, when the stock was purchased, and how much it cost. Stock holdings must be adjusted when shares are sold. The system must keep track of which shares are sold, when they are sold, for how much, and whether there is a gain or a loss on the sale.

Investors are not the only parties interested in the profits obtained from selling stock. The Internal Revenue Service is interested in the returns derived from investment (especially the positive returns). Under current tax law, gains on the sale of stock are taxable, but the applicable tax rate depends on how long the investor owned the stock. If the shares have been part of the portfolio for less than a year, then the gain on the sale of the stock is taxed at the same tax rate as that applied to the investor's regular income. The gain on the sale of such stock is called a *short-term capital gain*. In contrast, a *long-term capital gain* is the gain from a sale of stock that has been held for more than a year prior to the sale. Long-term gains are taxed at an effective rate that is significantly less than the regular income-tax rate.

In 1983 the maximum effective tax rate for a long-term gain was 20 percent.

Although the taxperson usually taketh, the taxperson sometimes giveth away, or at least taketh less. If stock is sold for a loss, then the loss may be deducted from taxable income.

Thus, it is important for a stock-tracking system to compute the short- and long-term gains and losses on the sale of stock. The tax implications of long-term versus short-term gains and losses are significant enough that the system should report the type of gain or loss whenever a sale is made. Moreover, there is benefit from having a year-end calculation of short-term and long-term gains. Having 1-2-3 do this automatically would lift a tedious burden from the investor's shoulders when it comes time to prepare the tax return.

Information to Be Stored
In the Portfolio Database

What information should be stored in the portfolio database? The birth of our portfolio occurs with the first purchase of stock. Consideration of the items of information involved in a stock purchase suggests what data should be stored in the worksheet. Obviously, the name of the stock is necessary. The date that the stock was purchased is also important; when it is time to sell the stock, the original purchase date will be needed to determine the short-term or long-term status of the sale.

The stock name and purchase date are not enough to identify a group of shares. Suppose you bought 50 shares of Modex Corporation this morning at $10 and another 50 shares later at $12. After a month, you sell 20 shares of stock. Which shares should you sell? This is an important question, because the answer determines the amount of gain or loss. Assigning identification (ID) numbers to each group of shares purchased would solve this problem. An ID number will therefore be another item to store in the worksheet, but this number will have to be generated by the system. You cannot trust a human being, even yourself, to assign a unique identifier to each group of shares.

The number of shares and the cost of the stock purchased must also be retained. The cost of the stock has two components. There is the price that the buyer must pay for each share involved in the transaction. Frequently, there is also the broker's commission, the fee charged by the trading middleman to execute the stock transaction. (Actually, the broker earns a commission not only for purchasing stock on the buyer's behalf, but also for selling stock.)

The purchase transaction suggests six items to be recorded: name, ID number, date, purchase price per share, commission, and total cost. A stock sale generates additional items: the number of shares sold, the date of sale, the sale price per share, the sales commission paid to the broker, the proceeds of the sale, the gain or loss, and the type of gain or loss (short-term or long-term).

A stock purchase creates an inventory of a particular group of stocks in the portfolio. Selling the stock decreases this inventory. In order to keep track of the portfolio holdings and the sale of shares separately, we design two unique types of records: a *holdings* record and a *sell* record. The holdings record contains information pertaining to current holdings—such as the amount of shares on hand, the date they were purchased, and their total cost. The sell record contains information that relates specifically to the shares sold. The distinction will become more clear when we begin using the database, but for now we note only that there must be an additional data field in the database representing the record type (holdings or sell).

Figure 11-1 shows the layout of the data fields just discussed. Before entering the field headings,

1. Assign column widths to the worksheet as follows:

COLUMN	WIDTH
A	15
B	3
C	5
D	3
E	3
F	3
G	6
H	10
I	8
J	13
K	9
L	9
M	13
N	12
O	8

2. Enter the column headings exactly as shown in Figure 11-1. Use /Range Label Center to center the column headings.

3. Put underscores in row 4 beneath all of the headings.

A	B	C	D	E	F	G	H	I	J	K	L	M	N	O
1		HOLD OR					PURCHASE PRICE PER SHARE	COMM'N PER SH: PURCHASE	TOTAL COST	SALE PRICE PER SH	COMM'N PER SH: SALE	SALE PROCEEDS	GAIN/ (LOSS)	SHORT/ LONG TERM
2														
3	NAME	ID	SELL	MO	DA	YR	QTY							
4	------													

Figure 11-1. Data fields for portfolio database

You may wish to turn ahead to Figure 11-4 to see how the database looks with data in it. The fields will make sense as we proceed to develop the transactions that affect the portfolio.

The Buy Transaction

In Chapter 10, we used electronic forms to enter records into a database. The Range Input command directed input into unprotected cells of an input form, and a macro copied the input cells to the database itself. We will use a similar method in this application to process portfolio transactions.

Structuring the Buy Input Form

We will begin by building an input form for purchasing stock, as displayed in Figure 11-2. Notice the string of asterisks above and below the title of the form. You can create these in the same way you create an underscore, using the \ (repeating label) prefix in combination with an asterisk. We will place the input form to the right of the database so that it will not interfere with the portfolio section of the worksheet. To put the form on your worksheet,

1. Place a string of asterisks in cells U1 and U3 using *, and type the centered label ^BUY in cell U2.

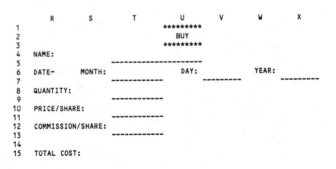

Figure 11-2. An input form for stock purchases

2. Enter the form headings as follows:

CELL	LABEL
R4	NAME:
R6	DATE -
S6	"MONTH:
U6	"DAY:
W6	"YEAR:
R8	QUANTITY:
R10	PRICE/SHARE:
R12	COMMISSION/SHARE:
R15	TOTAL COST:

3. Place underscores in the following cells: T5, U5, T7, V7, X7, T9, T11, and T13.

Underscored cells mark the input areas.

Next, attach range names to the input fields. This will facilitate copying the input cells to the database later. The range names are preceded by the letter *B* to indicate that they are associated with the Buy input form.

4. Use the Range Name command to assign the following names to the associated cells:

CELL	RANGE NAME
T4	BNAME
T6	BMONTH
V6	BDAY
X6	BYEAR
T8	BQUANTITY
T10	BPRICE
T12	BCOMM
T15	BCOST

5. Assign a currency format with three decimal places to cells T10 (the BPRICE cell), T12 (the BCOMM cell), and T15 (the BCOST cell). You can do this by typing **/Range Format Currency 3** ENTER *rangename* ENTER.

Next, to make room for large numbers, widen column T:

6. With the pointer in column T, type **/Worksheet Column Set-Width 12** ENTER.

Observe that no underline was placed below the TOTAL COST cell. The cost of the purchase is derived from a rather cumbersome calculation, (*purchase price per share + purchase commission per share) × number of shares purchased*. Why require the user to make this calculation when 1-2-3 can do it more quickly within the macro we will later develop? Likewise, the macro will automatically generate the ID number. Because there is no need for the investor to see the ID number during input, we will not include it in the Buy input form.

The Buy Input Macro

Seven steps are involved in processing a purchase transaction. These are as follows:

. First, display the input form on the screen.

. Second, fill out the form.

. Third, calculate the total cost of the shares and display them on the form.

. Fourth, ask the user if the input is correctly entered. If correct, then proceed to the next step; otherwise, go back to the first step and begin again.

. Fifth, incorporate the input form into the database.

. Sixth, erase the input fields of the form.

. Seventh, ask the user whether to continue data entry. To continue entry, go back to the first step; otherwise, stop.

The Buy input macro we build in the next few pages follows these seven steps, starting with displaying the input form on the screen.

Displaying the Input Form
On the Screen

The input form is designed so that when its top-left corner (cell R1) is the top left of the window, the form itself is the only section of the worksheet displayed on the screen. If the top-left corner of the form is not aligned with the top left of the window, then part of the form is not displayed, and the user is forced to scroll the window.

We can avoid this inconvenience with the help of the F5 (GoTo) key. The F5 (GoTo) key transfers the pointer directly to a specific coordinate. If that coordinate already appears in the window, the pointer changes position but the window does not budge. However, if the destination coordinate is outside of the window when the GoTo key is pressed, then 1-2-3 positions the window so that the destination cell becomes the top-left cell of the window — precisely what we want.

Therefore, to position the window the way we want it, we may press the F5 (GoTo) key to direct the pointer to cell R1. As long as the destination is outside the window when this key is pressed, cell R1 will be the top-left cell of the window. You can test this method for yourself by pressing the HOME key. The input form is now offscreen. Press the F5 (GoTo) key, and specify R1 as the destination cell. No matter where the pointer is, pressing HOME and F5 and then specifying R1 puts the input form on the screen properly.

Remember, however, that a cardinal rule of macros is to avoid direct cell references (such as R1). If the Buy form is moved, then cell R1 will no longer be the top left of the form, and a macro referring to cell R1 will malfunction. It is far safer to attach a range name to cell R1.

1. Assign the name **BUYFORM** to cell R1.

The macro to input a purchase will be named \A.

2. Move to cell R50, and enter the label

MACRO A: INPUT PURCHASE INTO DATABASE

3. In cell R51, enter the macro label containing the keystrokes to set up the form display: {HOME}{GOTO}BUYFORM~.

4. Assign the name \A to cell R51.

Using /XL and /XN for Data Entry

The Range Input command is one way of supervising data entry, as we saw in Chapter 10. There are effective alternatives, however. These are {GET-NUMBER *message, location*} (/XN) and {GETLABEL *message, location*} (/XL). We use the GETNUMBER command in Chapters 8 and 10 to prompt the user with *message* and store the user's numeric reply in *location*. GETLABEL works similarly to accept text as the user's response.

The advantage of GETNUMBER and GETLABEL is that they can enhance data entry by providing the user with descriptive prompts. Prompting guides the user through the input form in a dynamic way. Lotus 1-2-3 will be programmed to ask the user for each and every input. When the last field is filled out, 1-2-3 instantly proceeds to the next step, copying the input form into the database.

Where will the prompting commands store the user responses? The input fields of the purchase form, each of which has a range name, will be the destinations of the user's entries. Next we enter the command labels that fill out the purchase form. Figure 11-3 shows the completed \A macro.

1. Enter the following macro labels into cells R52 through R58:

V 2.0:   {GETLABEL "ENTER STOCK NAME:",BNAME}
   {GETNUMBER "ENTER PURCHASE DATE MONTH
      (NUMERIC):",BMONTH}
   {GETNUMBER "ENTER PURCHASE DATE DAY
      (NUMERIC):",BDAY}
   {GETNUMBER "ENTER PURCHASE DATE YEAR
      (2 DIGITS):",BYEAR}
   {GETNUMBER "HOW MANY SHARES PURCHASED?:",
      BQUANTITY}
   {GETNUMBER "PRICE PER SHARE:",BPRICE}
   {GETNUMBER "COMMISSION PER SHARE
      (0 IF NONE):",BCOMM}

```
                  R         S         T         U         V
50 MACRO A: INPUT PURCHASE INTO DATABASE
51 {HOME}{GOTO}BUYFORM~
52 {GETLABEL "ENTER STOCK NAME:",BNAME}
53 {GETNUMBER "ENTER PURCHASE DATE MONTH (NUMERIC):",BMONTH}
54 {GETNUMBER "ENTER PURCHASE DATE DAY (NUMERIC):",BDAY}
55 {GETNUMBER "ENTER PURCHASE DATE YEAR (2 DIGITS):",BYEAR}
56 {GETNUMBER "HOW MANY SHARES PURCHASED?:",BQUANTITY}
57 {GETNUMBER "PRICE PER SHARE:",BPRICE}
58 {GETNUMBER "COMMISSION PER SHARE (0 IF NONE):",BCOMM}
59 {GOTO}BCOST~+BQUANTITY*(BPRICE+BCOMM)~
60 {GETNUMBER "STORE IN DATEBASE? (1=YES, 0=NO):",SCRATCH}
61 {IF SCRATCH=0}{BRANCH \A}
62 {HOME}{END}{DOWN}{END}{DOWN}{DOWN}/CBNAME~~
63 {RIGHT}@MAX({UP}{END}{UP}.{END}{DOWN})+1~{EDIT}{CALC}~
64 {RIGHT}HOLD~{RIGHT}/CBMONTH~~{RIGHT}/CBDAY~~
65 {RIGHT}/CBYEAR~~{RIGHT}/CBQUANTITY~~
66 {RIGHT}/CBPRICE~~{RIGHT}/CBCOMM~~
67 {RIGHT}+{LEFT}{LEFT}{LEFT}*({LEFT}{LEFT}+{LEFT})~/RFC3~~
68 /REBNAME~/REBMONTH~/REBDAY~/REBYEAR~/REBQUANTITY~
69 /REBPRICE~/REBCOMM~/REBCOST~
70 {GETNUMBER "CONTINUE BUY INPUT? (1=YES, 0=NO):",SCRATCH}
71 {IF SCRATCH=1}{BRANCH \A}
```

Figure 11-3.   Macro \A stores purchases in the database

```
/X:   '/XLENTER STOCK NAME:~BNAME~
      '/XNENTER PURCHASE DATE MONTH (NUMERIC):
        ~BMONTH~
      '/XNENTER PURCHASE DATE DAY (NUMERIC):
        ~BDAY~
      '/XNENTER PURCHASE DATE YEAR (2 DIGITS):
        ~BYEAR~
      '/XNHOW MANY SHARES PURCHASED?:
        ~BQUANTITY~
      '/XNPRICE PER SHARE:~BPRICE~
      '/XNCOMMISSION PER SHARE (0 IF NONE):
        ~BCOMM~
```

We have divided these commands into separate labels for the purpose of clarity only. There is nothing to prevent you from combining the commands according to your own whim. Notice that the stock name is entered by a GETLABEL (/XL) command because the name is a label, not a value. The other prompts are for values, and they require the GETNUMBER (/XN) command.

Invoke macro \A to try it out. Make up any information you wish. Notice that you must press ENTER to end your response to each prompt.

The last item, commission per share, does not apply to all stock purchases. If there is no commission, the user must enter 0, even though it may seem natural simply to press ENTER without a response. This is because GET-NUMBER (/XN) expects a numeric response. Pressing ENTER without a preceding number does not work; the computer only beeps. In contrast, the label prompt GETLABEL (/XL) does accept ENTER as the sole response.

One more note before continuing. Commissions are not always charged on a per-share basis. The broker may apply a fee to the total purchase, depending on how many shares are bought. For example, the broker may charge $1 for buying 100 shares or $1.50 for buying 200 shares. For reasons we will explain later, the commission must be entered on a per-share basis even if it is not charged by the share. You are allowed to enter arithmetic expressions in response to GETNUMBER (/XN), so entering 1.5/200 is a valid way of converting the fixed fee into a per-share amount.

Computing and Displaying the Total Purchase Cost

The total purchase cost is equal to the total cost of a share (the price plus the commission) times the quantity. The pointer must be positioned at BCOST (cell T15) before entering the formula.

1. In the next macro cell (R59), enter the label

{GOTO}BCOST~+BQUANTITY*(BPRICE+BCOMM)~

Getting Permission to Store the Form

At this point in the macro's execution, the form has been filled out and the cost has been computed and displayed. The input may have errors in it, so we will ask the user whether to go ahead and register the purchase in the portfolio or to go back and reenter the information.

To do this, we can again use the GETNUMBER (/XN) command—this time to display a prompt in the control panel:

STORE IN THE DATABASE? (1=YES, 0=NO):

If the user's answer is 1 (yes), then execution will proceed to the next step. Otherwise, 1-2-3 will go back to the beginning of the macro (the cell named \A) to restart data input.

The user's response should be stored in a designated cell, which we will name SCRATCH. We can then use the IF (/XI) command, introduced in Chapter 8, to discern whether the response was 0 or 1. If the SCRATCH cell contains 0, then BRANCH (/XG) will send 1-2-3 to the beginning of the macro to continue reading keystrokes.

1. In cell R78, enter the label **SCRATCH**.

2. Move down once, and type /Range Name Create **SCRATCH** ENTER **R79** ENTER to assign the range name SCRATCH to cell R79.

3. Beginning with the next available macro cell (R60), enter the following macro labels:

> *V 2.0:* {GETNUMBER "STORE IN DATABASE? (1=YES, 0=NO):", SCRATCH}
> {IF SCRATCH=0}{BRANCH \}

> */X:* '/XNSTORE IN DATABASE? (1=YES, 0=NO):
> ~SCRATCH~
> '/XISCRATCH=0~/XG\A~

Copying the Stock Name
Into the Database

The next step is to transfer the input to the database. To do this, we must move the pointer to the first cell of the next available record of the portfolio. Pressing HOME END DOWN END DOWN DOWN (where DOWN represents the down arrow key) will do the trick. Verify that these keystrokes work. When you have finished, the pointer rests on the destination of the first cell to be copied, the stock name entered on the purchase form (BNAME). Adding /CBNAME~~ to the macro label will copy the stock name.

1. In the next macro cell (R62), enter the label

{HOME}{END}{DOWN}{END}{DOWN}{DOWN}/CBNAME~~

Assigning an ID Number

The next field of the database is the ID number. A unique ID number must be attached to each group of shares added to the database. The ID will be assigned on a sequential basis; the first group of shares is assigned 1, the next group is assigned 2, and so forth.

Pretend that this database has been filled with a number of holdings records that already have ID numbers. When the next purchase occurs, how would 1-2-3 determine its ID? If the records were in order of ID number, 1-2-3 could simply look at the previous holdings record and add 1 to its ID. But suppose the records were out of order. Then it would be necessary to examine the preceding records, choose the highest ID number from these, and add 1 to it.

The @MAX function returns the highest value among a group of values, so it can be used to determine the ID number for any record. Its format is @MAX(*list*), where *list* may be a single cell, a range, or a list of cells and ranges separated by commas. The idea is to instruct the macro to issue an @MAX, using as a list the column of ID numbers above the new record being processed.

To indicate the correct range, the macro must automatically move to the beginning of the ID column, anchor the range with a period, and point to the last-used ID cell (the one above the new record). The pointer was last placed on the NAME cell of the new record. Attempt the following. With the pointer at A5, press the right arrow key to move the pointer to the new ID cell. Now press the up arrow key, the END key, and the up arrow key again. This moves the pointer to the field heading, ID, which is two cells above the first ID number of the database.

If this label, or the underscore below it, were included in the @MAX range, it would be interpreted as a 0 because a label has no value. There is no harm, then, in designating this cell as the beginning of the range. From here, pressing END and the down arrow key transfers the pointer to the ID just above the new ID, which is where the end of the @MAX range will be. Thus, there is a way to instruct the macro to designate the correct range for the @MAX function.

With @MAX returning the highest ID number used so far, adding 1 to this value yields the next ID in the sequence. To enter the macro label that implements the ID assignment,

1. Move to cell R63, and type

{RIGHT}@MAX({UP}{END}{UP}.{END}{DOWN})+1~

Converting a Formula to a Value
With Edit Calc

Looking ahead to a time when the portfolio contains several stocks, we will probably want the ability to sort it. Unfortunately, the possibility of a sort throws a wrench into the ID assignment we just completed. The macro step contains a formula that refers to cells in other rows of the worksheet. If these rows are displaced in a sort procedure, the references of the ID formula may also change. The range in the @MAX function may no longer refer to the cells between the top of the column and the ID of the previous record. In sum, a sort could ruin the entire numbering scheme of the database because the ID formulas depend on the position of other cells in the worksheet.

What we really need to do is "freeze" the current value obtained by the formula at this point. Unlike a formula, a number does not change, no matter how cells are reorganized. We can solve the problem by computing the ID number with a formula, then storing the *value* of the formula instead of the formula itself.

Converting a formula to a value is a three-step process. First, placing the pointer on a cell containing a formula and pressing the F2 (Edit) key invokes Edit Mode, which permits the formula to be changed. Second, pressing the F9 (Calc) key *while in Edit Mode* displays the current value of the formula in the control panel. Third, pressing ENTER while in Edit Mode causes the number to replace the formula as the stored contents of the cell. Once it is stored, there is no way to bring back the formula.

To try this out, invoke macro \A. After you fill out the purchase form, allow the macro to copy the form to the database. You will see 1-2-3 copy the stock name, then generate the ID number 1 because this is the first record of the portfolio. The pointer rests on the ID cell. Press the F2 (Edit) key. Observe the ID formula in the control panel. Now press the F9 (Calc) key. The ID formula in the control panel is replaced by the number 1. Now press ENTER. The ID cell now contains a number instead of a formula. Before going on, erase the NAME and ID from this record. Now add this procedure to the macro.

1. Move the pointer to the macro label containing the ID formula (cell R63).

2. Press the F2 (Edit) key, then type {**EDIT**}{**CALC**}~ and press ENTER.

The revised macro label should look like this:

{RIGHT}@MAX({UP}{END}{UP}.{END}{DOWN})+1~{EDIT}{CALC}~

Completing the Purchase Record

The next field in the database is the record type. A purchase initiates a new inventory. It is a holdings record, as opposed to a sell record. The code for a holdings record is HOLD, which is stored as a label in this field. The commands to copy the purchase date, quantity, price, and commission are straightforward.

1. In cells R64, R65, and R66, respectively, enter the following labels:

**{RIGHT}HOLD~{RIGHT}/CBMONTH~~{RIGHT}/CBDAY~~
{RIGHT}/CBYEAR~~{RIGHT}/CBQUANTITY~~
{RIGHT}/CBPRICE~~{RIGHT}/CBCOMM~~**

The next field is total cost. This has already been calculated and stored in the BCOST cell (T15) on the input form. Could we simply copy it to the database record as we did for the other fields? Unlike the previous fields, BCOST is a formula: +BQUANTITY*(BPRICE+BCOMM). If BCOST is copied to the database field, its cell references will be copied in relative fashion. In the input form, the cost formula takes the cell that is seven cells up (BQUANTITY) and multiplies it by the sum of the cells that are five cells up (BPRICE) and three cells up (BCOMM). Copying BCOST to the TOTAL COST field would result in a TOTAL COST depending on cells that are seven, five, and three rows above it in the database, and this is not our intention.

Making the cell references of BCOST absolute would not help. This would cause the database TOTAL COST cell to refer to the cells of the input form, but when those cells are changed (when a new form for a different stock is filled out), the TOTAL COST cell would be recalculated using the values of a different stock; the original calculation would be lost.

Instead of copying a formula from the Buy form to the record, we will go directly to the database record itself and enter the formula for total cost. With the pointer on the TOTAL COST field, the macro would instruct 1-2-3 to multiply the QTY field (three cells to the left) by the sum of PURCHASE

PRICE PER SHARE (two cells to the left) plus COMM'N PER SH: PUR-CHASE (one cell to the left). The cell should also be formatted with a currency format. (The reason we format this field explicitly for each record, rather than simply assigning a format to the entire range in a single Range Format command, is that we do not know how many records will be in the database. How far down should we assign a format? If we format the entire column down to, say, row 500, we will be using up free memory that we may never need.)

2. In cell R67, enter the label

{RIGHT}+{LEFT}{LEFT}{LEFT}*({LEFT}{LEFT}+{LEFT})~
/RFC 3~~

Preparing for the Next Purchase Form

Before filling out the next input form, we must erase the previous one. To do this,

1. Enter the following two labels in cells R68 and R69:

'/REBNAME~/REBMONTH~/REBDAY~/REBYEAR~/
REBQUANTITY~
'/REBPRICE~/REBCOMM~/REBCOST~

Next the macro should ask the user whether to create another purchase entry and should store the reply in SCRATCH. If SCRATCH is equal to 1 (yes), 1-2-3 should loop back to the beginning of the macro. Otherwise, the macro should terminate.

2. In cells R70 and R71, respectively, enter the macro labels

V 2.0: **{GETNUMBER "CONTINUE BUY INPUT? (1=YES,**
0=NO):",SCRATCH}
{IF SCRATCH=1}{BRANCH \A}

/X: **'/XNCONTINUE BUY INPUT? (1=YES, 0=NO):**
~SCRATCH~
'/XISCRATCH=1~/XG\A~

Testing the Buy Input Macro

Now try out the macro. Invoke \A, and enter the transactions that follow. If you make a mistake before pressing ENTER in response to a prompt, use the BACKSPACE key to backspace and erase whatever you typed. If you already pressed ENTER, finish up the form, but reply 0 (no) when asked if you want to store the input in the database.

1. Buy 100 shares of Modex on 11/2/83 at $10.00 per share plus $0.10 commission per share. Be sure *not* to enter the $ sign (enter 10 for price and .1 for commission). Store the information in your database.

2. Next buy 10 shares of Rags-to-Riches on 2/15/83 at $50.00 per share, no commission. Again store the input.

3. Now buy an additional 100 shares of Modex on 11/2/83 at $12 per share, with a $10 commission charged for the group of 100 shares as a whole. Store the input.

The results appear in Figure 11-4.

Now that we have taught the system how to buy stock, we can move on to selling stock.

The Sell Transaction

In selling stock, your primary interest is the gain or loss resulting from the sale. You will want to know some of the original purchase information about the stock sold: the ID number, the original purchase price, and the commission. You also need to record new information: the quantity sold, the selling price, the sales commission, the sale date, the cost of the shares sold, the proceeds of the sale, the gain or loss, and the type of capital gain or loss (short-term or long-term). Also, you will need to update the inventory of the stock in the database to reflect the sale of shares.

We will use a Sell form to handle the sell transaction. Like the Buy form, the Sell form will be filled out under macro control. Then its contents will be transferred to the database. However, we will interrupt the macro procedure in the Sell form in order to benefit from some human intervention by the user.

	A	B	C	D	E	F	G	H	I	J	K	L	M	N	O
	NAME	ID	HOLD OR SELL	MO	DA	YR	QTY	PURCHASE PRICE PER SHARE	COMM'N PER SH: PURCHASE	TOTAL COST	SALE PRICE PER SH	COMM'N PER SH: SALE	SALE PROCEEDS	GAIN/ (LOSS)	SHORT/ LONG TERM
1															
2															
3															
4															
5	MODEX	1	HOLD	11	2	83	100	$10.000	$0.100	$1,010.000					
6	RAGS	2	HOLD	2	15	83	10	$50.000	$0.000	$500.000					
7	MODEX	3	HOLD	11	2	83	100	$12.000	$0.100	$1,210.000					

Figure 11-4. Database showing results of buy transactions

Structuring the Sell Input Form

Figure 11-5 shows the input form for selling shares from the portfolio. Only the underscored items will be entered by the user as input. All other items are provided by a macro. The six items on the top left of the form contain information about the stock to be sold, gleaned from the existing portfolio. The five items on the right are computed.

To enter the form on your worksheet,

1. Type the following labels in the specified cells:

CELL	LABEL
U23	^SELL
R25	NAME:
R26	ID NUMBER:
R27	BUY DATE-
S27	"MONTH:
U27	"DAY:
W27	"YEAR:
R28	ORIGINAL HOLDINGS:
R29	PURCHASE PRICE/SH:
R30	COMMISSION/SH:
R32	QUANTITY TO SELL:
R34	SELL PRICE/SHARE:
R36	COMMISSION/SH:
R38	SELL DATE
S38	"MONTH:
U38	"DAY:
W38	"YEAR:
V30	HOLDINGS:
V31	COST:
V32	PROCEEDS:
V33	GAIN/(LOSS):
V34	SHORT/LONG-TERM:

2. Use * to put a string of asterisks in cells U22 and U24.

3. Place underscores in the following cells: T33, T35, T37, T39, V39, and X39.

4. Assign the following range names to the associated cells by typing /**R**ange Name Create *rangename* ENTER *celladdress*.

```
            R       S       T       U       V       W       X
22                                  *********
23                                  SELL
24                                  *********
25  NAME:
26  ID NUMBER:
27  BUY DATE-  MONTH:                   DAY:            YEAR:
28  ORIGINAL HOLDINGS:
29  PURCHASE PRICE/SH:
30  COMMISSION/SH:                           HOLDINGS:
31                                           COST:
32  QUANTITY TO SELL:                        PROCEEDS:
33                  ------------             GAIN/(LOSS):
34  SELL PRICE/SHARE:                        SHORT/LONG-TERM:
35                  ------------
36  COMMISSION/SH:
37                  ------------
38  SELL DATE  MONTH:                    DAY:           YEAR:
39                  ------------             ---------       -------------
```

Figure 11-5. An input form for stock sales

CELL	RANGE NAME
R22	**SELLFORM**
T25	**SNAME**
T26	**SID**
T27	**SPURCHMONTH**
V27	**SPURCHDAY**
X27	**SPURCHYEAR**
T28	**SORIGHOLD**
T29	**SPURCHPRICE**
T30	**SPURCHCOMM**
T32	**SQUANTITY**
T34	**SPRICE**
T36	**SCOMM**
T38	**SMONTH**
V38	**SDAY**
X38	**SYEAR**
X30	**SHOLDINGS**
X31	**SCOST**
X32	**SPROCEEDS**
X33	**SGAIN**
X34	**STYPE**
X35	**SPLACE**

5. Assign currency format with three decimal places (/**R**ange Format Currency **3** ENTER *rangename* ENTER) to the following named cells: SPRICE, SCOMM, SCOST, SPROCEEDS, and SGAIN.

The Sell Input Macro

The first step in selling shares is to designate which shares are the ones being sold. Once 1-2-3 knows which stock the user wants to sell, it can retrieve information about current holdings of that stock and display it on the form. The user will then be prompted for information about the sale: the quantity sold, the selling price, the commission, and so forth. Given this information, 1-2-3 computes the gain from the sale and updates the database's inventory.

Determining Which Holdings to Sell: The {?} Command

How can the macro determine which holdings the user wants to sell? It is insufficient to prompt the user for the stock name, because there might be several groups of stock with the same name. Does the investor want to sell the group purchased at $10 per share rather than the group purchased at $8 per share? Then again, the user may not remember the precise name of the stock or whether there is currently an inventory of the stock in the portfolio.

The safest approach is to have the macro ask the user to point to the holdings record containing the shares to be sold. This provides the flexibility of being able to scroll through the portfolio to see what shares are available. Once the user moves the pointer to the correct cell and presses ENTER, the macro will take over.

The macro begins by placing the window on the top-left section of the portfolio; it then prompts the user to point to the shares to be sold.

1. In cell R80, enter the label

   MACRO B: INPUT SELL RECORD INTO DATABASE

2. In cell R81 enter {HOME}{END}{DOWN}.

3. In cell R82 type:

   V 2.0: {GETLABEL "PRESS ENTER: POINT TO SHARES SOLD:", SCRATCH}

   /X: '/XLPRESS ENTER: POINT TO SHARES SOLD: ~SCRATCH~

4. Assign the name \B to cell R81.

In this case, the SCRATCH cell has no significance. If you examined it, you would find an apostrophe followed by nothing else (because you never press anything except the ENTER key when you respond to the GETLABEL (/XL) message). We use the GETLABEL (/XL) command here only for its ability to display a prompt, not to retrieve a response. In addition, be aware that the message displayed by GETLABEL or GETNUMBER is limited to 39 characters.

When the user presses ENTER, the macro should wait until the user has pointed to a record and pressed ENTER again before it continues to execute other keystrokes. However, the macros we have developed thus far have been relentless. We have seen no way of stopping a macro from going on to the next step. The macro pause command, {?}, causes 1-2-3 to stop processing the macro until the user has pressed the ENTER key. The macro pause command is useful in developing interactive macros. For example, the macro might begin a command, pause, and then allow the user to continue the command. Putting {?} in the Sell macro at this point will allow the user to peruse the database and select a record.

5. In cell R83, enter {?}.

Again, this label could have been combined with the previous one with the same effect. Note: In executing this macro, when you point to a holdings record, you must place the pointer on the first field of that record (NAME) in order for the macro to work properly.

Transferring Original Purchase Data To the Input Form

When the user has selected a record and pressed ENTER, the macro should copy the stock name, ID, purchase date, original holdings, purchase price, and purchase commission to the Sell input form. The macro automatically places the pointer on each of these fields in the selected holdings record, copying each one to the appropriate cell of the input form. When done, the macro shifts the pointer to the Sell form to accept the user's input. When the form is complete, its information must be transferred back to the database in the form of a new sell record.

In addition, the macro must go back to the original holdings record and adjust the holdings. Now suppose that the holdings record is somewhere in the middle of the portfolio. The pointer is in the input form. How will the macro know where to find the holdings record? Lotus 1-2-3 does not remember every place the pointer has been. Therefore, must we prompt the user to find the holdings record again? Will the user remember which record it was?

What is needed is a "placeholder" in the database that can be inserted immediately after the user points to the holdings record at the beginning of the macro, *before* the pointer moves to the input form. When it comes time to go back to the holdings record, we simply use the F5 (GoTo) key to go to the placeholder. No new commands are necessary; just attach a range name to a cell in the holdings record after the user has identified the shares to sell.

The placeholder is named SPLACE. It is one of the cells you named earlier. With each sell, the assignment of SPLACE changes, depending on the position of the holdings record. Range Name Create assigns SPLACE to a cell. If SPLACE was assigned previously to another cell, 1-2-3 remembers and recommends the previous assignment. To unstick 1-2-3's memory, you would have to press ESC or the BACKSPACE key, then move the pointer to the correct cell. Usually 1-2-3's memory is helpful, but here it is a nuisance.

A more convenient way to avoid this problem is to delete the range name just before creating it. In this way, 1-2-3 will forget about the previous assignment of SPLACE and will recommend the current position of the pointer.

1. In cell R84, enter '/RNDSPLACE~/RNCSPLACE~~.

The following labels copy the holdings information to the Sell input form.

2. In cells R85, R86, R87, and R88, enter these labels:

```
'/C~SNAME~{RIGHT}/C~SID~
{RIGHT}{RIGHT}/C~SPURCHMONTH~{RIGHT}
  /C~SPURCHDAY~
{RIGHT}/C~SPURCHYEAR~{RIGHT}/C~SORIGHOLD~
{RIGHT}/C~SPURCHPRICE~{RIGHT}/C~SPURCHCOMM~
```

Here is a good place to stop and try out the macro yourself by invoking \B. Select a stock to sell, and move to the Sell input form (beginning at cell R22) to examine how the information was copied from the database.

Filling Out the Sell Input Form

To get the Sell input form on the screen, you would have to go to the top-left corner of the form, which is offscreen. The macro also must do this. This corner cell is named SELLFORM. The system should then prompt the user for the sell entries.

1. In cell R89 enter {GOTO}SELLFORM~.

2. In cell R90 type

   V 2.0: {GETNUMBER "ENTER QUANTITY SOLD:",
   SQUANTITY}

   /X: '/XNENTER QUANTITY SOLD:~SQUANTITY~

If the user tries to sell more than the holdings of this group of shares, the system issues a warning that the quantity is too much, and 1-2-3 loops back to the prompt for quantity.

3. In cell R91, type the following label on one line:

   V 2.0: {IF SQUANTITY>SORIGHOLD}{GETLABEL "TOO
   MUCH! PRESS ENTER & TRY AGAIN", SCRATCH}
   {BRANCH BPOINT1}

   /X: '/XISQUANTITY>SORIGHOLD~/XLTOO MUCH!
   PRESS ENTER & TRY AGAIN~SCRATCH~
   /XGBPOINT1~

4. Assign cell R90 the name **BPOINT1**.

Actually, it is conceivable that an investor would sell more shares than the portfolio has. This is called "selling short." This macro does not handle short sales, but it is certainly possible to do so in a macro. Someday you might try your hand at enhancing the macro with a short-sales capability.

5. Enter the following command labels in cells R92 through R96:

   V 2.0: {GETNUMBER "ENTER SELLING PRICE:", SPRICE}
   {GETNUMBER "ENTER COMMISSION:", SCOMM}
   {GETNUMBER "ENTER SELL DATE—MONTH
   (NUMERIC):", SMONTH}
   {GETNUMBER "ENTER SELL DATE—DAY
   (NUMERIC):", SDAY}
   {GETNUMBER "ENTER SELL DATE—YEAR
   (2 DIGITS):", SYEAR}

   /X: '/XNENTER SELLING PRICE:~SPRICE~
   '/XNENTER COMMISSION:~SCOMM~
   '/XNENTER SELL DATE—MONTH (NUMERIC):
   ~SMONTH~
   '/XNENTER SELL DATE—DAY (NUMERIC):~SDAY~
   '/XNENTER SELL DATE—YEAR (2 DIGITS):~SYEAR~

The macro will fill out the rest of the form.

Computing the Number
Of Shares Remaining

The first item to be computed and displayed on the form is the inventory of shares remaining after the sale, which is named SHOLDINGS. The formula is +SORIGHOLD−SQUANTITY, but with this formula we run into the same problem we confronted with ID's in the Buy input macro. Namely, when the formula entry is copied to the database, it is copied relatively, and the database will refer to the wrong cells. We can "freeze" the formula value by using {EDIT}{CALC}~ to convert the formula to a number. The same problem and solution apply to the other calculations that follow.

1. In cell R97, enter

   {GOTO}SHOLDINGS~+SORIGHOLD−SQUANTITY~{EDIT}
   {CALC}~

Cost of Shares Sold, Proceeds,
And Gain

The cost of the shares sold is equal to the original purchase price plus the purchase commission per share, multiplied by the number of shares purchased. Expressed as a formula, this is

   +SQUANTITY*(SPURCHPRICE+SPURCHCOMM)

Adding {EDIT}{CALC} to this formula converts the result to a number.

1. In cell R98, enter (on one line)

   {GOTO}SCOST~+SQUANTITY*(SPURCHPRICE+
   SPURCHCOMM)~{EDIT}{CALC}~

The proceeds of the sale are computed as the number of shares sold times the price per share less sales commission:

2. In cell R99, enter

   {GOTO}SPROCEEDS~+SQUANTITY*(SPRICE−SCOMM)~
   {EDIT}{CALC}~

The gain on the sale is simply proceeds minus cost:

3. In cell R100, enter

   {GOTO}SGAIN~+SPROCEEDS−SCOST~{EDIT}{CALC}~

Type of Sale

When the shares to be sold are more than a year old, the capital gain or loss on the sale is called long-term. You can determine whether the sale is eligible for long-term or short-term tax treatment by comparing the date of purchase to the date of sale, both of which are available on the input form. If the date of the sale (@DATE(SYEAR,SMONTH,SDAY)) is later than or equal to one year after the purchase date, (@DATE(SPURCHYEAR+1, SPURCHMONTH,SPURCHDAY)), then the sale is long-term, and the long-term code, LT, should be stored in the STYPE cell. Otherwise, the STYPE code is ST.

1. Enter '{GOTO}STYPE~ in cell R101.

2. In cell R102, enter on one line

> *V 2.0:*   {IF @DATE(SYEAR,SMONTH,SDAY>@DATE
> (SPURCHYEAR+1,SPURCHMONTH,SPURCHDAY)}
> "LT"{BRANCH BPOINT2}

> */X:*   '/XI@DATE(SYEAR,SMONTH,SDAY)>@DATE
> (SPURCHYEAR+1,SPURCHMONTH,SPURCHDAY)~
> "LT~/XGBPOINT2~

3. Enter "ST~ in cell R103.

4. Assign the name **BPOINT2** to cell R104.

Both LT and ST are right-justified within the field because of the double quotes used as a prefix. If the type is long-term, 1-2-3 skips down to BPOINT2 (two cells down) to continue reading keystrokes. Otherwise, 1-2-3 types the ST code and continues reading.

With the sell input complete, we ask the user whether to store the input in the database.

5. In cells R104 and R105, respectively, type

> *V 2.0:*   {GETNUMBER "STORE INPUT? (1=YES, 0=NO):",
> SCRATCH}
> {IF SCRATCH=0}{BRANCH \B}

> */X:*   '/XNSTORE INPUT? (1=YES, 0=NO):~SCRATCH~
> '/XISCRATCH=0~/XG\B~

Transferring the Input Form To the Database

The next concern is to update the inventory of shares. This is where our placeholder, SPLACE, comes in handy. We direct 1-2-3 to go to SPLACE, move right as many times as it takes to get to the QUANTITY field (which stores the holdings), and set this field equal to SHOLDINGS. An {EDIT} {CALC} is necessary to convert the QUANTITY to a number so that when SHOLDINGS changes on the next sell entry, this holdings field stays constant.

1. In cell R106, enter (on one line)

    {GOTO}SPLACE~{RIGHT}{RIGHT}{RIGHT}{RIGHT}{RIGHT}
    {RIGHT}+SHOLDINGS~{EDIT}{CALC}~

The remainder of the macro follows the same pattern as the purchase macro. Lotus 1-2-3 moves the pointer to the next available record, copies the input cells to the database (and enters SELL as the record type in the HOLD OR SELL field), erases the input form fields, and asks whether to process another sell. If the user responds with 0, the macro is finished. Otherwise, it loops back to the beginning of the macro (\B).

2. In cells R107 through R119, enter the following labels:

    {HOME}{END}{DOWN}{END}{DOWN}{DOWN}
    '/CSNAME~~{RIGHT}/CSID~~{RIGHT}SELL~
    {RIGHT}/CSMONTH~~{RIGHT}/CSDAY~~{RIGHT}
      /CSYEAR~~
    {RIGHT}/CSQUANTITY~~{RIGHT}/CSPURCHPRICE~~
    {RIGHT}/CSPURCHCOMM~~{RIGHT}/CSCOST~~
    {RIGHT}/CSPRICE~~{RIGHT}/CSCOMM~~
    {RIGHT}/CSPROCEEDS~~{RIGHT}/CSGAIN~~
    {RIGHT}/CSTYPE~~
    '/RESNAME~/RESID~/RESPURCHMONTH~
      /RESPURCHDAY~
    '/RESPURCHYEAR~/RESORIGHOLD~/RESPURCHPRICE~
    '/RESPURCHCOMM~/RESQUANTITY~/RESPRICE~
      /RESCOMM~
    '/RESMONTH~/RESDAY~/RESYEAR~/RESHOLDINGS~
      /RESCOST~
    '/RESPROCEEDS~/RESGAIN~/RESTYPE~

3. In cell R120 and R121, enter the following two labels:

V 2.0: {GETNUMBER "CONTINUE SELL ENTRY? (1=YES,
   0=NO):", SCRATCH}
   {IF SCRATCH=1}{BRANCH \B}

/X: '/XNCONTINUE SELL ENTRY? (1=YES, 0=NO):~
   SCRATCH~
   '/XISCRATCH=1~/XG\B~

Testing the Sell Input Macro

Figure 11-6 shows macro \B in its entirety. Invoke macro \B now and execute the following three sell transactions based on the purchases that you made earlier in this chapter (see Figure 11-4).

1. Sell 50 shares of Modex, ID number 3, on 11/1/84 at $13 per share plus $0.05 sales commission per share. Store the input in your database.

2. Next sell 50 shares of Modex, ID number 1, on 11/2/84 at $14 per share plus $0.05 sales commission per share. Store the input in your database.

3. Now sell two shares of Rags-to-Riches, ID number 2, on 1/15/84 at $60 per share. There is no commission on the sale. Again, store the input in your database.

The first transaction sells Modex (which was purchased on 11/2/83) on 11/1/84, just one day short of the long-term date. The input form should display ST as the type of sale. The second transaction sells Modex on the next day, 11/2/84. This is the first day of long-term status, so the display should register LT. The third transaction, the sale of Rags shares, should register as another short-term sale because it takes place only a few months after the original purchase. When you have finished filling out the forms, examine the database. Observe how the original holdings of the stocks were adjusted to reflect the sale and how the TOTAL COST column reflects the total cost of the new holdings. The results appear in Figure 11-7.

Total cost is derived from the new inventory of shares multiplied by the price and commission per share. Although the purchase commission may have been a flat fee applied to the total number of shares originally purchased, storing commissions on a per-share basis allows us to compute the portion of the commission applied to the shares that were sold even though some shares may be retained.

The ability to tell 1-2-3 *not* to store the sell record in the database is quite useful for testing hypothetical sell transactions, for it allows you to try out

```
                        R              S              T              U              V              W              X              Y              Z
80  MACRO B: INPUT SELL RECORD INTO DATABASE
81  {HOME}{END}{DOWN}
82  {GETLABEL "PRESS ENTER: POINT TO SHARES SOLD:",SCRATCH}
83  {?}
84  /RNDSPLACE~/RNCSPLACE~~
85  /C~SNAME~{RIGHT}/C~SID~
86  {RIGHT}{RIGHT}/C~SPURCHMONTH~{RIGHT}/C~SPURCHDAY~
87  {RIGHT}/C~SPURCHYEAR~{RIGHT}/C~SORIGHOLD~
88  {RIGHT}/C~SPURCHPRICE~{RIGHT}/C~SPURCHCOMM~
89  {GOTO}SELLFORM~
90  {GETNUMBER "ENTER QUANTITY SOLD:",SQUANTITY}
91  {IF SQUANTITY>SORIGHOLD}{GETLABEL "TOO MUCH! PRESS ENTER & TRY AGAIN",SCRATCH}{BRANCH BPOINT1}
92  {GETNUMBER "ENTER SELLING PRICE:",SPRICE}
93  {GETNUMBER "ENTER COMMISSION:",SCOMM}
94  {GETNUMBER "ENTER SELL DATE-MONTH (NUMERIC):",SMONTH}
95  {GETNUMBER "ENTER SELL DATE-DAY (NUMERIC):",SDAY}
96  {GETNUMBER "ENTER SELL DATE-YEAR (2 DIGITS):",SYEAR}
97  {GOTO}SHOLDINGS~+SORIGHOLD-SQUANTITY~{EDIT}{CALC}~
98  {GOTO}SCOST~+SQUANTITY*(SPURCHPRICE+SPURCHCOMM)~{EDIT}{CALC}~
99  {GOTO}SPROCEEDS~+SQUANTITY*(SPRICE-SCOMM)~{EDIT}{CALC}~
100 {GOTO}SGAIN+SPROCEEDS-SCOST~{EDIT}{CALC}~
101 {GOTO}STYPE~
102 {IF @DATE(SYEAR,SMONTH,SDAY)>=@DATE(SPURCHYEAR+1,SPURCHMONTH,SPURCHDAY)>"LT"{BRANCH BPOINT2}
103 "ST~
104 {GETNUMBER "STORE INPUT? (1=YES, 0=NO):",SCRATCH}
105 {IF SCRATCH=0}{BRANCH \B}
106 {GOTO}SPLACE~{RIGHT}{RIGHT}{RIGHT}{RIGHT}{RIGHT}+SHOLDINGS~{EDIT}{CALC}~
107 {HOME}{END}{DOWN}{END}{DOWN}{DOWN}
108 /CSNAME~{RIGHT}/CSID~{RIGHT}SELL~
109 {RIGHT}/CSMONTH~{RIGHT}/CSDAY~{RIGHT}/CSYEAR~~
110 {RIGHT}/CSQUANTITY~{RIGHT}/CSPURCHPRICE~~
111 {RIGHT}/CSPURCHCOMM~{RIGHT}/CSCOST~~
112 {RIGHT}/CSPRICE~{RIGHT}/CSCOMM~~
113 {RIGHT}/CSPROCEEDS~~{RIGHT}/CSGAIN~~
114 {RIGHT}/CSTYPE~~
115 /RESNAME~/RESID~/RESPURCHMONTH~/RESPURCHDAY~
116 /RESPURCHYEAR~/RESORIGHOLD~/RESPURCHPRICE~
117 /RESPURCHCOMM~/RESQUANTITY~/RESPRICE~/RESCOMM~
118 /RESMONTH~/RESDAY~/RESYEAR~/RESHOLDINGS~/RESCOST~
119 /RESPROCEEDS~/RESGAIN~/RESTYPE~
120 {GETNUMBER "CONTINUE SELL ENTRY? (1=YES, 0=NO):",SCRATCH}
121 {IF SCRATCH=1}{BRANCH \B}
```

Figure 11-6. Macro \B is used for sell transactions

	A	B	C	D	E	F	G	H	I	J	K	L	M	N	O
	NAME	ID	HOLD OR SELL	MO	DA	YR	QTY	PURCHASE PRICE PER SHARE	COMM'N PER SH: PURCHASE	TOTAL COST	SALE PRICE PER SH	COMM'N PER SH: SALE	SALE PROCEEDS	GAIN/ LOSS	SHORT/ LONG TERM
1															
2															
3															
4															
5	MODEX	1	HOLD	11	2	83	50	$10.000	$0.100	$505.000					
6	RAGS	2	HOLD	2	15	83	8	$50.000	$0.000	$400.000					
7	MODEX	3	HOLD	11	2	83	50	$12.000	$0.100	$605.000					
8	MODEX	3	SELL	11	1	84	50	$12.000	$0.100	$605.000	$13.000	$0.050	$647.500	$42.500	ST
9	MODEX	1	SELL	11	2	84	50	$10.000	$0.100	$505.000	$14.000	$0.050	$697.500	$192.500	LT
10	RAGS	2	SELL	1	15	84	2	$50.000	$0.000	$100.000	$60.000	$0.000	$120.000	$20.000	ST

Figure 11-7. Database showing results of sell transactions

different prices to see the resulting gain without altering the actual portfolio. You can use the same feature to enter a market price from the newspaper to find out the current market value of your holdings.

Reporting Gains and Losses At Year End

At the end of the year, you will need to report your gains or losses on the sale of stock on your tax return. Using the Data Sort command with a Primary sort key of the record type (HOLD OR SELL, column C), you can separate the two types of transactions so that printing the sell transactions alone will be easy. Descending order will put the sell transactions on the top of the file.

Using a Secondary sort key of the type of sale (SHORT/LONG TERM), you can separate the long-term gains and losses from the short-term gains and losses. The report is so easy to develop that it is probably not worth writing a macro for, though you may wish to do so as an exercise. Here are the steps involved:

1. Press HOME.

2. Select /Data Sort Data-Range.

The data range begins with the first field of the first record of the database.

3. Point to the first field of the first record (cell A5).

4. Type the . key to anchor the range.

5. Point to the last field of the last record of the portfolio (cell O10), and press ENTER.

6. Select Primary-Key, point to the HOLD OR SELL field (column C), press ENTER, and select Descending sort order.

7. Select Secondary-Key, point to the last field of the file (SHORT/LONG TERM, column O), press ENTER, and then select Ascending sort order. Select Go.

8. Move the pointer to the first short-term sell record in column O, and use /Worksheet Insert Row to insert four rows above the short-term records.

9. Use @SUM to store a net total of long-term gains/losses in cell N7. Assign the cell a Currency format with three digits.

	A	B	C	D	E	F	G	H	I	J	K	L	M	N	O
	NAME	ID	HOLD OR SELL	MO	DA	YR	QTY	PURCHASE PRICE PER SHARE	COMM'N PER SH: PURCHASE	TOTAL COST	SALE PRICE PER SH	COMM'N PER SH: SALE	SALE PROCEEDS	GAIN/ LOSS	SHORT/ LONG TERM
1															
2															
3															
4															
5	MODEX	1	SELL	11	2	84	50	$10.000	$0.100	$505.000	$14.000	$0.050	$697.500	$192.500	LT
6															
7														$192.500	
8															
9															
10	MODEX	3	SELL	11	1	84	50	$12.000	$0.100	$605.000	$13.000	$0.050	$647.500	$42.500	ST
11	RAGS	2	SELL	1	15	84	2	$50.000	$0.000	$100.000	$60.000	$0.000	$120.000	$20.000	ST
12															
13														$62.500	

Figure 11-8. Year-end report of gains and losses

10. Move down to the first HOLD record, and insert four rows above it.

11. Use **@SUM** to store a net total of short-term gains/losses in cell N13, and assign the cell the Currency format with three digits.

That concludes the year-end report, illustrated in Figure 11-8. To print it, you will need wider margins than the 1-2-3 defaults, so use the Options menu of the Print command to set the left margin to 0 and the right margin to 132. If your printer cannot fit 132 characters across in 10-character-per-inch mode, you may have to condense the print using the Setup option.

We have discussed only the tip of the iceberg when it comes to the applicability of 1-2-3 to portfolio management. This model can be expanded almost infinitely. For instance, you could develop a parallel file of market prices, gleaned from the newspaper or downloaded through a database service, to produce a report of market values for all holdings in the portfolio. Graphs based on market data could suggest trends of the stock price. The model could be expanded to handle other types of securities, such as bonds or options.

Entire books have been written on the microcomputer applications of portfolio management. Undoubtedly an entire book could be devoted to 1-2-3's usefulness in this area.

Chapter 12
Financial Functions
And
Sensitivity Analysis

A Model for Evaluating
Acquisitions

Opportunity Costs

"What If" Calculations

Lotus 1-2-3 is a multifunctional program, but it is first and foremost an electronic spreadsheet. Chapters 2 and 3 described how the spreadsheet commands would be applied to forecasting a pro forma income statement. In this chapter that same income statement will be used as the basis for a more ambitious project: a decision model to analyze the financial effects of acquiring a new product or an entire company. The model's purpose is to evaluate an acquisition based on forecast assumptions and accepted valuation methods.

The model incorporates two of 1-2-3's special financial functions, @NPV and @IRR. These functions are not only essential to acquisitions; they also apply to a wide variety of investment decisions, such as lease-versus-buy decisions, bond valuation, and IRA accounts. The chapter also uses the data table facility, discussed in Chapter 9, to introduce 1-2-3's suitability to sensitivity analysis.

A Model for Evaluating Acquisitions

The acquisition of a new product or company can be a quick, efficient, yet risky means of growth for a corporation. Through acquisition, a firm can buy its way into a new line of business without expending the resources required to develop a market on its own. An acquisition is one way of strengthening a firm's market position in its own industry, through acquiring firms with complementary product lines and through economies of scale. A manufacturing firm might buy out one of its suppliers in order to lower the cost of raw materials or to maintain greater control over the availability of supplies.

An acquisition model poses a great challenge. Acquisition analysis demands flexibility. In the first place, each acquisition has a character of its own. The purchase of a widget producer is different from the purchase of a private hospital, which in turn is different from the purchase of an investment bank. Thus, each acquisition requires its own, customized analysis. However, it is possible to develop a model that is adaptable to many different situations—a model that minimizes the amount of necessary customization.

Another requirement of the model is that any single acquisition should be adaptable to various scenarios. After all, a forecast of how the fledgling division or product will fare in the next five years is only a calculated prophecy; acquisition analysis is not an exact science.

The key point to keep in mind is that, although an organized printout of forecasted financial statements suggests precision and definitiveness, no acquisition analysis is complete without an awareness of the risks involved in the purchase. A forecast is only as good as its underlying assumptions.

Considerations in Evaluating A Candidate

Although each acquisition has its own unique features, the method of evaluating the earnings potential of a candidate is common to all acquisitions. Our primary task is to establish the worth of the product or company under consideration, so that we can determine a fair (or better yet, unfair!) offering price for the candidate.

Corporate acquisitions come in two forms. A corporation can acquire a company's assets, such as its equipment, inventories, and receivables; or it can purchase a company's stock. In the example that follows, we will investigate a corporate acquisition of the second type, the purchase of a company's entire stock in exchange for cash.

As analysts for Conglomerated Consolidated Inc., we have been asked by the chairperson to look into the possibility of acquiring none other than the Rags-to-Riches Company, that promising, young dishtowel company introduced in Chapters 1 and 2. An appropriate acquisition price will reflect the expected profitability of the company throughout its economic life. But how long is the life of a firm, and how well can one predict its lifetime earnings? Rags may be in business for 100 years. Can we make a reasonable prediction about its earnings 99 years from now?

To circumvent these uncertainties, we limit the horizons of the analysis to a more reasonable time frame, five years. For the purposes of comprehending financial statements and implementing a model, this time period is much more manageable.

We will approach the acquisition as a sort of temporary purchase. We buy the company today and hold it for five years. At the end of the holding period, we sell the company for a predicted amount, the *terminal value.*

The terminal value represents the amount that the company will be worth on the market at the end of the five-year holding period. Equivalently, it represents our guess as to the value of the company's earnings potential from Year 6 to eternity. Thus, our five-year picture of the acquisition candidate actually constitutes an evaluation of the firm's earnings over its entire corporate life. By combining the five years of money outflows and inflows, we can arrive at a purchase price. This is done by developing a financial worksheet detailing the amount of financial resources expended or received over the five-year period.

Where does this information come from? Fortunately, Chapter 3 happens to have the most up-to-date, accurate data available for Rags-to-Riches Company. We will utilize the pro forma income statement developed in that chapter to create a five-year forecast of the flow of funds into and out of Rags.

The Flow of Funds Statement

A report of the flow of money into and out of the acquisition is called the *flow of funds statement,* or funds flow statement. The flow of funds statement is our basis for determining the value of Rags-to-Riches because it reports the annual amounts that Conglomerated stands to invest in (that is, lose) or gain from its prospective subsidiary.

The flow of funds statement that we will develop is shown later in Figure 12-2. You may want to take a minute to look ahead at that figure. We will place Rags' income statement in the top section of the worksheet, and then we will add the flow of funds statement below it. Note: If you do not have the income statement developed in Chapters 2 and 3 on disk, then you may generate it by following the numbered steps of those chapters.

1. Retrieve the Rags-to-Riches income statement by typing /File Retrieve **IS** ENTER.

2. In cell D35, enter the label **FUNDS FLOW ANALYSIS**.

3. In cell D36, press the space bar two times and enter the label **$ IN THOUSANDS**.

Copy the column headings of the income statement down to the funds flow statement as follows:

4. Move to cell C4; type /Copy; press END, the right arrow key, the down arrow key, and ENTER; and then move to cell C38, and press ENTER again.

Net Income

How do we begin to measure the flow of money into and out of the acquisition? We start with the closest measure at hand: net income.

1. Enter the label **NET INCOME** in cell B40.

Once we have acquired Rags, net income (or loss) will affect the parent company starting in Year 1. We must bring down the YEAR 1 NET INCOME from the income statement by setting the flow of funds statement's NET INCOME equal to the income statement's NET INCOME.

2. Move to Year 1 NET INCOME of the funds statement (cell D40).

3. Type the + key, point to Year 1 NET INCOME of the income statement (cell D31), and press the ENTER key. (This is a one-item formula.)

4. Copy this Year 1 formula to Years 2 through 5 in cells E40..H40.

Non-Cash Charges

One might think that after-tax income is all we require to describe the flows of funds that are relevant to the purchase. However, net income includes certain non-cash items that are not actual out-of-pocket expenses for the firm. In the Rags example, we deducted $20,000 of depreciation expense in Year 1, but this expense did not represent $20,000 in cash that Rags paid out to creditors. It represents the use and wear of the plant and equipment bought and paid for sometime in the past. Cost of Goods Sold, on the other hand, represents a cash cost to the company. Therefore, to determine the actual flow of funds, we must add back any non-cash items that were deducted in the income statement.

1. Enter the label **NON-CASH CHARGES** in cell B41.

Next bring down the depreciation line from the income statement.

2. Move to Year 1 NON-CASH CHARGES of the funds statement (cell D41).

3. Type the + key, move up to Year 1 DEPRECIATION of the income statement (cell D20), and press the ENTER key.

4. Copy this formula to Years 2 through 5 (cells E41..H41).

Capital Investment

We are now closer to the actual funds figure, but we are not there yet. The income statement measures income from operations as a result of sales, but certain cash expenditures are not immediately reflected in it. Capital investment in fixed assets is the amount of funds expended to upgrade the plant and buy new equipment. This equipment is paid for before it is reflected as depreciation. According to the owners of Rags-to-Riches, new equipment will be necessary over the next five years to accommodate the firm's growth and to replace aging machines. These equipment expenditures will not be reflected in the funds statement unless we deduct them explicitly to reflect a use of funds.

1. Enter the label **CAPITAL INVESTMENT** in cell B42.

Capital expenditures, rounded to the nearest thousand, are expected to appear as shown.

YEAR	AMOUNT
1	50
2	40
3	28
4	45
5	45

2. Beginning with the Year 1 CAPITAL INVESTMENT cell (D42), enter these annual investment amounts as *negative* values (because they are deductions from funds).

Thus, cell D42 should contain the value −50, cell E42 should contain −40, and so forth.

Calculating Change In Working Capital

We must still make one adjustment in order to arrive at a real funds figure. The income statement treats current revenues as inflows of funds, even if the inflows are not cash in hand. For example, suppose Rags sold $80 million worth of designer dishtowels to cash-paying customers and sold $8 million worth to charge customers. The income statement would recognize $88 million of income, the total of cash and charge sales. For purposes of funds flow, however, we are concerned merely with the receipt of cash. If the cash is received in the following year, it must be added to the funds statement then, not now. Similarly, materials expense is fully recognized in the income statement even if a significant number of purchases were made on the company's credit account and thus were recorded as part of the company's accounts payable at the end of the year.

Accounts receivable is an example of a *current asset*, an asset that will be used up or converted into cash within one year. Other current assets are cash itself (how much more current can you get?), marketable securities owned by the company (these can be quickly sold for cash), and inventories.

In contrast, accounts payable is a *current liability* because it is payable within a year. Other current liabilities include short-term notes and short-term loans, which the company must pay back within a year.

The difference between current assets and current liabilities is called *net working capital*. If net working capital has increased in the current year, then current assets have increased more than current liabilities, and funds are needed to pay for the increase. This net growth in working capital should be deducted from income in the funds statement. Conversely, if the year's change in current liabilities exceeds the change in current assets, then the reduction in working capital that was not really paid for in cash must be added to income. As a result, an increase in working capital decreases funds, while a decrease in working capital increases funds. The adjustment to income thus consists of deducting the net change in working capital.

Rags' owners did not want to admit it, but a portion of their sales forecast did include purchases by charge customers. At the same time, some of Rags' materials expense was charged by the company and has not yet been paid in cash. On balance, however, the amount of outstanding receivables from charge customers exceeds the amount of credit that the company owes its creditors at the end of each year of the forecast. These facts account for the net increases in working capital that are shown in Step 2 of the following procedure. The increase in working capital represents a reduction in funds (primarily because the company has not received the funds from its credit customers).*

To incorporate the change in working capital into the funds statement,

1. Move to cell B43, and type the label **CHANGE IN WORKING CAPITAL**.

2. Enter the following values into Years 1 through 5 (cells D43..H43):

YEAR	VALUE
1	−10
2	−5
3	−15
4	−17
5	−14

The Acquisition Payment...Almost

The funds flow statement will reflect the costs and benefits that the acquisition of Rags will bring to Conglomerated. So far, we have amassed all of the items necessary to create a net funds flow for the forecast years. However, we have omitted one major expenditure of funds in our analysis: the cost of acquisition itself, the purchase price. Whereas the adjusted net income of

---

*Remember, we are making adjustments to net income. Net income would have been the "right" funds flow number if it did not include any non-cash transactions. But we know that that was not the case.

Rags will not affect its prospective parent until Year 1, the purchase price will affect Conglomerated in Year 0, the year of its takeover of Rags. Therefore, we must include a line beneath CHANGES IN WORKING CAPITAL to register this solitary flow of funds in Year 0.

1. Enter the label **ACQUISITION PAYMENT** ------> in cell B44.

The last eight characters of the label, seven dashes and a right arrowhead (the SHIFT key combined with the . key), are used to draw attention to this most important feature of the funds statement.

Now there is one minor problem. The net funds outflow in Year 0 is the acquisition purchase price. But the acquisition price is precisely the figure that we are attempting to derive by calculating the net funds flow. How can we calculate the net funds flow in Year 0 if we cannot first obtain the purchase price?

This problem is beyond control at this stage, so we will do the same as any red-blooded financial analyst in the same situation: throw up our hands, shrug, and skip to the next step. Actually, with some patience and a bit of 1-2-3's magic, the paradox will remedy itself.

Computing Net Funds Flow

We are now ready to compute the net funds flow for the startup year and the forecast period.

1. Enter the label **NET FUNDS FLOW** at cell B46.

In the Year 0 column, we will enter the formula to accumulate all of the items of the funds statement.

2. Move to the Year 0 NET FUNDS FLOW cell (C46).

3. Type **@SUM(** and point to the Year 0 NET INCOME cell (C40) to start the formula. Next type the . key to anchor the range, point to Year 0 ACQUISITION PAYMENT in cell C44, type the **)** key, and press ENTER.

4. Copy this formula to the remaining years in cells D46..H46.

Computing Terminal Value

We have not yet taken into account the terminal sale value received as an additional funds flow in Year 5. In some instances you may have a reasonable guess as to an appropriate terminal value. For Rags, we will make the simplified assumption that the terminal value is seven times the Year 5 operat-

	A	B		C	D	E	F	G	H
35					FUNDS FLOW ANALYSIS				
36					$ IN THOUSANDS				
37									
38				0	1	2	3	4	5
39				---					
40		NET INCOME			2429	3304	4045	4449	4894
41		NON-CASH CHARGES			20	20	20	20	20
42		CAPITAL INVESTMENT			-50	-40	-28	-45	-45
43		CHANGE IN WORKING CAPITAL			-10	-5	-15	-17	-14
44		ACQUISITION PAYMENT ------->							
45									
46		NET FUNDS FLOW		0	2389	3279	4022	4407	38839

Figure 12-1. Funds flow analysis for acquisition model

ing funds flow.* Thus, the estimated funds flow for Year 5 is the original calculation of the funds derived from operating the subsidiary plus seven times that amount.

The formula for funds in Year 5 (cell H46) is currently @SUM(H40..H44). The funds flow formula should be @SUM(H40..H44)+(7*@SUM(H40..H44)). This is equivalent to eight times the Year 5 funds. However, to show that this formula represents the year's funds flow plus a residual value, we write the formula the long way.

To update the formula,

1. Move the pointer to the Year 5 NET FUNDS FLOW cell (H46).

2. Press the F2 (Edit) key to enter Edit Mode.

3. Type +(7*@SUM(H40.H44)) and press the ENTER key.

Figure 12-1 shows the results. Now that we have the funds flows for the forecast years, we are in a position to compute the maximum purchase price, the maximum amount that Conglomerated will pay Rags in order to achieve its requisite level of profit.

*See the explanatory footnote following "The @NPV Function."

Opportunity Costs

Acquisitions can be exciting, but there are certainly more reliable and predictable ways to turn a buck. The millions of dollars that Conglomerated is thinking of investing in designer dishtowels could be channeled instead into a U.S. Treasury bond, and at considerably less risk. Alternatively, Conglomerated could invest its money in one of its other subsidiaries, which currently provides the corporation with a known percentage return on each dollar invested in it.

Why would Conglomerated invest in a new business? Aside from any business-strategy rationale, the additional risk of an acquisition could be well worthwhile if the return on the investment is higher than what Conglomerated might have earned on another investment. Investing in the acquisition involves an *opportunity cost*, the cost of *not* investing in something else. The value of investing in the acquisition must take this opportunity cost into account.

Present Value

Conglomerated's treasurer claims that the corporation can invest its money in an alternative investment earning a 15% return. If the corporation invests $100 today, this will yield $100*(1+.15), or $115 in a year. If it leaves the money tied up in the investment for two years, then at the end of the second year this will yield a 15% return on the $115, totaling $137.50.

This can be expressed as follows:

$$\$115*(1+.15)=\$137.50$$

Still another way of deriving the value of the investment is to replace the $115 in the formula with the formula by which *it* was derived:

$$\$100*(1+.15)*(1+.15)=\$137.50$$

In other words, invest $100 today at 15% interest, compound the initial investment for the number of years in which the money is invested, and the result is the value of the investment two years from now. Banks calculate the interest on savings in a similar way.

How much money is the investment worth after the third year?

$$\$100*(1+.15)*(1+.15)*(1+.15)=100*(1+.15)^3=\$158.125$$

The value of the investment at some future date (for example, $158.125) is called the *future value*. The initial investment ($100) is called the *present value*. Substituting financial lingo into the example, *present value* $*(1+rate)^N=$

future value, where N is the number of years for which the investment is compounded.

How does this discussion relate to the present application? The funds that Rags is expected to earn in the future are the *future values* of the investment. The *rate* (return) that these funds earn must be at least 15% in order for this investment to be financially sound. If we know the future values and the required minimum rate of return, then we can derive the *present value* of the investment. The present value of the investment is the amount we pay for Rags today; it is the acquisition price.

Take a look at the forecast of Rags' flow of funds over the next five years:

YEAR	RETURN
1	2389
2	3279
3	4022
4	4407
5	38839

When corporate management sees these numbers, they will ask whether Conglomerated should avoid the risk of acquisition by making a more secure investment. Should they invest in Rags, or should they choose an alternative that earns the same (or better) annual returns as those we have projected?

To answer this question, we must first know how much the treasurer would have to invest at 15% in another acquisition in order to yield the same returns as the Rags acquisition. In more technical terms: What is the present value of $2389 thousand (earned one year hence)? What is the present value of $3279 thousand (earned two years hence)? What is the present value of each of the other three returns? If we calculate each of these present values and then add them together, the result will be the amount that Conglomerated needs to invest today, at 15% compound interest, in order to earn $2389 thousand in one year, $3279 thousand in two years, and so forth. The answer is $29 million ($29032 thousand), but it is not as "easy as 1-2-3" to compute manually. Luckily, 1-2-3 has a function that lets us painlessly calculate present values, and we will introduce it shortly.

Maximum Purchase Price

The present value, $29032 thousand, is the amount that Conglomerated must invest in the 15% alternative in order to earn the equivalent of the Rags acquisition. And $29032 is also the magic number that we have worked so diligently to derive: it is the *maximum purchase price.*

Why is $29032 the *maximum* purchase price? If the price that Conglomerated is asked to pay for the acquisition equals the present value of the alternative investment at 15%, then the corporation will be financially indifferent to choosing one investment over the other. If it has $29032 thousand to invest, it can achieve the same returns over five years either way. However, if Rags' management is willing to sell their company for $10000 thousand, Conglomerated would be most happy to accept this gift, because it will get the same returns for far less than the investment in the 15% alternative. On the other hand, if Rags asks for $50000 thousand, Conglomerated will shop elsewhere. Better to put its money into the safer and cheaper 15% investment than to pay that price.

The @NPV Function

Now we know how to find the maximum purchase price of the acquisition: it is equal to the present value of the funds flows, which we calculate by using the rate of return on the alternative investment. If the offered price is higher than the maximum computed price, the acquisition is financially inadvisable. If the proposed price is lower than the computed price, the acquisition is favorable, even accounting for the opportunity cost of rejecting the alternative.

The rate used to compute the present value is called the *discount rate.* The funds flows are said to be discounted at the discount rate in order to derive the present value. (We will refer to these terms throughout our discussion of 1-2-3's financial functions.)

Lotus 1-2-3 provides a function, *@NPV,* that computes the present value of a range of cash flows. The @NPV function requires two arguments: a discount rate, and a range of cells containing the funds flows. The first cell of the range is discounted one year, the second cell is discounted two years, and so on through the nth coordinate (which is discounted n years).

The format of the @NPV function is @NPV (*discount rate, range of cells*). The *discount rate* can be a number or a cell containing a number. The range of cells (and the discount rate, if it is stored in a cell) can be referred to by address or by range name. In our own case, we are interested in discounting the net funds flows for Years 1 to 5. As for the discount rate, let us store it in a coordinate below the funds statement. That way, if we decide to change it later on, we can simply enter a new number into the coordinate.

1. Move to cell B50, and enter the label **DISCOUNT RATE.**

Conglomerated's required discount rate is 15%. To use this rate in the @NPV function, we would have to store it as a decimal number, .15. Actually, there are two ways to enter the value .15. You can type .15, or you can type 15%. When 1-2-3 is in Value Mode, it recognizes the % symbol and divides whatever you have entered by 100. Thus, if you enter 15%, the number is stored as .15.

2. Move to the next column over (cell C50), and enter Conglomerated's rate by typing **15%** and pressing the ENTER key. (You will see 0 displayed, because the global format is set to integer.)

3. To give this cell a percent format, select **/Range Format Percent** ENTER ENTER.

At long last,

4. Move up to cell B48, and enter the label **MAXIMUM PURCHASE PRICE**.

5. Move to cell C48, and type **@NPV(** to begin the formula.

6. Point to the DISCOUNT RATE cell (C50), and press the , key.

7. Point to the first value to be discounted, the Year 1 NET FUNDS FLOW in cell D46.

8. Press the . key to anchor the range.

9. Point to the Year 5 NET FUNDS FLOW cell (H46), press the) key, and press ENTER.

The maximum purchase price is $29032 thousand. Now that it has been calculated, the funds statement may be concluded. Remember the sticky problem of the Year 0 outflow of funds that we could not calculate because the maximum purchase price was unavailable? Now that we have pinned down the maximum purchase price, we can plug it into the funds statement.

10. Move the pointer up to the Year 0 ACQUISITION PAYMENT cell (C44).

Bring up the purchase price as a negative value, because it is a reduction from income:

11. Type the − key, move the pointer to the MAXIMUM PURCHASE PRICE indicated in cell C48, and press ENTER.

Now sit back for a moment and admire the results, as shown in Figure 12-2. We began with an income statement that linked to the funds flow statement by providing five years of after-tax net income and the adjustments for non-cash charges. We made adjustments in the form of investment

	A	B	C	D	E	F	G	H
35				FUNDS FLOW ANALYSIS				
36				$ IN THOUSANDS				
37								
38			0	1	2	3	4	5
39			---					
40		NET INCOME		2429	3304	4045	4449	4894
41		NON-CASH CHARGES		20	20	20	20	20
42		CAPITAL INVESTMENT		-50	-40	-28	-45	-45
43		CHANGE IN WORKING CAPITAL		-10	-5	-15	-17	-14
44		ACQUISITION PAYMENT ------>	-29032					
45								
46		NET FUNDS FLOW	-29032	2389	3279	4022	4407	38839
47								
48		MAXIMUM PURCHASE PRICE	29032					
49								
50		DISCOUNT RATE	15.00%					

Figure 12-2. Calculation of maximum purchase price at 15% rate

in fixed assets and changes in working capital. Adding the line items and including a terminal value in the last year of the forecast, we obtained a net funds flow.* Next we recognized that the acquisition payment, which is the funds outflow in Year 0, is equivalent to the amount that must be invested today in order to earn the funds flows of Years 1 through 5. Therefore, the price of purchasing these future funds is equal to the present value of the funds flows.

In using a discount rate of 15%, we have built an opportunity cost into the purchase-price calculation. Once we determined the maximum purchase price, we factored it into Year 0 of the funds statement, resulting in a complete picture of the gains and losses involved in Conglomerated's purchase decision, including the timing of these gains and losses. What a grand model!

---

*For expedience, we assumed the terminal value to be seven times the Year 5 funds flow. However, a more reasonable assumption is that the firm's value reflects its earnings potential, and that its earnings return will be maintained by Conglomerated at the corporate discount rate, to perpetuity. Thus, Rags becomes an annuity. The formula for valuing an annuity is *funds flow**(1/*discount rate*). Therefore, the Year 5 funds flow is not multiplied by 7; it should be multiplied by 1/*discount rate*, with the formula for Year 5 funds flow adjusted accordingly. If the discount rate were 15%, the Year 5 funds flow would be multiplied by a factor of 1/.15, or 6.7, to obtain the terminal value.

"What If" Calculations

Now we are ready to call the chairperson of Conglomerated to recommend a maximum offer of $29032 thousand. However, while we were patting ourselves on the back in the previous paragraph, the corporate treasurer phoned to say that Conglomerated can get a higher return on bonds than was originally anticipated. The new alternative investment rate is 17%. This higher rate will have the effect of decreasing the maximum purchase price, because the funds flows should be discounted by a greater factor. The lower maximum purchase price may increase the gap between what we are willing to pay and what Rags' owners are willing to accept.

What is the lower purchase price? Will it be as elusive as the one we just finished calculating? In the old days, we would have had to grab our calculators, derive the present value of Year 1, the present value of Year 2, and so on, add up the present values, and finally update the funds statement. But with our 1-2-3 model, our task is almost ridiculously easy.

1. Move the pointer to the discount rate cell (C50), and enter 17%.

Presto! The result is $27016 thousand, a reduction of more than two million dollars in the maximum purchase price.

This is only the beginning of our model's utility. Remember all that flexibility we built into the income statement? If we are unsatisfied with the growth projections for any of the income statement items, we can change the rates in the RATE column. The changes will carry through to net income, which will transfer to the funds statement, which will translate into a new funds flow, which will yield a revised maximum purchase price. Obviously, the potential for "what if" analysis is expansive.

Calculating Internal Rate of Return:
The @IRR Function

Don't relax yet; our model is not complete. It is quite doubtful that the chairperson will call up Rags' owner and admit that Conglomerated will pay a maximum of $27016 thousand. Rather, the chairperson will attempt to pay less. If this effort is successful, Conglomerated will earn a higher rate of return on the acquisition investment than the 17% rate upon which the maximum price was predicated. The chairperson would like to know exactly how much higher this return will be. The answer lies in a financial measure called the *internal rate of return* (IRR).

The internal rate of return is the discount rate that makes the present value of the future returns exactly equal to the Year 0 investment. The chairperson is asking, "If I give you the price I want to pay (presumably less than the maximum purchase price), what rate of interest should be used to obtain a present value equal to my offer?"

One way of finding out would be by trial and error with a calculator: Guess an interest rate, use it to figure out the present value of each of the five annual returns, total the five present values, and hope that the total equals the purchase price. It stands to reason that with so many cash flows and a high probability of making the wrong guess, we might resort to shrugging our shoulders and rounding to the nearest 50%. However, there is a better way: we can utilize the @IRR function of 1-2-3.

The @IRR function requires two arguments: a guess as to the resulting IRR (we will use .17 as a rough guess) and the range of coordinates containing the funds flows. Lotus 1-2-3 uses the guess as a first approximation of the true IRR, then refines this guess until it converges onto the correct value. For now, let us forget about trying out a new purchase price. If we use $27016 thousand as the proposed purchase price, we can check whether we have done the IRR calculation correctly. Given the maximum purchase price and the funds flows, we already know that the return is 17%. And at 17%, the net present value (present value of the returns minus initial investment) is zero, because the discounted returns equal the investment.

1. At cell B52, enter the label **INTERNAL RATE OF RETURN**.

2. Move to the YEAR 0 column (cell C52).

3. Type **@IRR(** to begin the formula.

Specify the estimate of the IRR:

4. Type **.17** to continue the formula.

Specify the range of funds flows, which must include the initial investment of Year 0:

5. Point to Year 0 NET FUNDS FLOW (cell C46); anchor the range by typing the . key; press END and the right arrow key to expand the pointer to the Year 5 NET FUNDS FLOW cell (H46); and then type **)** ENTER to end the formula.

6. Give the cell a percent format by selecting **/Range Format Percent** ENTER ENTER.

The result, shown in Figure 12-3, is 17%—proof that the @IRR function works. Now for some alternative purchase prices.

	A	B	C	D	E	F	G	H
35				FUNDS FLOW ANALYSIS				
36				$ IN THOUSANDS				
37								
38			0	1	2	3	4	5
39								
40		NET INCOME		2429	3304	4045	4449	4894
41		NON-CASH CHARGES		20	20	20	20	20
42		CAPITAL INVESTMENT		-50	-40	-28	-45	-45
43		CHANGE IN WORKING CAPITAL		-10	-5	-15	-17	-14
44		ACQUISITION PAYMENT ------>	-27016					
45								
46		NET FUNDS FLOW	-27016	2389	3279	4022	4407	38839
47								
48		MAXIMUM PURCHASE PRICE	27016					
49								
50		DISCOUNT RATE	17.00%					
51								
52		INTERNAL RATE OF RETURN	17.00%					

Figure 12-3. Calculation of internal rate of return

Sensitivity Analysis

Sensitivity analysis examines how a model reacts to a constant change in an input. As an example, we will see how changes in the maximum purchase price affect the acquisition's internal rate of return.

Using Data Table 1 for Sensitivity Analysis

The Data Table 1 command introduced in Chapter 9 is an extremely potent tool for sensitivity analysis. Recall that the left-hand column of the table is a range of coordinates containing input values—in this case, a set of potential purchase prices for which we would like to evaluate contingent internal rates of return. The top row of the table consists of formulas that depend upon the input value, such as the IRR formula that is a function of the proposed purchase price. The other element necessary for Data Table 1 is the input cell, the cell in the worksheet where we will substitute the values of the substitution column. For our example, we would like to substitute the MAXIMUM PURCHASE PRICE formula at cell C48. The resulting data table is shown in Figure 12-4.

The input cell is not a part of the data table; it is a part of the main worksheet—in our case, the funds statement. Data Table 1 will perform the

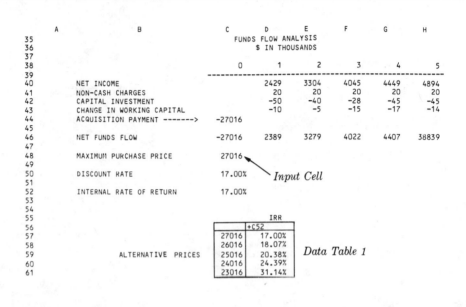

Figure 12-4. Data Table 1 shows IRR values for alternative purchase prices

analysis using the substitution values and store the results into the result matrix, but it will leave the remainder of the worksheet unaltered. Implementing Data Table 1 is easy once you know what kind of scenarios you want to generate.

1. Move to cell C57, where we will enter the first substitution value for the acquisition payment.

The first substitution will be the maximum purchase price, so that we will be able to check the data table's results against those of the model.

2. Type the + key to begin the formula; then point to the MAXIMUM PURCHASE PRICE (cell C48) and press ENTER.

We will test four additional acquisition prices, each one 1000 thousand (one million) lower than its predecessor.

3. Move to the next substitution-entry cell (C58).

4. Type the + key, move the pointer to the previous entry (cell C57), type −1000, and press ENTER.

The next substitution cell will be 1000 thousand less than the one just defined, as will each of the other three, so copy the formula down the substitution-entries column:

5. Select /Copy ENTER; move down once to cell C59, and type . to anchor the target range; then move down twice to cell C61, and press ENTER.

(By the way, we could also have used the Data Fill command to enter the substitution entries, because the substitutions are a sequence of numbers decreasing by a constant step.)

The formula to be evaluated is the internal rate of return, which will be entered at cell D56. (Remember that the top-left coordinate, C56, is not used with Data Table 1. Formulas are placed starting at the next column.) We could enter the same formula that we typed into the INTERNAL RATE OF RETURN cell, or we could take the easy route: merely refer to the INTERNAL RATE OF RETURN cell (C52) and let 1-2-3 examine the formula contained in that cell. We will take the easy route.

6. Move to cell D56, type +, point to the @IRR formula in cell C52, and press ENTER.

7. Now give the formula cell a text format by typing /Range Format Text ENTER ENTER.

Because the cells in the result column below will contain percentages,

8. Move down once to cell D57, and select /Range Format Percent ENTER PG DN ENTER.

To keep things tidy,

9. Move up once to cell D55, and enter the right-justified label "IRR.

10. At cell B59, enter the right-justified label "ALTERNATIVE PRICES.

Now other people will be able to understand the table, and we can understand it the next time we use this worksheet.

After Data Table 1 is constructed, we can implement it.

11. Select /Data Table 1.

1-2-3 asks for the table range, the top-left and bottom-right coordinates of the data table.

12. Move the pointer to the top left of the data table, cell C56.

13. Type the . key to anchor the range, expand the pointer to the bottom right of the table (cell D61), and press the ENTER key.

In response to the prompt for the input cell,

14. Move to the funds statement for MAXIMUM PURCHASE PRICE at cell C48, and press ENTER.

That is all. The WAIT message appears at the top right of the screen for a short time while 1-2-3 substitutes the various purchase prices into the worksheet. The table calculation takes a few seconds, longer than a normal calculation because 1-2-3 must factor in the entire worksheet for each of the substitution entries. In the end, the table discloses how sensitive the internal rate of return is to each million-dollar decrease in the proposed purchase price. In this case, each million-dollar decrease in the purchase price results in a substantial increase in internal rate of return.

The substitution-entries column need not contain formulas. We could accomplish a standard "what if" analysis by filling one or more of the entries with specific values instead of formulas. For example, we could exchange the value 20000 thousand for the maximum purchase price in cell C57. However, be aware that changing substitution values, or formulas, will not of itself cause the data table to be reevaluated. Even pressing the F9 (Calc) key will not affect the data table. To rerun a data table, we must reexecute the Data Table command. But as we will see, 1-2-3 gives us an even faster way.

Updating Data Tables
With the F8 (Table) Key

The F8 (Table) key provides an extremely convenient way of calculating a data table several times. Pressing the F8 (Table) key causes 1-2-3 to reexecute the last Data Table command you issued, using the same table range and input cell(s). For example, suppose we want to do a sensitivity analysis for decreases of $3 million in the acquisition price, then $2 million, then $.5 million. We enter the substitutions for $3 million; then instead of selecting the Data Table 1 command again, we simply press the F8 (Table) key and the table will be updated. We can do the same for the other two sensitivity analyses. With the F8 (Table) key, these types of analyses take only a few keystrokes.

If you create several data tables on one worksheet, remember that the F8 (Table) key recalculates only the one you used most recently.

This application incorporates many of 1-2-3's advanced spreadsheet capabilities into a sophisticated model. The acquisition simulation is a powerful decision-making tool. Yet because of the flexibility of 1-2-3's command set, the model can be adapted readily to most acquisition analyses. Moreover, results from the model can be obtained quickly—an important feature in situations that, more often than not, involve pressure and urgency.

Chapter 13
Using Character Strings, Logical Functions, And the System Command (Version 2.0 Only)

Among the most important additions to 1-2-3 in Version 2.0 are the ability to halt the worksheet session temporarily to perform operating system tasks, and the ability to manipulate textual information. In this chapter you will discover the potency of these new features. Functions will be the foundation of the model you are about to create—a purchase-order tracking system. You will not make use of all or even most of 1-2-3's functions, but you will get a clear idea of how much work you can save by making clever use of them. These new functions allow the program to be used for projects that were once inappropriate for 1-2-3.

Building a Purchase-Order Tracking System

Joe Doe is the supplies manager of Fidget Widget Manufacturing. Every few weeks, Joe takes stock of the company's office supplies and issues requisitions, called *purchase orders*, to replenish supplies of paper clips, paper pads, and other office paraphernalia. Keeping track of all the orders is a job that has gotten out of hand, and Joe needs a computerized system that tells him what items have been ordered and from whom, and whether or not orders have been filled.

Inquiring about the feasibility of developing such a system on Fidget Widget's mainframe computer, Joe found out that the firm's Systems Development Group would charge $500,000 and six free lunches to complete the job. Joe has the impression that the application would be appropriate for 1-2-3 Version 2.0—and that's where you come in.

The supplies analysis portion of the purchase-order tracking system that you will be developing is shown in Figure 13-1. Joe lists each item ordered, the date it was ordered and received, the vendor with whom the order was placed, the quantity of the item ordered, and the price of the order. Each purchase order is assigned a unique purchase-order code, which helps the accounting department identify the order. The analysis also indicates whether a particular order is closed (that is, whether the shipment has been received) or open (not received). In addition, the analysis flags the open orders that are late.

Using DOS to Change the System Date

Remember that you answer date and time prompts when you first boot the system prior to entering the 1-2-3 environment. If you enter the real date and time, they will appear at the bottom left corner of the screen. If you press ENTER in response to the date and time prompts (and if your system does not include an internal clock), an incorrect default date and time are used.

	H	I	J	K	L	M	N	O	P	Q	R	S	T	U	V
1		DATE			DATE										
2		ORDERED			RECEIVED				UNIT	TOTAL		PURCHASE ORDER		P.O.	ORDER
3	ITEM	M	D	Y	M	D	Y	QUANTITY	PRICE	PRICE	VENDOR	PREFIX	SUFFIX	CODE	STATUS
4	PENCILS	2	1	85				50	$2.50	$125.00	PENCIL PUSHER	JPEN	1	JPEN1	LATE
5	PAPER	3	27	85	3	29	85	30	$2.00	$60.00	PAPER TIGER	JPAP	2	JPAP2	CLOSED
6	CLIPS	3	6	85				100	$0.50	$50.00	YANKEE CLIPPER	JCLI	3	JCLI3	OPEN
7	STAPLES	1	3	85				75	$1.50	$112.50	STAPLETON	JSTA	4	JSTA4	LATE

Figure 13-1. Preview of Fidget Widget's supplies analysis sheet

If the correct date and time is not currently displayed, or if you want to change the current date and time, you need to use the *System* command to exit into the DOS (Disk Operating System) environment, as well as the @NOW date function.

1. Boot up the system and press ENTER in response to the DOS prompts for the date and time.

2. Enter the 1-2-3 worksheet environment.

This chapter's figures use the current date April 1, 1985, so pretend that 4/1/85 actually is the current date to make your results match those of the figures. To reset the date, you must suspend your 1-2-3 session and enter the DOS environment. After issuing the command to set the system date in DOS, you will resume your 1-2-3 session where you left off. This is the function of the System command.

The System command permits you to leave 1-2-3, perform a DOS function (such as formatting a diskette or setting the system date and time), and return to 1-2-3. To use this command, you must first

3. Type / and select System from the main menu.

1-2-3 is now ready to run DOS and asks you to press ENTER or enter a DOS program name. 1-2-3 is about to search the disk for the DOS system or for a particular DOS program, and you must ensure that DOS is available before 1-2-3 begins its search. Therefore, if you have a diskette drive system,

4. In drive A, replace the 1-2-3 System Disk with a disk containing the DOS operating system (such as the DOS System Disk).

1-2-3 displays a message informing you that issuing the Exit command in your DOS session will return you to the place you left off in 1-2-3. Then 1-2-3 pretends to relinquish control of the DOS system. Don't be fooled, though. 1-2-3 still remains in RAM, and it eagerly awaits your return.

If you have done any work in 1-2-3, it is a good idea to save the worksheet before issuing the System command and exiting into DOS, just in case something sinister happens before you get a chance to reenter 1-2-3.

Issuing the DOS Date Command

The DOS "A>" prompt should appear on the screen. To specify a system date, issue the *DOS Date* command as follows.

1. Type **DATE** and press ENTER.

Next, type the date in mm-dd-yy or mm-dd-yyyy format:

2. Type **4-1-85** and press ENTER.

To resume 1-2-3,

3. Type **EXIT** and press ENTER.

The new date now appears in the lower-left corner of the screen. The next task is to put this date into the spreadsheet. The time for @NOW is now.

Using @NOW to Obtain the Current Date and Time

The @*NOW* function is a formula that checks the calendar and clock to produce the current moment (that is, the moment that 1-2-3 thinks is current, based on the system date and time). There are two aspects of @NOW: the current date and the current time of day. The @NOW function checks the calendar to count the number of days from December 31, 1899, to the current date; and it checks the clock to determine how much of the day has elapsed since midnight. You used @NOW in Chapter 6 to obtain the system date. To place the current date in cell A1,

1. Move to cell A1, type @**NOW**, and press ENTER.

The resulting value is a decimal number. The digits to the left of the decimal point (31138) comprise the numerical equivalent of April 1, 1985. The digits to the right of the decimal point correspond to the current time of day.

Your immediate interest is in the date portion of the @NOW value. To display the system date, assign the cell a date format.

2. Type **/Range Format Date 1** and press ENTER.

A string of asterisks appears. The asterisks are 1-2-3's way of indicating that the selected date format is too wide to fit into a nine-character column. To solve the problem, widen the column.

3. Type **/Worksheet Column Set-Width**; then press the right arrow key to widen the column.

The asterisks disappear, and the format is displayed correctly.

4. Press ENTER to finalize the change.

Format	Example (for 1:15:30 PM)
1 (HH:MM:SS AM/PM)	01:15:30 PM
2 (HH:MM AM/PM)	01:15 PM
3 (Long International)	13:15:30
4 (Short International)	13:15

Table 13-1.   Time formats

Perhaps some day, when the ultimate perfection of machines is more generally recognized, 31138 will gain greater acceptance as a date stamp for reports. For now, though, 01-Apr-85 is the more practical format.

The @NOW Function Using Time Format

If you run reports several times a day, it may be important to time-stamp the spreadsheet. The @NOW function can be used for this purpose, too. You will store another @NOW formula in the spreadsheet and use its result to display the current time of day.

1. Move the pointer to cell B1.

2. Type **@NOW** and press ENTER.

The Date format command operates on the date-related digits of the @NOW value. To display the time-related digits in Time format, you use the Time option of the Format Date menu.

3. Type /**R**ange Format **D**ate Time.

Table 13-1 shows the four time formats and the results of applying them to a time of 1:15 P.M. and 30 seconds (13:15:30 on a 24-hour clock). The 1-2-3 serial number for 13:15:30 is 0.552430. Note that International format uses a 24-hour clock.*

---

*Using the /Worksheet Global Default Other International Time command makes three other international formats available for the Format Date Time command: HH.MM.SS, HH,MM,SS, and HHhMMmSSs.

Try option 1.

4. Select option 1 (HH:MM:SS AM/PM).

5. Press ENTER to apply this format to the range B1..B1.

The result is too wide to fit into the column, so you will need to widen the column.

6. Type /Worksheet Column Set-Width, and press the right arrow key repeatedly until the asterisks disappear and the format is displayed correctly; then press ENTER to lock in the change.

The current time now appears in cell B1. Note that because 1-2-3 recalculates formulas automatically whenever you enter a new value or label, the @NOW formulas in A1 and B1 will be automatically recalculated as time goes by and as the spreadsheet is recalculated. This means that the time displayed in B1 will change.

Developing the Analysis Sheet

Now that you have established the current date, you can proceed to the report itself. The first step is to enter a title to identify your work.

1. Press the CAPS LOCK key, if necessary, to commence all-caps typing.

2. In cell C1, enter the label **FIDGET WIDGET SUPPLIES ANALYSIS**.

The purchase-order analysis will consist of two parts. A table of the supplies to be tracked will be on the far left. It contains the names of the supplies, their unit prices, and their vendors. The right portion of the spreadsheet, columns H through V as shown in Figure 13-1, is the tracking system. Joe Doe, with your assistance, will record orders and receipts in this area, as well as formulas that allow him to keep track of delinquent orders and costs of supplies.

Entering the Table of Supplies

Your first task is to create the table of supplies. The table should include columns for the name of the supply, the price per unit of the item, and the name of the vendor. When Joe Doe is ready to make an order for a particular supply, such as paper, 1-2-3 will determine the total cost of the order by multiplying the quantity ordered by the unit price stored in the table. Joe can also use the table to look up the vendor that sells the item.

Place the table of supplies in the first three columns of the spreadsheet, as follows:

1. Enter the label **ITEM** in cell A4, **UNIT** in B3, **PRICE** in B4, and **VENDOR** in C4.

Figure 13-2 shows the current supplies table as it should be stored in the spreadsheet. The values in the UNIT PRICE column (column B) have been formatted in Currency format, which displays numbers with dollar signs. (Currency format also inserts commas into numbers greater than 999 and encloses negative values in parentheses.)

2. In rows 5 through 8, enter the table information as shown in Figure 13-2. The currency values should be entered as decimal values.

Next, assign Currency format to the unit prices.

3. Move to cell B5, type **/R**ange **F**ormat **C**urrency, press ENTER to specify two decimal places, expand the pointer down to the last cell in the column (B8), and press ENTER.

Entering the Tracking Spreadsheet

Now you are ready to set up the tracking system itself. The column titles of the tracking system are stored in the first three rows of columns H through V of the spreadsheet. First you should adjust the column widths to accommodate the headings you'll be entering.

```
              A          B          C          D          E          F
1 01-Apr-85 11:04:47 AM FIDGET WIDGET SUPPLIES ANALYSIS
2
3              UNIT
4 ITEM         PRICE              VENDOR
5 CLIPS               $0.50 YANKEE CLIPPER
6 PAPER               $2.00 PAPER TIGER
7 PENCILS             $2.50 PENCIL PUSHER
8 STAPLES             $1.50 STAPLETON
```

Figure 13-2. The supplies table

1. Use the Worksheet Column Set-Width command to change the column widths. Set columns I, J, K, L, M, and N to **3**; column R to **15**; and T to **7**. The remaining columns (H, O, P, Q, and S) should remain at the default width of 9.

2. Next, enter the headings in cells H1..V3 as they appear in Figure 13-1.

Now you are ready to enter the data and formulas necessary to track a purchase. Because you may wish to use the same formula in several portions of the spreadsheet, you will design the formulas so they may be copied easily. In applications like this one, it pays to spend time planning each formula so that things go smoothly later on.

On February 1, 1985, Joe Doe ordered 50 boxes of pencils. This is all the information you need to begin tracking the order. Begin by entering the name of the item, PENCILS, in the first row of the analysis:

3. In cell H4, enter the label **PENCILS**.

The next entry item, DATE ORDERED, consists of three fields: M (month), D (day), and Y (year). To enter a date of February 1, 1985,

4. Enter **2** in the M field (I4), **1** in the D field (J4), and **85** in the Y field (K4).

Since the pencils have not yet arrived, you should skip the DATE RECEIVED field. This brings you to the last input field, QUANTITY. After this field is completed, all other fields can be derived from entries in the first four fields of the analysis.

5. Enter the value **50** in the QUANTITY field (O4).

Using @VLOOKUP to Determine Unit Price

The next item in the spreadsheet, UNIT PRICE, will be calculated in cell P4. This information is contained in the table of supplies that you stored in the top left corner of the spreadsheet. Using the @VLOOKUP function, you can look up the item being tracked (pencils) in this table in order to retrieve information related to that item, such as its unit price.

You were introduced to the @VLOOKUP function in Chapter 5. The function takes the form @VLOOKUP(*item to look up, range containing vertical lookup table, offset*). In this case, the first argument (the item to look up) is the item in cell H4 of the spreadsheet. The second argument required by @VLOOKUP is the range containing the vertical lookup table, which is

A5..C8. The third argument, the offset, is 1 for UNIT PRICE because that column is one column to the right of the table's first column. VENDOR has an offset of 2.

Making the Lookup Table Range Absolute

One correct way to enter the lookup formula for UNIT PRICE is @VLOOKUP(H4,A5..C8,1). However, it is possible to develop a more flexible @VLOOKUP formula.

Remember that you will be copying this formula down to the next line of the spreadsheet (cell P5) when you post the next order of supplies. Copying the formula @VLOOKUP(H4,A5..C8,1) relatively from P4 down to P5 would result in @VLOOKUP(H5,A6..C9,1). The item to be looked up, H5, would be appropriate for the next line, which would be in row 5. However, copying the formula relatively would move the table range from A5..C8 to A6..C9, but the table is always stored in A5..C8. To ensure that the table range does not change when the formula is copied down the column, you must make the cell references to the table range absolute. The corrected formula would be @VLOOKUP(H4,$A$5..$C$8,1).

1. Move the cell pointer to P4 and type **@VLOOKUP(** to begin the formula.

2. Point to the item in column H (cell H4).

3. Type , to separate this argument of the function from the next one.

Begin specifying the table range.

4. Point to the top left corner of the table range (A5).

Make the range specification absolute.

5. Press the ABS (F4) key once.

The control panel now contains @VLOOKUP(H4,$A$5.

6. Type . to anchor the range.

7. Move to the end of the table range (cell C8).

8. Type , to separate the argument.

9. Type **1** to indicate the offset; then type **)** and press ENTER to end the formula.

The result, 2.5, should be formatted to indicate that it represents dollars and cents.

10. Type **/Range Format Currency** and press ENTER twice.

Entering Total Price and Vendor Formulas

Now that both QUANTITY and PRICE are available, TOTAL PRICE can be computed as the product of the two.

1. Move to the TOTAL PRICE column (Q4).

2. Type + to begin the formula entry.

3. Point to the QUANTITY cell (O4).

4. Type * to indicate multiplication.

5. Point to the UNIT PRICE cell (P4) and press ENTER.

Format the result, 125, using Currency format.

6. Type /Range Format Currency and press ENTER twice.

Determining the vendor of the pencils is simply another @VLOOKUP function: here, 2 is used as the offset. Keeping in mind that the structure of the function is @VLOOKUP(*item to look up, range containing vertical lookup table, offset*),

7. Move to the VENDOR column (R4) and type **@VLOOKUP(** to begin the formula.

8. Point to the item in column H (H4).

9. Type , and then point to the first cell of the table range (A5); press the ABS (F4) key, type . to anchor the range, and point to the bottom right cell of the table range (C8).

10. Type ,2) and press ENTER to end the formula.

The result is shown in Figure 13-3. As you can see, @VLOOKUP may be used to retrieve alphabetic information as well as numeric information, a capability not available prior to Version 2.0.

At this point, pause to save your work.

11. Type /File Save **PURCHASE** and press ENTER.

Figure 13-3. The unfinished purchase-order tracking spreadsheet

Strings and String Functions

At this point, the spreadsheet records purchasing information and looks up information in the supply lookup table. The next few items in the spreadsheet concern the purchase-order code, the code that identifies each order of supplies. Joe Doe, the purchasing clerk of Fidget Widget, was an encryption expert in World War II, and he has put his experience to use by establishing a coding system for purchase orders (P.O.s). The coding system not only identifies each of Fidget Widget's P.O.s but also keeps the P.O. system secure from enemy hands. Incorporating this coding scheme into your spreadsheet will provide you with opportunities to make use of 1-2-3's extensive character-string manipulation functions.

Fidget's P.O. code is composed of two parts, a *prefix* and a *suffix*. The prefix is a combination of a code letter and the first three letters of the item. The code letter indicates the type of supply being purchased. Office supplies use "J" P.O. codes, and product material purchases use "Z" codes. Since the example model deals exclusively with "J" purchases, you will not work with other codes here; however, it would be easy to adapt this model to use multiple codes.

Each purchase order has a unique number that is used as the suffix of the P.O. code. The spreadsheet will automatically assign the first P.O. a value of 1, the next a value of 2, and so on.

The prefix for the current order is the letter J followed by the first three letters of the item, PEN. The prefix JPEN is called a *character string* and is made up of two substrings, "J" and "PEN", that are concatenated, or joined, to form a single string. A character string is a group of alphanumeric characters. Entering a character string within a cell formula permits you to use string functions or to perform string manipulations, such as combining two strings into one string.

You will begin by experimenting with strings and then proceed to deriving the P.O. code.

Combining two strings is similar to adding two numbers in a numeric formula. For example, to add 4 and 6 you would enter the formula 4+6. As you typed the 4, 1-2-3 would be thrown into Value Mode and expect you to enter either a number or a numeric formula. The + sign between the two numbers is an arithmetic operator indicating addition.

To combine two strings you would specify the first string, followed by a string operator, followed by the second string. The *string operator* is the & (ampersand) character, and it does to strings what the + operator does to numbers: it combines them. For example, entering the string formula +"J"&"PEN" into cell S4 would produce a result of JPEN.

There are two important things to keep in mind about the string formula entry +"J"&"PEN". First, the formula entry begins when you press the + key. A string formula is different from a label entry, because a string formula is a value—it must be entered in Value Mode. To throw 1-2-3 into Value Mode you can type the + key, just as you would in entering a numeric formula that begins with a cell address.

Second, when you enter character strings directly into a formula, you must enclose the strings in double quotation marks. That is why the two strings J and PEN are entered as "J" and "PEN".

To see how 1-2-3 handles a string formula,

1. Move to cell S4 and type + to begin a formula entry.

2. Type " (double quotation marks).

3. Type J; then type ".

4. Type **&**; then type "**PEN**".

Make sure the control panel contains +"J"&"PEN". Then

5. Press RETURN.

Cell S4 should display the string value JPEN.

Using &, you can also combine a string with a cell containing a label, or you can combine two label cells. For example:

6. Type +"**J**"**&** and then move the pointer to the ITEM cell, H4.

The control panel displays the formula +"J"&H4.

7. Press RETURN.

The result is JPENCILS, which is quite close to the string that you are trying to derive, the P.O. prefix.

What you really want is the concatenation of "J" and the first three characters in cell H4. You can accomplish this with a number of string functions that are capable of extracting a subset, or *substring*, of characters from a string. One of these functions is @LEFT.

Using @LEFT for the P.O. Code Prefix

The structure of the *@LEFT* function is @LEFT (*string, num*). The first argument, *string*, is the string (or the address of a cell containing a string) from which you want to extract a substring. The second argument, *num*, is the number of characters, starting from the leftmost character, that you want to extract. For example, @LEFT("BASEBALL",4) returns the string "BASE"—the leftmost four characters of BASEBALL. There is also an @RIGHT (*string, num*) function that extracts the rightmost *num* characters of a string.

In the purchase-order example, the first three characters of the item in cell H4 would be derived with the formula @LEFT(H4,3). Therefore, the elusive P.O. prefix would be returned by the formula +"J"&@LEFT(H4,3).

1. You can destroy the evidence of the experiment you just performed in cell S4 by either erasing it or overwriting it. Then type the + sign to begin the formula entry.

2. Type "**J**"&@**LEFT(** to begin the entry.

3. Point to the ITEM cell (H4).

4. Type , to continue the entry.

5. Type **3)** and press RETURN.

The P.O. prefix is JPEN.

Using @N for the P.O. Code Suffix

The P.O. code suffix is a unique number assigned to the purchase order. The first suffix will be 1, and succeeding suffixes will increase sequentially, so that the formula for a particular suffix is the value of the previous suffix plus 1. For example, the suffix of the second purchase would be 1 plus 1 (the value of the previous suffix), which equals 2.

Therefore, if you are going to copy the formulas from the first record to the second record, the formula you should enter for the first suffix is 1 + the previous cell (or in this case, 1+T3). Right away, though, you hit a snag. Instead of a numeric value, the previous cell contains a label, SUFFIX.

Try using the formula 1+T3 in cell T4: the displayed result is "ERR". As things stand, you may not add a number to a label. If only you could convert the SUFFIX label to the numeric value of 0 so that the formula can be used in cell T4.

Fortunately, 1-2-3 comes to the rescue with the @*N* function. The @N function converts a label or string to a value. The structure of the function is @N (*range*), where the argument *range* specifies a cell that contains a label or string. Using the single-cell range of T3..T3, the function @N(T3..T3) returns a value of 0. Observe that the argument of @N must be a range; it may not be a single cell address, such as @N(T3).

Thus, a working formula for the P.O. suffix is 1+@N(T3..T3). When copied down to the next cell, this formula correctly adds 1 to the numeric value of the previous cell.

1. In cell T4, type **1+@N(** to begin the formula.

2. Move up to the previous cell (T3).

3. Type . to anchor the range.

The control panel shows 1+@N(T3..T3—just the range you wanted.

4. Type **)** and press RETURN to complete the formula.

This may seem like an elaborate way to obtain the value 1, but the effort will pay off when you enter the next purchase with the Copy command.

Using @STRING to Combine the Prefix and Suffix

The next step is to derive the P.O. code and place it in column U. The P.O. code itself is the concatenation of the prefix and suffix. This would indicate using the & operator to combine the prefix cell, S4, with the suffix cell, T4. However, 1-2-3 only permits concatenation of strings or cells containing strings. The prefix stores a string, "JPEN"; but the suffix contains a value, 1.

To combine the prefix and suffix into a single string, it is necessary to reference the suffix as a string. You can do this by using the *@STRING* function, whose format is @STRING (*num1, num2*). The *num1* argument is the value, or cell address of a value, that will be used as a string. The *num2* argument specifies how many decimal places should be shown in that string. Since all of the suffixes are integers, you will use a *num2* argument of 0.

Note that if you use a cell reference as your *num1* argument, it must be a single-cell reference (such as T4). Compare this with the argument of the @N function, which must be a range (such as T3..T3).

1. Move to cell U4.

2. Type **+** and then move to the prefix in cell S4.

3. Type **&@STRING(** to continue the entry.

4. Move to the suffix in cell T4; then type **,0)** and press RETURN.

The P.O. code for the first purchase order is JPEN1.

The @IF Function

The next item of the analysis is ORDER STATUS, in column V. This column is the real payoff of this spreadsheet. It indicates which orders are still open and which are closed. At a glance, this column tells Joe Doe which orders to keep an eye on.

The formula for this cell is fundamentally different from the formulas you've seen thus far. Previously, a given formula generated a particular result. In this case, the formula may have one of two results. If the order has been received, it is closed, and the ORDER STATUS cell displays the label CLOSED. If the order is open, ORDER STATUS displays the label OPEN. The result displayed in the ORDER STATUS cell depends on whether a *condition* is satisfied: whether or not the order has been received.

What data in the worksheet indicates whether the order was received? The answer lies in the DATE RECEIVED columns (L, M, and N). If there are values in the month, day, or year columns of DATE RECEIVED, the order must be closed; otherwise, the order is open.

In Chapter 5 you used logical formulas to develop formula criteria, and in Chapter 8 you used them to create conditional IF statements in macros. Now you will use a logical formula with the @IF function to create a conditional result in a cell entry.

The @IF function makes full use of logical formulas, so it is considered a *logical function*. Using @IF, you may instruct 1-2-3 to display a particular result if a condition is TRUE and a different result if a condition is FALSE.

The structure of the function is @IF (*condition, arg1, arg2*), where *condition* is the condition being tested, *arg1* is the result if the condition is TRUE, and *arg2* is the result if the condition is FALSE. Both *arg1* and *arg2* may be values, formulas, or strings.

For example, suppose you stored the formula @IF(A1>B1,100,0) in cell Z55. If the contents of cell A1 were greater than the contents of cell B1, the condition would be true, and the value of cell Z55 would be 100 (*arg1*). Otherwise, the value would be 0 (*arg2*).

The @IF function for ORDER STATUS in cell V4 is entered as @IF(N4 >0,"CLOSED","OPEN"). This formula instructs 1-2-3 to display the string "CLOSED" if N4 is greater than 0 (that is, if the result is TRUE) and otherwise to display "OPEN". Here, *arg1* and *arg2* are strings; and in accordance with the rules of specifying strings in formulas, the characters of the string are enclosed in double quotation marks. To enter the conditional formula,

1. Move to cell V4 and type **@IF(** to begin the formula.

2. Point to the DATE RECEIVED Y field (N4).

3. Type **>0,** to continue the formula.

4. Type **"CLOSED","OPEN")** and press RETURN.

The result is OPEN because the condition is FALSE.

Nested @IF Functions

It is useful to know whether an order is open or closed, but it would be even more valuable to have a warning system that identifies orders that are truly late. For example, you might want to have three possible values for ORDER STATUS: CLOSED if the order is received, OPEN if the order is unfilled but less than 30 days old, and LATE if the order is unfilled for 31 or more days.

Such a warning system would require two @IF functions. The first @IF would test whether the order was open or closed, as before. If the order were open, the second @IF would test whether the difference between the date ordered and the current date (the date the orders are being analyzed) is greater than or equal to 31. If it is, the result would be LATE; otherwise (that is, if the order were open but less than 31 days old), the status would be OPEN.

You already know that the format of the @IF function is @IF (*condition, arg1, arg2*), and you know that *arg1* and *arg2* may be values, strings, or formulas. Formulas may include functions, and @IF is a function. Therefore, you may use a second @IF function for one of the two arguments or for both. This is called *nesting* @IF functions.

Instead of the functional but simplistic logical construct

> *If* there exists a DATE RECEIVED,
>   *then* display CLOSED;
>   *otherwise* display OPEN

by using nested @IF functions you can employ the more powerful construct

> *If* there exists a DATE RECEIVED,
>   *then* display CLOSED;
>   *otherwise*
>   *If* the difference between the ORDER
>   DATE and today's date is >= 31,
>   *then* display LATE;
>   *otherwise* display OPEN

In @IF format, this structure is expressed as

@IF (*condition1, arg1,* @IF (*condition2, arg1, arg2*))

The second @IF is actually *arg2* of the first @IF function. So long as you have the right number of arguments and the right number of parentheses, the nested functions work well. Now it is time to translate this @IF format to an actual formula entry.

Date Arithmetic and the @DATE Function

The first part of the formula, @IF *(condition1, arg1,* translates into @IF(N4>0,"CLOSED". The second part of the formula, the nested @IF, must include a condition to test the age of the order. You can derive the age of the order by subtracting the serial number of the date ordered from the serial number of the current date. The current date is already stored in the @NOW formula at the top left corner of the spreadsheet, in cell A1. You derive a serial number for the date ordered using the @*DATE* function. The structure of the function is @DATE *(year, month, day)*. In the case of DATE ORDERED, *year* is in cell K4, *month* is in I4, and *day* is in J4.

Calculating P.O. Status
For the First Order

Now you have all of the ingredients for the nested @IF formula. The condition is @NOW−@DATE(K4,I4,J4)>=31; *arg1* is LATE, and *arg2* is OPEN. Enter this formula into cell V4 as follows:

1. Move to cell V4.

2. Type @IF(N4>0,"CLOSED", to begin the formula.

Next enter the nested @IF function:

3. Type @IF(@NOW−@DATE(K4,I4,J4)>=31,"LATE","OPEN").

4. Type an additional) to close the first @IF function, and press RETURN to end the formula.

As shown in Figure 13-4, the ORDER STATUS for pencils is LATE. You have successfully tracked the first purchase order of the spreadsheet.

Entering Other Purchase Orders

Now that you've developed the formulas you need for the first purchase order, appending additional purchase orders to the analysis is a cinch. Just type in the information for ITEM, DATE ORDERED, DATE RECEIVED,

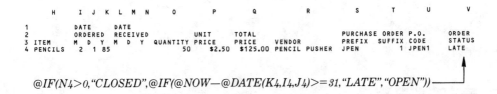

```
        H   I J K L M N     O      P       Q         R       S      T   U       V
1               DATE     DATE
2             ORDERED  RECEIVED            UNIT    TOTAL             PURCHASE ORDER P.O.   ORDER
3  ITEM       M  D  Y  M  D  Y  QUANTITY PRICE    PRICE   VENDOR     PREFIX SUFFIX CODE   STATUS
4  PENCILS    2  1 85                50   $2.50  $125.00 PENCIL PUSHER JPEN          1 JPEN1 LATE
```

$@IF(N4>0,\text{``CLOSED''},@IF(@NOW-@DATE(K4,I4,J4)>=31,\text{``LATE''},\text{``OPEN''}))$

Figure 13-4. Purchase order showing nested @IF formula

and QUANTITY. Then use the Copy command to copy the formulas from the previous record to the current one.

Try entering a purchase order for 30 reams of paper ordered on March 27, 1985, and received on March 29, 1985.

1. Store the appropriate values for ITEM, DATE ORDERED, DATE RECEIVED, and QUANTITY in cells H5..O5 of the spreadsheet, as shown in Figure 13-5.

```
        H   I J K L M N     O      P       Q         R       S      T   U       V
1               DATE     DATE
2             ORDERED  RECEIVED            UNIT    TOTAL             PURCHASE ORDER P.O.   ORDER
3  ITEM       M  D  Y  M  D  Y  QUANTITY PRICE    PRICE   VENDOR     PREFIX SUFFIX CODE   STATUS
4  PENCILS    2  1 85                50   $2.50  $125.00 PENCIL PUSHER JPEN          1 JPEN1 LATE
5  PAPER      3 27 85  3 29 85       30
```

Figure 13-5. The second purchase-order calculation

H	I J K L M N	O	P	Q	R	S	T	U	V
1	DATE DATE								
2	ORDERED RECEIVED		UNIT	TOTAL		PURCHASE ORDER		P.O.	ORDER
3 ITEM	M D Y M D Y	QUANTITY	PRICE	PRICE	VENDOR	PREFIX	SUFFIX	CODE	STATUS
4 PENCILS	2 1 85	50	$2.50	$125.00	PENCIL PUSHER	JPEN		1 JPEN1	LATE
5 PAPER	3 27 85 3 29 85	30	$2.00	$60.00	PAPER TIGER	JPAP		2 JPAP2	CLOSED
6 CLIPS	3 6 85	100	$0.50	$50.00	YANKEE CLIPPER	JCLI		3 JCLI3	OPEN

Figure 13-6. Results of the third purchase-order calculation

The rest of the items of information, from UNIT PRICE to ORDER STA-TUS, are formulas that can be replicated in a single Copy command from the previous record to the current one.

2. Move the pointer to the beginning of the FROM range, the previous record's unit price (cell P4).

3. Press MENU (F10) and select Copy.

To expand the pointer over the rest of the row of formulas to copy,

4. Press the END key; then press the right arrow key and the RETURN key to designate P4..V4 as the FROM range.

The TO range is specified by the first cell of the current record, the unit price in cell P5.

5. Point to the current record's unit price (P5) and press RETURN to complete the Copy command.

Cell V5 shows that this order is closed because it lists the date received. Also, notice that the purchase-order prefix is JPAP, and the suffix has been increased from 1 to 2.

To test whether the ORDER STATUS works properly for an order less than 31 days old,

6. Use row 6 to enter an order for 100 units of clips ordered on March 6, 1985, but not yet received.

7. Repeat steps 2 through 5, using row 5 as the previous purchase order.

Figure 13-6 shows the results. As expected, the order status is OPEN. Now that you have verified the results, you can rest assured that the Copy command functions correctly—and so does the model.

Appendix A
Keys Used
In Different Versions
Of Lotus 1-2-3

This appendix provides a useful cross-reference of key codes for all major systems using Lotus 1-2-3 at the time of writing. The key codes used in this book are based on those used for the IBM PC, XT, and AT. The key codes used on systems other than the IBM PC, XT, and AT may vary from those listed here.

KEY CODES USED IN THIS BOOK	IBM PC, XT, AND AT	TI PROFESSIONAL	WANG PROFESSIONAL	IBM 3270
ENTER	↵	RETURN	RETURN or EXEC	↵
ESC	Esc	ESC	CANCEL or 12/ESCAPE	Esc
CTRL and BREAK (SCROLL LOCK/BREAK key)	Ctrl and Scroll Lock/Break	CTRL BRK	SHIFT CANCEL	Break
DEL	Del	DEL	DELETE	Del
BACKSPACE	←	BACKSPACE	BACKSPACE and ERASE	←
up arrow key	↑	▲	↑	↑
down arrow key	↓	▼	↓	↓
left arrow key	←	◄	←	←
right arrow key	→	►	→	→
PG UP	PgUp	ALT ▲	SHIFT ↑	PgUp
PG DN	PgDn	ALT ▼	SHIFT ↓	PgDn
TAB (page right)	|⇄| or Ctrl →	TAB or ALT ►	TAB or SHIFT →	|⇄| or Ctrl →
TAB used with SHIFT (page right)	Shift |⇄| or Ctrl ←	SHIFT TAB or ALT ◄	BACKTAB or SHIFT ←	Shift |⇄| or Ctrl ←
END	End	F12/End	NEXT/END	End
HOME	Home	HOME	HOME	Home
F1 (Help)	F1/Help	F1/Help	HELP	PF1/Help
F2 (Edit)	F2/Edit	F2/Edit	2/Edit	PF2/Edit
F3 (Name)	F3/Name	F3/Name	3/Name	PF3/Name
F4 (Abs)	F4/Abs	F4/Abs	4/Abs	PF4/Abs
F5 (GoTo)	F5/GoTo	F5/GoTo	GO TO or 5/GoTo	PF5/GoTo
F6 (Window)	F6/Window	F6/Window	6/Window	PF6/Window
F7 (Query)	F7/Query	F7/Query	7/Query	PF7/Query
F8 (Table)	F8/Table	F8/Table	8/Table	PF8/Table
F9 (Calc)	F9/Calc	F9/Calc	9/Calc	PF9/Calc
F10 (Graph)	F10/Graph	F10/Graph	10/Graph	PF10/Graph
CAPS LOCK	Caps Lock	CAPS LOCK	LOCK	Caplk
NUM LOCK	Num Lock	——	——	Numlk

(VI)CTOR 9000	ZENITH Z-100	GRID COMPASS	HP 150	HYPERION	DEC RAINBOW
(RE)TURN	RETURN or ENTER	RETURN	Return	Rtn	Return or Enter
	ESC	ESC	ESC	Esc	F11/Esc
(..)R/HOME	SHIFT BREAK	CODE CTRL ↓	Break or Shift Stop	Ctrl Brk	Break
(..)L	DELETE	CODE —	Delete Char	Del	Remove
(..)CKSPACE	BACKSPACE	BACKSPACE	Backspace	Rubout	, ⟨x⟩ or F12/Backspace
	↑	↑	▲	↑	⇧
	↓	↓	▼	↓	⇩
	←	←	◀	←	⇦
	→	→	▶	→	⇨
(..)FT ↑	SHIFT ↑	CODE ↑	Prev or Ctrl ▲	PgUp	Prev Screen or Shift ⇧
(..)FT ↓	SHIFT ↓	CODE ↓	Next or Ctrl ▼	PgDn	Next Screen or Shift ⇩
(.. or) SHIFT →	TAB	TAB or CTRL →	Tab or Ctrl ▶	Tab or Ctrl →	Tab
(..)FT TAB or (..)FT ←	SHIFT TAB	SHIFT TAB or CTRL ←	Shift Tab or Ctrl ◀	Shift Tab or Ctrl ←	Shift Tab
(..)RD →	F11/End or DEL LINE	CODE TAB or CODE SHIFT ↓	Select	End	Select/End
(..)RD ←	HOME	CODE SHIFT ↑	▷	Home	Find/Home
(..)Help	F1/Help	CODE 1/Help	f1/Help	F1/Help	Help
(..)Edit	F2/Edit	CODE 2/Edit	f2/Edit	F2/Edit	Do/Edit
(..)Name	F3/Name	CODE 3/Name	f3/Name	F3/Name	Name
(..)Abs	F4/Abs	CODE 4/Abs	f4/Abs	F4/Abs	Abs
(..)GoTo	F5/GoTo	CODE 5/GoTo	f5/GoTo	F5/GoTo	GoTo
(..)Window	F6/Window	CODE 6/Window	f6/Window	F6/Window	Window
(..)Query	F7/Query	CODE 7/Query	f7/Query	F7/Query	PF1/Query
(..)Table	F8/Table	CODE 8/Table	f8/Table	F8/Table	PF2/Table
(..)Calc	F9/Calc	CODE 9/Calc	/Calc	F9/Calc	PF3/Calc
(..)/Graph	F10/Graph	CODE 0/Graph	/Graph	F10/Graph	PF4/Graph
(..)K	CAPS LOCK	SHIFT ESC	Caps	Caps Lock	Lock
(..)	——	——	——	Num Lock	——

(continued)

KEY CODES USED IN THIS BOOK	IBM PC, XT, AND AT	TI PROFESSIONAL	WANG PROFESSIONAL	IBM 3270
SCROLL LOCK	Scroll Lock	F11/Scroll	11/Scroll Lock	Scrlk
SHIFT	⇧	SHIFT	SHIFT	⇧
ALT	Alt	ALT	GL/Alt	Alt
Single-Step Modes	Alt F1	ALT F1	SHIFT HELP	Alt PF1
space bar	space bar	space bar	space bar	space bar
\	\	\	2ND /	\
{	{	{	2ND [	{
}	}	}	2ND]	}
~	~	~	2ND -	~
¦	¦	¦	2ND !	¦

CTOR 9000	ZENITH Z-100	GRID COMPASS	HP 150	HYPERION	DEC RAINBOW
SCRL	F12/Scroll Lock	——	/Scroll Lock	Brk	Addtnl Options/ Scroll
FT	SHIFT	SHIFT	Shift	Shift	Shift
r	CTRL SHIFT	CODE	Ctrl Shift	Alt	Ctrl Shift
[1]/Help	SHIFT F1/Help	CODE SHIFT 1	Shift f1	Alt F1	Shift Help
ace bar	space bar	space bar	space bar	space bar	space bar
	\	CODE SHIFT '	\	\	\
	{	CODE SHIFT ,	{	{	{
	}	CODE SHIFT .	}	}	}
	~	CODE ;	~	~	~
	¦	CODE SHIFT ;	¦	¦	¦

About the Author

Edward M. Baras is the author of *The Symphony Book, Symphony: The Expert's Guide*, and *The Jazz Book*. Mr. Baras received a B.A. in computer science from Columbia University and an M.B.A. in finance from New York University.

Index

G

H

I

K

L

M